Test authors: Alyssa Coburn, Nicole Burmingham, Amanda Ratzloff, Daniel Melko, Julia Dopp, and Leslie Guthrie.

Test editors: Sarah Phillips, Colleen Gronkiewicz, Daniel Melko, Jessica Bowman, Erin Doyle, Karen Sheehan, Anna Holland, Alicia Sanfillippo, Amanda Ratzloff, and Jenna Flink.

ISBN: 978-1-7323159-2-1
Library of Congress Control Number: 2020910852

Nurturing Wisdom Tutoring's Practice Tests: The Upper Level ISEE

By Nurturing Wisdom Tutoring, Inc.®

www.nurturingwisdom.com

About Nurturing Wisdom Tutoring

Nurturing Wisdom Tutoring offers one-on-one, in-home and online tutoring in Chicagoland and beyond. Since 2005, we've customized tutoring for students of all ages for test prep, academics, and executive functioning. Our team of tutors, directors, and coaches works closely together to develop curious and independent learners.

The Nurturing Wisdom team helps students increase their scores on college admission tests including the ACT and SAT, and on high school entrance tests including the ISEE, SSAT, HSPT, and CPS exam. Our proven curriculum is comprehensive, helping students develop skills across four important areas: test-taking strategies, timing strategies, overcoming test anxiety, and overall academic skills.

Nurturing Wisdom also helps students improve their performance in their academic classes. Not only do they earn better grades, but they also become more confident learners, develop a growth mindset, and transfer what they've learned to other areas of their lives.

Our executive functioning tutoring helps students truly take ownership of their learning. Tutors teach strategies around physical and digital organization, time management, study skills, and self-advocacy.

Visit our website, nurturingwisdom.com, to learn more!

Table of Contents

ISEE Test 5

ISEE Test 6

ISEE Test 7

ISEE Test 8

ISEE Test 9

ISEE Test 10

Blank Answer Sheets

Overview of the Upper Level ISEE

Used for admission to many independent high schools, the ISEE (Independent School Entrance Exam) assesses students' verbal, math, and reading skills. The Upper Level ISEE is taken by students in eighth through eleventh grades.

Because of that range of grade levels, this is not an easy test, especially for younger students. The content is high level, the question types are challenging, and some topics may be unfamiliar. That said, once you're familiar with the type of material and questions on the ISEE, you'll be able to confidently work your way through it!

The practice tests in this book will help you identify which parts of the test are most difficult for you, and give you the chance to sharpen your skills. Beyond learning content and understanding questions types, you'll also get a better feel for pacing. When you pace well, it means that you know when to spend a little extra time on a question and when to make a best guess and move on. That skill is critical on this test!

Before jumping into taking the practice tests, learn more about the Upper Level ISEE below. Understanding the test will help you make the most of your practice time!

Test Structure and Timing

The ISEE is divided into five sections, as outlined in the chart below.

Section	Number of Questions	Time Allotted
Verbal	40	20 minutes
Quantitative	37	35 minutes
Reading	36	35 minutes
Math	47	40 minutes
Writing Sample	1	25 minutes

Section Overviews

The five sections of the ISEE test a variety of skills, some you'll recognize, and others you won't. Below are descriptions of the question types and some notes about what makes each section challenging.

Verbal

The verbal section assesses vocabulary and verbal reasoning skills and is comprised of two question types:

Synonyms: Each question presents a word, and you have to choose a word from the answer choices that most closely matches the original word's meaning.

Sentence Completions: For this question type, you will be given a sentence with one or two words missing. Your job is to figure out which word(s) best fits the missing portion(s) of the sentence.

What makes this section challenging?

Vocabulary: The verbal section includes challenging high school level vocabulary. Since there isn't a specific list of words that are tested, you can't simply memorize a word list to prepare for the section. In general, building up a strong vocabulary through reading will go a long way!

Answer Choices: Sometimes there are subtle distinctions between the answer choices. Often, you can narrow it down to two possible answers which both seem correct.

Sentence Completions: The sentence completions can be misleading, and at times it can be challenging to figure out what type of word belongs in the blank.

Quantitative

The quantitative section tests your mathematical reasoning skills. Problems typically require minimal computation and instead focus on conceptual understanding. That means you'll be doing a lot of tricky word problems, interpreting data, estimating, and predicting.

What makes this section challenging?

Abstract Word Problems: The word problems are not asked in a straightforward way. It can be difficult to determine which information you need and how to work with it. You also need to make sure that you understand the question being asked!

Quantitative Comparisons: The format of the quantitative comparison questions can be intimidating! In these problems students are asked to compare two quantities and determine which is larger (or determine if there is not enough information).

Reading

The reading section contains six nonfiction and fiction passages on topics like science, history, contemporary life, and literature. After reading each passage, you'll answer six multiple choice questions.

What makes this section challenging?

Unfamiliar Terms: The nonfiction passages often use academic language, like science vocabulary, that can throw you off.

Passage Length: The passages on the test can be quite long - each ranges between 300 and 600 words. This can make the timing on this section feel short!

Math

The questions cover a variety of math topics in algebra, geometry, measurement, data analysis and statistics.

What makes this section challenging?

Wide Variety of Math and Question Types: The math section covers a lot of ground, requiring a broad range of mathematical knowledge.

Higher Level Math: The ISEE math can be quite challenging and includes a handful of math skills typically covered in Algebra 2, such as matrices and imaginary numbers. The good news is that only the most simple versions of these concepts are covered, but they can be intimidating if you haven't encountered them before!

No Calculator Allowed: Ugh, not what you want to hear, we know. You'll need to get comfortable rattling off your math facts, as well as working out problems mentally and with pencil and paper.

Essay

You'll be asked to complete an essay which is unscored but sent directly to schools. You will be given a writing prompt which you must respond to in thirty minutes. The prompts are on relatively straightforward and age appropriate topics.

What makes this section challenging?

Timing: The thirty minutes will go quickly! You'll want to devote a few minutes to brainstorming and organizing your ideas.

Experimental Questions

Each section of the ISEE includes experimental questions. These questions are being tested out for future ISEEs and will not count toward your score. However, you won't know which questions are experimental and which are part of the scored portion of your test. Therefore, it's important to give your best effort to every question you encounter.

ISEE Test 1

Section 1: Verbal
40 Questions, 20 Minutes

Synonyms
Instructions: Select the word whose meaning is closest to the word in capital letters.

1. ABSTRUSE:

    a. angry
    b. hard
    c. perplexing
    d. stormy

2. ALLIANCE:

    a. alege
    b. enemy
    c. union
    d. war

3. PROTRUDE:

    a. bend
    b. bulge
    c. concave
    d. hip

4. VIBRANT:

    a. good
    b. extreme
    c. spirited
    d. quiet

5. VELOCITY:

    a. car
    b. speed
    c. torque
    d. violence

6. TRUNCATE:

    a. broke
    b. crop
    c. prop
    d. twist

7. EVICT:

    a. abstain
    b. elicit
    c. remove
    d. residence

8. TOLERATE:

    a. acknowledge
    b. permit
    c. quite
    d. tempt

9. SUBLIME:

    a. candid
    b. heavenly
    c. music
    d. super

10. PRUDENT:

    a. calm
    b. leery
    c. shy
    d. stoic

11. OMINOUS:

    a. anger
    b. cloudy
    c. menacing
    d. weather

12. MEMENTO:

    a. answer
    b. keepsake
    c. knickknack
    d. memory

13. IMPERIL:

    a. hazard
    b. important
    c. interest
    d. war

14. THRIVE:

    a. afloat
    b. live
    c. prosper
    d. still

15. PECULIAR:

    a. loud
    b. new
    c. strange
    d. timid

16. PESTER:

    a. bore
    b. bother
    c. interrogate
    d. rouse

17. OPULENT:

    a. eye
    b. bland
    c. lavish
    d. oval

18. MALICE:

    a. fight
    b. hatred
    c. pain
    d. tool

19. KINDLE:

    a. book
    b. friend
    c. ignite
    d. stance

Sentence Completion

Instructions: Select the word or pair of words that best completes the sentence.

20. Always -------, the event planner made everyone feel welcome.

    a. affable
    b. contagious
    c. irate
    d. unbiased

21. University of Chicago climate scientist David Archer is ------- thousands of articles and videos about global warming on his website to help people find reliable and useful information on climate change.

    a. assembling
    b. portraying
    c. reading
    d. writing

22. Normally nervous, Marissa shocked her dance instructor when she ------- to demonstrate a new pose to the class.

    a. attempted
    b. refused
    c. tried
    d. volunteered

23. Not wanting to seem insensitive, Carla attempted to ------- her crying friend.

    a. console
    b. interrupt
    c. please
    d. reprimand

24. It is the job of custodial staff to ------- the school's after hours activities, interior rooms, and exterior grounds.

    a. clean
    b. obliterate
    c. oversee
    d. use

25. As people demand more seafood at lower prices, overfishing becomes a real problem and many species of fish are at risk of extinction or severe -------.

    a. depletion
    b. exhaustion
    c. resistance
    d. starvation

26. Bears hibernate in the winter to ------- in the cold and dark without having to search for food and warmth.

    a. battle
    b. flourish
    c. subsist
    d. survive

27. Apart from the occasional moment of regret, Arthur never really had feelings of ------- when he thought about the end of his friendship with Terrell.

    a. anger
    b. blame
    c. remorse
    d. sadness

28. Stepping onto the campus of an Ivy League institution can be an intimidating, yet -------, experience.

    a. anxious
    b. inspiring
    c. raucous
    d. solmen

29. Despite having been incarcerated for years in the United States penal system, the rate of ------- is alarmingly high for former prisoners.

    a. disobedience
    b. improvement
    c. loss
    d. recidivism

30. Redistricting in the community has led to much conflict between the town's political -------.

    a. adversaries
    b. allies
    c. policies
    d. proponents

31. Doctors must declare a(n) ------- or specific area of study at some point during medical school.

    a. example
    b. minor
    c. speciality
    d. verdict

32. Traveling throughout Europe, Delia was surprised by the stark contrast of ------- and ------- architecture that were often times right next to one another.

    a. beautiful . . . ornate
    b. classical . . . modern
    c. opulent . . . rare
    d. primitive . . . ancient

33. Reassuring her friend that they had -------, Petra did not leave the hospital until the two had -------.

    a. connected . . . prayed
    b. prevailed . . . cried
    c. reconciled . . . embraced
    d. reunited . . . discussed

34. Wanting to accomplish the task alone, Sharon values ------- over -------.
    a. academics . . . athletics
    b. independence . . . dependence
    c. private . . . public
    d. wealth . . . poverty

35. Our behaviors are often thought to be learned rather than -------; however, most experts believe the two work in ------- together.

    a. devised . . . harmony
    b. inherent . . . concert
    c. native . . . time
    d. taught . . . contrast

36. Martha does not ------- cheating even during a ------- game.

    a. hate . . . humorous
    b. condone . . . friendly
    c. endorse . . . angry
    d. tolerate . . . competitive

37. Despite having a theory of evolution that is very ------- to Charles Darwin, Alfred Russel Wallace gets little of the -------.

    a. advanced . . . ridicule
    b. divergent . . . praise
    c. similar . . . acclaim
    d. unique . . . contempt

38. Dental surgery can be a(n) ------- experience, but the benefits far outweigh the -------.

    a. daunting . . . wait
    b. distressing . . . pain
    c. expensive . . . recovery
    d. positive . . . negatives

39. Acting positive when you really feel -------, can actually help you feel -------.

     a. anxious . . . inspired
     b. depressed . . . better
     c. intrepid . . . calm
     d. passive . . . active

40. Marcel Proust wrote great works of fiction blended with ------- on how to ------- life.

     a. analogies . . . extend
     b. examples . . . dispel
     c. philosophy . . . live
     d. stories . . . explain

Section 2: Quantitative
37 Questions, 35 Minutes

The section is divided into two parts: problem solving and quantitative comparison. Directions for each part are provided.

Part 1 - Problem Solving

Instructions: Each question is followed by four possible answers. Select the best answer.

1. Carly has a jar of red and blue marbles. She has 3 times as many red marbles as blue marbles. If the total number of marbles in the jar is 24, how many red marbles does Carly have?

    a. 6
    b. 9
    c. 12
    d. 18

2. A rectangle's height is 6 centimeters. If the area of the rectangle is smaller than 45 centimeters squared, and the base of the rectangle is an integer, which of the following could be the perimeter of the rectangle?

    a. 12 cm
    b. 13 cm
    c. 26 cm
    d. 48 cm

3. If x is a factor of a and y is a factor of c, which of the following statements is true?

    a. c is a multiple of xy
    b. ac is a multiple of xy
    c. c is a factor of xy
    d. ac is a factor of xy

4. Mr. Smith wants to reward the hard work all of his students demonstrated all semester, so he has decided to add four points to everyone's final grade. If the range of grades before he added on the extra points was 26, what will the range of grades be after he adds on the extra points?

    a. 22
    b. 26
    c. 30
    d. 34

5. If $*z = 5z - 25$, what is the value of $*3 + *7$?

    a. -10
    b. 0
    c. 10
    d. 25

6. Which of the following is equivalent to the expression $\dfrac{2x^3y^5z^8}{6x^3y^6z^7}$?

    a. $\dfrac{3y}{z}$
    b. $\dfrac{z}{3y}$
    c. $\dfrac{1}{3xyz}$
    d. $\dfrac{x^6y^{11}z^{15}}{3}$

7. If $a + b = 7$, which of the following is equal to b?

    a. $-a - 7$
    b. $-a + 7$
    c. $a - 7$
    d. $a + 7$

8. The length of the base of a parallelogram is decreased by 40% and the height is increased by 10%. What is the percent decrease in the area of the parallelogram?

    a. 24%
    b. 30%
    c. 34%
    d. 66%

9. What is the product of all prime factors of 40?

    a. 5
    b. 7
    c. 10
    d. 20

10. The graph below could represent the change in temperature of

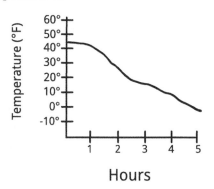

Hours

    a. a pot of cold water brought to a boil.
    b. a scoop of ice cream on a hot day.
    c. an ice sculpture that is left outside in sub zero temperatures.
    d. a package of food that is moved from the refrigerator to the freezer.

11. Samantha, Julian, and Kenmar are competing in a board game tournament. Each player has an equal chance of winning any given game. Which of the following events has the highest probability?

    a. Samantha will win the tournament
    b. Kenmar will come in second place
    c. Either Julian or Samantha will win the tournament
    d. Kenmar will win and Julian will come in second place

12. If $x^2 + y^2 = 10$ and $2xy = 6$, what is the value of $(x + y)^2$?

    a. 4
    b. 8
    c. 16
    d. 60

13. Two parallel lines must have

    a. the same slope.
    b. different slopes.
    c. intersecting points.
    d. the same y intercept.

14. Javier is riding a stationary bike at the gym. The graph below shows his heart rate as a function of time.

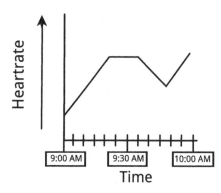

During his workout, he tires and takes a break. He then restarts his workout. At what time does he restart his workout?

    a. 9:20 AM
    b. 9:35 AM
    c. 9:50 AM
    d. 10:00 AM

15. If x is an odd number greater than 1 or smaller than -1, x squared minus three must result in a number that is

    a. positive and even.
    b. positive and odd.
    c. negative and even.
    d. negative and odd.

16. Malia is selling wrapping paper for a school fundraiser. She tracks the number of rolls of wrapping paper she sells to each person in the chart below. What is the mode of the data?

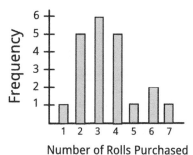

Number of Rolls Purchased

    a. 1
    b. 3
    c. 5
    d. 6

17. If △ABC is similar to △XYZ, which of the following must be true?

    a. ∠A + ∠B = ∠C
    b. ∠A ≅ ∠B ≅ ∠C
    c. AB = XY
    d. ∠A ≅ ∠X

18. The pyramid shown below has a square base and sides made up of four equilateral triangles.

    Which of the following could NOT be a net of the pyramid?

    a.

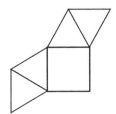

    b.

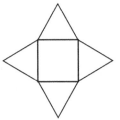

    c.

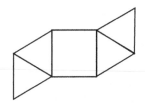

    d.

19. Dylan and Jesse were both running down the same track at constant speeds, though Dylan was running at a slower constant speed than Jesse. When Jesse had started running at the start of the track, Dylan was already 300 meters down the track. What additional piece of information is necessary to determine how long it would take for Jesse to catch up with Dylan?

    a. Jesse's speed
    b. Dylan's speed
    c. The difference between Jesse's and Dylan's speeds
    d. The sum of Jesse's and Dylan's speeds

Part 2 - Quantitative Comparisons

Instructions: In each question, use the information provided to compare the quantity in Column A with the quantity in Column B. All quantitative comparison questions have the same answer choices:

    a. The quantity in column A is greater.
    b. The quantity in column B is greater.
    c. The two quantities are equal.
    d. The relationship cannot be determined from the information given.

Consider the following dataset: 1, 1, 3, 5, 8, 8, 8, 12, 15

20.   **Column A**   **Column B**

The median of the dataset   The mode of the dataset

---

21.   **Column A**   **Column B**

$2 + 5 \times 2 - 3 + \dfrac{12}{2}$ $\dfrac{12}{2} + 5 \times 2 + 2 - 3$

---

22.   **Column A**   **Column B**

The smallest integer larger than 2.4.   The greatest integer smaller than $\dfrac{9}{4}$.

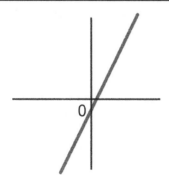

23.   **Column A**   **Column B**

The slope of the line pictured above.   3

Let x and y represent distinct positive integers.

24.   **Column A**   **Column B**

$(x + y)^3$ $x^3 + y^3$

$x < 1$

25.   **Column A**   **Column B**

$2x + 3$ $x - 7$

---

26.   **Column A**   **Column B**

25% of 60   30% of 50

---

x is an integer less than or equal to -1

27.   **Column A**   **Column B**

x^3 x^4

The area of a rectangle is 48 cm².

28.   **Column A**   **Column B**

The height of the rectangle.   The length of the base of the rectangle.

Let h(x) = 10 – 3x.

29. Column A   Column B

   h(4)   h(-4)

A coin is tossed three times.

30. Column A   Column B

   The probability that all   The probability that
   three tosses land on   none of the tosses land
   heads   on heads

Rectangle A   Rectangle B

Note: The images are not drawn to scale.

31. Column A   Column B

   The area of rectangle A.   The area of rectangle B.

y = -2x - 5

32. Column A   Column B

   The maximum value   The maximum value of y
   of y when -3 < x < 0 when 0 < x < 3

The formula for the volume of a cone is $V = \frac{1}{3}\pi r^2 h\, x$, where r represents the radius of the cone's base and h represents the height of the cone. The radius of cone F is larger than the radius of cone G, and the height of cone G is larger than the height of cone F.

33. Column A   Column B

   The volume of cone F   The volume of cone G

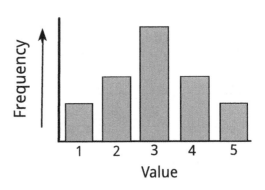

34. Column A   Column B

   The mean of the data.   The median of the
                          data.

Triangle ABC is inscribed in the circle. The diameter of the circle is 12 centimeters.

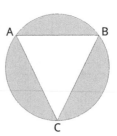

35. Column A   Column B

   The circumference of   The area of the shaded
   the circle.   region.

Charlie rolls two 6-sided number cubes with sides labeled 1-6, then adds the results together.

36. <u>Column A</u>   <u>Column B</u>

If the first roll results in a 5, the probability that the sum will be less than 10

If the first roll results in a 5, the probability that the sum will be 10 or greater

---

The measure of an exterior angle of a regular polygon with n sides is $\frac{360°}{n}$.

37. <u>Column A</u>   <u>Column B</u>

The measure of an exterior angle of a regular hexagon.

The measure of an exterior angle of a regular pentagon.

Section 3: Reading
36 Questions, 35 Minutes

Instructions: Carefully read each passage and answer the questions that follow it. For each question, decide which of the choices best answers the question based on the passage.

Questions 1 - 6

1　　The dense white cheese known as halloumi
2　originated in Cyprus, a small Mediterranean island
3　country located off the southern coast of Turkey.
4　Halloumi resembles mozzarella in appearance but
5　has a sturdier texture and a tangier, saltier flavor
6　profile compared to its milder Italian cousin. It
7　has found a particular niche amidst vegetarian-
8　friendly and sustainable food movements, offering
9　a meatless protein choice that can be fried,
10　barbecued, and grilled with ease. It is perhaps best
11　known for its ability to withstand high cooking
12　temperatures without losing its characteristic
13　rubbery firmness and is often referred to as a
14　"squeaky" cheese due to this unique texture.
15　　Until recently, halloumi was a relatively
16　obscure product that could only be found in
17　ethnic specialty stores. However, it has surged in
18　popularity over the past few years. In fact, global
19　sales more than doubled from 2014 to 2017 alone,
20　largely due to halloumi's skyrocketing appeal
21　in British, Swedish, and German markets. It has
22　become a mainstay dairy item in Western European
23　grocery stores and is beginning to gain traction in
24　Chinese and American food culture as well.
25　　Halloumi is customarily made using milk
26　from sheep and goats, which are both among
27　the scant 17 mammal species that are native to
28　the mediterranean island. These hardy animals
29　thrive in Cyprus' mountainous environment and
30　are able to withstand the infamously hot, dry
31　summer season far better than other domesticated
32　ungulates. Unfortunately, sheep and goats are
33　pitiful milk producers compared to cattle (which
34　were conspicuously absent from the island for most
35　of Cypriot history), and the exploding demand for
36　halloumi rapidly outstripped the production ability
37　of suppliers using traditional methods.

38　　Supplementing with milk from imported
39　cows has allowed halloumi suppliers to increase
40　their yields, but critics claim that the resulting
41　product is adulterated and cannot justifiably
42　be marketed as halloumi. Furthermore, cheese
43　manufacturers outside of Cyprus have begun to
44　cash in on the trend by creating their own versions
45　of halloumi. As cow's milk is the cheapest and most
46　readily-available option for non-Cypriot suppliers,
47　the majority of extranational would-be halloumi
48　cheese contains an extremely high proportion of it.
49　　In the attempt to retain control of the
50　rapidly expanding market, Cyprus has become
51　embroiled in a series of legal efforts to gain
52　exclusive rights to halloumi production by
53　designating it as a uniquely Cypriot cheese. If
54　halloumi is granted protected status, foreign
55　competitors would not be able to label their cheese
56　as halloumi. Instead, they would have to market
57　under a new name, distinct from the product they
58　sought to emulate. Ostensibly, this differentiation
59　would safeguard the quality of the cheese by
60　preventing inferior producers from slipping
61　in cheap, mass-produced versions that might
62　ultimately damage halloumi's overall status in the
63　market. Naturally, Cyprus also stands to benefit
64　financially from monopolizing halloumi, now that
65　the cheese has gone from small-time specialty to a
66　lucrative industry.

1. The purpose of the last paragraph (lines 49 - 66) is to

    a. explain the effect of designating halloumi a uniquely Cypriot cheese.
    b. compare and contrast the pros and cons of halloumi's protected status.
    c. safeguard halloumi cheese from would be copycats.
    d. persuade readers to only buy halloumi cheese from Cyprus.

2. In line 27, "scant" most nearly means
    a. small.
    b. sturdy.
    c. few.
    d. sufficient.

3. According to the passage, Halloumi has increased in popularity for all of these reasons EXCEPT

    a. sustainability.
    b. vegetarianism.
    c. price.
    d. texture.

4. Which of the following characterises the structure of the first paragraph (lines 1 - 14)? The author

    a. acknowledges a similarity, then offers a comparison.
    b. states a thesis, then gives supporting evidence.
    c. affirms one perspective, then considers others.
    d. persuades a reader to think about one idea, then provides a contrast.

5. Halloumi is most likely originally made from sheep and goats because

    a. it tastes better.
    b. that was all that was available.
    c. they produce less milk.
    d. they are cheaper than cows.

6. The author's tone towards Halloumi is best described as

    a. indifferent.
    b. admiring.
    c. informative.
    d. hesitant.

Questions 7 - 12

1   Although it's widely accepted in many
2   circles that John Shepherd-Barron invented the
3   ATM (automated teller machine), the truth is far
4   more complicated. It's said that Shepherd-Barron, a
5   British engineer, came up with the idea for an ATM
6   when he was frustrated that he was unable to make
7   it to the bank before it closed on a Saturday. As he
8   was sitting in the bath, lamenting his misfortune,
9   he dreamt up the concept of a machine that would
10   securely supply money to consumers outside of
11   business hours. Soon thereafter, he approached
12   Barclay's bank with the idea of the ATM and was
13   hired to create the machine. In 1967, Barclay's
14   unveiled the device, which used a paper check and
15   PIN (personal identification number), to much
16   fanfare.

17   In reality, most banks, including Barclay's,
18   had been working on ATM-like cash machines for
19   many years prior to the invention of the ATM. In
20   1960, nearly a decade before Shepherd-Barron's
21   epiphany, American Luther George Simjian
22   invented the Bankograph machine which allowed
23   customers to deposit checks and cash. The
24   Bankograph machine was used at a bank in New
25   York, primarily by a small minority of customers
26   (mainly gamblers), who preferred not to interact
27   with tellers. However, the average consumer was
28   not interested in this unfamiliar apparatus, and it
29   never became widely used.

30   By the mid to late 1960's, many banks
31   tasked engineering teams with finding a way for
32   customers to deposit and withdraw money without
33   the expense of a human bank teller. In fact, a
34   month after Barclay's unveiled its ATM, Britain's
35   Westminster Bank began using their own cash
36   machine. This machine had been in development
37   for several years, and although it was released
38   after Shepherd-Barron's ATM, it was patented by
39   Scottish inventor James Goodfellow in 1966. This
40   machine, like Shepherd-Barron's, used a PIN.
41   However, it also had the added innovation of an
42   ATM card.

43   But the story of the ATM's invention
44   doesn't end there. In 1968, American Don Wetzel,
45   tired of standing in line for a teller, invented his
46   own version of the ATM. Unlike Goodfellow's
47   machine, Wetzel's ATM used a magnetic card,
48   similar to cards used in ATMs today, which
49   improved security. This ATM was first used in 1969,
50   and Wetzel still holds the American patent for the
51   ATM.

52   What's most surprising is that none of
53   the inventors seemed to have known about each
54   other, yet they all came up with almost the same
55   invention within a few years of one another. So
56   who was the true inventor of the ATM? It's hard to
57   say. The invention of the ATM is a great example
58   of "multiple discovery," a hypothesis which states
59   that many new inventions are simultaneously
60   and independently developed by several different
61   inventors.

7. Which inventor's machine primarily accepted cash and checks?

    a. John Shepherd-Barron
    b. Luther George Simjian
    c. James Goodfellow
    d. Don Wetzel

8. In line 17, the author uses the phrase "In reality" in order to

    a. support the idea that John Shepherd-Barron invented the modern ATM.
    b. prove that American Luther George Simjian was the real inventor.
    c. dissuade people from appreciating the contributions of John Shepherd-Barron.
    d. describe how banks helped to develop the ATM.

9. What was one commonality among many of the inventors?

    a. They were leery of using the ATM themselves.
    b. They wanted to improve the traditional banking system.
    c. They had engineering backgrounds.
    d. They were all bankers.

10. In line 8, "lamenting" most nearly means
    a. crying.
    b. bemoaning.
    c. stressing.
    d. worrying.

11. The primary purpose of this passage is to

    a. provide a detailed history of the invention of the ATM.
    b. explain how multiple people unknowingly collaborated on the invention of the modern day ATM.
    c. persuade readers on the importance of teamwork when inventing new technology.
    d. evaluate the pros and cons of automating things like a bank teller.

12. The author infers that many people did not use the Bankograph machine because

    a. they did not want to be associated with gambling.
    b. they did not need to deposit cash.
    c. they found it too novel.
    d. they preferred human interaction.

Questions 13 - 18

1   While "hibernation" is a familiar term,
2 it's often misunderstood to mean "a long sleep."
3 Hibernation is more complex than slumber
4 and varies among species. Certain animals
5 hibernate, or essentially shut down their bodies
6 in the cold winter months, in order to conserve
7 energy. Some animals experience a state of deep
8 unconsciousness while others simply reduce their
9 activity. Bears actually give birth during this period
10 of hibernation. However, the bear cubs do not join
11 their mother in hibernation; they sleep, nurse, and
12 lie next to her for the duration of the season.
13   Because hibernating animals use very
14 little energy, their breathing and metabolism slows,
15 and heart rate and body temperature drops. The
16 temperature of some animals, such as the ground
17 squirrel, can fall as low as -2 degrees Celsius. Some
18 cold-blooded animals, like frogs, produce natural
19 antifreezes to avoid being frozen solid in frigid
20 environments.
21   Hibernation is a dangerous business. If an
22 animal does not store up enough fat in the summer
23 and autumn, they may starve. If the weather is
24 severe enough or they are prematurely awoken,
25 they will die. Hibernating creatures are also easy
26 prey.

27   Aestivation is a less well-known process
28 but quite similar to hibernation. Some animals
29 in hot climates use aestivation to escape heat
30 and drought. During aestivation, animals such as
31 the Nile crocodile, snails, and the lungfish bury
32 themselves in the ground and wait for cooler
33 and wetter weather to return. Sometimes, snails
34 climb trees to get off the hot ground and then
35 shut themselves into their shells using mucus.
36 Unfortunately, if a drought is prolonged many of
37 these aestivating animals will perish as they use up
38 all of their stored energy.
39   Climate change poses a risk to both
40 hibernating and aestivating animals. Many
41 animals, such as the marmot, rely on air
42 temperature to tell them when to emerge from
43 hibernation. Warmer temperatures cause animals
44 to rise from their reduced-energy state too early.
45 Prolonged periods of heat and reduced rainfall put
46 animals that aestivate at great risk. Climate change
47 is a particular concern to bears as they are easily
48 woken during stretches of warm weather and then
49 may not have enough energy to survive the rest of
50 the winter.

13. The author's description of hibernation as a "dangerous business" (line 21) is an example of

    a. irony.
    b. metaphor.
    c. simile.
    d. personification.

14. It can be inferred from the passage that animals that are woken too early from hibernation may

    a. return to hibernation eventually.
    b. compete with humans for resources.
    c. not be able to get enough food and water.
    d. be easily irritable and attack humans.

15. Based on the passage, a tortoise in a desert likely

    a. hibernates during the long winter.
    b. aestivates during the colder months.
    c. hibernates during the hot summer.
    d. aestiviates during the dry months.

16. The author's attitude toward climate change can best be described as

    a. skeptical.
    b. concerned.
    c. surprised.
    d. angry.

17. In the second paragraph the author explains that an animal's heart rate goes down because

    a. they are using less energy.
    b. they are cold.
    c. their metabolism is slower.
    d. their breathing has slowed.

18. As used in line 19, "frigid" most nearly means

    a. harsh.
    b. cold.
    c. hostile.
    d. sweltering.

Questions 19 - 24

1   The camp was in a glade and the spring
2 was just at the edge of the woods. Near the spring
3 some of the horses and two of the oxen were
4 tethered to stout saplings. As Henry approached, a
5 horse neighed, and he noticed that all of them were
6 pulling on their ropes. The two careless guards were
7 either asleep or so near it that they took no notice of
8 what was passing.
9   Henry walked among the animals but
10 was still unable to find the cause of the trouble. He
11 knew them well and he patted their backs, rubbed
12 their noses, and tried to soothe them. They became
13 a little quieter, but he could not remain any longer
14 with them because his sister was waiting at the
15 wagon for the water. So he went to the spring and,
16 stooping down, filled his cup.
17   When Henry rose to his full height, his eyes
18 happened to be turned toward the forest, and there,
19 about seven or eight feet from the ground, and
20 not far from him he saw two coals of fire. He was
21 so startled that the cup trembled in his hand, and
22 drops of water fell splashing back into the spring.
23 But he stared steadily at the red points, which he
24 now noticed were moving slightly from side to side,
25 and presently he saw behind them the dim outlines
26 of a long and large body. He knew that this must
27 be a panther. Either it was a very hungry or a very
28 ignorant panther to hover so boldly around a camp
29 full of men.

30   The panther was crouched on a bough
31 of a tree as if ready to spring, and Henry was the
32 nearest living object. But when a minute passed
33 and the panther did not move, save to sway gently,
34 his courage rose, especially when he remembered
35 that it was the natural impulse of all wild animals
36 to run from man. So he began to back away, and
37 he heard behind him the horses trampling about
38 in alarm. The lazy guards still dozed. Now Henry
39 made a resolve to show what he really could do. He
40 dropped his cup, rushed to the fire, and picked up a
41 long brand, blazing at one end.
42   Swinging his torch around his head until
43 it made a perfect circle of flame he ran directly
44 toward the panther, uttering a loud shout as he ran.
45 The animal gave forth a shriek of terror and leaping
46 from the bough sped with cat-like swiftness into the
47 forest.
48   All the camp was awake in an instant,
49 the men springing out of the wagons, ready for
50 any trouble. When they saw only a boy, holding a
51 blazing torch above his head, they were disposed
52 to grumble, and the two sleepy guards, seeking
53 an excuse for themselves, laughed outright at the
54 tale that Henry told. But Mr. Ware believed in the
55 truth of his son's words, and the guide, who quickly
56 examined the ground near the tree, said there could
57 be no doubt that Henry had really seen the panther,
58 and had not been tricked by his imagination. The
59 great tracks of the beast were plainly visible in the
60 soft earth.

19. It can be concluded that the animals are acting strangely because they

    a. were in an unfamiliar glade.
    b. sensed Henry approaching.
    c. were startled by the guards.
    d. knew the panther was nearby.

20. It can be inferred that the guards
    a.
    b. were frightened and didn't want to fight off any wild animals
    c. disliked Henry and wanted him to fend for himself.
    d. didn't believe that there was much danger to the camp.
    e. were exhausted because they had been out hiking all day.

21. In line 20, the author describes Henry seeing "two coals of fire" to describe the

    a. eyes of the panther.
    b. blazing torches.
    c. ensuing forest fire.
    d. fury in the horses.

22. As it is used in line 33, "save" most nearly means

    a. except
    b. furthermore
    c. rescue
    d. store

23. Henry decided to attempt to frighten the panther for all of the following reasons EXCEPT

    a. there was no one readily available to help him.
    b. he believed the panther might attack him.
    c. he knew that panthers were predisposed to be afraid of men.
    d. he wanted to impress the men who were watching him.

24. According to the passage, the men at the camp view Henry

    a. with deep respect as a skilled horseman.
    b. with contempt for rousing them from their slumber.
    c. as an imaginative child.
    d. as someone they must tolerate since his father is the leader.

Questions 25 - 30

1   Oxytocin is a polypeptide hormone
2 and neurotransmitter that is produced in the
3 hypothalamus and secreted by the pituitary gland
4 in mammals, though molecules with similar
5 structures and functions are found in many non-
6 mammalian species. The English scientist Sir Henry
7 Dale discovered oxytocin in 1906, and derived its
8 name from Greek words for "swift birth" after he
9 observed that the hormone induced labor in the
10 cats he was studying. 47 years later the American
11 biochemist Vincent du Vigneaud successfully
12 replicated its structure in the lab, making oxytocin
13 the first synthetically available polypeptide
14 hormone.
15   Though oxytocin was originally recognized
16 and utilized as a therapeutic agent during
17 childbirth and maternal bonding, its influence on
18 social attachment extends far beyond mother-child
19 relationships. In fact, its impact on connectedness
20 has become well known in recent years, earning
21 it monikers like "the cuddle chemical" and "the
22 love hormone." While this common perspective
23 offers a comparatively broader understanding of
24 oxytocin's effects, it still falls far short of capturing
25 the complex reality at work.
26   The popular understanding of oxytocin as
27 an indiscriminately positive and pro-social force
28 is actually quite misleading. Continued research
29 has shown that oxytocin-induced responses are
30 highly dependent on context. While oxytocin can
31 bring about feelings of affection, contentment,
32 and trust, these responses tend to be conditional.
33 Under different circumstances, oxytocin can
34 induce emotions that are far less desirable, such
35 as prejudice, envy, and even hatred. This extreme
36 variance in oxytocin's expression appears to stem
37 from a singular effect: increased tribalism instincts.
38   Tribalism, at its most basic, can be
39 understood as the urge to form communities.
40 However, this is a rosy oversimplification not
41 unlike depictions of oxytocin as "the cuddle
42 chemical." Humans are innately social beings,
43 and the formation of groups has long been
44 established as one of mankind's most primal drives.
45 Unsurprisingly, people tend to form close-knit
46 bonds with fellow group members, such as family,
47 friends, and romantic partners. However, scientists
48 posit that the inevitable complement to this in-
49 group favoritism is out-group derogation. In other
50 words, deeper attachments between individuals in
51 the same group may also cause increased hostilities
52 towards outsiders.

53   Expression of this intergroup bias appears
54 to be strongly linked to the presence of oxytocin in
55 humans. Some research has even indicated that
56 oxytocin is a factor in cross-species relationships;
57 for example, several studies have shown a direct
58 relationship between interaction time (specifically,
59 petting and eye contact) and oxytocin levels
60 in dogs and their owners. Importantly, this
61 correlation was not observed when the humans
62 and dogs in the study did not know each other.
63 This selective response was found even when
64 oxytocin was administered to the dogs via nasal
65 spray. This artificial administration of oxytocin did
66 lead to the dogs behaving affectionately towards
67 their owners, but not towards strangers. In fact,
68 some dogs exhibited higher degrees of wariness
69 towards strangers, seemingly corroborating the
70 link between oxytocin and tribalism even in non-
71 humans.
72   Despite more than a century of research,
73 the role that oxytocin plays in the cognitive,
74 emotional, and physical systems of humans and
75 other animals is still a mystery in many ways.
76 Above and beyond its apparent ability to heighten
77 both positive and negative responses to social
78 stimuli, studies indicate that oxytocin factors into
79 everything from anxiety, depression, and addiction
80 to wound healing and bone formation. One thing is
81 clear: this polypeptide may be tiny, but its impact is
82 enormous.

25. The primary purpose of the passage is to

    a. persuade readers to increase their oxytocin levels.

    b. provide a detailed explanation of the complexities of oxytocin.

    c. explain why oxytocin is a harmful chemical.

    d. describe tribalism's impact on the body's production of oxytocin.

26. According to the passage, oxytocin is found only in

    a. land animals.

    b. humans.

    c. mammals.

    d. non-mammalian species.

27. The author's statement that oxycontin's effects are "highly dependent on context" suggests that oxytocin

    a. has an unknown effect on the body.

    b. brings about positive feelings such as trust and affection.

    c. can elicit either positive or negative emotions depending on the circumstances.

    d. can have different effects depending on the dosage.

28. According to the author, the attachments formed through tribalism can also cause

    a. antagonism toward outsiders.

    b. favoritism of one individual.

    c. fighting within closely knit communities.

    d. welcoming of new group members.

29. The author included the second to last paragraph (lines 53 - 71) to show that oxycontin

    a. makes dogs affectionate toward unfamiliar dogs and humans.

    b. causes dogs to mistrust their human owners.

    c. works more effectively as a nasal spray.

    d. functions almost identically in dogs and humans.

30. As it is used in the passage, corroborating (line 69) most nearly means

    a. allowing

    b. confirming

    c. refuting

    d. summarizing

Questions 31 - 36

1   Lobsters have been a part of North
2   American coastal ecosystems for millenia, but their
3   status as a posh and pricey commodity dates back
4   a mere century or two. At the time of European
5   colonization, the bottom-dwelling crustaceans
6   were so populous that they were regularly washed
7   ashore by storms, littering New England beaches
8   in piles up to 2-feet high. Their extreme abundance
9   created a nuisance and even a minor hazard, which
10 was made worse by the shellfish's size. Modern
11 American lobsters typically weigh around 1-1.5lbs,
12 while the average colonial-era lobster was 4 to 5
13 times that size!
14 Due to their unfortunate resemblance
15 to giant insects and overwhelming prevalence,
16 lobsters were considered highly unappetizing by
17 indigenous populations and American colonists
18 alike. Until the 19th century, lobster meat was
19 relegated to the role of cheap and plentiful (albeit
20 disgusting) protein source in times of desperation,
21 rather than a luxurious treat. The only people who
22 consumed lobster on a regular basis were those
23 who were forced to: the enslaved, the destitute,
24 and/or the imprisoned.
25 Antiquated preparation and preservation
26 methods further cemented lobster's reputation
27 as an unsavory last resort among food options.
28 Historically, lobster was baked or boiled post-
29 mortem, like other meats. Unlike most other meats,
30 however, lobster flesh is laden with bacteria that
31 rapidly multiply and release poisonous toxins
32 upon the death of the host. As a result, lobster is
33 considerably more perishable than most meats.
34 Unbeknownst to early cooks, preparing dead
35 lobster frequently meant preparing spoiled lobster,
36 which led to extremely high instances of lobster-
37 related food poisoning.

38 Lack of sterilization and imperfect canning
39 processes exacerbated lobster's high spoilage
40 rates. In the era before food safety regulations,
41 handwashing and glove-wearing, workers pulled
42 the lobster's meat from the shell by hand before
43 packing it, introducing innumerable contact germs.
44 Flaws in the cans themselves (e.g. incomplete
45 seals, inadequate heat treatment, etc.) also enabled
46 spoiling.
47 In the mid-19th century, advancements
48 in the hermetically-sealed canning process
49 combined with the advent of American railroads
50 began to transform lobster's status into that of a
51 lux delicacy. Improvements in preparation and
52 storage dramatically lowered spoilage rates, but the
53 longstanding bias against lobster meat remained
54 a barrier to sales. However, anti-lobster sentiment
55 was largely limited to the coastal regions of the
56 United States; inland consumers were naive to
57 lobster's notoriety as a poor man's protein, and
58 charmed by the novelty of having access to "fresh"
59 seafood from the shores of New England. Seizing
60 the untapped market, railroad operators began
61 acquiring lobster from New England canneries and
62 served it in cross-country dining cars. Markups
63 were tremendous, as landlocked passengers were
64 just as naive about lobster's price point as they were
65 about its history as prison fare. Railroads profited
66 immensely, and Americans developed a lasting
67 taste for lobster thanks to its association with high
68 class travel and leisure.

31. It can be inferred that one reason the lobster accumulated in such large quantities on the shore was that they

    a. had no marine predators.
    b. were only popular in inland regions.
    c. weighed between 1 and 1.5 pounds.
    d. weren't being eaten by humans in large numbers.

32. The passage is primarily concerned with

    a. defending the reputation of the lobster.
    b. demonstrating how to properly prepare lobster.
    c. describing how repulsive lobster meat was before the 19th century.
    d. explaining how the lobster went from being undesirable to a delicacy.

33. In line 23, "destitute" most nearly means

    a. angry.
    b. fortunate.
    c. poor.
    d. resistant.

34. Based on the information in the passage, it can be inferred that the safest way to eat lobster is to

    a. cook a fresh lobster and eat it immediately.
    b. heat up a lobster that was canned in the era before safety regulations.
    c. cook a recently deceased lobster and eat it within a few days.
    d. eat a fresh lobster uncooked.

35. According to the author, improved canning and transportation made lobster

    a. seem like more of a delicacy.
    b. less likely to spoil.
    c. popular in coastal regions.
    d. more likely to be consumed by the poor.

36. According to the passage, train passengers' lack of knowledge about the lobster allowed the trains to

    a. refuse to sell lobster in train dining cars.
    b. serve fresh lobster on the trains.
    c. sell lobster for more than it was worth.
    d. market the lobster as a poor man's protein.

Section 4: Math
47 Questions, 40 Minutes

Instructions: Each question is followed by four answer choices. Select the best answer.

1. What is the value of the numerical expression $5.7 \times 10^2 - 4.0 \times 10^{-2}$?

   a. 1.7
   b. 5.3×10^2
   c. 5.6996×10^2
   d. 1.7×10^4

2. There are 5 people waiting for the bus. If only two can fit on the next bus, how many different combinations of people could ride the next bus?

   a. 5
   b. 10
   c. 15
   d. 20

3. Which of the following is the most reasonable unit to use when measuring the weight of a coin?

   a. kilograms
   b. millimeters
   c. grams
   d. centimeters

4. Diana squeezes 8 oranges to make 2 cups of juice. How many oranges will she need to squeeze to make 3 cups of juice?

   a. 9
   b. 12
   c. 16
   d. 24

5. The first four terms of an algebraic sequence are shown below.

   2, -4, -10, -16

   Which expression represents the nth term in this sequence?

   a. 2 - 6n
   b. 2 + 6n
   c. 8 - 6n
   d. 8 + 6n

6. How many lines of symmetry are in the regular polygon?

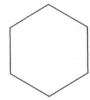

   a. 2
   b. 4
   c. 6
   d. 8

7. The graph below shows the number of movies watched by students in a film class over the course of a month. What is the range of the data?

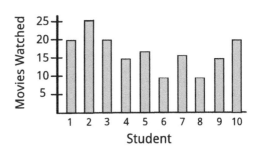

   a. 10
   b. 15
   c. 20
   d. 25

8. What is the value of the numerical expression $\sqrt{36 + 64}$?

   a. 10
   b. 14
   c. 48
   d. 50

9. Two vertices of a triangle are shown below. Which of the following could NOT be the coordinates of the third vertex?

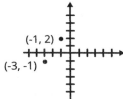

   a. (-2, -3)
   b. (1, -3)
   c. (1, 5)
   d. (5, 2)

10. The day after Halloween, the price of candy bars dropped from $1.40 per ounce to $1.12 per ounce. What was the percent decrease in the price of candy bars?

   a. 14%
   b. 20%
   c. 25%
   d. 28%

11. Four cubed plus seven is equal to what number?

   a. 21
   b. 23
   c. 64
   d. 71

12. The function g is defined as $g(x) = x^2 + 3$. What is the value of $g(-1)$?

   a. 1
   b. 2
   c. 4
   d. 5

13. A student surveyed her classmates to determine which color was their favorite. The results are displayed in the pie chart below. What is the central angle of the portion of the circle represented by students whose favorite color is blue?

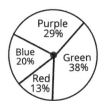

   a. 36°
   b. 50°
   c. 60°
   d. 72°

14. What is the prime factorization of 120?

   a. $2 \times 3 \times 5$
   b. $2^2 \times 3 \times 5$
   c. $2^3 \times 3 \times 5$
   d. $2^4 \times 3 \times 5$

15. A researcher surveys a random sample of 2,000 Illinois high school students to determine how many hours a day they spend doing homework. 40% of the students surveyed did at least three hours of homework a day. It can reasonably be concluded that

   a. exactly 40% of all high school students in the United States study for at least three hours a day
   b. approximately 40% of high school students in Illinois study for at least three hours a day
   c. approximately 40% of high school students in Illinois study for exactly three hours a day
   d. approximately 40% of all students in Illinois study for at least three hours a day

16. Which number is equivalent to $\frac{7}{6}$?

   a. .86
   b. 1.14
   c. $1.1\overline{6}$
   d. 1.2

17. Which inequality is shown in the solution set below?

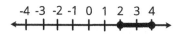

   a. $-3 \le 2x - 1 \le -7$
   b. $-3 \le 2x - 1 \le 7$
   c. $3 \le 2x - 1 \le -7$
   d. $3 \le 2x - 1 \le 7$

18. If $6x + 12 = 3(xy + 2y)$, what is the value of y?

   a. 2
   b. 3
   c. 4
   d. 6

19. The solution to $4x = 5$ is a

    a. irrational number
    b. natural number
    c. integer
    d. real number

20. Which expression is equivalent to the expression $3x^2y^3 - 2xy^3 - (-4xy^3 + 2x^2y^3)$?

    a. $x^2y^3 - 2xy^3$
    b. $x^2y^3 + 2xy^3$
    c. $5x^2y^3 + 2xy^3$
    d. $5x^2y^3 - 2xy^3$

21. There are 1,760 yards in a mile and 91.44 centimeters in a yard. Isla swims at a speed of 2 miles an hour. Which expression shows how many centimeters she swims per second?

    a. $\dfrac{60 \times 60}{1,760 \times 91.44 \times 2}$

    b. $\dfrac{1,760 \times 91.44 \times 2}{60 \times 60}$

    c. $\dfrac{60 \times 60 \times 2}{1,760 \times 91.44}$

    d. $\dfrac{1,760 \times 91.44 \times 60}{60 \times 2}$

22. A student records the number of sports each of her classmates plays. The data is summarized in the table below. What is the mean of the data?

    Note: Round to the nearest hundredth.

Number of Sports	Number of Students Playing That Number of Sports
1	4
2	8
3	3
4	1

    a. 2.06
    b. 2.2
    c. 4
    d. 8.25

23. Which expression is equivalent to $\sqrt{36y^4}$?

    a. $6y^2$
    b. $6y^4$
    c. $18y^2$
    d. $18y^4$

24. Which expression is equivalent to $(x + 3)(x - 4)$?

    a. $x^2 - 12$
    b. $x^2 - 1$
    c. $x^2 - x - 12$
    d. $x^2 + x + 12$

25. Jamar spins a prize wheel comprised of 15 equal sized wedges at his local arcade. Eight wedges result in a reward of 10 tickets, four wedges result in a reward of 25 tickets, two wedges result in a reward of 50 tickets, and one wedge results in a reward of 100 tickets. If Jamar spins the price wheel only once, what is the probability that he will win at least 50 tickets?

    a. $\dfrac{1}{4}$

    b. $\dfrac{1}{5}$

    c. $\dfrac{3}{5}$

    d. $\dfrac{2}{15}$

26. The radius of the cylinder below is one-third of its height. What is the cylinder's surface area?

    Note: The formula used to determine the surface area of a cylinder is $SA = 2r^2\pi + 2rh\pi$ where r is the cylinder's radius and h is the cylinder's height.

    a. 18 in^2
    b. 54 in^2
    c. 60 in^2
    d. 72 in^2

27. The box-and-whisker plot below shows test scores for an Algebra 1 class. What score represents the first quartile?

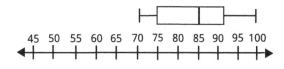

    a. 70
    b. 75
    c. 85
    d. 92

28. What is the slope of the line pictured below?

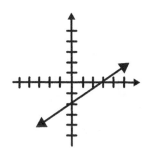

    a. $\frac{3}{2}$

    b. $\frac{2}{3}$

    c. $-\frac{2}{3}$

    d. $-\frac{3}{2}$

29. For what value of b is the equation
    $(6 - 2b) - 2(3 - b) = 0$ true?

    a. -3
    b. 3
    c. All real numbers
    d. There are no values for b that make the equation true

30. What is the height of a triangle with an area of 48 inches² and a base of 6 inches?

    a. 4 in
    b. 6 in
    c. 12 in
    d. 16 in

31. While saving up his allowance, Franco tracks the price of the new skateboard he wants to buy. In January, the skateboard costs $72.00. In both February and March, the skateboard costs $75.00. In April, the skateboard goes on sale for $50.00. What is the mean cost of the skateboard over these 4 months?

    a. $65.67
    b. $68.00
    c. $72.00
    d. $90.67

32. What is the equation of a circle with center (-2, 3) and radius 6?

    a. $(x + 2)^2 + (y - 3)^2 = 36$
    b. $(x - 2)^2 + (y + 3)^2 = 36$
    c. $(3 + x)^2 + (-2 + y)^2 = 36$
    d. $(3 - x)^2 + (2 - y)^2 = 36$

33. Quadrilateral ABCD is similar to quadrilateral EFGH. The length of $\overline{AD}$ is 5 inches and the length of $\overline{EH}$ is 7 inches. What is the length of $\overline{DC}$ if the length of $\overline{HG}$ is 21 inches?

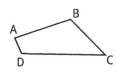

    a. 10 inches
    b. 12 inches
    c. 14 inches
    d. 15 inches

34. What is the result of the expression

$$\begin{bmatrix} 2 & 0 \\ 5 & -1 \end{bmatrix} + \begin{bmatrix} 2 & 8 \\ -9 & 6 \end{bmatrix}?$$

    a. $\begin{bmatrix} 2 & 8 \\ 5 & -1 \end{bmatrix}$

    b. $\begin{bmatrix} 4 & 8 \\ 4 & -5 \end{bmatrix}$

    c. $\begin{bmatrix} 2 & 8 \\ -4 & 5 \end{bmatrix}$

    d. $\begin{bmatrix} 4 & 8 \\ -4 & 5 \end{bmatrix}$

35. Solve: $x^2 - 12x + 35 = 0$.

    a. $x = -7, -5$
    b. $x = -7, 5$
    c. $x = 7, -5$
    d. $x = 7, 5$

36. A high school surveys their 9th and 10th grade students regarding their preferred class. The results of the survey are below.

Favorite Class	9th Graders	10th Graders	Total Number of Students
English	35	43	78
History	29	32	61
Math	27	38	65
Science	39	27	66
Total	130	140	270

What is the probability that a 10th grader's favorite class is history?

    a. $\dfrac{29}{130}$

    b. $\dfrac{8}{35}$

    c. $\dfrac{29}{61}$

    d. $\dfrac{32}{61}$

37. Nikki and Jorge are playing with a standard deck of 52 cards. Exactly half of the cards are red and half are black. If Nikki and Jorge each randomly draw one card from the deck, what is the probability that they both get a red card?

    a. $\dfrac{1}{2} \times \dfrac{1}{2}$

    b. $\dfrac{1}{2} \times \dfrac{25}{51}$

    c. $\dfrac{1}{2} \times \dfrac{25}{52}$

    d. $\dfrac{1}{2} \times \dfrac{26}{51}$

38. What is the measure of $\angle x$?

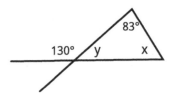

    a. $47°$
    b. $50°$
    c. $57°$
    d. $130°$

39. A square with a side length of 8 inches is inscribed in the circle below. If the area of the circle is 81π in², what is the area of the shaded region?

    a. $(81\pi - 64)$ in²
    b. $(81\pi - 32)$ in²
    c. $(64 - 81\pi)$ in²
    d. $(32 - 81\pi)$ in²

40. Triangle ABC is shown below. What is the cosine of $\angle A$?

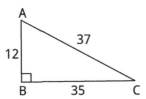

    a. $\dfrac{12}{37}$

    b. $\dfrac{12}{35}$

    c. $\dfrac{35}{37}$

    d. $\dfrac{37}{35}$

41. What is the solution set for $x^2 + 18 = 9$?

    a.   3
    b.   3i
    c.   -3i
    d.   ±3i

42. Which of the following describes all values for x for which $|3x - 4| \le 8$?

    a. $x \le 4$

    b. $x \ge -\dfrac{4}{3}$

    c. $-\dfrac{4}{3} \le x \le 4$

    d. $x \le 4 \text{ or } x \ge -\dfrac{4}{3}$

43. The equation for the perimeter of a regular hexagon is $P = 6s$, where s represents the length of one side. Which of the following shows the equation in terms of s?

    a. $s = \dfrac{6}{P}$

    b. $s = 6P$

    c. $s = P - 6$

    d. $s = \dfrac{P}{6}$

44. Kelsey subscribes to a movie streaming service. The service charges $9.00 a month for the first 15 movies and $0.50 for each additional movie after the first 15. If Kelsey watches 22 movies in a month, how much will she pay for the service that month?

    a. $9.00
    b. $11.00
    c. $12.50
    d. $20.00

45. The stem-and-leaf plot below represents the number of minutes it takes for employees of a business to drive to work. What is the median of the data?

Stem	Leaf
1	5 6 8 9
2	3 5 5 6 8
3	1 2 4
4	1 3 7 8
5	5 7 9

    a.   28
    b.   31
    c.   32
    d.   34

46. What is the solution set to the inequality $5 \le -3x - 1 \le 14$?

    a. $-5 \le x \le -2$
    b. $-2 \le x \le -5$
    c. $x \le -2 \text{ or } x \le -5$
    d. $x \ge -2 \text{ or } x \ge -5$

47. A sphere has a radius of 3 inches. What is the sphere's volume in inches³?

Note: The formula used to determine the volume of a sphere is $V = \dfrac{4}{3}\pi r^3$, where r is the sphere's radius.

    a. 4π
    b. 36π
    c. 81π
    d. 108π

Essay
1 Question, 30 Minutes

Instructions: You have 30 minutes to write an essay on the topic below. It is not permitted to write an essay on a different topic. Your essay must be written in blue or black pen.

Please be aware that the schools you apply to will receive a copy of your essay. Your essay should be longer than a paragraph and use specific examples and details.

Write your response on this page and the next page.

Your school will allow you to propose a new class on any topic. What topic would you choose and why?

Test 1 Answer Key

Section 1: Verbal

1.	C	9.	B	17.	C	25.	A	33.	C
2.	C	10.	B	18.	B	26.	D	34.	B
3.	B	11.	C	19.	C	27.	C	35.	B
4.	C	12.	B	20.	A	28.	B	36.	B
5.	B	13.	A	21.	A	29.	D	37.	C
6.	B	14.	C	22.	D	30.	A	38.	B
7.	C	15.	C	23.	A	31.	C	39.	B
8.	B	16.	B	24.	C	32.	B	40.	C

Section 2: Quantitative

1.	D	9.	C	17.	D	25.	D	33.	D
2.	C	10.	D	18.	D	26.	C	34.	C
3.	B	11.	C	19.	C	27.	B	35.	D
4.	B	12.	C	20.	C	28.	D	36.	A
5.	B	13.	A	21.	C	29.	B	37.	B
6.	B	14.	C	22.	A	30.	C		
7.	B	15.	A	23.	D	31.	C		
8.	C	16.	B	24.	A	32.	A		

Section 3: Reading

1.	A	9.	B	17.	A	25.	B	33.	C
2.	C	10.	B	18.	B	26.	C	34.	A
3.	C	11.	B	19.	D	27.	C	35.	B
4.	A	12.	C	20.	C	28.	A	36.	C
5.	B	13.	B	21.	A	29.	D		
6.	C	14.	C	22.	A	30.	B		
7.	B	15.	D	23.	D	31.	D		
8.	A	16.	B	24.	C	32.	D		

Section 4: Math

1.	C	11.	D	21.	B	31.	B	41.	D
2.	B	12.	C	22.	A	32.	A	42.	C
3.	C	13.	D	23.	A	33.	D	43.	D
4.	B	14.	C	24.	C	34.	D	44.	C
5.	C	15.	B	25.	B	35.	D	45.	B
6.	C	16.	C	26.	D	36.	B	46.	A
7.	B	17.	D	27.	B	37.	B	47.	B
8.	A	18.	A	28.	B	38.	A		
9.	C	19.	D	29.	C	39.	A		
10.	B	20.	B	30.	D	40.	A		

ISEE Test 2

Section 1: Verbal
40 Questions, 20 Minutes

Synonyms

Instructions: Select the word whose meaning is closest to the word in capital letters.

1. BANISH:

   a. admonish
   b. attack
   c. expel
   d. ignore

2. PLAUSIBLE:

   a. far-fetched
   b. obvious
   c. reasonable
   d. thoughtful

3. TEDIOUS:

   a. challenging
   b. dull
   c. sad
   d. swift

4. VALIDATE:

   a. aggravate
   b. agree
   c. motivate
   d. prove

5. IMPARTIAL:

   a. hesitant
   b. opinionated
   c. unbiased
   d. uncertain
   e.

6. SOLITARY:

   a. bashful
   b. lonely
   c. serene
   d. watchful

7. RETREAT:

   a. enjoy
   b. give
   c. relax
   d. withdraw

8. OBSTRUCTION:

   a. blockage
   b. coerison
   c. complication
   d. error

9. LOATHE:

   a. condescend
   b. detest
   c. exhaust
   d. refute

10. LUSTER:

    a. beauty
    b. confidence
    c. fatigue
    d. sheen

11. ARDUOUS:

    a. heavy
    b. oppressive
    c. strange
    d. strenuous

12. HASTEN:

    a. forget
    b. lighten
    c. quicken
    d. widen

13. COWER:

    a. climb
    b. crouch
    c. hide
    d. walk

14. DEBACLE:

    a. accident
    b. disagreement
    c. disaster
    d. misunderstanding

15. CULTIVATE:

    a. describe
    b. desire
    c. encourage
    d. plant

16. EXULTANT:

    a. elated
    b. poised
    c. relaxed
    d. revered

17. TACITURN:

    a. furious
    b. morose
    c. polite
    d. reticent

18. HUBRIS:

    a. altruism
    b. doubt
    c. frustration
    d. pride

19. CONTRITE:

    a. hopeful
    b. petulant
    c. remorseful
    d. shrewd

Sentence Completion

Instructions: Select the word or pair of words that best completes the sentence.

20. The professor's lectures were so ------- that very few of his students could follow them.

    a. condescending
    b. disjointed
    c. informative
    d. persuasive

21. In 2003, a genetics researcher concluded that one in every 200 men alive today is a ------- of the Mongolian Emperor Gengis Khan.

    a. confidant
    b. descendant
    c. enemy
    d. son

22. In light of the recent extreme heat, it seems ------- that the outdoor festival will take place this weekend.

    a. absurd
    b. inevitable
    c. improbable
    d. likely

23. Daniel Steibelt, a renowned piano -------, once challenged Beethoven to a musical duel.

    a. concerto
    b. builder
    c. tuner
    d. virtuoso

24. Although they anticipated that the transition would be -------, Jamal's parents agreed that relocating to a larger city would be beneficial in the long run.

    a. difficult
    b. impossible
    c. manageable
    d. tedious

25. The opulent palaces of St. Petersburg contrast sharply with the ------- Soviet era apartment buildings found throughout the city.

    a. dingy
    b. elaborate
    c. elegant
    d. hulking

26. Known for being -------, the old man kept to himself and avoided unnecessary conversations.

    a. boisterous
    b. passive
    c. pious
    d. reclusive

27. A debate moderator ------- discussion by asking questions, keeping participants on topic, and holding participants to time limits.

    a. critiques
    b. impedes
    c. facilitates
    d. forbids

28. The 1933 Double Eagle $20 coin was sold by Christie's for a(n) ------- 7.6 million dollars, making it the most expensive coin ever auctioned.

    a. exorbitant
    b. paltry
    c. reasonable
    d. unimpressive

29. After losing every tennis match to Ava, Marcus recognized that she was a(n) ------- opponent.

    a. adaptable
    b. formidable
    c. frightening
    d. novice

30. The United States sometimes uses ------- to restrict trade with foreign countries who violate international law.

    a. allies
    b. embargos
    c. negotiations
    d. treaties

31. A(n) ------- writer, Agatha Christie published 69 novels, 14 short story collections, and 19 plays during her lifetime.

    a. expert
    b. insightful
    c. nuanced
    d. prolific

32. Unlike Miranda, who ------- spending time with friends and social interaction, Damian ------- quiet and solitude.

    a. circumvents. . . values
    b. savors . . . detests
    c. thrives on . . . treasures
    d. tolerates . . . shirks

33. The company found that there were ------- benefits to letting their employees work from home: sales increased, employees took fewer sick days, and administrative tasks were completed 50% more -------.

    a. few . . . quickly
    b. several . . . laboriously
    c. substantial . . . efficiently
    d. unexpected . . . slowly

34. Tasmanian devils are ------- hunters and spend the daylight hours burrowed in a dark hole or under dense -------.

    a. fierce . . . shade
    b. nocturnal . . . foliage
    c. savage . . . conditions
    d. solitary . . . sunlight

35. Typically -------, Aria took a deep breath, gathered all of her courage, and stood up to the ------- bully.

    a. brave . . . frightened
    b. meek . . . malicious
    c. quiet . . . loud
    d. spiteful . . . cowering

36. David didn't mean to ------- his job responsibilities: he simply ------- his boss's instructions.

    a. fulfill . . . misunderstood
    b. meet . . . followed
    c. neglect . . . transcended
    d. shirk . . . misconstrued

37. Terrell was unsure about what to study in college: while he had ------- math and science grades, he had always been more interested in -------.

    a. exceptional . . . sports
    b. exemplary . . . literature
    c. mediocre . . . the arts
    d. superlative . . . chemistry

38. Kiersten was a ------- supporter of the new highway funding proposal, despite her initial ------- about the viability of the plan.

    a. fervent . . . excitement
    b. reluctant . . . hesitations
    c. staunch . . . concerns
    d. steadfast . . . confidence

39. Samantha's ------- question unintentionally offended some of the more ------- members of the group.

    a. benign ... thoughtful
    b. friendly ... impervious
    c. inconsiderate ... incorrigible
    d. innocuous ... sensitive

40. Jaxon liked to think that he was ------- to persuasion; however, when he purchased every item the salesman suggested, he realized that he was more ------- to it than he liked to admit.

    a. hostile ... averse
    b. immune ... susceptible
    c. predisposed ... resistant
    d. privy ... vulnerable

Section 2: Quantitative
37 Questions, 35 Minutes

The section is divided into two parts: problem solving and quantitative comparison. Directions for each part are provided.

Part 1 - Problem Solving

Instructions: Each question is followed by four possible answers. Select the best answer.

1. Jonah has 5 dimes and 5 nickels in his pocket. He takes out two random coins and determines their combined value. Which of the following events has the highest probability?

   a. The combined value of the coins will be $0.10
   b. The combined value of the coins will be $0.15
   c. The combined value of the coins will be $0.20
   d. The combined value of the coins will be $0.25

2. A golf course tracked the number of times each member came to the course in a given year. They then calculated the mean, median, mode, and range of the data. That information is collected in the table below.

Measure	Value
Mean	38
Median	41
Mode	37
Range	28

   If the member who went the least number of times decided to go four more times over the course of the year, and still went fewer times than any other member, how would that affect the data?

   a. It would decrease the range by 4.
   b. It would increase the range by 4.
   c. It would decrease the mode by 4.
   d. It would increase the mode by 4.

3. If $(x + 4)^2 = x^2 + kx + 16$, what is the value of k?

   a. 4
   b. 8
   c. 12
   d. 16

4. During her freshman year on the soccer team, Mindy scored a total of 12 goals. As a sophomore, she scored 25% more goals than she did as a freshman. How many goals did Mindy score during her sophomore year?

   a. 3
   b. 9
   c. 15
   d. 16

5. Joshua's final biology grade is calculated by averaging his scores on the five tests given over the length of the class. Joshua is hoping for a final grade greater than 92. If his grades on the first four tests were 96, 88, 97, and 85, what grade would he have to earn on the last test to achieve his goal?

   a. 92
   b. 93
   c. 94
   d. 95

6. Lines A and B are perpendicular. The equation of line A is $y = -\frac{1}{3}x - 1$. Two points on line B are $(-1, 4)$ and $(2, y)$. What is y?

   a. -5
   b. -13
   c. 5
   d. 13

7. A math teacher offered extra help to his students before and after school. He recorded the number of students who came to his office for extra help before school for a total of 25 days. On how many days did at least 3 students show up?

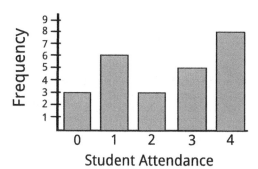

a. 5
b. 7
c. 13
d. 15

8. The sum of all integers from 1 to 299, inclusive, is x. What is the sum of all integers from 1 to 300, inclusive?

a. x - 299
b. x - 300
c. x + 299
d. x + 300

9. The circumference of a circle is 8. If the radius of the circle is reduced by 25%, what is the area of the new circle?

a. 6π
b. 8π
c. 9π
d. 12π

10. The net for a cube is shown below. Which of the following is a possible view of the folded cube?

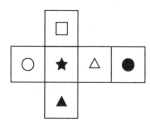

a.

b.

c.

d.

11. If az + bz = ac, which of the following expresses a, b, and c in terms of z?

a. $\dfrac{ac}{a+b}$

b. $\dfrac{c}{b}$

c. ac - a - b

d. $a^2c + abc$

12. Nathan is standing and holding a ball. He throws the ball up in the air and lets it fall to the ground. Which of the following graphs best represents this scenario?

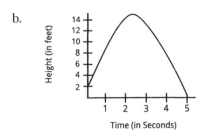

a.

b.

c.

d.

13. A 50 yard field has cone markers placed at the 10, 20, 30, 40, and 50 yard lines. A student in a gym class is instructed to run to the first cone, then back to the starting point, then to the second cone, then back to the starting point, and so on with this pattern until she has run to the last cone and back to the starting point. After she has completed this exercise, how many yards will the student have run total?

    a. 50 yards
    b. 100 yards
    c. 150 yards
    d. 300 yards

14. The sum of three consecutive even integers is 30. What is the largest of the integers?

    a. 8
    b. 10
    c. 12
    d. 14

15. There are five different styles of blue jeans on sale at the store. They cost $65, $35, $50, $60, and $35 per pair, respectively. If Monika wants to purchase a pair in the style that is the median price, how much will she spend on her pair of blue jeans before taxes?

    a. $30
    b. $35
    c. $50
    d. $65

16. The formula for the surface area of a cube is $A = 6s^2$, where s represents the side length. Cube A has side lengths that are half the side lengths of cube B. Which of the following statements regarding the surface areas of the cubes is true?

    a. The surface area of cube A is half the surface area of cube B.
    b. The surface area of cube A is half the surface area of cube B.
    c. The surface area of cube A is 2 times the surface area of cube B.
    d. The surface area of cube A is 4 times the surface area of cube B.

17. If $f(x) = (x - 3)^2$, what is the value of $f(-1)$?

    a. -16
    b. -4
    c. 4
    d. 16

18. In the rectangle below, $\overline{AB}$ is 4 inches and $\overline{AC}$ is 5 inches. What is the perimeter of the rectangle below?

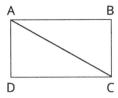

    a. 14 inches
    b. 16 inches
    c. 18 inches
    d. 20 inches

19. What is the maximum value for y if $y = -1x^3 + 3$
    for $-2 \leq x \leq 2$?

    a. 0
    b. 3
    c. 7
    d. 11

20. The sum of the interior angles of a regular
    polygon with n sides is $180°(n - 2)$. What type
    of polygon's interior angles have a sum of
    1080°?

    a. octagon
    b. pentagon
    c. hexagon
    d. decagon

Part 2 - Quantitative Comparisons

Instructions: In each question, use the information provided to compare the quantity in Column A with the quantity in Column B. All quantitative comparison questions have the same answer choices:

    a.   The quantity in column A is greater.
    b.   The quantity in column B is greater.
    c.   The two quantities are equal.
    d.   The relationship cannot be determined from the information given.

21. Column A   Column B

    x^2 $2x$

---

22. Column A   Column B

    The largest prime   The largest prime
    factor of 84.   number smaller than
                       10.

---

23. Column A   Column B

    $7 - 5 \times (3+2)^2$ $7 - 5 \times 3 + 2^2$

$\triangle ABC$ is similar to $\triangle QRS$.

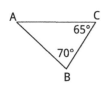 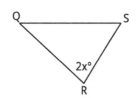

24. Column A   Column B

    $\angle A$ x

---

x is an integer greater than 1

25. Column A   Column B

    $\sqrt{2x}$ $2\sqrt{x}$

Two bags of chips and two candy bars cost a total of $3.50. Three bags of chips and four candy bars cost a total of $6.25.

26. Column A   Column B

    The cost of one candy $1.00
    bar

$x < -1$

27. Column A   Column B

    $-|x|$ $|x|$

A jar contains a mix of red and yellow candies. Two random candies are taken from the jar.

28. Column A   Column B

    The probability that   The probability that
    both candies chosen   one red candy and
    are red   one yellow candy are
                       chosen.

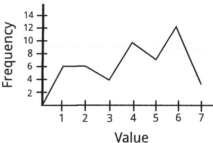

29.

    Column A   Column B

    The mode of the   The range of the
    frequency of the   frequency of the data.
    data.

Let $y^* = \dfrac{1}{y}$.

30. | Column A | Column B |
| --- | --- |
| 3^* | 6^* |

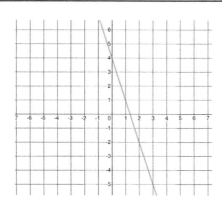

31. | Column A | Column B |
| --- | --- |
| The slope of the graph. | 3 |

32. | Column A | Column B |
| --- | --- |
| $(x-5)(x^2 +5x + 25)$ | $x^3 - 5^3$ |

The area of a rectangle is 108 in². One side of the rectangle is three times the length of the other side.

33. | Column A | Column B |
| --- | --- |
| The length of the shorter side of the rectangle. | 4 in. |

34. | Column A | Column B |
| --- | --- |
| The least common multiple of 2 and 6 | The greatest common factor of 24 and 30 |

Mr. Franklin selects students to answer questions by randomly pulling their names out of a jar. He returns the chosen names to the jar after every 5 questions. Molly is a student in Mr. Franklin's class.

35. | Column A | Column B |
| --- | --- |
| The probability that Molly is chosen to answer a question first | If Molly is not chosen first, the probability that Molly is chosen second |

The area of square A is 25 cm². The area of rectangle B is 20 cm². Note: The images are not drawn to scale.

Square A	Rectangle B

36. | Column A | Column B |
| --- | --- |
| The perimeter of square A. | The perimeter of rectangle B. |

The circle below has a radius of x.

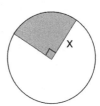

37. | Column A | Column B |
| --- | --- |
| The area of the unshaded region. | $x^2 \pi - \dfrac{1}{4}x^2 \pi$ |

Section 3: Reading
36 Questions, 35 Minutes

Instructions: Carefully read each passage and answer the questions that follow it. For each question, decide which of the choices best answers the question based on the passage.

Questions 1 - 6

1　　　With the arrival of the 21st century, global
2　warming became an urgent threat that could
3　no longer be ignored. This warming has caused
4　climate change, which leads to extreme weather
5　events like hurricanes, typhoons, and heat waves.
6　The United Nations Intergovernmental Panel
7　on Climate Change warned that if the planet's
8　temperature increases an additional 2.7 degrees
9　Fahrenheit, it would be catastrophic for millions of
10　people and animals. Shockingly, it is estimated that
11　the earth will approach that number by 2035.
12　　　The Jane Goodall Institute believes
13　the work they do can change that trajectory. In
14　addition to protecting animals and empowering
15　communities, they fight global warming in an effort
16　to slow down and mitigate the effects of climate
17　change. The organization, named for its founder
18　and renowned primatologist and anthropologist
19　Jane Goodall, knows that nature is surprisingly
20　resilient. The Jane Goodall Institute strives to
21　literally save the world.
22　　　To thwart climate change, the institute
23　recommends four key solutions: eliminate poverty,
24　change unsustainable lifestyles, abolish corruption,
25　and consider the growing population. This is
26　accomplished through a variety of initiatives,
27　and with the help of new technology that allows
28　humans to live in harmony with the natural world.
29　The group also recognizes that social media has
30　allowed people around the globe to connect and
31　share information in ways they never have before.
32　Especially meaningful, young people have the
33　power to help turn the tide. One of the Goodall
34　Institute's key programs, Roots & Shoots, brings
35　together students of all ages to carry out various
36　conservation projects.

37　　　Roots and Shoots is active in over one
38　hundred countries. Working with schools,
39　educators, and youth programs, the group
40　empowers young people as they identify and
41　solve problems in their own communities. In the
42　United States, Roots and Shoots has a National
43　Youth Leadership Council that provides leadership
44　training so that students can support the Jane
45　Goodall Institute operations as well as community-
46　based programs. Mini-grants are available for
47　students who create youth-led service-learning
48　campaigns. The projects range from small (e.g.
49　constructing birdhouses for wintering birds) to
50　large (building a barge that filters an invasive plant
51　species out of waterways). Jane Goodall believes, "If
52　we all get together, we can truly make a difference.
53　But we must act now. The window of time is
54　closing."

1. According to the passage, one can likely infer that Jane Goodall had previously been known for her work

   a. on climate change.
   b. with primates.
   c. children.
   d. indigenous people.

2. Which of the following best describes how the passage is organized?

   a. Individual causes of a problem are fully analyzed.
   b. An emotional appeal is used to make others care about a problem.
   c. A problem is explained and potential solutions are presented.
   d. A historical perspective is provided to help readers understand the origins of the issue.

3. In line 20, "resilient" most nearly means

   a. flexible.
   b. fragile.
   c. springy.
   d. strong.

4. The author's tone when describing climate change is best described as

   a. ambivalent.
   b. doomed.
   c. restrained.
   d. hopeful.

5. According to the passage, climate change has caused all of the following EXCEPT

   a. heat waves.
   b. hurricanes.
   c. tornadoes.
   d. typhoons.

6. It is clear from the passage that Jane Goodall believes

   a. that young people are essential in the fight against climate change.
   b. technology is hurting the environment.
   c. increasing the population will help slow global warming.
   d. the world's temperature will increase 2.7 degrees by 2030.

Questions 7 - 12

1   The unequal treaty terms that concluded
2   the first Opium War (1839-1842) ushered in a
3   decades-long period of economic exploitation
4   of China by Western powers and Japan. By the
5   end of the century most of China had been
6   partitioned into spheres of foreign influence, with
7   Britain controlling the south, France controlling
8   the southeast, Japan controlling the north,
9   Germany controlling the northeast, and Russia
10   controlling the northwest. Impositions ranged
11   from disadvantageous stipulations regarding trade
12   (including the seizure of Chinese ports and control
13   over tariffs) to extraterritorial rights that exempted
14   foreigners from following Chinese law. An influx of
15   Christian missionaries added insult to injury for the
16   primarily Confucian and Buddhist population.
17   The Qing dynasty initially attempted to
18   mitigate further damage by balancing a series of
19   humiliating concessions with a push for internal
20   reforms that were designed to make China more
21   competitive. This approach, known as the self-
22   strengthening movement, allowed the Qing
23   government to retain some semblance of authority
24   even as Western colonialism chipped away at
25   China's sovereignty.
26   Unfortunately, strained international
27   relations were accompanied by a succession of
28   domestic trials. Extreme weather led to a cyclical
29   pattern of floods and droughts, creating food
30   shortages that (due to the exploding population)
31   soon became full-scale famine. These dire
32   conditions fostered discontent among the public,
33   and sporadic riots ensued. By the mid-19th
34   century, this civil unrest culminated in the bloody
35   10-year Taiping Rebellion, which the Qing regime
36   finally quelled after an estimated 10-30 million
37   lives were lost. For four years of the rebellion, China
38   was also embroiled in the Second Opium War,
39   surrendering to Britain and France in 1860.

40   After the Sino-Japanese War of 1894-1895
41   ended in yet another disastrous defeat, the reigning
42   Qing emperor, Emperor Guangxu, decided that
43   desperate measures were warranted. In 1898, he
44   launched the infamous Hundred Days' Reform,
45   which sought to rapidly Westernize key institutions
46   across the country. To subvert opposition to the
47   initiative, he planned to oust conservative officials,
48   including his own aunt. The radical nature of the
49   Hundred Days' Plan, combined with Guangxu's
50   furtive approach, led to speculation that Guangxu
51   was actually being manipulated into sacrificing
52   China's independence to Western conspirators. The
53   emperor's aunt, Dowager Empress Cixi, got wind
54   of her nephew's plan to depose her and arranged a
55   successful coup d'etat instead. Although Guangxu
56   retained his official title, he was exiled and kept
57   under virtual house arrest while Cixi seized all
58   practical control of the throne.
59   Backlash against the Hundred Days'
60   Reform fanned the flame of the pre-existing anti-
61   Western sentiment. The Chinese people once again
62   began to riot, but this time they focused their ire
63   squarely on foreign intruders. In the northern
64   province of Shandong, a secret society called the
65   Righteous and Harmonious Fists began to brutalize
66   missionaries, diplomats, merchants, and any other
67   Westerners they could find (along with Chinese
68   citizens who had converted to Christianity). The
69   group practiced calisthenic exercise routines
70   that they believed would render them physically
71   invincible, and became known as the Boxers due
72   to the resemblance between these workouts and
73   shadowboxing.
74   The Boxer movement quickly gained
75   momentum and formed militias, which roamed
76   the countryside with explicit intent to execute
77   foreigners. Dowager Empress Cixi initially
78   denounced them as unruly agitators, despite her
79   own antipathy towards the West. However, as the
80   group expanded, she saw their potential and shifted
81   her position to one of endorsement. In June of
82   1900 the Boxers swarmed the capital city of Beijing,
83   while Empress Cixi declared war on all nations
84   with diplomatic ties in China. The Boxers occupied
85   Beijing for nearly 2 months, until an international
86   coalition of nearly 20,000 Western troops captured
87   it on August 14th and ended the rebellion.

7. In line 15, the author uses the idiomatic expression "added insult to injury" to describe

    a. how many of the Chinese felt about Christian missionaries.

    b. the pain inflicted upon the Chinese by the Christian missionaries.

    c. the conflict between Buddhism and Confucianism.

    d. the inequality created by Western expansion into China.

8. What did the Qing Dynasty initially do in order to preserve some of their power?

    a. They declared war on Western powers.

    b. They started the Sino-Japanese War.

    c. They made internal reforms.

    d. They forced missionaries out of China.

9. All of the following are examples of domestic problems suffered by the Qing dynasty, EXCEPT

    a. food shortages.

    b. famine.

    c. riots.

    d. war.

10. Based on the information in the final paragraph, why did the Dowager Empress Cixi come to support the boxers?

    a. She believed they would protect the Western powers in China.

    b. She thought they would help to depose her nephew.

    c. She saw them as political allies against the West.

    d. She viewed them as unruly agitators.

11. In lines 3 - 4, the author uses the phrase "exploitation of China" to

    a. show respect for how other nations treated China.

    b. describe the unfair way other nations treated China.

    c. portray the violence inflicted upon China from other nations.

    d. show the demarcation of a divided China.

12. According to the passage, which of the following nations were victorious in the Second Opium War?

    a. France

    b. Germany

    c. Russia

    d. China

Questions 13 - 18

1   Over the last decade, almond milk has
2   become an increasingly popular substitute for
3   cow's milk. In fact, between 2010 and 2015, almond
4   milk consumption grew by over 250% and demand
5   for the drink has continued to rise in recent years.
6   Its popularity is driven primarily by consumers
7   who do not drink cow's milk for dietary or ethical
8   reasons. Almond milk is seen by these consumers
9   as a low calorie and healthy alternative to drinking
10   dairy.
11   However, almond milk is not without
12   controversy. Almonds are a very "thirsty" nut:
13   it takes over 23 gallons of water to make just
14   one gallon of almond milk. This is especially
15   problematic because over 80% of the world's
16   almonds are grown in drought-stricken California.
17   In an effort to have enough water to produce
18   almonds, farmers are drilling thousands of feet
19   down into aquifers to retrieve it. There are concerns
20   that this drilling may unintentionally destabilize the
21   land, making the area more prone to earthquakes
22   or reducing infrastructure stability. In some almond
23   growing regions of California, the land is already
24   starting to sink due to this heavy drilling.
25   Proponents of almond milk are correct
26   to point out that producing a gallon of almond
27   milk actually uses less water than producing a
28   gallon of cow's milk (it takes about 30 gallons of
29   water to make one gallon of cow's milk). However,
30   the dairy industry argues that the higher level
31   of consumption is sustainable since it's spread
32   throughout farms all over the country, rather than
33   farms in a small, drought-stricken area.

34   Another concern with the increase in
35   almond production is the impact on honey bees,
36   whose numbers are declining at an alarming rate.
37   One survey of beekeepers found that more than
38   50 billion bees died in the winter of 2018-19 due to
39   almond milk production. This amounts to one-
40   third of all the bee colonies in the United States.
41   The high mortality rate is due mainly
42   to heavy pesticide use by almond farmers, but
43   other factors are at play as well. To grow almonds,
44   billions of bees must be transferred into a very
45   small geographic area to pollinate the crops. The
46   close proximity of such a high number of bees
47   makes it easier for disease to spread. What's
48   more, pollinating almond crops is especially
49   taxing because bees must be awoken from their
50   winter dormancy one to two months early. The
51   abbreviated period of inactivity makes bees less
52   healthy and more prone to disease.
53   Both beekeepers and almond farmers
54   recognize the need to address these issues. Some
55   California almond producers are taking steps
56   already to increase the biodiversity of their almond
57   groves, planting wildflowers, clover, and mustard
58   around their almond trees. Honey bees thrive on
59   this variety, and, theoretically, it should improve
60   the health of the bees. Also, in 2019, California
61   passed a bee protection law as part of the state's
62   "Bee Where" initiative. This law requires farmers to
63   inform bee keepers of any plans to spray pesticides
64   so that they can limit the bees' exposure to harm.

13. The primary purpose of the passage is to

    a. suggest that almond milk production be discontinued.
    b. advocate for the consumption of almond milk.
    c. discuss the effect of almond milk on honey bees.
    d. outline the controversies surrounding the production of almond milk.

14. According to the author, aquifer drilling has already caused

    a. earthquakes.
    b. harm to the bee population.
    c. drought.
    d. sinking land.

15. In line 25, "proponents" most nearly means

    a. advocates.
    b. critics.
    c. drinkers.
    d. questioners.

16. According to the passage, the dairy industry argues that cow's milk is more sustainable than almond milk because

    a. more water is used to produce a gallon of almond milk than is used to produce a gallon of cow's milk.
    b. dairy farms use less farmland than almond farms.
    c. dairy farms' water use is spread over a larger geographical area than almond farm's water use.
    d. almond farms kill honey bees and dairy farms do not.

17. Which best describes the organization of paragraph 5?

    a. A series of justifications for an action.
    b. An explanation of the causes of a problem.
    c. An opinion supported by facts.
    d. A description of how a problem is being resolved.

18. It can be concluded that the "Bee Where" intuitive hopes to empower beekeepers to

    a. expose their bees to more biodiverse flora and fauna.
    b. relocate or protect their bees if pesticides are being used nearby.
    c. pass laws against pesticide use.
    d. advocate for fewer bees to be used during almond production.

Questions 19 - 24

1   The influenza pandemic of 1918-1919
2 known as the Spanish flu was arguably the most
3 devastating outbreak of communicable disease
4 in recorded history, comparable to the infamous
5 bubonic plague of the Middle Ages. Roughly 1 in
6 3 of the 1.8 billion people in the world at the time
7 were infected, of which an estimated 50-100 million
8 died. This death toll from the Spanish flu was more
9 than double the number of casualties from World
10 War One, and represented a total global population
11 loss of 3-5%.
12   Due in part to its generalized symptoms,
13 the Spanish flu was not immediately recognized
14 as the distinct threat that it was. On the contrary,
15 reports of infection in the early months of 1918
16 were attributed to typical bouts of various seasonal
17 illnesses and were largely dismissed. Although
18 the outbreak's origins cannot be pinpointed with
19 certainty, many historians believe that the first
20 instances of Spanish flu can be traced to a military
21 base near Haskell County, Kansas. A local doctor
22 even logged a report with the Public Health Service
23 when a mysteriously virulent sickness began
24 spreading through the otherwise healthy young
25 soldiers in February and March of 1918, but no
26 follow-up investigation was conducted. On the
27 contrary, when the initial wave of illness appeared
28 to pass, many of the men were sent off to Europe
29 to fight. World War One was in its fourth and final
30 year, and the mass movements of troops perfectly
31 facilitated the virus' international spread.
32   Tight media censorship was another
33 consequence of the war that allowed the flu to
34 flourish; warring countries forbade news outlets
35 from reporting on the virus for fear of damaging the
36 war effort. In a disgraceful and tragic endangerment
37 of public health, the governments of Allied and
38 Central Powers alike continued to suppress public
39 knowledge of Spanish flu for months, even as the
40 disease ravaged their citizens. Spain was one of
41 the few places that still had an uncensored press,
42 due to the country's neutral status in the war. In

43 May of 1918, Spanish newspapers became the first
44 to publicly raise the alarm, giving rise to the false
45 impression that the virus had originated there and,
46 in turn, Spanish flu's misleading name.
47   In most other countries, including the
48 United States, inadequate government response
49 continued to escalate the crisis. When the first
50 wave of Spanish flu waned over the summer, the
51 dwindling number of new cases was taken as
52 evidence that the pandemic had ended. Rather
53 than taking advantage of the respite by preparing
54 for the virus' return, countries largely dropped what
55 little precautionary measures they'd taken.
56   In a tragic example of this kind of
57 complacency, Philadelphia held a Liberty
58 Loan parade to raise funds for the war effort on
59 September 28th, 1918 (despite being urged by
60 doctors to cancel the event). It was the largest
61 parade in the city's history, and the 200,000-person
62 crowd that gathered in support of American troops
63 provided the perfect environment for the Spanish
64 flu to spread. Within 6 weeks of the parade, 12,000
65 Philadelphians had died. By October, apathy and
66 denial finally gave way to panic as the second wave
67 of the virus continued to spread with a vengeance
68 that could not be ignored.

19. This passage is primarily concerned with the

    a. devastating effects of the Spanish flu.
    b. origins of the Spanish flu.
    c. causes of the accelerated spread of Spanish flu.
    d. symptoms of the Spanish flu.

20. As it is used in the passage, the word "facilitated" (line 31) most nearly means

    a. enabled
    b. hindered
    c. mangled
    d. represented

21. It can be concluded that many governments censored media coverage of the Spanish flu because they

    a. didn't realize how serious it was.
    b. wanted their citizens to take precautions to avoid getting sick.
    c. thought that media coverage wouldn't help slow the spread of the flu.
    d. didn't want to hurt their chances at winning the war.

22. According to the passage, the pandemic was named "Spanish" flu because

    a. it originated in Spain.
    b. Spain experienced the worst flu outbreak.
    c. the flu was first reported in Spanish newspapers.
    d. the second outbreak of the flu occurred only in Spain.

23. The author implies that the public began taking the Spanish flu seriously when

    a. the flu began to spread in a Kansas military base.
    b. American troops spread the flu overseas.
    c. the flu got worse over the summer.
    d. thousands of people in Philadelphia died of the disease.

24. The author's tone when discussing the United States government's response to the Spanish flu can best be described as

    a. apprehensive
    b. disapproving
    c. remorseful
    d. skeptical

Questions 25 - 30

1   Although hydraulic fracturing has been
2   around since the late nineteenth century, it became
3   increasingly popular in the early twenty-first
4   century as the United States began to run out of
5   conventional oil reservoirs produced using vertical
6   wells. Hydraulic fracturing, colloquially referred
7   to as "fracking," is an unconventional method of
8   production used to pull natural gas and petroleum
9   from shale reservoirs. Fracking is the process of
10   pumping pressurized liquid through a wellbore
11   in order to create fractures, or cracks, in shale
12   formations. The liquid, made up of water and sand
13   with some chemical additives, serves as a way to
14   create and sustain the fractures so that oil and
15   natural gas can escape the shale formation.
16   Fracking is often combined with horizontal
17   drilling to maximize the amount of product
18   extracted. In the early 2000's, horizontal drilling
19   technology came down in price, and it went up
20   in precision. This relationship naturally gave way
21   to a boom in the use of fracking and horizontal
22   drilling in the United States, increasing oil and
23   gas production by more than 100% over a ten-
24   year period. Since this boom, the United States
25   has become a leader in global oil and natural gas
26   production, exporting more than it imports.

27   There is some controversy regarding
28   the practice of hydraulic fracturing. Much of this
29   sensitivity comes from the disposal of the liquid
30   used to create the fractures. Once the liquid
31   has served its purpose to create and sustain
32   fractures, it returns to the surface through the
33   well as "flowback." A popular disposal method for
34   flowback is to inject it back into the ground after it
35   is treated. This is not allowed at every well site, and
36   in the places it is allowed, there is concern over its
37   effect on groundwater. There is also the chance that
38   flowback may be pumped back into the ground
39   near pre-existing faults that may cause localized
40   earthquakes.
41   There is no doubt that fracking has
42   revolutionized the energy industry in the United
43   States. It provides thousands of jobs to scientists,
44   engineers, and on-site personnel. It helps stimulate
45   small-town economies, and it has made the
46   United States the leading producer of oil and
47   natural gas globally. However, it comes at a cost.
48   Not only is there concern over the possible effects
49   on groundwater and the localized aftershocks of
50   flowback disposal, but many argue that the United
51   States should focus on more sustainable energy
52   production. A shift toward renewable energy
53   resources, like solar and wind, provides just as great
54   an opportunity for global leadership as fracking
55   and horizontal drilling did nearly twenty years ago.

25. According to the passage, fracking became widely used

    a. in the 1800s.
    b. when oil reserves became scarce.
    c. when technology for vertical wells improved.
    d. in the late nineteenth century.

26. The primary purpose of the passage is to

    a. warn against the dangers of fracking.
    b. provide a global overview of fracking.
    c. explain the rise of and concern with fracking in the United States.
    d. analyze the pros and cons of hydraulic fracturing.

27. In line 20, "precision" most nearly means

    a. accuracy.
    b. fidelity.
    c. loyalty.
    d. value.

28. All of the following are reasons fracking increased EXCEPT

    a. global demand for oil.
    b. reduced oil reserves.
    c. improved technology.
    d. oil surpluses.

29. Which best describes the organization of lines 41 - 52?

    a. The pros and cons of fracking are passionately debated.
    b. The positive effects of fracking are acknowledged as well as the downsides.
    c. A problem is presented and a solution is offered.
    d. A dire warning is giving to supporters of fracking.

30. In the final sentence of the passage, the author suggests that society

    a. should continue to balance the positive impacts of fracking with the negative effects.
    b. abandon new pursuits of energy.
    c. look for more durable sources of energy.
    d. aim for total energy independence.

Questions 31 - 36

1 One night I had roamed into the city, and was
2 walking slowly on in my usual way, musing upon
3 a great many things, when I was arrested by an
4 inquiry, the purport of which did not reach me, but
5 which seemed to be addressed to myself, and was
6 preferred in a soft sweet voice that struck me very
7 pleasantly. I turned hastily round and found at my
8 elbow a little girl who begged to be directed to a
9 certain street at a considerable distance.
10
11 'It is a very long way from here,' I said.
12
13 'I know that, sir,' she replied timidly. 'I am afraid it is
14 a very long way, for I came from there tonight.'
15
16 'Alone?' said I, in some surprise.
17
18 'Oh, yes, I don't mind that, but I am a little
19 frightened now, for I had lost my road.'
20
21 'And what made you ask it of me? Suppose I should
22 tell you wrong?'
23
24 'I am sure you will not do that,' said the little
25 creature,' you are such a very old gentleman, and
26 walk so slow yourself.'
27
28 I cannot describe how much I was impressed by
29 this appeal and the energy with which it was made,
30 which brought a tear into the child's clear eye, and
31 made her slight figure tremble as she looked up
32 into my face.
33
34 'Come,' said I, 'I'll take you there.'

35 She put her hand in mine as confidingly as if she
36 had known me from her cradle, and we trudged
37 away together; the little creature accommodating
38 her pace to mine, and rather seeming to lead and
39 take care of me. I observed that every now and then
40 she stole a curious look at my face, as if to make
41 quite sure that I was not deceiving her, and that
42 these glances seemed to increase her confidence at
43 every repetition.
44
45 For my part, my curiosity and interest were at least
46 equal to the child's, for child she certainly was,
47 although I thought that her very small and delicate
48 frame imparted a peculiar youthfulness to her
49 appearance.
50
51 'Who has sent you so far by yourself?' said I.
52
53 'Someone who is very kind to me, sir.'
54
55 'And what have you been doing?'
56
57 'That, I must not tell,' said the child firmly.
58
59 There was something in the manner of this reply
60 which caused me to look at the little creature
61 with an involuntary expression of surprise; for I
62 wondered what kind of errand it might be that
63 had her prepared for questioning. Her quick eye
64 seemed to read my thoughts, for as it met mine she
65 added that there was no harm in what she had been
66 doing, but it was a great secret—a secret which she
67 did not even know herself.

31. In line 7, the man turned "hastily" toward the little girl because he was

    a. startled.
    b. irritated.
    c. helpful.
    d. angry.

32. According to the passage, the little girl asked for help because she

    a. was scared of the dark.
    b. wants companionship.
    c. was tired.
    d. was lost.

33. It can be inferred that the little girl approached the narrator, rather than another passerby, because he was

    a. the only person around.
    b. older and did not seem intimidating.
    c. smiling and seemed friendly.
    d. looking curiously at her since she was walking alone.

34. What figure of speech is used in lines 35 - 39?

    a. hyperbole
    b. irony
    c. personification
    d. simile

35. As it is used in line 39, "accommodating" most nearly means

    a. accelerating
    b. encouraging
    c. matching
    d. pausing

36. What caused the man to have an "involuntary expression of surprise"(line 61)?

    a. The realization that the little girl was asked to keep a secret.
    b. The determination the little girl showed in keeping her secret.
    c. The manner in which the little girl reassured the man that not doing anything wrong.
    d. The trust that the little girl had that the man would keep her secret.

Section 4: Math
47 Questions, 40 Minutes

Instructions: Each question is followed by four answer choices. Select the best answer.

1. What is the seventh number in this sequence?

   26, 19, 12, 5, -2

   a. -8
   b. -9
   c. -15
   d. -16

2. The product of two rational numbers must be

   a. irrational
   b. an integer
   c. rational
   d. complex

3. The stem-and-leaf plot below represents the number of minutes each student in a class studied for a science test. What is the mode of the data?

Stem	Leaf
1	5 7
2	7 8 8
3	4 5 5
4	2 7 7 7 9
5	4 6 6
6	3 7 9 9
7	2 2 8

   a. 35
   b. 47
   c. 69
   d. 72

4. The formula for the surface area of a sphere is $4\pi r^2$, where r is the radius of the sphere. If a sphere has a circumference of 12π inches, what is the surface area of the sphere?

   a. 36π in^2
   b. 48π in^2
   c. 144π in^2
   d. 576π in^2

5. Which of the following describes all values for x for which $|2x - 1| > 9$?

   a. $x < -4$ or $x > 5$
   b. $x > -4$ or $x < 5$
   c. $-4 < x < 5$
   d. $-4 > x > 5$

6. What is the distance between $(4, 5)$ and $(1, -3)$?

   a. $\sqrt{29}$
   b. $\sqrt{56}$
   c. $\sqrt{73}$
   d. $\sqrt{89}$

7. If $\frac{10}{m} = 0.01$, what is the value of m?

   a. 1
   b. 10
   c. 100
   d. 1000

8. Louisa and Milly are making t-shirts for a fundraiser. Milly makes half as many t-shirts as Louisa does each day. If they made a total of 48 t-shirts yesterday, how many did Milly make?

   a. 16
   b. 17
   c. 32
   d. 34

9. What is the solution set to the inequality $-4 \leq 2x - 6 \leq 8$?

    a. $-5 \leq x \leq 1$
    b. $1 \leq x \leq 7$
    c. $1 \leq x \leq 5$
    d. $5 \leq x \leq 7$

10. What is the solution set for $x^2 + 36 = 0$?

    a. 6
    b. ±6
    c. ±6i
    d. ±6i, 6

11. Triangle ABC is shown below. What is the tangent of $\angle$ B?

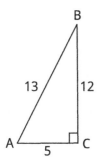

    a. $\frac{5}{13}$
    b. $\frac{5}{12}$
    c. $\frac{12}{13}$
    d. $\frac{12}{5}$

12. Point (9, -2) is on a circle with center (1, -7). What is the radius of the circle?

    a. $\sqrt{13}$ grid units
    b. $\sqrt{89}$ grid units
    c. 13 grid units
    d. 89 grid units

13. Julien can make up his own locker combination. If he can choose from digits 1-6 to create a 4 digit combination without any numbers repeating, how many different combinations could he make?

    a. 72
    b. 180
    c. 360
    d. 1,296

14. A scale model of a train car is 7 inches long and 3 inches tall. The real train car the model is based on measures 35 feet long. How tall is the real train car?

    a. 10 ft
    b. 15 ft
    c. 21 ft
    d. 31 ft

15. A smaller square is inscribed in the larger square below. The side length of the smaller square is half of that of the larger square. What is the area of the shaded region?

    a. 36 cm²
    b. 48 cm²
    c. 96 cm²
    d. 108 cm²

16. Marcus is shopping at his local market. Which of the following equations represents the amount of change (c) Marcus will receive if he purchases n items at $4.50 each and pays with a $20 bill?

    a. $c = 20 - 4.5n$
    b. $c = 4.5n - 20$
    c. $c = 20 + 4.5n$
    d. $c = 20n - 4.5$

17. Akil is trying to determine if most pet owners in his neighborhood own cats, dogs, or another pet. What sample will give him the best and most reliable information about his pet owning neighbors?

    a. all of the neighbors he knows well
    b. all neighbors
    c. all pet owners in his neighborhood
    d. all pet owners in his town

18. Find the third quartile of the following data set:

    6, 8, 8, 9, 10, 11, 15

    a. 8
    b. 9
    c. 10
    d. 11

19. What is the value of the expression $\sqrt{4} \times \sqrt{36}$

    a. 4
    b. 8
    c. 12
    d. 16

20. A clothing store displayed some new items in their store. The price of the 22 new items is noted in the chart below. If all 22 items are displayed, what is the median price of these items?

    a. $20.00
    b. $30.00
    c. $40.00
    d. $50.00

21. What is the result of the expression below?

$$2 \begin{bmatrix} 3 \\ 4 \\ 1 \\ 0 \end{bmatrix}$$

    a. $\begin{bmatrix} 1 \\ 6 \\ 3 \\ 0 \end{bmatrix}$

    b. $\begin{bmatrix} 6 \\ 8 \\ 2 \\ 2 \end{bmatrix}$

    c. $\begin{bmatrix} 3 \\ 1 \\ 5 \\ 1 \end{bmatrix}$

    d. $\begin{bmatrix} 6 \\ 8 \\ 2 \\ 0 \end{bmatrix}$

22. If the function f is defined as f(x) = 6x - 2, for what value of x is f(x) equal to 22?

    a. 4
    b. 5
    c. 6
    d. 7

23. In the xy-coordinate plane, segment $\overline{AB}$ is to be shifted 2 units up and 2 units right. What will be the new coordinates of the point A?

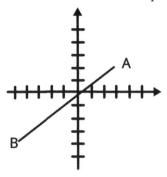

    a. $(1, 0)$
    b. $(4, 5)$
    c. $(5, 4)$
    d. $(6, 4)$

24. How many unique prime factors does the number 324 have?

    a. 1
    b. 2
    c. 3
    d. 4

25. Which expression is equivalent to the expression $4a^2b^2c - 5a^2b^3 + (6a^2b^2c + 2a^3b^2)$?

    a. $10a^2b^2c - 3a^2b^3$
    b. $10a^2b^2c - 7a^2b^3$
    c. $-2a^2b^2c - 5a^2b^3 + 2a^3b^2$
    d. $10a^2b^2c - 5a^2b^3 + 2a^3b^2$

26. Solve: $x^2 - 4 = 0$.

    a. $x = -2$
    b. $x = 0$
    c. $x = 2$
    d. $x = 2, -2$

27. Matteo flips a coin 5 times and records whether each flip results in heads or tails. What is the probability that the coin lands on heads for all 5 coin flips

    a. $\frac{1}{32}$

    b. $\frac{1}{10}$

    c. $\frac{1}{5}$

    d. $\frac{1}{2}$

28. The height of the cone pictured below is 2 more than its diameter. What is the volume of the cone?

Note: The formula used to determine the volume of a cone is $V = \frac{1}{3}\pi r^2 h$, where r is the cone's radius and h is the cone's height.

10 cm.

   a. 100π in^3
   b. 120π in^3
   c. 200π in^3
   d. 400π in^3

29. What is the value of the expression $6.7 \times 10^6 + 5.3 \times 10^3$?

   a. 6.7053×10^6
   b. 6.753×10^6
   c. 6.7053×10^9
   d. 14.0×10^9

30. A quadrilateral is shown below. What is the measure of the missing angle?

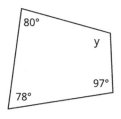

   a. 87°
   b. 95°
   c. 105°
   d. 107°

31. Point A is a point on line S (not pictured) which is parallel to line R. What is another point on line S?

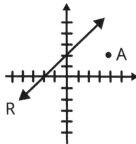

   a. (4, 0)
   b. (3, 3)
   c. (0, 0)
   d. (2, 0)

32. If $5(y - 1) + 3 = y(5 + 2) - 8$, what is the value of y?

   a. 2
   b. 3
   c. 5
   d. 6

33. The price of a laptop increased from $450 to $600. What was the percent increase in the price of the laptop?

Note: round to the nearest percent

   a. 20%
   b. 25%
   c. 33%
   d. 40%

34. A class is measuring the weight of various insects. What is the most reasonable unit of measure to use?

   a. milliliters
   b. kilograms
   c. centimeters
   d. milligrams

35. Which of the following is equivalent to $\frac{9}{16}$?

   a. .55
   b. .5625
   c. .57
   d. .6

36. The box-and-whisker plot below represents a class's grades, in percentages, on a math test. What is the range of the data?

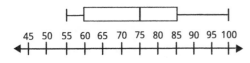

   a. 45
   b. 50
   c. 55
   d. 60

37. The area of the rectangle below is 27 cm². What is the length of the shorter side of the rectangle?

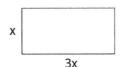

   a. 3 cm
   b. 6 cm
   c. 7 cm
   d. 9 cm

38. A real estate agency tracks the number of homes sold by their realtors each month. The probability of selling a given number of homes is outlined in the table below.

Number of homes sold	Probability
1	$\frac{3}{6}$
2	$\frac{1}{6}$
3	$\frac{1}{6}$
4	$\frac{1}{6}$

What is the expected number of homes sold?

   a. 1
   b. 2
   c. 3
   d. 4

39. Harris collects comic books. He has 10 superhero comics, 5 animal comics, and 6 action/adventure comics. The rest of his collection is made up of sports comics. If Harris randomly selects one comic from his collection, the probability of selecting a sports comic is $\frac{1}{8}$. How many total comic books does Harris own?

   a. 21
   b. 22
   c. 24
   d. 27

40. Simplify: $3xy^2 \times 4x^3y^4$.

   a. $12xy$
   b. $12x^3y^6$
   c. $12x^4y^6$
   d. $12x^3y^8$

41. The graph below is the solution set for which inequality?

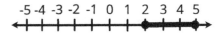

   a. $-15 \leq 5x - 11 \leq 24$
   b. $-15 \leq 5x + 11 \leq 24$
   c. $-1 \leq 5x + 11 \leq 14$
   d. $-1 \leq 5x - 11 \leq 14$

42. Which expression is equivalent to $\sqrt{100x}$?

   a. $\frac{10}{x}$

   b. $10\sqrt{x}$

   c. $50x$

   d. $50\sqrt{x^2}$

43. ∠A is congruent to ∠C. What is the measure of ∠B?

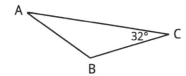

a. 32°
b. 64°
c. 104°
d. 116°

44. There are 5,280 feet in a mile. Brianna walks at a speed of 440 feet per minute. Which expression shows how many miles she walks per hour?

a. $\dfrac{5,280 \times 440}{60}$

b. $\dfrac{440 \times 60}{5,280}$

c. $\dfrac{5,280 \times 60}{440}$

d. $\dfrac{60}{5,280 \times 440}$

45. Clarissa tracked the high temperatures every day during the first week of summer. The high temperatures for Monday through Saturday were 79 degrees, 82 degrees, 83 degrees, 86 degrees, 81 degrees, and 77 degrees. If the mean high temperature for the week was 81 degrees, what was the high temperature on Sunday?

a. 76 degrees
b. 79 degrees
c. 81 degrees
d. 85 degrees

46. Which expression is equivalent to $(x - 5)(x - 6)$?

a. $x^2 + 30$
b. $x^2 - x + 30$
c. $x^2 - 11x - 30$
d. $x^2 - 11x + 30$

47. A librarian tracks the average number of books checked out by 6th to 12th grade students during the first semester. That data is represented in the line graph below. According to the data, 9th grade students check out how many more books than 12th grade students?

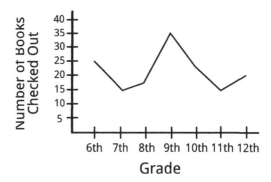

a. 5
b. 10
c. 15
d. 20

Essay
1 Question, 30 Minutes

Instructions: You have 30 minutes to write an essay on the topic below. It is not permitted to write an essay on a different topic. Your essay must be written in blue or black pen.

Please be aware that the schools you apply to will receive a copy of your essay. Your essay should be longer than a paragraph and use specific examples and details.

Write your response on this page and the next page.

What do you have in common with your closest friends? How are you different?

Test 2 Answer Key

Section 1: Verbal

1. C	9. B	17. D	25. A	33. C
2. C	10. D	18. D	26. D	34. B
3. B	11. D	19. C	27. C	35. B
4. D	12. C	20. B	28. A	36. D
5. C	13. B	21. B	29. B	37. B
6. B	14. C	22. C	30. B	38. C
7. D	15. C	23. D	31. D	39. D
8. A	16. A	24. A	32. C	40. B

Section 2: Quantitative

1. B	9. C	17. D	25. B	33. A
2. A	10. A	18. A	26. C	34. C
3. B	11. A	19. D	27. B	35. B
4. C	12. B	20. A	28. D	36. D
5. D	13. D	21. D	29. B	37. C
6. D	14. C	22. C	30. A	
7. C	15. C	23. B	31. B	
8. D	16. B	24. A	32. C	

Section 3: Reading

1. B	9. D	17. B	25. B	33. B
2. C	10. C	18. B	26. C	34. D
3. D	11. B	19. C	27. A	35. C
4. D	12. A	20. A	28. D	36. B
5. C	13. D	21. D	29. B	
6. A	14. D	22. C	30. C	
7. A	15. A	23. D	31. A	
8. C	16. C	24. B	32. D	

Section 4: Math

1. D	11. B	21. D	31. D	41. D
2. C	12. B	22. A	32. B	42. B
3. B	13. C	23. C	33. C	43. D
4. C	14. B	24. B	34. D	44. B
5. A	15. D	25. D	35. B	45. B
6. C	16. A	26. D	36. A	46. D
7. D	17. C	27. A	37. A	47. C
8. A	18. D	28. A	38. B	
9. B	19. C	29. A	39. C	
10. C	20. C	30. C	40. C	

ISEE Test 3

Section 1: Verbal
40 Questions, 20 Minutes

Synonyms

Instructions: Select the word whose meaning is closest to the word in capital letters.

1. RATIONAL:

    a. agreeable
    b. logical
    c. smart
    d. thoughtful

2. EXTRACT:

    a. comply
    b. precise
    c. remove
    d. stop

3. DISPERSE:

    a. dispute
    b. scatter
    c. summon
    d. throw

4. CHRONIC:

    a. acute
    b. convenient
    c. occasional
    d. persistent

5. CAPSIZE:

    a. crash
    b. enlarge
    c. overturn
    d. sail

6. GARGANTUAN:

    a. enormous
    b. frightening
    c. mammalian
    d. rocky

7. LETHARGIC:

    a. catatonic
    b. discreet
    c. peevish
    d. sluggish

8. INDIGNANT:

    a. aggrieved
    b. noxious
    c. vagrant
    d. serious

9. ENLIGHTEN:

    a. brighten
    b. inform
    c. perplex
    d. ponder

10. BELLIGERENT:

    a. combative
    b. disappointed
    c. humble
    d. impetuous

11. AMORPHOUS:

    a. circular
    b. large
    c. mysterious
    d. shapeless

12. JOCULAR:

    a. frightened
    b. gleeful
    c. pleased
    d. responsible

13. OBLIVIOUS:

    a. childish
    b. indolent
    c. relaxed
    d. unaware

14. FRIGID:

    a. chilly
    b. freezing
    c. rainy
    d. tepid

15. EXTRAPOLATE:

    a. deduce
    b. join
    c. recognize
    d. think

16. AUSTERE:

    a. dull
    b. greedy
    c. recalcitrant
    d. strict

17. OBSTINATE:

    a. defiant
    b. morose
    c. stubborn
    d. witty

18. LOQUACIOUS:

    a. funny
    b. inconsiderate
    c. silent
    d. talkative

19. LEXICON:

    a. dictionary
    b. game
    c. library
    d. word

Sentence Completion

Instructions: Select the word or pair of words that best completes the sentence.

20. The district attorney was confident that she had ------- evidence to successfully bring charges against the man.

    a. inconsistent
    b. little
    c. stunning
    d. sufficient

21. With a paltry 1-12 record, the Smithville Jaguars were clearly the ------- going into the game.

    a. favorites
    b. observers
    c. underdogs
    d. visionaries

22. Eighth century Persian mathematician Muhammad ibn Musa al-Khwarizmi is celebrated for ------- Arabic numerals to the West.

    a. introducing
    b. involving
    c. leaving
    d. suggesting

23. In the Battle of Lexington, the patriot troops successfully ------- the invading British forces.

    a. angered
    b. assisted
    c. noticed
    d. repelled

24. Abdul lived his life with -------, always sticking to his values even when it was difficult.

    a. empathy
    b. integrity
    c. positivity
    d. thoughfulness

25. The ------- jewelry thief was arrested by police after he accidentally set off a silent alarm at a high end jewelry store.

    a. lethargic
    b. notorious
    c. renowned
    d. wealthy

26. Paul couldn't believe that he was hired for a job for which he was so clearly -------.

    a. competent
    b. knowledgeable
    c. uncertain
    d. unqualified

27. On August 25th, 1944, Allied troops ------- Paris from the German occupation.

    a. controlled
    b. destroyed
    c. evaluated
    d. liberated

28. The ocean was surprisingly ------- after the previous night's tempestuous storm.

    a. cold
    b. grimy
    c. placid
    d. turbid

29. Progeria, a rare genetic condition, is a medical ------- in which children's bodies age very quickly.

    a. anomaly
    b. eccentricity
    c. norm
    d. procedure

30. Technology advances at such a fast pace that within just a few years, a phone or computer can become -------.

    a. broken
    b. fashionable
    c. obsolete
    d. reworked

31. Typically -------, Kiana was stunned into silence when she met the president of the United States.

    a. exuberant
    b. indefatigable
    c. polite
    d. verbose

32. Fariq ------- hoped to go scuba diving on his vacation to the Caribbean, but he ------- settled on snorkeling instead.

    a. initially . . . ultimately
    b. once . . . first
    c. never . . . hopelessly
    d. really . . . eagerly

33. Scaring tourists with stories of the ------- drop bear, described as an aggressive and predatory koala bear, is a popular ------- in Australia.

    a. amiable . . . prank
    b. easygoing . . . tactic
    c. fictional . . . hoax
    d. frightening . . . greeting

34. Although Alexander Fleming is ------- with the invention of penicillin, Howard Flory and Ernst Chain were responsible for its use in -------.

    a. busy . . . cooking
    b. credited . . . medicine
    c. familiar . . . design
    d. trusted . . . healing

35. AT&T held a(n) ------- on phone service in the United States and Canada until 1982 when the company was ------- into seven smaller companies.

    a. authority . . . connected
    b. monopoly . . . divided
    c. patent . . . combined
    d. training . . . branched

36. Her new boss's ------- tone made Millie feel ------- and unimportant.

    a. condescending . . . resentful
    b. dismissive . . . valued
    c. encouraging . . . introspective
    d. respectful . . . angry

37. Gianna was in a tough -------: should she stay in Iowa to be near her family or move to California for a(n) ------- job opportunity?

    a. market . . . amazing
    b. position . . . disappointing
    c. predicament . . . prestigious
    d. world . . . unremarkable

38. Even when he spotted a hammerhead shark in the distance, the ------- scuba diver did not become -------.

    a. ardent . . . enthused
    b. experienced . . . emboldened
    c. intrepid . . . panicked
    d. timid . . . alarmed

39. Like many of her -------, Susan couldn't
    understand why the younger generations
    preferred to communicate using email rather
    than handwritten -------.

    a. contemporaries . . . letters
    b. children . . . novellas
    c. peers . . . text messages
    d. elders . . . transcripts

40. The con artist ------- Logan's ------- by
    promising him that he would double his
    investment in just a few days.

    a. boosted . . . ignorance
    b. deflated . . . eagerness
    c. enriched . . . money
    d. exploited . . . naivete

Section 2: Quantitative
37 Questions, 35 Minutes

The section is divided into two parts: problem solving and quantitative comparison. Directions for each part are provided.

Part 1 - Problem Solving

Instructions: Each question is followed by four possible answers. Select the best answer.

1. Freight train A leaves Central Station for Springfield at 11:00am going at a constant speed of 60 miles per hour. Two hours later, freight train B leaves the same station for Springfield on a neighboring track going at a constant speed of 90 miles per hour. At what time will freight train B catch up with freight train A?

    a. 3:00pm
    b. 4:00pm
    c. 5:00pm
    d. 6:00pm

2. What is the product of 3 and the lowest common multiple of 6, 10, and 14?

    a. 210
    b. 630
    c. 840
    d. 2,520

3. Ebony is sewing a tablecloth for her round kitchen table. Her table has a diameter of 36 inches. If she wants the tablecloth to hang over all edges of the table by six inches, what circumference does she need to make the tablecloth?

    a. 42π inches
    b. 48π inches
    c. 212π inches
    d. 242π inches

4. What is the value of the expression $\dfrac{42\left(\frac{4^{3}}{4^{1}}\right)}{16(18 - 2)}$?

    a. 0
    b. 1
    c. 2
    d. 4

5. Which of the following is equal to $\sqrt[3]{x^{2}}$?

    a. $x^{\frac{2}{3}}$
    b. x
    c. $x^{\frac{3}{2}}$
    d. x^{6}

6. A jar contains a collection of 30 marbles that are either blue, green, yellow, or orange. If one marble is chosen at random, the probability that the chosen marble is blue is $\frac{1}{5}$. The probability that the chosen marble is green is $\frac{1}{3}$. Which of the following is greatest?

    a. The number of green marbles in the bag
    b. The number of blue marbles in the bag
    c. The combined number of orange and yellow marbles in the bag
    d. There is not enough information given to determine the answer.

7. In the chart below, the mean and the median of the data are both 5. If the data is symmetric about the mean, what is the frequency of value 2?

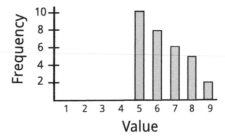

    a. 2
    b. 4
    c. 5
    d. 6

8. If $\frac{xy}{1} = \frac{y}{z}$, which of the following is equal to x?

    a. $\frac{1}{zy^2}$

    b. $\frac{1}{z}$

    c. z

    d. zy

9. For any positive integer n, n! is the product of all integers from 1 to n, inclusive. What is the value of the expression below?

    5!

    a. 20
    b. 60
    c. 100
    d. 120

10. If $g(x) = \sqrt{g}$, which inequality is true?

    a. $g(0.25) < g(0.5) < g(1)$
    b. $g(1) < g(0.5) < g(0.25)$
    c. $g(0.25) < g(1) < g(0.5)$
    d. $g(1) < g(0.25) < g(0.5)$

11. If $(x - m)(x - 5) = x^2 - 11x + 30$, what is the value of m?

    a. -6
    b. -1
    c. 6
    d. 11

12. Raquel decided to change the prices of a couple of candy bars in her shop. She raised the price of the cheapest candy bar by five cents and lowered the price of the most expensive candy bar by three cents. If the range of candy bar prices was 35 cents before she adjusted the prices, what is the new range?

    a. 27 cents
    b. 30 cents
    c. 38 cents
    d. 42 cents

13. Which equation represents the statement below?

    The sum of a number and its cube is seven times the number.

    a. $x - x^2 = 7$
    b. $x - x^3 = 7x$
    c. $x + x^2 = 7$
    d. $x + x^3 = 7x$

14. A school records the types of bakery items sold (cakes, cookies, pies, and brownies) at an annual bake sale in the pie chart below. If twice as many cakes were sold as pies and the most popular item sold was cookies, which part of the pie chart represents brownies?

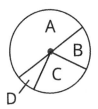

    a. A
    b. B
    c. C
    d. D

15. The sum of two integers is 15, and the difference between those same two integers is 3. What is the product of the integers?

    a. 15
    b. 36
    c. 54
    d. 69

16. Which graph's slope is undefined?

a.

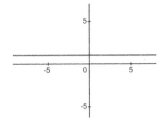

b.

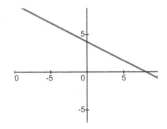

c.

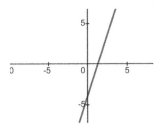

d.

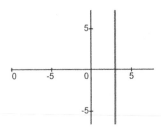

17. The formula for the volume of a cylinder is $V = r^2 \pi h$, where r represents the radius of the cylinder's base and h represents the height. If the height of a given cylinder is reduced by $\frac{1}{3}$ and the radius remains the same, which of the following will be the effect on the volume of the cylinder?

    a. The volume of the cylinder will be reduced by $\frac{1}{3}$.

    b. The volume of the cylinder will be reduced by $\frac{1}{9}$.

    c. The volume of the cylinder will be increased by $\frac{1}{3}$.

    d. The volume of the cylinder will be increased by $\frac{1}{9}$.

18. Ira was trying to determine the mean amount he spent on groceries per week over a four week period. He forgot to write down how much he spent on groceries each week for the first three weeks, but he knows he spent $360 total over that three week period. If he spent $80 on groceries during the fourth week, what was the mean amount spent per week over four weeks?

    a. $90
    b. $110
    c. $120
    d. $125

19. The base of a rectangle is 8, and the area of the rectangle is 56 inches². If three inches are added to the rectangle's height and one inch is subtracted from the base, what is the area of the new rectangle?

    a. 30 in
    b. 66 in
    c. 70 in
    d. 90 in

20. Which of the following figures could NOT be a net of the rectangular prism shown?

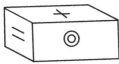

21. What is the range of possible values for y if y = 4x - 1 and $-1 \leq x \leq 2$?

    a. $-5 \leq y \leq 8$
    b. $-5 \leq y \leq 7$
    c. $-1 \leq y \leq 7$
    d. $-1 \leq y$

a.

b.

c.

d.

Part 2 - Quantitative Comparisons

Instructions: In each question, use the information provided to compare the quantity in Column A with the quantity in Column B. All quantitative comparison questions have the same answer choices:

    a.   The quantity in column A is greater.
    b.   The quantity in column B is greater.
    c.   The two quantities are equal.
    d.   The relationship cannot be determined from the information given.

Raj tosses a coin 10 times in a row and tracks the results. After 9 tosses, he has counted 5 heads and 4 tails.

22.

Column A	Column B
The probability that the final coin toss will result in heads	The probability that the final coin toss will result in tails

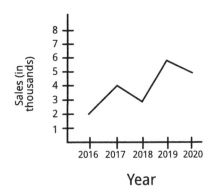

Year

23.

Column A	Column B
The sales for the year with the highest sales.	The sales for the year with the lowest sales plus the sales for the year with the second lowest sales.

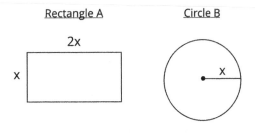

24.

Column A	Column B
The area of rectangle A	The area of circle B

25.

Column A	Column B
$-3\,|{-7} + 4|$	$-3(-7 + 4)$

$x < 0$

26.

Column A	Column B
$9 \times x - \dfrac{2^3}{4}$	-11

$x > 1$

27.

Column A	Column B
$(2x + 1)^2$	$2(x+1)^2$

$\triangle ABC$ is similar to $\triangle DEF$.

28.

Column A	Column B
$\overline{AB}$	$\overline{DE}$

x and y are consecutive integers $(x < y)$

Column A	Column B
$y - x - 1$	0

Lines X and Y are graphed on the same coordinate plane and the two lines intersect at point (3, 2). The slope of line X is 4.

30.

Column A	Column B
4	The slope of line Y.

The perimeter of a triangle is 15 inches.

31.

Column A	Column B
5 inches.	The length of the base of the triangle.

Let c◇d = (c + d)².

32.

Column A	Column B
6◇4	8◇2

Maya rolls two 6-sided number cubes with sides labeled 1-6. She then multiplies the results together.

33.

Column A	Column B
If the first roll results in an even number, the probability that the product will be an even number.	If the first roll results in an odd number, the probability that the product will be an even number.

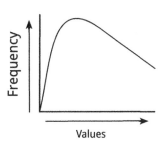

34.

Column A	Column B
The value of the mean.	The value of the mode.

In March, the cost of gas was $3.10 per gallon. In April, the cost of gas was 20% higher than the cost in March. In May, the cost was 20% lower than the cost in April.

Column A	Column B
The cost of one gallon of gas in May	$3.10

ABCE is a rectangle. △CDE is an isosceles triangle with base $\overline{EC}$.

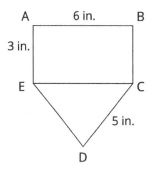

35.

Column A	Column B
The perimeter of ABCDE.	The area of ABCE.

Polygon A   Polygon B

36.

Column A	Column B
The sum of the interior angles in regular polygon A.	The sum of the exterior angles of regular polygon B.

Section 3: Reading
36 Questions, 35 Minutes

Instructions: Carefully read each passage and answer the questions that follow it. For each question, decide which of the choices best answers the question based on the passage.

Questions 1 - 6

1　　　For decades, people have had practically
2　only two choices when it comes to cooking
3　appliances: gas or electric. Gas cooktops have been
4　more popular by far among chefs, home cooks, and
5　self-described foodies for their preciseness and
6　cooking ability. Recently, though, the induction
7　cooktop has wedged its way into the kitchen scene.
8　　　Surprisingly, induction cooking first
9　debuted in the 1900's and was even featured at the
10　1933 Chicago World's Fair. However, it did not catch
11　on, and induction cooktop production was delayed
12　until the 1970's. Even then the appliance was very
13　expensive, and manufacturing ultimately stopped
14　in the U.S. In Europe, however, where energy is
15　more expensive, companies continued to develop
16　induction cooking. In 2000, European companies,
17　along with DuPont, made a technological
18　breakthrough in the design. This, coupled with a
19　reduction in fabrication costs, drastically reduced
20　the price of induction cooktops.
21　　　Induction cooking creates heat in the
22　pan, negating the need for an outside source
23　like fire. This method of cooking involves the
24　electromagnetic induction principle. Electricity
25　is generated using magnetism: two wires carrying
26　fluctuating currents that either repel or attract one
27　another. When the cooktop is activated, a current
28　flows through the metal coil inside. It produces a
29　magnetic field all around the cooktop and directly
30　above it where the pan sits. The molecules in the
31　pan start moving rapidly, resisting one another. All
32　of that movement quickly generates heat.

33　　　This is actually similar to how an electric
34　toothbrush operates. When the toothbrush
35　is attached to its plastic charging station,
36　electromagnetic energy flows via induction from
37　the charger to the battery housed in the toothbrush.
38　Since both the charger and toothbrush are covered
39　in plastic, there is no direct electrical connection
40　between them. Instead, a coil of wire in the charger
41　produces a magnetic field that induces an electrical
42　current in a similar coil in the toothbrush.
43　　　There are several pros to induction
44　cooking; it's more energy efficient than traditional
45　gas cooking and also can be powered by solar
46　panels. Food heats up as much as 50% faster,
47　and the machine is easier to clean than its gas
48　counterparts. Regarding safety, the cooktop itself
49　never gets hot. There is also no chance of fire or
50　carbon monoxide leaks.
51　　　Of course, there are some drawbacks to
52　owning an induction cooktop. Unlike a gas cooktop,
53　an induction version will be rendered useless if
54　the power goes out. Some people may be irked by
55　the soft buzz produced by induction. Others find it
56　inconvenient that the electromagnetic energy used
57　by induction cooktops only work with certain types
58　of pans.

1. What is the purpose of including the third paragraph (lines 21 - 32) in this passage?

    a. to explain the mechanism of induction in toothbrushes
    b. to illustrate how induction works in an object readers may have more familiarity with
    c. to convince readers that induction is safe
    d. to provide contrast in how induction functions in different objects

2. Which of the following conclusions can be drawn about gas cooktops?

    a. Gas cooktops can cause fires.
    b. Gas cooktops are noisy.
    c. Gas cooktops cook food faster than induction cooktops.
    d. Gas cooktops are not commonly used in restaurants.

3. In line x, wedged most nearly means

    a. arrived.
    b. crushed.
    c. pushed.
    d. stowed.

4. The sentence, "In Europe, however, where energy is more expensive, companies continued to develop induction cooking" (lines 14 - 16) is included to

    a. demonstrate why induction cooking is better in Europe.
    b. compare European cooking to American cooking.
    c. show that electricity is very pricey in Europe.
    d. explain why the induction cooktop has improved over time.

5. What would happen on an induction cooktop if it were turned on without a pan?

    a. The heat would escape into the air.
    b. Nothing would happen.
    c. The cooktop would be warm.
    d. Carbon monoxide would surround the cooktop.

6. According to lines 27-30, "When the cooktop is activated, a current flows through the metal coil inside. It produces a magnetic field all around the cooktop and directly above it where the pan sits", and " the electromagnetic energy used by induction cooktops only work with certain types of pans" (lines 56-58), what type of pan would likely work on an induction cooktop?

    a. metal
    b. clay
    c. glass
    d. stone

Questions 7 - 12

1   John Brown was a lifelong abolitionist.
2 He grew up helping his father, Owen Brown,
3 participate in the Underground Railroad by
4 hiding fugitive enslaved persons on the family's
5 Ohio property. As an adult, he exhibited a racial
6 egalitarianism that was exceedingly rare among
7 white abolitionists. He and his family lived in
8 a black community in upstate New York, and
9 he forcefully advocated for racial equality and
10 integration whenever possible. In one famous
11 example, Brown was expelled from his church for
12 standing up during services to offer his family's pew
13 to a family of black congregants (who had been
14 ordered to stand at the back of the chapel).
15   When the Kansas-Nebraska Act of 1854
16 allowed settlers to decide whether the areas would
17 be established as free or slave states, Brown and
18 three of his sons joined many other abolitionists
19 who flocked to Kansas to attempt to sway the vote.
20 When a band of pro-slavery Missourians (called
21 "border ruffians") ransacked the anti-slavery town
22 of Lawrence on May 21, 1856, Brown decided
23 to retaliate. Three nights later, he and his sons
24 murdered five pro-slavery settlers with swords
25 in Pottowatamie, Kansas. Prior to this bloody
26 event, Brown had been a pacifist (as were most
27 abolitionists). The Pottawatomie Massacre, as it
28 came to be known, propelled Brown to fame and
29 notoriety among an increasingly divided American
30 public. He was portrayed as a heroic visionary, as
31 a fanatical madman, and as a depraved terrorist by
32 various factions.
33   Brown parlayed his fame into financial
34 support, notably from members of the artistic and
35 philosophical Transcendentalist movement of the
36 Northeast. With their backing, he devised a plan to
37 eradicate slavery by forming an army of liberated
38 former slaves who would, in turn, inspire those who
39 were currently enslaved to join their ranks. Brown
40 had become convinced that a slave revolution was
41 looming, but hoped that his planned snowball
42 effect would minimize bloodshed by destabilizing
43 the institution of slavery so rapidly that it would
44 become too impractical for pro-slavery forces to
45 fight back for long.

46   In December of 1858, Brown tested his
47 plan on a small scale by leading a raid in which
48 liberated 11 enslaved people from two Missouri
49 farms. Encouraged by this successful mission, he
50 began training his followers to conduct an attack
51 on the federal arsenal at Harpers Ferry, Virginia.
52 Brown hoped to use Harpers Ferry as a strategic
53 home base while his men infiltrated nearby
54 plantations to sound the rallying cry and distribute
55 weapons from the arsenal's plentiful stores. Brown
56 felt sure that enslaved people would rise up and
57 free themselves. Then, they could gather at Harpers
58 Ferry to regroup before retreating to the nearby
59 mountains, which Brown believed were put in
60 place by God for exactly this purpose.
61   Though Brown and his men were able to
62 initially seize the arsenal, Brown had overestimated
63 the speed with which he would be able to recruit
64 an army, and underestimated the response of
65 Virginia's pro-slavery government. Within two days,
66 the arsenal was surrounded by troops led by Robert
67 E. Lee. Brown refused to surrender, so Lee retook
68 the arsenal by force. Though a few of Brown's
69 raiders managed to escape, and a few others
70 (including Brown) were captured, most were killed.
71 Brown remained unrepentant upon his sentencing,
72 and passed an eerily prophetic note to his jailor on
73 the morning of his execution. In part, it read that he
74 was "now quite certain that the crimes of this guilty
75 land will never be purged away, but with blood."
76 The American Civil War broke out two years later.

7. The sentence "He exhibited a racial egalitari-anism that was exceedingly rare among white abolitionists" (lines 5 - 7) is included to show that while abolitionists wanted to end slavery, most

    a. disliked African Americans.
    b. did not believe in equality.
    c. supported separate but equal laws.
    d. used pacifism to accomplish their goals.

8. Which event most divided the public's opinion regarding John Brown?

    a. giving up his pew in church to a black family
    b. the Pottawatomie Massacre
    c. participation in the underground railroad
    d. execution of John Brown

9. The author states that John Brown's last note was "eerily prophetic" (line 72) to show that Brown

    a. had been grossly mistaken in his actions.
    b. succeeded in scaring the American public.
    c. knew what the future held.
    d. felt guilty for breaking his pacifistic ways.

10. This passage is primarily concerned with

    a. exonerating the actions of John Brown.
    b. portraying John Brown as a true hero.
    c. criticizing the decisions made by John Brown.
    d. explaining the actions John Brown took to end slavery.

11. The point of view of the passage's author can best be described as

    a. someone who has personally been affected by the actions of John Brown.
    b. an admirer who has long been frustrated with the lack of information about John Brown.
    c. someone knowledgeable in the actions of the abolition movement.
    d. someone confused by John Brown's use of violence.

12. According to the passage, what was one of Brown's biggest mistakes at Harpers Ferry?

    a. the assumption that many slaves would join his army
    b. his use of violence
    c. his refusal to enlist the help of other abolitionists
    d. his distrust of the federal government

Questions 13 - 18

1   More than half of the human body is made
2 of water. While the percentage is higher in younger
3 populations, and even slightly higher in men than
4 in women, in general an adult's body is about 60%
5 water. Vital organs like the brain, the heart, and
6 the lungs are made of an even higher percentage
7 of water. Even bones are about 30% water. Clearly,
8 H20 is an important building block of human
9 anatomy. But how much water do humans need to
10 consume in order to support overall health?
11   Many people are familiar with the popular
12 statistic that humans need to consume at least
13 eight glasses, or sixty-four ounces, of water on
14 a daily basis to maintain their personal health.
15 However, many experts agree that this is a myth
16 because there is no science to prove it. This
17 erroneous statistic can be traced back to a 1945
18 recommendation from the Food and Nutrition
19 Board that said people should consume about two
20 liters of water daily. However, the line that follows
21 this recommendation includes an often forgotten
22 caveat: most of the water humans consume is
23 through mixed liquids like tea, coffee, and even
24 beer or through foods like fruits and vegetables.
25 Greens such as spinach, cucumbers, and broccoli
26 are at least 90% water! So the eight-glasses-a-day
27 myth can be traced back to 1945, but why hasn't it
28 been debunked? It actually has been, but because
29 it's a reasonable goal and easy to remember, the
30 recommendation persists.

31   The actual amount of water one must
32 consume to maintain their well being depends on
33 their personal health. Some other factors are one's
34 sex, lifestyle choices, and even weather conditions.
35 Men need to drink more water than women. The
36 more a person exercises, the more water they will
37 need to consume. Those living in hot and humid
38 climates or environments higher in altitude are
39 more prone to dehydration, and therefore should
40 consume more water. Women who are pregnant
41 and/or breastfeeding need to drink more water as
42 well. The fact remains: there is no one-size-fits-all
43 rule for how much water humans should consume
44 on a daily basis.
45   The human body is a complex system,
46 but when it comes to hydration, there is built-in
47 regulation: thirst. The human body is fine-tuned
48 to send biological signals to our brains to trigger
49 actions, like the flight or fight response. The
50 biological signal that is sent when one is thirsty
51 drives them to drink water. In fact, the body sends
52 this message long before it is near the point of
53 dehydration. It is a fool-proof system. Regardless
54 of what media and advertisers suggest, listening to
55 and acting on these important biological signals is
56 the best way to maintain homeostasis in the body.

13. The primary purpose of the passage is to

  a. convince readers that they should not drink eight glasses of water per day.
  b. describe the biological processes that occur when humans drink water.
  c. explain why water is important in the human body.
  d. explore the complexities of how much water should be consumed by humans.

14. In line 22, "caveat" most nearly means

  a. clarification
  b. inaccuracy
  c. justification
  d. warning

15. Which best describes the organization of lines 1 - 9?

  a. A scientific theory is described and then debunked.
  b. A set of facts is presented and followed by a conclusion.
  c. An opinion is stated and then supported with facts.
  d. Several statistics are presented and then contradicted.

16. It can be inferred that the recommendation made by the Food and Nutrition board

  a. was made based on the results of a scientific study.
  b. has been widely misinterpreted.
  c. did not gain popularity after 1945.
  d. is followed by all doctors in the United States today.

17. According to the passage, all of the following can impact the amount of water a person should drink to maintain health EXCEPT the

  a. person's age.
  b. amount of exercise the person does.
  c. climate the person lives in.
  d. person's sex.

18. The "fool proof system" described to in line 53 refers to the

  a. biological systems of the human body.
  b. human body's fight or flight response.
  c. processes the body uses to avoid dehydration.
  d. ability of the body to maintain the sensation of thirst.

Questions 19 - 24

1 Cries of alarm and protest, mingled with fierce
2 cheering, had reached the house from the garden
3 just beyond the broad veranda. Then, just as Tom
4 stepped out on the veranda, a sudden stream of
5 water from a garden hose caught him directly in the
6 left ear.
7
8 "Stop that!" cried Tom, doing his best to dodge the
9 water. "What do you mean by wetting me this way?"
10
11 "It wasn't my fault, Dad," came from a boy standing
12 on the lawn, both hands clutching a rubber hose
13 held, also, by another boy of about the same age. "It
14 was Fred who turned the hose that way."
15
16 "Nothing of the sort! It was John that twisted it that
17 way trying to get it away from me," cried Fred. "And
18 he isn't going to do it!" and thereupon ensued a
19 struggle between the two boys which caused the
20 stream of water to fly over the garden first in one
21 direction and then another.
22
23 Meanwhile, another stream of water was issued
24 from a hose held by two other boys. This, as well
25 as the water from the first hose, had been directed
26 towards the back of the garden, where two elderly
27 men were trying to shelter themselves behind a low
28 hedge to keep from becoming drenched.
29
30 "Make the boys stop" cried out Aleck, one of the old
31 men, when he caught sight of Tom. "They have no
32 reason to touch those hoses!"
33
34 "Why! We didn't know you were behind the hedge,
35 Aleck" came from Andy, one of the boys holding
36 the second hose. "We thought you were both down
37 at the barn."
38
39 "You can't make believe like that, Andy!" replied
40 Ness, shaking his head vigorously. "You knew I was
41 going to trim this hedge a bit and that Aleck was
42 going to help me."

43 "You boys let up with this nonsense," came sternly
44 from Tom. "It's a shame for you boys to drench
45 Ness and Aleck. Both of them might catch cold or
46 get rheumatism."
47
48 "We didn't start to do anything like that," answered
49 Andy. "We were going to have a little fight between
50 ourselves playing rival firemen. We didn't see Ness
51 and Aleck until they let out a yell."
52
53 "But I saw you aiming the water in that direction,"
54 cried Tom.
55
56 "Oh, well, what was the harm after they were all
57 wet?" pleaded Fred. "They'd have to change their
58 clothing anyway."
59
60 "That's just it," added Andy quickly, with his eyes
61 twinkling from merriment. "A little more water
62 won't hurt a person when he's already soaked. It's
63 just like spoiling a rotten egg—it can't be done."
64
65 At this reply Tom had to turn away to hide his
66 amusement. Nevertheless, he sobered his face
67 almost instantly as he answered, "Well, these
68 pranks around the farm have got to stop. It's a
69 fortunate thing that your mothers went down to the
70 town to do some shopping. Otherwise I think all of
71 you would be in for quite some punishment."

19. Tom got sprayed with water because

   a. he tried to take the hose from John and Fred.
   b. John and Fred were fighting over the hose.
   c. he got in between the hose and the old men.
   d. John and Fred were playing a practical joke on him.

20. The boys can be described as

   a. arrogant.
   b. cruel.
   c. mischievous.
   d. lazy.

21. The boys admit that they were aiming their hoses at the old men when

   a. Tom reveals that he saw them doing it.
   b. Aleck accuses the boys of targeting him and Ness.
   c. the boys are shamed by Tom.
   d. Tom reminds them that their mothers will be angry.

22. The phrase "like spoiling a rotten egg" (line 63) is an example of a(n)

   a. irony.
   b. hyperbole.
   c. metaphor.
   d. simile.

23. As it is used in the passage, "sobered" (line 66) most nearly means

   a. ignored.
   b. hid.
   c. relaxed.
   d. restrained.

24. Based on the final paragraph, it's likely that the boys will

   a. not be punished.
   b. forced to go indoors.
   c. be punished by their mothers.
   d. not be allowed to use the hose again.

Questions 25 - 30

1   A staple in the canon of American
2 literature is Ernest Hemingway. Famous for his
3 sparse style of writing as both a journalist and
4 an author, Hemingway was also a bull-fighter,
5 boxer, fisherman, hunter, and a veteran of World
6 War I. He is popularly known for his unflinching
7 narratives of masculinity and brutality. Many of his
8 novels feature a brooding but sensitive protagonist
9 who shares many common characteristics with
10 Hemingway himself.
11   Born to well-educated parents in
12 1899, Hemingway had an idyllic childhood and
13 adolescence, spending his summers lakeside in
14 Michigan learning to hunt, fish, and rejoice in
15 the splendors of outdoor life. Perhaps an early
16 indication of his adoration with adventure,
17 Hemingway joined the Italian Army after the
18 United States entered World War I. There he would
19 find his inspiration for his 1929 novel A Farewell
20 to Arms. After he was injured in the war, he briefly
21 returned home to the United States before falling
22 in love and moving with his new wife to Paris,
23 where he worked as a foreign correspondent for an
24 American newspaper.
25   This time in Paris, detailed in Hemingway's
26 memoir A Moveable Feast, led to the creation of
27 the "Lost Generation." The term was coined by
28 Gertrude Stein but popularized by Hemingway
29 who used it as an epigraph in The Sun Also Rises.
30 He and Stein were only just a couple members of
31 what came to be a large social circle of writers like
32 F. Scott Fitzgerald, T.S. Eliot, and Ezra Pound, who
33 lived as expatriates in Paris during the 1920's. The
34 "lost generation" label is used to describe both
35 this specific group of artists and more broadly
36 to describe the generation that came of age after
37 World War I, full of disillusionment and pessimism.

38   Many critics believe Hemingway's status
39 as an icon of American literature is not due to his
40 talents as a writer, but instead depends in large part
41 upon his status as a celebrity during his career. His
42 four marriages were widely reported on in gossip
43 magazines and newspapers, and Hemingway
44 himself became somewhat of a character known for
45 his hard-drinking and love of adventure. Of course
46 it was not all fun and games for Hemingway. He is,
47 after all, a once-in-a-generation talent. He won the
48 Pulitzer Prize for fiction in 1953 for his novel The
49 Old Man and the Sea, and in 1954, he was awarded
50 the Nobel Prize for Literature. The Nobel Prize was
51 awarded for, among other things, the influence
52 that he had on the American style of writing.
53 These prizes, won in consecutive years, cemented
54 Hemingway's legacy as one not dependent upon
55 his fast-paced lifestyle, but one worthy of critical
56 acclaim.
57   In October of 1960, after recent
58 deterioration of his mental state, Hemingway
59 moved with his fourth wife to Idaho. He had
60 become increasingly paranoid and was unable
61 to focus for long periods of time, making writing
62 difficult. In July of 1961, after enduring multiple
63 rounds of electroshock therapy throughout the
64 preceding months, Hemingway died by suicide.
65 The tragic end to his life does not tarnish his
66 influence on American culture both past and
67 present. Hemingway's works are fundamental to
68 contemporary American high school curriculum.
69 He is revered as a defining voice of the Lost
70 Generation. His writing style is singular, and his
71 literary voice remains unparalleled.

25. In lines 7 - 10, the author implies that Hemingway

    a. was not a kind person.
    b. wrote about himself.
    c. was a complex character.
    d. was unhappy.

26. In line 12, "idyllic" most nearly means

    a. active.
    b. educational.
    c. ideal.
    d. peaceful.

27. The "lost generation" mentioned in line 27 refers to all of the following EXCEPT

    a. Ernest Hemingway.
    b. a social circle of writers.
    c. soldiers who experienced the depravity of the First World War.
    d. those who became adults after World War I.

28. Which of the following choices best supports the author's view of Ernest Hemingway?

    a. He has received undue credit.
    b. His popularity has stemmed from his romantic liaisons.
    c. He is a true literary genius.
    d. He is not as well known as he should have been.

29. What does the first line of the passage, "a staple in the canon of American literature" (lines 1 - 2) imply about Hemingway's work?

    a. It is pretty basic.
    b. It is a foundation.
    c. It is an eccentric example.
    d. It is complicated and academic.

30. Which of the following would be a good title for the passage?

    a. Hemingway's Lost Generation
    b. The Wins and Losses in Hemingway's Life
    c. How to Win a Nobel Prize
    d. Hemingway: An American Icon

Questions 31 - 36

1   Although wild tigers are an endangered
2 species, the buying and selling of captive tigers is
3 a thriving industry. In fact, there are more tigers
4 living in captivity than there are living free. It's
5 appalling. Many captive tigers are kept as pets by
6 exotic animal enthusiasts and pseudo-sanctuaries.
7 Experts estimate that out of the more than 5,000
8 captive tigers in the United States, only about 300 of
9 those are living in accredited zoos.
10   Many captive tigers in the U.S. are used
11 for profit. Businesses are built around the practice
12 of breeding baby tigers for financial gain, and
13 business is booming. People pay up to $700 to pet,
14 hold, swim, and take pictures with tiger cubs at
15 private zoos and "sanctuaries." The reality is that
16 a tiger cub is only profitable at this level for about
17 twelve weeks of its life, after which it becomes
18 too big to exploit in this regard. Owners must
19 continually breed cubs to maintain profit margins
20 because tigers become increasingly more expensive
21 as they age out of cub-petting experiences. For
22 this reason, older tigers are often sold on the black
23 market for parts or to individual owners who keep
24 them in backyards and basements. Even worse,
25 there is no legislation dictating statewide oversight
26 or mandatory reporting of dead tigers and their
27 disposal, so many of them wind up unaccounted
28 for altogether.

29   In general, the United States laws dealing
30 with exotic animal ownership are complicated
31 and vague. Many of the businesses that house big
32 cats like tigers are operating under the guise of
33 rescue and conservation. However, none of the
34 profits these places make go toward alleviating the
35 consequences of wild tigers being endangered. The
36 fact remains that tigers are meant to live in the wild.
37 They retain their wildlife instincts even when born
38 and raised in captivity, posing a risk to individuals
39 and their communities. The practice of breeding
40 and exploiting tigers for financial gain needs to be
41 outlawed in the United States, and the so-called
42 conservation of them in pseudo-sanctuaries must
43 be regulated more strictly.

31. The author uses the statistic in lines 7 -9 to show

    a. why people want to own tigers.
    b. the scope of the captive tiger problem.
    c. why tigers should be put into accredited zoos.
    d. the reason that tigers are considered endangered.

32. The author's attitude toward the captive tiger trade can be described as

    a. hesitant.
    b. disinterested.
    c. dismissive.
    d. outraged.

33. According to the author, tiger breeders sell older cubs on the black market

    a. because they don't profit from tigers who are younger than 12 weeks old.
    b. so the government can not track what happens to their tiger cubs.
    c. so they have the money to breed more young cubs.
    d. because they don't have the space to keep the older cubs.

34. The author of this passage appears to care deeply about

    a. the welfare of tigers involved in the captive tiger trade.
    b. ensuring that breeders keep their tiger cubs for more than 12 weeks.
    c. the importance of supporting sanctuaries that take good care of tigers.
    d. removing unnecessary regulations of the captive tiger trade.

35. Based on the information in the final paragraph, the author believes to be considered a true rescue organization, a zoo or sanctuary must

    a. advocated for clearer exotic animal ownership laws.
    b. use volunteers only.
    c. release its captive tigers into the wild.
    d. devote some profits to helping endangered wild tigers.

36. As it is used in line 42, "pseudo" most nearly means

    a. sham
    b. unimpressive
    c. illegal
    d. overpriced

Section 4: Math
47 Questions, 40 Minutes

Instructions: Each question is followed by four answer choices. Select the best answer.

1. A circle has a circumference of 16π feet. What is the circle's area?

    a. $8\ \text{ft}^2$
    b. $8\pi\ \text{ft}^2$
    c. $64\ \text{ft}^2$
    d. $64\pi\ \text{ft}^2$

2. The value of $\sqrt{28}$ falls between which of the following pairs of integers?

    a. 4 and 5
    b. 5 and 6
    c. 6 and 7
    d. 7 and 8

3. What is the surface area of the rectangular prism below?

    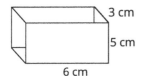

    a. $90\ \text{cm}^2$
    b. $108\ \text{cm}^2$
    c. $126\ \text{cm}^2$
    d. $136\ \text{cm}^2$

4. A sandwich shop tracks the number of sandwiches purchased by customers one afternoon. What is the mode of the data?

Number of Sandwiches	Number of Customers Purchasing That Number of Sandwiches
1	5
2	6
3	8
4	6
5	4

    a. 2
    b. 3
    c. 4
    d. 5

5. $\triangle ABC$ is a right triangle. If line segment $\overline{BD}$ is added to the figure and bisects $\triangle ABC$, what is the measure of $\triangle ABD$?

    a. $30°$
    b. $45°$
    c. $90°$
    d. $180°$

6. Which graph represents the solution set of the inequality $|2x - 2| \geq 6$?

    a.

    b.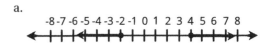

    c.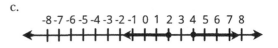

    d.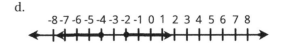

7. Noelle is celebrating her 6th birthday. If Noelle has 8 friends and can only invite 6 of them, how many combinations of friends can attend?

   a. 14
   b. 48
   c. 28
   d. 720

8. Triangle PQR is shown below. Which expression is equal to the length of side $\overline{PR}$?

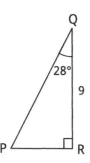

   a. $\cos\dfrac{28°}{9}$

   b. $9\cos 28°$

   c. $9\tan 28°$

   d. $\tan\dfrac{28°}{9}$

9. Which expression is equivalent to the expression $4a^4b^2 - 7ab^3 + 2(3a^4b^2 + 8ab^3)$?

   a. $10a^4b^2 + 9ab^3$
   b. $10a^4b^2 - 9ab^3$
   c. $7a^4b^2 + ab^3$
   d. $7a^4b^2 - ab^3$

10. A teacher noticed that students who were late to her class at least once a week had lower grades on tests than students who were on time more frequently. The teacher concluded that arriving late was the cause of her late students' low test scores. If true, which of the following is evidence that the teacher may be incorrect in her conclusion?

    a. Students who were on time enjoyed the class more.
    b. Students who were late also studied less for tests.
    c. Students who were late to her class were late to other classes as well.
    d. Students who were on time had higher quiz scores as well.

11. The base of a triangle is twice the triangle's height. If the area of the triangle is 16 in^2, what is the triangle's base?

    a. 2 in
    b. 4 in
    c. 6 in
    d. 8 in

12. A travel agency surveyed their clients about their favorite European city. The results of the survey are below.

Favorite Destination	Women	Men	Total Number of Clients
Barcelona	17	12	29
Paris	23	18	41
Venice	31	29	60
Vienna	19	27	46
Total	90	86	176

What is the probability that a client's favorite travel destination is Venice?

   a. $\dfrac{31}{176}$

   b. $\dfrac{29}{86}$

   c. $\dfrac{15}{44}$

   d. $\dfrac{31}{60}$

13. A cylinder has a height of 6 cm and volume of 216 cm^3. What is the cylinder's radius?

   Note: The formula used to determine the volume of a cylinder is $V = r^2h\pi$, where r is the cylinder's radius and h is the cylinder's height.

   a. 3 cm
   b. 6 cm
   c. 12 cm
   d. 36 cm

14. Amira wants to measure the amount of water held by her kitchen sink. What is the most reasonable unit for her to use?

    a. liters
    b. kilograms
    c. milliliters
    d. grams

15. Three vertices of a parallelogram are shown below. What are the coordinates of the fourth vertex?

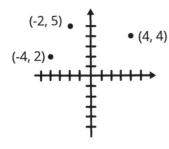

    a. (2, 1)
    b. (2, 2)
    c. (3, 1)
    d. (2, 2)

16. Sabrina and Jamar are playing a board game, and Jamar is just three spaces away from the finish. If he rolls a standard die containing the numbers 1-6, what is the probability that he will win the game on his next turn?

(Note: round to the nearest percent)

    a. 33%
    b. 50%
    c. 67%
    d. 76%

17. The first four terms of a geometric sequence are shown below.

    4, 12, 36, 108

Which value represents the 5th term of this sequence?

    a. 144
    b. 216
    c. 324
    d. 432

18. A piece of artwork that normally costs \$95 is on sale for 40% off. What is the new price?

    a. 35
    b. 57
    c. 70
    d. 89

19. If $\left(\frac{5}{4} + \frac{3}{4}\right)d = d - 6$, what is the value of d?

    a. -6
    b. -2
    c. 0
    d. 8

20. What is the result of the expression

$$\begin{bmatrix} 4 & -3 & 2 \\ 0 & 1 & 7 \end{bmatrix} + \begin{bmatrix} 3 & 8 & 0 \\ -1 & 8 & -1 \end{bmatrix}?$$

    a. $\begin{bmatrix} 7 & 11 & 2 \\ 1 & 9 & 8 \end{bmatrix}$

    b. $\begin{bmatrix} 3 & 9 & 7 \\ 3 & 5 & 2 \end{bmatrix}$

    c. $\begin{bmatrix} 7 & -5 & 2 \\ 1 & -9 & 6 \end{bmatrix}$

    d. $\begin{bmatrix} 7 & 5 & 2 \\ -1 & 9 & 6 \end{bmatrix}$

21. If x is a positive number, which expression is equivalent to $x\sqrt{x^8}$?

    a. x^4
    b. $\sqrt{x^{10}}$
    c. $\sqrt{x^{16}}$
    d. x^9

22. (6, -4) and (-2, 3) are two points on line S. What is the slope of line S?

    a. $-\frac{8}{7}$
    b. $-\frac{7}{8}$
    c. $\frac{7}{8}$
    d. $\frac{8}{7}$

23. For what values(s) of x does

    $(x - 4)(x + 3) = 0$

    $x^2 - 144$

    a. $x = -12, x = 12$
    b. $x = -4, x = 3$
    c. $x = 4, x = -3$
    d. $x = 12, x = 4, x = -3$

24. The sum of two numbers is 18. The smaller number is equal to half the larger number. What is the larger number?

    a. 6
    b. 8
    c. 10
    d. 12

25. A gumball machine contains 6 blue gumballs, 5 pink gumballs, 4 yellow gumballs, and 3 white gumballs. If Priya buys 2 random gumballs, what is the probability that both gumballs are pink?

    a. $\dfrac{5}{9}$

    b. $\dfrac{5}{18}$

    c. $\dfrac{5}{18} \times \dfrac{4}{17}$

    d. $\dfrac{5}{18} \times \dfrac{5}{18}$

26. The box-and-whisker plot below shows the heights, in inches, of a class of first grade students. What is the median height?

    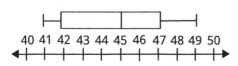

    a. 41
    b. 42
    c. 45
    d. 47

27. Brianna walks home from school each day at a speed of 4 miles an hour. Which expression shows how many feet she walks per second? Note: there are 5,280 feet in a mile.

    a. $\dfrac{5,280 \times 4}{60}$

    b. $\dfrac{5,280 \times 4}{60 \times 60}$

    c. $\dfrac{60}{5,280 \times 4}$

    d. $\dfrac{60 \times 60}{5,280 \times 4}$

28. The expression below is an example of which property?

    $(a + b) + c = a + (b + c)$

    a. commutative property
    b. identity property
    c. associative property
    d. distributive property

29. What is the solution set to the inequality $-3 \le 2x + 7 \le 7$?

    a. $-5 \le x \le 0$
    b. $-4/5 \le x \le 7$
    c. $4/5 \le x \le 0$
    d. $-5 \le x \le 7$

30. $\triangle ABC$ and $\triangle DEF$ are similar triangles. The length of $\overline{AB}$ is 5 inches and the length of $\overline{DE}$ is 3 inches. What is the length of $\overline{EF}$ if the length of $\overline{BC}$ is 15 inches?

    a. 1 in
    b. 5 in
    c. 6 in
    d. 9 in

31. For what value(s) of x is the equation $\dfrac{x-1}{1-x} = 1$ true?

    a. 0 only
    b. 1 only
    c. all real numbers
    d. there are no values for x that make the equation true

32. One half of eight squared is equal to what number?

    a. 4
    b. 8
    c. 32
    d. 64

33. The table below shows the relationship between x and f(x). Which of the following could be the equation for the function?

x	f(x)
1	4
2	7
3	10
4	13

    a. $f(x) = 2x + 2$
    b. $f(x) = 3x + 1$
    c. $f(x) = 4x$
    d. $f(x) = 5x - 1$

34. Which expression is equivalent to $x^2 - 11x + 24$?

    a. $(x - 6)(x - 4)$
    b. $(x - 6)(x + 4)$
    c. $(x - 3)(x - 8)$
    d. $(x - 3)(x + 8)$

35. What is the greatest common factor of 3ab, $12b^3$, and $15a^2b$ if a and b are both prime?

    a. $3b$
    b. $3a^2b^3$
    c. $60b$
    d. $60a^2b^3$

36. A study was done comparing the amount of time students spend playing sports and the amount of time they spend using electronics. The results are summarized in the scatterplot below. What pattern does the data show?

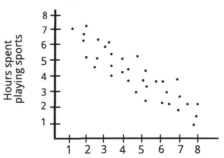

    a. The more time students spend playing sports, the less time they spend using electronics.
    b. The less time students spend playing sports, the less time they spend using electronics.
    c. Students who spend at least 6 hours a week playing sports spend the most time using electronics.
    d. Students who spend 3- 6 hours a week on sports spend the least amount of time using electronics.

37. The area of each grid square shown is 2 in². What is the area of the shaded area?

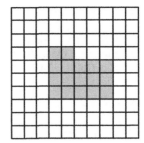

    a. 16 in²
    b. 17 in²
    c. 32 in²
    d. 34 in²

38. Mrs. Patel is reviewing the results of the most recent test she gave her algebra class. If the lowest score a student earned on the test was 64% and the range of the scores was 29, what was the highest score earned?

    a. 75%
    b. 83%
    c. 93%
    d. 99%

39. Which of the following is smaller than .64?

    a. $\frac{7}{9}$

    b. $\frac{5}{7}$

    c. $\frac{4}{3}$

    d. $\frac{3}{5}$

40. Which of the following describes all values for x for which $|2x + 6| < 4$?

    a. $x < -1$
    b. $x < -5$
    c. $x > -1$ or $x < -5$
    d. $-5 < x < -1$

41. On a map of the United States, 1 inch represents 250 miles. Chicago and Philadelphia are 3 inches apart on the map. How many miles apart are the two cities?

    a. 300 miles
    b. 500 miles
    c. 750 miles
    d. 1,000 miles

42. A car dealership decided to track the weekend car sales for three of its salesmen. The sales are detailed in the chart below. What is the mean number of cars sold by the salesman? Round your answer to the nearest hundredth.

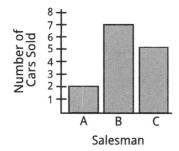

    a. 3.50
    b. 4.67
    c. 5.00
    d. 5.34

43. What is the first quartile of the data set below?

    16, 19, 20, 25, 30, 31, 34, 41, 44, 46, 51

    a. 19
    b. 20
    c. 25
    d. 30

44. What is the value of the numerical expression .000098723?

    a. 9.8723×10^{-9}
    b. 9.8723×10^{-5}
    c. 9.8723×10^{4}
    d. 9.8723×10^{5}

45. What is the solution set for $x^2 + 80 = -20$?

    a. $2\sqrt{15}$
    b. 10
    c. -10i
    d. ±10i

46. If $10n - 10 = nm - m$, which of the following is the value of m?

    a. -10
    b. 0
    c. 1
    d. 10

47. In the xy-coordinate plane shown, $\triangle ABC$ is to be translated 2 units left and 1 unit up to form $\triangle A'B'C'$. What are the coordinates of point B'?

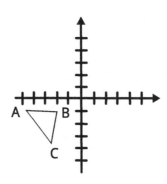

    a. (-4, 0)
    b. (-3, 1)
    c. (-1, 3)
    d. (1, -4)

Essay
1 Question, 30 Minutes

Instructions: You have 30 minutes to write an essay on the topic below. It is not permitted to write an essay on a different topic. Your essay must be written in blue or black pen.

Please be aware that the schools you apply to will receive a copy of your essay. Your essay should be longer than a paragraph and use specific examples and details.

Write your response on this page and the next page.

> If you had a million dollars to donate to a charity or cause of your choice, where would you donate your money and why?

Test 3 Answer Key

Section 1: Verbal

1. B	9. B	17. C	25. B	33. C
2. C	10. A	18. D	26. D	34. B
3. B	11. D	19. A	27. D	35. B
4. D	12. B	20. D	28. C	36. A
5. C	13. D	21. C	29. A	37. C
6. A	14. B	22. A	30. C	38. C
7. D	15. A	23. D	31. D	39. A
8. A	16. D	24. B	32. A	40. D

Section 2: Quantitative

1. C	9. D	17. A	25. B	33. A
2. B	10. A	18. B	26. D	34. A
3. B	11. C	19. C	27. A	35. B
4. B	12. A	20. D	28. D	36. A
5. A	13. D	21. B	29. C	37. B
6. C	14. C	22. C	30. D	
7. C	15. C	23. A	31. D	
8. B	16. D	24. B	32. C	

Section 3: Reading

1. B	9. C	17. A	25. B	33. C
2. A	10. D	18. C	26. C	34. A
3. C	11. C	19. B	27. C	35. D
4. D	12. A	20. C	28. C	36. A
5. B	13. D	21. A	29. B	
6. A	14. A	22. D	30. D	
7. B	15. B	23. D	31. B	
8. B	16. B	24. A	32. D	

Section 4: Math

1. D	11. D	21. B	31. D	41. C
2. B	12. C	22. B	32. C	42. B
3. C	13. B	23. C	33. B	43. B
4. B	14. A	24. D	34. C	44. B
5. B	15. A	25. C	35. A	45. D
6. A	16. C	26. C	36. A	46. D
7. C	17. C	27. B	37. D	47. A
8. C	18. B	28. C	38. C	
9. A	19. A	29. A	39. D	
10. B	20. D	30. D	40. D	

ISEE Test 4

Section 1: Verbal
40 Questions, 20 Minutes

Synonyms

Instructions: Select the word whose meaning is closest to the word in capital letters.

1. DECOY:

    a. lure
    b. hunt
    c. rabbit
    d. spy

2. VESSEL:

    a. delay
    b. receptacle
    c. time
    d. vase

3. TALON:

    a. bite
    b. end
    c. falcon
    d. nail

4. CACHE:

    a. chest
    b. jewels
    c. lock
    d. stockpile

5. RETORT:

    a. anger
    b. explain
    c. rejoinder
    d. snap

6. LATITUDE:

    a. beyond
    b. earth
    c. leeway
    d. long

7. IDLE:

    a. car
    b. deliberate
    c. inactive
    d. quiet

8. SLANDER:

    a. call
    b. defame
    c. snake
    d. speak

9. GUMPTION:

    a. adhesive
    b. initiative
    c. sticky
    d. transportation

10. NOMINEE:

    a. alien
    b. contender
    c. name
    d. politician

11. PRUNE:

    a. botanical
    b. plum
    c. trim
    d. wrinkle

12. EMPATHY:

    a. agitation
    b. commiseration
    c. emotion
    d. help

13. EQUILIBRIUM:

    a. equate
    b. balance
    c. fluctuate
    d. temper

14. HAMLET:

    a. afloat
    b. house
    c. long
    d. village

15. PERUSE:

    a. acknowledge
    b. ascertain
    c. browse
    d. tell

16. ETERNITY:

    a. limbo
    b. longevity
    c. perpetuity
    d. plausibility

17. TIMID:

    a. easy
    b. punctual
    c. skittish
    d. tired

18. FACADE:

    a. building
    b. exterior
    c. ornate
    d. supply

19. INAUSPICIOUS:

    a. alone
    b. forgotten
    c. skeptical
    d. unfortunate

Sentence Completion

Instructions: Select the word or pair of words that best completes the sentence.

20. Never a(n) ------, Marta eagerly joined in on the fun.

    a. extrovert
    b. intellectual
    c. naysayer
    d. optimist

21. The ------ dog hungrily eyed the forgotten plate of food on the kitchen table.

    a. angry
    b. lonely
    c. ravenous
    d. sick

22. During early voting, only a handful of ------ were cast.

    a. ballots
    b. decisions
    c. elections
    d. voters

23. The jury members were in ------; everyone agreed the plaintiff was guilty.

    a. aggrandizement
    b. consensus
    c. limbo
    d. shock

24. The young boy was ------ to miss school because he loved seeing his friends during recess.

    a. adjudicated
    b. distressed
    c. excited
    d. indifferent

25. The car wash must be ------ because it broke down during an automatic cleaning, trapping the customers in their car.

    a. crazy
    b. doomed
    c. malfunctioning
    d. possessed

26. Dr. Greene's presentation centered on building a ------ relationship between the parent and child in order for them to solve problems together.

    a. collaborative
    b. friendly
    c. hostile
    d. loving

27. One ------- among female leaders in America today is that almost all of them were once Girl Scouts.

    a. commonality
    b. personality
    c. tradition
    d. trait

28. The ------- of honeybees is particularly distressing to farmers who wonder how they will pollinate their fruit crops if bee colonies collapse.

    a. abundance
    b. journey
    c. life
    d. plight

29. When miniature pinscher dogs run, they often look like deer ------- in a meadow.

    a. jogging
    b. oscillating
    c. prancing
    d. reposing

30. The best coffee is grown at ------- altitudes such as those found in the Andes Mountains.

    a. base
    b. dense
    c. elevated
    d. subtropical

31. Certain Civil War monuments have been removed in cases where they seemed to celebrate ------- figures.

    a. controversial
    b. idealized
    c. meaningful
    d. obscure

32. In August, almost all Parisians ------- their tourist-filled city and travel to Il de Re, a ------- vacation island in the Atlantic.

    a. enjoys . . . beloved
    b. escapes . . . formidable
    c. flee . . . fashionable
    d. visits . . . small

33. Cell phone technology has ------- dramatically since its ------- almost forty-five years ago.

    a. ameliorated . . . commencement
    b. decreased . . . beginnings
    c. improved . . . genesis
    d. risen . . . inauguration

34. ------- birds fly south for the winter, leaving their nesting place behind in search of more ------- food.

    a. certain . . . delectable
    b. migratory . . . plentiful
    c. transitory . . . sustainable
    d. singular . . . abundant

35. Frederic Chopin's music is -------; he wrote unforgettable ------- including ballads, concertos, and nocturnes.

    a. abject . . . tunes
    b. infinite . . . poetry
    c. permanent . . . plays
    d. timeless . . . melodies

36. Cycling to work and school has two -------: it's good for your health, and it also helps the -------.

    a. benefits . . . heart
    b. concerns . . planet
    c. merits . . . environment
    d. positives . . . habitat

37. A plant-based diet is far more ------- for the environment than eating animal protein because it is estimated that one-third of greenhouse gas emissions comes from -------.

    a. detrimental . . . cattle
    b. helpful . . . farming
    c. strenuous . . . animals
    d. sustainable . . . livestock

38. The music of Tori Amos, while almost fanciful and ------- in nature, is also quite personal because she often writes of her own -------.

    a. funny . . . struggles
    b. harsh . . . difficulties
    c. mythical . . . experiences
    d. true . . . dreams

39. In order to keep her diabetes -------, Caroline
    visits her doctor -------, as much as three times
    a week.

        a. aside . . . regularly
        b. controlled . . . frequently
        c. drifting. . . occasionally
        d. subdued . . . intermittently
        e.

40. The family's new minivan, while -------, came
    at a -------, as they could no longer park in their
    garage.

        a. affordable . . . price
        b. appealing . . . sacrifice
        c. roomy . . . prize
        d. spacious . . . cost

Section 2: Quantitative
37 Questions, 35 Minutes

The section is divided into two parts: problem solving and quantitative comparison. Directions for each part are provided.

Part 1 - Problem Solving

Instructions: Each question is followed by four possible answers. Select the best answer.

1. What is the minimum value for y if $y = -2x^2 + 3$ and $-1 < x < 3$?

    a. -15
    b. -1
    c. 1
    d. 3

2. The most common price for a bottle of soda at a local convenience store is $1.93. If the store owner raises the price of every bottle of soda by four cents, what will the mode soda price be?

    a. $1.89
    b. $1.93
    c. $1.97
    d. Not enough information given to answer

3. If $a + b = c - d$, which of the following is equal to d?

    a. $-a - b + c$
    b. $a - b + c$
    c. $a + b - c$
    d. $a + b + c$

4. An author spends an hour one morning writing a chapter of her latest novel. At the beginning of the hour, the author had difficulty getting started and wrote very few words. She then had a burst of ideas and wrote quite a bit. Later in the hour, her writing began to slow. Which of the following graphs shows this progression?

a.
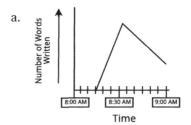

b.
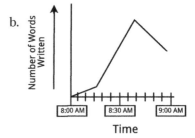

c.
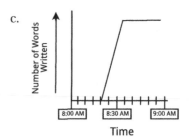

d.
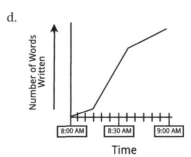

5. If $(x+y)^2 = 144$ and $x^2 + y^2 = 74$, what is the value of xy?

    a. 14
    b. 35
    c. 70
    d. 140

6. A total of 65 tickets have been purchased for the 3pm showing of a new movie. The number of adult tickets sold is 15 more than the number of child tickets sold. How many adult tickets have been purchased?

    a. 10
    b. 25
    c. 40
    d. 55

7. What is the product of all prime factors of 58?

    a. 2
    b. 18
    c. 29
    d. 58

8. The graph below tracks the increase in sales for a business. If the trend in the graph continues, what will be the increase in sales in 2021?

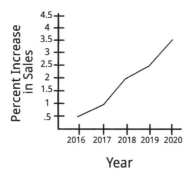

    a. 3%
    b. 3.5%
    c. 4%
    d. 4.5%

9. Which of the following is equivalent to 2y - 2?

    a. $\dfrac{2}{y^2}$

    b. $\dfrac{1}{2y^2}$

    c. $\sqrt{2y^2}$

    d. $\sqrt{2y^2}$

10. Theo and Heather are playing a board game. On his/her turn, each player will roll two 6-sided number cubes, determine the sum, and move forward that many spaces. A player must land on the final space exactly in order to win. Theo is 11 spaces away from the finish, and Heather is 7 spaces away. Who has a higher probability of winning?

    a. Theo
    b. Heather
    c. Theo and Heather have the same probability of winning.
    d. There is not enough information given to determine the answer.

11. The length of the base of a triangle is increased by 60% and the height is decreased by 30%. What is the percent increase in the area of the triangle?

    a. 12%
    b. 15%
    c. 24%
    d. 30%

12. If $f(x) = 7x + 1$ and $g(x) = \sqrt{x}$, what is the value of $f(g(9))$?

    a. 4
    b. 8
    c. 20
    d. 22

13. The two cylinders shown below have equal volumes. If the radius of cylinder A is half the radius of cylinder B, which of the following statements about the heights of the cylinders must be true?

A   B

Note: The formula for the volume of a cylinder is $V = \pi r^2 h$, where r represents the radius of the cylinder's base and h represents the height.

    a. The height of cylinder A is 2 times the height of cylinder B.
    b. The height of cylinder A is 3 times the height of cylinder B.
    c. The height of cylinder A is 4 times the height of cylinder B.
    d. The height of cylinder A is 5 times the height of cylinder B.

14. Lines X and Y are in the same coordinate plane. Line X has a slope of 3. Line Y has a slope of -3. What must be true about the lines?

    a. They are perpendicular.
    b. They intersect.
    c. They are parallel.
    d. They are the same line.

15. Gina is participating in a walkathon fundraiser in which participants continue to walk around a circular track from 6:00pm until 12:00am. If Gina walks at a constant speed of three miles per hour, what other piece of information would you need to calculate the total number of laps Gina walked around the track?

    a. The radius of the track
    b. The diameter of the track
    c. The circumference of the track
    d. Any of the above

16. The perimeter of square ABCD is 32 inches. What is the area of triangle ABC?

    a. 16 in²
    b. 24 in²
    c. 32 in²
    d. 64 in²

17. Which of the following figures could NOT be folded to form the cube shown below?

a.
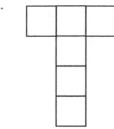

b.
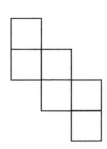

c.
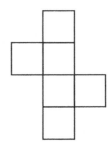

d.

18. In the graph below, each dot represents a different adult male. What pattern does the graph show?

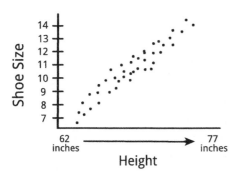

a. There is a weak negative correlation between a man's height and his shoe size.
b. There is a strong negative correlation between a man's height and his shoe size.
c. There is a weak positive correlation between a man's height and his shoe size.
d. There is a strong positive correlation between a man's height and his shoe size.

Part 2 - Quantitative Comparisons

Instructions: In each question, use the information provided to compare the quantity in Column A with the quantity in Column B. All quantitative comparison questions have the same answer choices:

    a. The quantity in column A is greater.
    b. The quantity in column B is greater.
    c. The two quantities are equal.
    d. The relationship cannot be determined from the information given.

$x > 0$

19. | Column A | Column B |
|---|---|
| 2x3 | 2x/x-2 |

Let $\heartsuit z = 3z + 5$.

20. | Column A | Column B |
|---|---|
| $\heartsuit 5$ | $\heartsuit 8 - \heartsuit 3$ |

Samantha uses a 30% off coupon to purchase a book that normally costs $21.

21. | Column A | Column B |
|---|---|
| The amount of money that Samantha saves. | $6.50 |

22. | Column A | Column B |
|---|---|
| 50 | $(5 - 2)^2 + 8 \times 4 - 1$ |

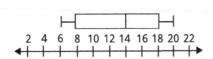

23. | Column A | Column B |
|---|---|
| The median of the data. | The range of the data. |

For any positive integer n, n! is the product of all integers from 1 to n, inclusive.

24. | Column A | Column B |
|---|---|
| $\dfrac{4!}{1!}$ | 3! |

$x < 0$

25. | Column A | Column B |
|---|---|
| (x+3)(x+3) | $x^2 + 32$ |

A bag contains a combination of quarters and nickels. If one coin is removed from the bag at random, the probability that the coin will be a quarter is $\frac{3}{7}$.

26. | Column A | Column B |
|---|---|
| The number of quarters in the bag. | The number of nickels in the bag. |

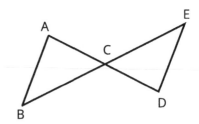

In the figure above, $\angle A$ is congruent to $\angle D$.

27. | Column A | Column B |
|---|---|
| The measure of $\angle E$. | The measure of $\angle B$. |

Lines A and B are parallel and are in the same coordinate plane.

28. Column A   Column B

The slope of line A.   The slope of line B.

_____

$z \leq 0$

29. Column A   Column B

2z + 5   -2z - 5

_____

Consider the following dataset: 1, 2, 2, 2, 3, 4, 5

30. Column A   Column B

2 less than the range of   The median of the
the dataset   dataset

_____

A circle has a radius of x.

31.
    Column A   Column B

The area of the circle.   The circumference of
                             the circle.

_____

y is an integer greater than 0. z is an integer less than 0.

32. Column A   Column B

$\dfrac{y}{z}$ $\dfrac{z}{y}$

_____

A jar contains 4 blue marbles, 6 green marbles, and 2 white marbles. One marble is randomly selected from the jar and put aside. Then a second marble is randomly selected.

33. Column A   Column B

The probability that   The probability that the
both marbles select-   first marble selected is
ed are blue.   blue and the second is
                             not blue.

The area of a square is 64 in^2

34. Column A   Column B

16   One side of the
                             square.

_____

35. Column A   Column B

The greatest common   The least common
factor of 48 and 72   multiple of 8, 6, and 2

_____

The measure of an interior angle of a regular polygon with n sides is $\dfrac{180° \, (n - 2)}{n}$. The measure of an exterior angle of a regular polygon with n sides is $\dfrac{360}{n}$.

36. Column A   Column B

The measure of an   The measure of an
interior angle of a   exterior angle of a
pentagon.   pentagon.

_____

ABCD is a square. A portion of ABCD is shaded.

37. Column A   Column B

The area of the shaded   The area of the unshaded
area.   area.

Section 3: Reading
36 Questions, 35 Minutes

Instructions: Carefully read each passage and answer the questions that follow it. For each question, decide which of the choices best answers the question based on the passage.

Questions 1 - 6

1   Indonesia, one of the largest countries in
2 the world, is made up of more than 17,000 islands.
3 Its size and complex cultural identity make it
4 uniquely qualified to be home to Borobudur, the
5 world's largest Buddhist temple. The pyramidal
6 monument, positioned on top of a hill, was built
7 between the 8th and 9th centuries and consists
8 of nearly two million cubic feet of volcanic stone.
9 The structure is made up of several layers: a large,
10 square base topped with five square terraces, three
11 circular platforms, and a massive stupa, or dome.
12 The walls of the temple are decorated with low
13 relief sculptures which contrast with the temple's
14 stupas, each of which contains a three dimensional
15 statue of Buddha. Overall, Borobudur contains
16 more than 2,600 panels with relief sculptures and
17 more than 500 Buddha statues!
18   The monument's design reflects the
19 Buddhist journey to enlightenment. Visitors are
20 meant to enter the temple at the eastern-most
21 stairway and travel clockwise through each of
22 the nine levels (square base, five terraces, three
23 platforms) to reach the top, where the monumental
24 stupa will greet them. On the first level, visitors
25 can view reliefs of earthly desires that depict
26 kama-dhatu, "the realm of feeling," and the first
27 of three realms on one's journey to Buddhist
28 enlightenment. The reliefs on the second level,
29 the five terraces, illustrate events from Buddha's
30 past lives. The third level, on which the famous
31 stupa rests, doesn't have reliefs, but is instead
32 decorated by dozens of smaller stupas, each of
33 which contains a Buddha partially visible through
34 patchy stonework. The entire trip, from the eastern
35 staircase to the final stupa, is more than three miles
36 long.

37   In 1991, UNESCO designated Borobudur
38 a World Heritage site after the Indonesian
39 government invested in massive renovations.
40 Today, the temple is a site for religious pilgrimages
41 and for tourists interested in the impressive art and
42 architecture. Borobudur is a point of pride for many
43 Indonesian people; they see the country's financial
44 investment and the temple's tourist popularity as
45 proof of Buddhism's rebirth in the country.

1. Borobudur can be described as all of the following EXCEPT

    a. massive.
    b. historic.
    c. ornate.
    d. dilapidated.

2. Based on the information in the passage, Borobudur is likely located

    a. on a volcanic island.
    b. on a mountainside.
    c. on a deserted island.
    d. in a tropical jungle.

3. Which of the following is a possible title for this passage?

    a. Borobudur: A Forgotten Relic
    b. Indonesian Historical Sites
    c. The Buddhist Temple of Borobudur
    d. Borobudur and the Rise of Buddhism

4. Based on the design of the temple, the journey to enlightenment is likely

    a. beautiful and easy.
    b. long and complex.
    c. dangerous and frightening.
    d. fast and thought provoking.

5. According to the passage, the third level is different from the others because it is

    a. more than three miles long.
    b. decorated with small and large stuptas.
    c. lower than the other levels.
    d. decorated with reliefs that depict Buddah's past lives.

6. As it is used in the passage, "low" (line 12) most nearly means

    a. modern.
    b. inexpensive.
    c. domed.
    d. shallow.

Questions 7 - 12

1   What motivates students? This question
2 has plagued educators since the dawn of time. It's
3 not unusual at all for a youngster to spend hours
4 trying to make it to the next level of a video game
5 and then fail to complete an easy math assignment.
6 This is frustrating for parents and teachers alike.
7 Some recommend that the best way to get a child
8 to complete tasks is to offer incentives. However,
9 a better outcome could be achieved by identifying
10 the cause of the lack of motivation. This can be
11 done using the Temporal Motivation Theory (TMT).
12   Temporal Motivation Theory examines
13 a person's motivation, or how likely they are to
14 procrastinate in a given moment. Dr. Piers Steel
15 based TMT on a formula which includes the
16 four factors that impact motivation: motivation =
17 expectancy x value / impulsiveness x delay. In other
18 words, motivation is expectancy multiplied by
19 value divided by impulsiveness multiplied by delay.
20   Let's look at the first part of the equation.
21 Expectancy is related to how capable someone feels
22 about completing a task. Value relates to how much
23 worth one attaches to a particular task. Therefore,
24 high expectancy and value leads to increased
25 motivation. If someone is confident that they'll
26 be able to complete a task, and they see purpose
27 in doing the work, the more likely they will be to
28 do it in a timely fashion. The inverse is also true. If
29 someone lacks skills or does not see the reason for
30 doing a task, then they tend to procrastinate.

31   The second part of the equation states that
32 impulsiveness and delay cause procrastination.
33 Impulsiveness is a susceptibility to distraction.
34 Delay is related to how urgent the task is. If a
35 student is easily distracted, and their assignment
36 isn't due for two weeks, it's likely they won't get to
37 work on it right away. As with the first part of the
38 equation, the reverse is also true for the second
39 part of the statement. If a person is good at avoiding
40 distractions and the assignment is due tomorrow,
41 they can focus and complete it rather than put it off.
42   Perhaps instead of calling students
43 lazy or unmotivated, we should consider how
44 to alter these four factors in order to maximize
45 motivation. If someone is feeling like they can't
46 meet given expectations, it would help to build
47 their skills. Teachers should be thoughtful about
48 assigning meaningful work. They can also help
49 students break up long term projects into smaller
50 parts. Finally, assisting students with establishing
51 routines and strategies in order to minimize
52 distractions will also reduce procrastination.

7. Which of the following best describes the author's perspective?

   a. The author is unconcerned with why a student lacks motivation instead the author wants to explore how to make a student motivated.
   b. The author does not believe that unmotivated students are lazy.
   c. The author thinks incentives will help motivate students.
   d. The author believes that motivation will continue to plague teachers for a long time.

8. Which best describes the organization of the passage?

   a. A problem is explained, and solutions are offered.
   b. An issue is debated, and a cause is agreed upon.
   c. An academic perspective is given on a common problem.
   d. A sequence of events is explained as to how a conclusion was drawn.

9. In line 2, "dawn of time" is used as

   a. alliteration.
   b. pun.
   c. imagery.
   d. hyperbole.

10. The passage is primarily concerned with

    a. helping people feel more motivated.
    b. explaining the temporal motivation theory.
    c. determining the prime moment of motivation.
    d. analyzing the impact that lack of motivation has on a person.

11. In line 28, "inverse" most nearly means

    a. decline.
    b. incline.
    c. opposite.
    d. transverse.

12. According to the author which of the following would lead to the most motivation?

    a. high expectancy, high value, low delay, and low impulsivity
    b. high expectancy, high value, high delay, and high impulsivity
    c. low expectancy, high value, low delay, and high impulsivity
    d. low expectancy, low value, low delay, and low impulsivity

Questions 13 - 18

1   Diogenes of Sinope was well known for
2 his highly unusual and provocative behavior. He
3 refused to wear shoes, lived in an old wine barrel
4 in a public marketplace, and ate raw meat. He
5 was perhaps history's original troll; he endlessly
6 harassed wealthy and powerful figures and mocked
7 society for adhering to the status quo. He was also
8 one of the greatest philosophers of Ancient Greece.
9 Even though none of his prolific writings survived
10 the ancient world, his legacy was nevertheless
11 ensured thanks to his wild antics.
12   Diogenes thought that most material
13 possessions and social norms were products of
14 human vanity and stupidity. He is considered
15 to be one of the founders of the Cynic school
16 of philosophy, which asserted that the key to
17 happiness and virtue was freedom from frivolous
18 concerns like wealth, pride and comfort. Diogenes
19 lived out his values in an extremely public and
20 confrontational fashion, and his disdain for and
21 mockery of conventional standards of behavior
22 made him a sort of counter-cultural icon.
23   One of Diogenes' favorite targets was the
24 elite philosopher Plato. Diogenes routinely taunted
25 the great thinker, and took every opportunity he
26 could to poke holes in Plato's teachings. When
27 Plato was applauded for developing a simplistic
28 definition of man as a "featherless biped," Diogenes
29 famously burst into one of his lectures wielding a
30 plucked chicken and yelling "Behold, a man!"
31   As Diogenes' reputation spread throughout
32 Greece, his disregard for social hierarchy became
33 increasingly dangerous. Alexander the Great, King
34 of the Greek Empire, became intrigued by the
35 stories of Digoenes' acerbic brilliance and went to
36 Athens to meet the notorious philosopher. Upon
37 seeking out Diogenes' barrel, Alexander offered
38 to bestow any gift that the man desired. Diogenes
39 retorted that he would greatly appreciate the gift
40 of Alexander stepping to the side, so that he would
41 stop blocking Diogenes' sunlight. Amazingly,
42 Alexander reportedly took the eccentric man's
43 insults with good humor and remarked that if
44 he weren't Alexander the Great, he'd wish to be
45 Diogenes. Diogenes replied that if he were anyone
   but Diogenes, he would also wish to be Diogenes.
   It is not unreasonable to think that Diogenes might
   have been put to death for speaking to Alexander
   in such a manner. Yet somehow his abrasive
   authenticity seemed to shield him from the
   penalties that befell others for committing similar
   (or lesser) offenses.

46   Near the end of his life, Diogenes was
47 captured by pirates and sold into slavery. When
48 asked what trades and aptitudes he had, Diogenes
49 said that his only skill was ruling other people, and
50 that he would best be sold to a man who wanted
51 a master. Incredibly, one buyer was so amused by
52 Diogenes' wit that he purchased him on the spot
53 as a tutor for his children. Diogenes was reportedly
54 quite content with these circumstances, and
55 remained with the family until his death. Ironically,
56 he remained immune to and exempt from the laws
57 of society even while he was technically enslaved.
58 He thus lived out his days in what he considered to
59 be the ultimate state of freedom.

13. According to the author, which of the following is the best example as to why Diogenes remained famous despite the fact that none of his writings survived?

    a. He insulted Plato.
    b. He had some very unusual habits and behaviors.
    c. He met Alexander the Great.
    d. He was captured by pirates and sold into slavery.

14. The author suggests that Diogenes was a "counter-cultural icon" (line 22). This most nearly means Diogenes was quite popular

    a. within Greek inner circles.
    b. despite living outside cultural norms.
    c. among the common Greek people.
    d. in places of high cultural importance.

15. The line, "Behold, a man." (line 30) represents Diogenes

    a. desire to belong.
    b. demeaning nature.
    c. defiance.
    d. frustration with scientific progress.

16. In line 35, "acerbic" most nearly means

    a. anguished.
    b. foolish.
    c. sharp.
    d. wit.

17. According to the passage, people viewed Diogenes in the all the following ways EXCEPT

    a. as an eccentric.
    b. as intelligent.
    c. as an imbecile.
    d. as humorous.

18. Which of the following lifestyle choices of Diogenes best corresponds to his belief in cynicism?

    a. He lived in an old wine barrel.
    b. He was a tutor.
    c. He met Alexander the Great.
    d. He was captured by pirates.

Questions 19 - 24

1   Of the fourteen different organelles
2 students learn about, one tends to stand out: the
3 "powerhouse of the cell," the mitochondria. The
4 mitochondrion is the organelle responsible for
5 creating energy in the cell, hence its nickname.
6 One can find mitochondria in nearly every
7 eukaryotic cell except for monocercomonoides.
8 Some cells, like those found in the human liver and
9 muscle, actually contain hundreds or thousands
10 of mitochondria. As might be expected of such a
11 well-known organelle, mitochondria are large in
12 comparison to other organelles. They are oval-
13 shaped and made up of two membranes. The inner
14 membrane's folds create cristae, or crests, that
15 resemble a maze and are not easily permeated.
16 The outer membrane is permeable to small
17 molecules and has processes for transporting
18 larger molecules. Mitochondria also contain their
19 own DNA which means that they can function
20 autonomously.
21   Respiration is the process of changing
22 food particles into energy, a process that would
23 be impossible without mitochondria. Specifically,
24 cellular respiration requires that the mitochondria
25 take molecules which have permeated both
26 membranes and convert them to energy through a
27 series of chemical reactions. The energy produced
28 by mitochondria has a special name: adenosine
29 triphosphate, simply called ATP. ATP powers every
30 biochemical action in the human body, from
31 breaking down glucose to building proteins.

32   Mitochondria's production of ATP is
33 relatively complex and full of scientific jargon,
34 but it can be simplified into three steps. First,
35 molecules that enter the mitochondria are broken
36 down into small pieces. This breakdown occurs
37 inside of both membranes where there's a gel-like
38 substance full of chemical compounds that prepare
39 the pieces to be moved to the inner membrane.
40 Second, the pieces from the jelly center proceed
41 to the inner membrane where they move along
42 the cristae, gaining and losing electrons through
43 a series of redox reactions. As a result of these
44 reactions, adenosine diphosphate (ADP) is created.
45 In the third and final step of ATP production, a
46 phosphoryl group of atoms is added to ADP thus
47 creating ATP and completing the cycle of cellular
48 respiration.

19. The author includes lines 6 - 10 in order to

    a. explain the purpose of mitochondria.
    b. describe the process of respiration.
    c. explain why mitochondria are so large.
    d. show the prevalence of mitochondria.

20. The inner membrane of the mitochondria is different than the outer membrane of the mitochondria because the inner membrane

    a. is not easily penetrated.
    b. is oval shaped.
    c. contains its own DNA.
    d. transports large molecules.

21. This passage is most concerned with the

    a. the 14 organelles of the body.
    b. a physical description of mitochondria.
    c. the creation of ADP.
    d. the function of the mitochondria.

22. In line 20, "autonomously" most nearly means

    a. carefully.
    b. inadequately.
    c. independently
    d. reliably.

23. According to the passage, what must be true of cellular respiration?

    a. It must create ATP.
    b. It must take place only in the mitochondria's inner membrane.
    c. It must use ADP to break apart molecules.
    d. It must maintain the cell's number of electrons.

24. According to the third paragraph, ADP is produced in

    a. an electron.
    b. the mitochondria's inner membrane.
    c. the mitochondria's outer membrane.
    d. a phosphoryl group of atoms

Questions 25 - 30

1 One Saturday afternoon an animated group of
2 boys was gathered at a large pond. Among them
3 was Frederic Hooper, a teacher at Center Grammar
4 School.
5
6 "Now, boys," he said, holding in his hand a
7 Waterbury watch, "I offer this watch as a prize to
8 the boy who can skate across the pond and back
9 in the least time. You will start together and make
10 your way to the mark which I placed at the end of
11 the lake, skate around it, and return here. Do you
12 understand?"
13
14 "Yes, sir!" exclaimed the boys.
15
16 Before proceeding, it may be best to introduce two
17 of the boys who were to engage in the contest.
18 The first was Randolph Duncan, whose father was
19 the president of the Groveton Bank. Randolph's
20 father was a rich man and lived in a style beyond
21 that of his neighbors. Randolph, his only son, was
22 an athletic boy of sixteen who believed his wealth
23 made him superior to the other boys.
24
25 Next came Luke Larkin, a boy similar in age and
26 physical strength, but in other respects different
27 from Randolph. Luke was the son of a carpenter's
28 widow and lived on narrow means. He had a warm
29 heart and was probably, in spite of his poverty, the
30 most popular boy in school. In this respect he was
31 the opposite of Randolph, whose assumption of
32 superiority prevented him from having any real
33 friends. Randolph had two or three companions
34 who flattered him because they thought it looked
35 good to be on friendly terms with the young
36 aristocrat.
37
38 These two boys were the chief contestants for the
39 prize. Opinions differed as to which would win.
40
41 "I think Luke will get the watch," said Fred.
42
43 "I don't know about that," said Tom. "Randolph
44 skates just as well, and he has a pair of club skates.
45 His father sent to New York for them."
46
47 "Of course that gives him the advantage," said
48 Percy. "Look at Luke's old-fashioned wooden
49 skates!"
50
51 "It's a pity Luke doesn't have a better pair," said
52 Linton. "I don't think the contest is fair."

53 Randolph had his friends near him, administering
54 the adulation he so much enjoyed.
55
56 "I have no doubt you'll get the watch, Randolph,"
57 said Sam. "You're a better skater any day than
58 Luke."
59
60 "Of course you are!" chimed in Tom.
61
62 "Are you ready?" asked Mr. Hooper.
63 Most of the boys responded promptly in the
64 affirmative; but Luke said quickly: "I am not ready,
65 Mr. Hooper. My strap broke!"
66
67 "Luke, I am sorry to hear it," said the teacher,
68 examining the fracture. "As matters stand, you can't
69 skate."
70
71 Randolph's eyes brightened. He knew that his
72 chances of success would be greatly increased by
73 Luke's withdrawal.
74
75 "The prize is yours now," whispered Tom.
76
77 "It was before," answered Randolph, conceitedly.
78 Luke looked disappointed. He knew that he had a
79 good chance of winning, and he wanted the watch.
80 Several of his friends had watches, and this seemed
81 his only chance of securing one.
82
83 "It's a pity you can't skate, Luke," said Mr. Hooper.
84 "You are one of the best skaters. Is anyone willing to
85 lend Luke his skates?"
86
87 "You can use my skates, Luke," said Linton.
88
89 "I don't think that's fair," said Randolph, with a
90 frown. "Each boy should use his own skates."
91
92 "There is nothing unfair about it," said the teacher,
93 "except that Luke is placed at a disadvantage in
94 using skates he is unaccustomed to."
95
96 Randolph did not dare gainsay the teacher, but he
97 looked sullen.
98
99 "You are very kind, Linton," said Luke, regarding his
100 friend affectionately.
101
102 "It's all right, Luke," said Linton. "Now go and win!"

25. The passage indicates that Randolph and Luke were very different in all of the following ways EXCEPT their

    a. personality.
    b. wealth.
    c. popularity.
    d. physical abilities.

26. Tom and Sam speak to Randolph with a tone of

    a. thoughtful encouragement.
    b. genuine concern.
    c. callous mockery.
    d. false deference.

27. It can be inferred that "club skates" (line 44) are

    a. antiques.
    b. embellished.
    c. high quality.
    d. widely available.

28. It can be concluded that the contest is Luke's "only chance of securing" (line 81) a watch because

    a. his parents won't allow him to have a watch.
    b. watches are difficult to find in stores.
    c. he can't afford to purchase one.
    d. he really wants his teacher's watch.

29. Randolph's comment "It was before" (line 77) is included to in order to show his

    a. arrogance.
    b. confusion.
    c. deference.
    d. fury.

30. As it is used in the passage, the word "gainsay" (line 96) most nearly means

    a. ask.
    b. contradict.
    c. glorify.
    d. threaten.

Questions 31 - 36

1　　　Since its introduction in 1991, the World
2　Wide Web has revolutionized people's lives, and
3　imagining a world without the internet feels nearly
4　impossible. Although that was the norm just thirty
5　years ago, today we rely on connectivity to navigate
6　daily life, from the route we take to work to the way
7　we consume media and share personal milestones;
8　it's all made easier, quicker, and more convenient
9　thanks to the internet. As anyone with social media
10　would tell you, a plethora of indulgent activities
11　also rely on the internet. Some might even be under
12　the impression that it was invented just to help
13　people waste time. What is perhaps less clear is
14　how essential a resource the internet is to industries
15　in every sector. Take education for example. Public
16　education in 2020 is a far cry from where it was
17　in 1991, and the internet is a crucial piece of that
18　evolution.
19　　　For many teachers, the internet is their first
20　stop when writing lesson plans. There are countless
21　resources teachers can access online which provide
22　them with reliable and engaging activities for their
23　classes. Once a teacher has written an original
24　lesson plan that meets standards and excites
25　students, they need some way for administrators
26　to access it. So what do they do? They upload it to a
27　school or district database for approval.
28　　　A lesson plan must meet various criteria
29　before earning administrator approval. In many
30　school districts, a big chunk of this criteria deals
31　with Common Core standards, which serve as
32　regulations aimed at establishing consistency in
33　education. Standards exist in every subject which
34　set forth the expectation that "digital media"
35　is provided to "enhance understanding." This
36　translates to having students watch documentaries
37　or videos, participate in lab simulations, play
38　educational games, create digital presentations,
39　and conduct research online. In short, it is now a
40　mandate that teachers implement some form of
41　those and other internet-based activities in their
42　curriculum.

43　　　In 2020, the implementation of digital
44　media in the classroom is a crucial part of a holistic
45　education. Along with all of the other content
46　students are expected to learn throughout school,
47　they will also need a basic level of technological
48　proficiency to enter the workforce after high school
49　or go on to college. For the more than 64% of
50　students who have access to the internet at home,
51　having that same access at school is somewhat
52　irrelevant. However, for the 36% of students who
53　don't have access to the internet at home, the
54　degree to which their teachers implement digital
55　media in class can make or break their success after
56　graduation.
57　　　The internet is an indispensable resource
58　for students and teachers. Yes, it helps shape
59　classroom culture and provides new ways for
60　students to absorb information, but it does even
61　more than that: it prepares students for what life
62　will be like outside of a classroom. The invention
63　of the internet has revolutionized the world we
64　live in today, and education is just one example of
65　how society is adapting to meet demands. In 2018
66　alone, the internet sector created six million jobs
67　and more than two trillion dollars in gross domestic
68　product. Educators are on the frontlines of
69　preparing young people to enter a workforce reliant
70　on technological fluency. The relationship between
71　education and technology will continue to evolve
72　to meet the changing demands of the twenty-first
73　century.

31. What best describes the organization of the passage?

    a. It introduces a topic and focuses on a specific aspect of that topic.
    b. It gives a wide array of information on a particular subject matter.
    c. It provides critical analysis on a topic.
    d. It explains one person's personal narrative on an issue.

32. As used in line 10, "plethora" most nearly means

    a. embarrassment.
    b. excess.
    c. succinct.
    d. sufficient.

33. In lines 49 - 56, the author uses percentages in order to demonstrate

    a. that most students have internet access at home.
    b. only a minority of students lack access to the internet.
    c. that internet usage at school is important for many students.
    d. that internet usage is not really relevant.

34. Which best expresses the main idea of the passage?

    a. The internet is a useful tool in a variety of economic sectors.
    b. Internet in the classroom prepares students for school and beyond.
    c. Too much emphasis is placed on technology and not enough on common core.
    d. Digital media is now a requirement for all educators.

35. The author's tone toward the internet can best be described as

    a. admiring.
    b. amused.
    c. curious.
    d. impartial.

36. The primary purpose of the last paragraph is to

    a. explain why education and technology are a lasting relationship.
    b. summarize the points made earlier in the passage.
    c. allow the reader to ponder what the future might be like.
    d. convince the reader that more needs to be done to fund access to the internet in low income countries.

Section 4: Math
47 Questions, 40 Minutes

Instructions: Each question is followed by four answer choices. Select the best answer.

1. A teacher recorded the number of questions her students missed on a recent quiz in the table below. What is the median number of answers missed?

Questions Missed	Numbers of Students Missing That Number of Questions
0	1
1	5
2	7
3	7
4	1

 a. 1
 b. 2
 c. 3
 d. 4

2. Find the midpoint of the line segment defined by the points A (6, -4) and B (8, 2).

 a. (1, -1)
 b. (1, 3)
 c. (7, -1)
 d. (7, 3)

3. What is the solution set to the inequality $1 \le 3x + 7 \le 10$?

 a. $-2 \le x \le -1$
 b. $-2 \le x \le 1$
 c. $x \le -2$ or $x \le 1$
 d. $x \le -2$ or $x \le -1$

4. If $2(4k - k) = 24$, what is the value of k?

 a. 4
 b. 6
 c. 8
 d. 12

5. A pair of jeans is on sale for 30% off. If the sale price is $28.00, what was the original price of the jeans?

 a. $27.70
 b. $36.40
 c. $40.00
 d. $58.00

6. A pharmaceutical company developed a new acne medication for people with moderate to severe acne. To get the most reliable data on the effectiveness of the medication, the company should test it on a group of volunteers who

 a. have mild acne.
 b. are already taking acne medications.
 c. live near the pharmaceutical company.
 d. are comprised of a variety of ages, races, and genders.

7. Which expression is equivalent to $x^2 - 3x - 28$?

 a. $(x - 7)(x - 4)$
 b. $(x - 7)(x + 4)$
 c. $(x - 6)(x - 4)$
 d. $(x - 6)(x + 4)$

8. What is the value of the expression $\dfrac{5.8 \times 10^4}{8.0 \times 10^3}$?

 a. 7.25×10
 b. 7.25×10^3
 c. 7.25×10^6
 d. 7.25×10^7

9. Two angles, which measure 3x and x degrees respectively, are arranged on a line. Solve for x.

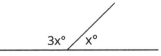

 a. 45°
 b. 50°
 c. 60°
 d. 135°

10. The equation for a given line is y = 6x - 1. Which of the following shows the equation in terms of x?

   a. $x = \dfrac{y+1}{6}$

   b. $x = \dfrac{y}{6} + 1$

   c. $x = 6y - 1$

   d. $x = 6y$

11. When measuring the height of a tree, it would be most reasonable to use which of the following units?

   a. millimeters
   b. meters
   c. kilograms
   d. grams

12. The solution to $-2 = x^2$ is which type of number?

   a. integer
   b. natural number
   c. complex number
   d. real number

13. What is the solution set for $2x^2 = -8$?

   a. -4i
   b. -2i
   c. ±2
   d. ±2i

14. ∠Z is congruent to ∠Y. What is the measure of ∠X?

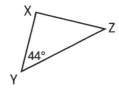

   a. 44°
   b. 88°
   c. 92°
   d. 104°

15. Put the following numbers in order, from least to greatest: -3.4, $\dfrac{9}{2}$, $-\dfrac{15}{4}$, 4.75, -3.9

   a. -3.9, $-\dfrac{15}{4}$, -3.4, $\dfrac{9}{2}$, 4.75

   b. $-\dfrac{15}{4}$, -3.9, -3.4, $\dfrac{9}{2}$, 4.75

   c. $-\dfrac{15}{4}$, -3.9, -3.4, 4.75, $\dfrac{9}{2}$

   d. -3.4, $-\dfrac{15}{4}$, -3.9, 4.75, $\dfrac{9}{2}$

16. If the function f is defined as f(x) = 2x + 11, for what value of x is f(x) equal to 5?

   a. -6
   b. -3
   c. -2
   d. 8

17. What is the sixth number in this sequence?

   -27, -21, -15, -9, -3

   a. -2
   b. 0
   c. 2
   d. 3

18. At the local dog show only four dogs can move on to the final round. If there are ten dogs showing, how many different groups of dogs could make it to the final round?

   a. 24
   b. 90
   c. 210
   d. 5,040

19. Four cubed minus three squared is equal to what number?

   a. 3
   b. 9
   c. 55
   d. 64

20. A school tracks how many students from each grade level come for extra math help after school. The data is summarized in the dot plot below. What is the mean number of students per grade level that come in for extra help?

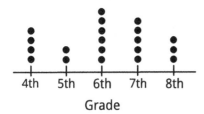

Grade

a. 3
b. 4
c. 5
d. 6

21. Which expression is equivalent to $\sqrt{25x^2y^4}$?

a. $5xy^2$
b. $5x^2y$
c. $5x4y^8$
d. $25xy^2$

22. The formula for the surface area of a square pyramid is $s^2 + 2sl$, where s is the length of a side of the base and l is the slant height. What is the surface area of a square pyramid where s = 3 inches and l = 5 inches?

a. $24\ in^2$
b. $36\ in^2$
c. $39\ in^2$
d. $55\ in^2$

23. Which inequality is shown in the solution set below?

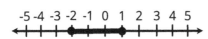

a. $-1 \leq 3x - 7 \leq 10$
b. $-1 \leq 3x + 7 \leq 10$
c. $1 \leq 3x - 7 \leq 10$
d. $1 \leq 3x + 7 \leq 10$

24. Joe's cookie recipe calls for 3 cups of flour and makes 2 dozen cookies. He needs to make 12 dozen cookies for the bake sale. How many cups of flour will he need?

a. 8 cups
b. 13 cups
c. 18 cups
d. 24 cups

25. The area of each grid square shown is $3\ cm^2$. What is the area of the shaded area?

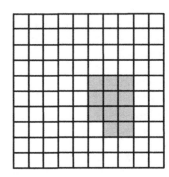

a. $11\ cm^2$
b. $12\ cm^2$
c. $22\ cm^2$
d. $33\ cm^2$

26. Lamar measured his body temperature every 8 hours during the two days he had a fever. On the first day he recorded temperatures of 101.2 degrees, 100.6 degrees, and 99.9 degrees. On the second day, he recorded temperatures of 100.4 degrees , 99.1 degrees, and 101.0 degrees. What was the range of Lamar's recorded temperatures?

a. 1.1 degrees
b. 1.3 degrees
c. 1.9 degrees
d. 2.1 degrees

27. In the xy-coordinate plane if point (4,-3) is reflected over the y-axis, what are the coordinates of the resulting point?

a. (-4, -3)
b. (-4, 3)
c. (4, 3)
d. (4, 6)

28. Carlos has a stack of number cards containing the numbers 1-15. If Carlos selects one number card at random, what is the probability that he will choose a prime number?

   a. $\frac{1}{2}$

   b. $\frac{2}{5}$

   c. $\frac{3}{7}$

   d. $\frac{7}{15}$

29. Siobhan bought a circular kitchen table. When she measured from the exact center of the table to the edge of the table, she found it was 18 inches. What is the table's circumference?

   a. 36 inches
   b. 18π inches
   c. 36π inches
   d. 324π inches

30. A data set is represented in the box-and-whisker plot below. What is the third quartile of the data?

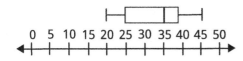

   a. 20
   b. 25
   c. 35
   d. 38

31. What is the value of the numerical expression $\sqrt{25 - 9}$?

   a. 2
   b. 4
   c. 6
   d. 8

32. For what value(s) of y is the equation $5 + y = 5 - y$ true?

   a. -4 only
   b. 0 only
   c. all real numbers
   d. there are no values for y that make the equation true

33. What is the least common multiple of $9g^3h$, $18gh^4$, and $56g^2$ if g and h are both prime?

   a. $9g$
   b. $9g^3h^4$
   c. $504g$
   d. $504g^3h^4$

34. Which expression is equivalent to the expression $\dfrac{2c^4 - 8c^2d^3}{4c^4 - 4c^2d^3}$?

   a. $\dfrac{c^2 - 4d^3}{2c^2 - 2d^3}$

   b. $\dfrac{c^2 - 2d^3}{2c^2 - d^3}$

   c. $\dfrac{c^2 - 4d^3}{c^2 - d^3}$

   d. $\dfrac{c^4 - 4d^3}{c^4 - d^3}$

35. A grocery store wants to determine the most common number of items purchased by customers. To gather that information, the store tracks the number of purchases made by its first 10 customers of the day. That data is shown in the graph below. What is the mode of the data?

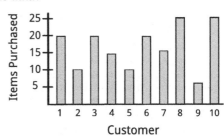

   a. 10
   b. 15
   c. 20
   d. 25

36. A cyclist is cycling at a speed of 250 meters per minute. If there are .305 meters per foot and 5,280 feet in a mile, which expression represents the cyclist's speed in miles per hour?

   a. $\dfrac{.305 \times 5,280 \times 60}{250}$

   b. $\dfrac{250 \times 60}{.305 \times 5,280}$

   c. $\dfrac{.305 \times 5,280}{250 \times 60}$

   d. $\dfrac{.305 \times 5,280 \times 250}{60}$

37. The sum of two numbers is 36. The larger number is eight more than the smaller number. What is the measure of the larger number?

    a. 14
    b. 16
    c. 20
    d. 22

38. Which of the following describes all values for x for which $|8x - 4| > 12$?

    a. $x < -1$ or $x > 2$
    b. $x > -1$ or $x < 2$
    c. $x > -1$
    d. $x < 2$

39. A bag contains 7 blue marbles, 3 green marbles, and 5 red marbles. Jill randomly chooses one marble, returns it to the bag, and then chooses another marble. What is the probability that her first choice was blue and her second choice was NOT blue?

    a. $\frac{7}{15} \times \frac{7}{14}$
    b. $\frac{7}{15} \times \frac{8}{14}$
    c. $\frac{7}{15} \times \frac{7}{15}$
    d. $\frac{7}{15} \times \frac{8}{15}$

40. A food delivery service tracks the number of orders each customer makes in a given month. The results are summarized in the table below.

Number of orders per month	Probability
1	$\frac{2}{7}$
2	$\frac{1}{7}$
3	$\frac{3}{7}$
4	$\frac{2}{7}$

What is the expected number of orders placed per month?

    a. 1
    b. 2
    c. 3
    d. 4

41. A parallelogram has a base of 8 inches and height of 9 inches. What is the area of the parallelogram?

    a. $17 \, in^2$
    b. $34 \, in^2$
    c. $36 \, in^2$
    d. $72 \, in^2$

42. What is the result of the expression

$$\begin{bmatrix} 4 & 5 & 3 \\ 9 & 0 & 4 \end{bmatrix} - \begin{bmatrix} 8 & 3 & 1 \\ 7 & 6 & 3 \end{bmatrix}$$

    a. $\begin{bmatrix} 4 & 2 & 2 \\ 2 & -6 & 1 \end{bmatrix}$

    b. $\begin{bmatrix} 4 & 2 & 2 \\ 2 & 6 & -1 \end{bmatrix}$

    c. $\begin{bmatrix} 12 & 8 & 4 \\ 16 & 6 & 7 \end{bmatrix}$

    d. $\begin{bmatrix} 4 & 8 & 4 \\ 9 & -6 & 1 \end{bmatrix}$

43. Solve: $x^2 - 7x - 18 = 0$.

    a. $x = -9, -2$
    b. $x = -6, -3$
    c. $x = 6, 3$
    d. $x = 9, -2$

44. The height of the prism pictured below is 3 centimeters less than its length and the base of the prism is 2 centimeters less than its length. What is the volume of the prism?

Note: The formula used to determine the volume of a triangular prism is $V = \frac{1}{2} lbh$, where l is the prism's length, b is the prism's base and h is the prism's height.

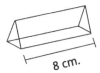

8 cm.

    a. 24
    b. 48
    c. 120
    d. 240

45. An animal rescue organization tracks the number of volunteer hours logged each year. Between 2017 and 2020, the hours increased by how much?

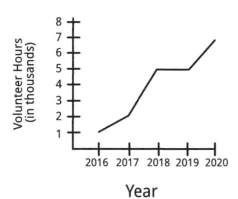

a. 2
b. 5
c. 2,000
d. 5,000

46. Line S is perpendicular to line Q (not pictured). If point A is a point on line Q, what is another point on line Q?

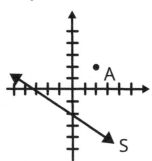

a. (-6, -2)
b. (-5, 1)
c. (-3, 0)
d. (-2, -4)

47. Triangle XYZ is shown below. What is the sine of ∠Z?

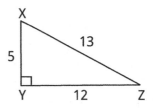

a. $\frac{5}{13}$

b. $\frac{5}{12}$

c. $\frac{12}{13}$

d. $\frac{12}{5}$

Essay

1 Question, 30 Minutes

Instructions: You have 30 minutes to write an essay on the topic below. It is not permitted to write an essay on a different topic. Your essay must be written in blue or black pen.

Please be aware that the schools you apply to will receive a copy of your essay. Your essay should be longer than a paragraph and use specific examples and details.

Write your response on this page and the next page.

If you could make any change to your school, what would you change and why?

Test 4 Answer Key

Section 1: Verbal

1. A	9. B	17. C	25. C	33. C
2. B	10. B	18. B	26. A	34. B
3. D	11. C	19. D	27. A	35. D
4. D	12. B	20. C	28. D	36. C
5. C	13. B	21. C	29. C	37. D
6. C	14. D	22. A	30. C	38. C
7. C	15. C	23. B	31. A	39. B
8. B	16. C	24. B	32. C	40. D

Section 2: Quantitative

1. A	9. A	17. D	25. B	33. B
2. C	10. B	18. D	26. B	34. A
3. A	11. A	19. C	27. C	35. C
4. D	12. D	20. A	28. C	36. A
5. B	13. C	21. B	29. D	37. D
6. C	14. B	22. A	30. C	
7. D	15. D	23. C	31. D	
8. C	16. C	24. A	32. D	

Section 3: Reading

1. D	9. D	17. C	25. D	33. C
2. A	10. B	18. A	26. D	34. B
3. C	11. C	19. D	27. C	35. A
4. B	12. A	20. A	28. C	36. A
5. B	13. B	21. D	29. A	
6. D	14. B	22. C	30. B	
7. B	15. C	23. A	31. A	
8. A	16. C	24. B	32. B	

Section 4: Math

1. B	11. B	21. A	31. B	41. D
2. C	12. C	22. C	32. B	42. A
3. B	13. D	23. D	33. D	43. D
4. A	14. C	24. C	34. A	44. C
5. C	15. A	25. D	35. C	45. D
6. D	16. B	26. D	36. B	46. D
7. B	17. D	27. A	37. D	47. A
8. C	18. C	28. B	38. A	
9. A	19. C	29. C	39. D	
10. A	20. B	30. D	40. C	

ISEE Test 5

Section 1: Verbal
40 Questions, 20 Minutes

Synonyms
Instructions: Select the word whose meaning is closest to the word in capital letters.

1. DURABLE:

    a. enduring
    b. modest
    c. thoughtful
    d. weak

2. FOE:

    a. child
    b. enemy
    c. friend
    d. peer

3. PRESERVE:

    a. absorb
    b. maintain
    c. produce
    d. reconstruct

4. ADHERE:

    a. give
    b. listen
    c. stick
    d. touch

5. EXEMPLIFY:

    a. alter
    b. critique
    c. dismantle
    d. embody

6. PERPLEX:

    a. confuse
    b. disagree
    c. embarrass
    d. remove

7. ALOOF:

    a. arrogant
    b. distant
    c. intolerant
    d. punctual

8. LULL:

    a. boring
    b. discourse
    c. pause
    d. stroll

9. RECTIFY:

    a. amend
    b. enlighten
    c. intensify
    d. trim

10. MERCIFUL:

    a. agreeable
    b. forgiving
    c. friendly
    d. persevering

11. INSTINCTIVE:

    a. automatic
    b. forced
    c. perceptive
    d. sudden

12. HAUGHTY:

    a. ardent
    b. extroverted
    c. pompous
    d. shameful

13. IMPETUOUS:

    a. bold
    b. momentum
    c. motivated
    d. reckless

14. PUTRID:

    a. adverse
    b. broken
    c. hostile
    d. rancid

15. REBUKE:

    a. confuse
    b. mock
    c. reprimand
    d. seize

16. SNEER:

    a. abhor
    b. brag
    c. complain
    d. snicker

17. AMELIORATE:

    a. enhance
    b. frustrate
    c. illuminate
    d. surge

18. COGENT:

    a. gloomy
    b. persuasive
    c. reserved
    d. versatile

19. SOMBER:

    a. irritable
    b. pensive
    c. solemn
    d. vulnerable

Sentence Completion

Instructions: Select the word or pair of words that best completes the sentence.

20. The little girl's high-pitched squeal ------- around the empty hallway.

    a. boomed
    b. diminished
    c. ran
    d. reverberated

21. In 2019, the ------- mathematician Karen Uhlenbeck became the first woman to win the prestigious Abel Prize.

    a. esteemed
    b. poised
    c. lethargic
    d. sociable

22. While Vlad didn't exactly lie, he had a tendency to ------- the truth when talking to his friends about his athletic feats.

    a. attack
    b. embellish
    c. negate
    d. tell

23. Carol's ------- personality made even her most apathetic middle school students excited to come to school each day.

    a. adventurous
    b. ebullient
    c. nervous
    d. serious

24. Australians observe National Sorry Day on May 26th of each year to formally recognize and ------- the mistreatment of indigenous Australians.

    a. commemorate
    b. continue
    c. dismiss
    d. heighten

25. Over the past 40 years, humans have ------- more than 20% of the Amazon rainforest, resulting in massive deforestation.

    a. explored
    b. harvested
    c. impacted
    d. razed

26. Although Hans was convinced that purchasing a new vehicle was by far the best option, he also recognized that repairing his current car was a ------- possibility.

    a. fantastic
    b. terrible
    c. viable
    d. worrisome

27. ------- influenza viruses primarily affect birds but have been spread to humans who are in contact with infected poultry.

    a. Avian
    b. Seasonal
    c. Serious
    d. Swine

28. Despite the community's concerns about the dismal condition of the local playground, there was ------- interest in funding the playground's renovation.

    a. fervent
    b. much
    c. reasonable
    d. scant

29. A(n) ------- student, Viola rarely did homework and never studied for tests.

    a. agreeable
    b. apathetic
    c. unconventional
    d. zealous

30. As he walked into his office, the disgraced politician was flooded by a(n) ------- of questions from reporters.

    a. assortment
    b. handful
    c. smattering
    d. torrent

31. The restaurant critic wrote a ------- review of the new seafood restaurant after he got serious food poisoning at the establishment.

    a. neutral
    b. somber
    c. vitriolic
    d. wise

32. Upset that his boss ------- to give him an early raise, Malcolm ------- his boss's authority and complained to the president of the company.

    a. agreed . . . usurped
    b. consented . . . honored
    c. was forced . . . realized
    d. refused . . . undermined

33. The ------- farmhouse partially collapsed due to years of -------.

    a. damaged. . . care
    b. decrepit . . . neglect
    c. rustic . . . stability
    d. stout . . . use

34. The steel ------- built his ------- fortune by creating a more efficient, less expensive method to make steel.

    a. apprentice . . . inconsiderable
    b. magnate . . . negligible
    c. tycoon . . . immense
    d. worker . . . expected

35. As a child, Tyler was a(n) ------- Chicago Bears fan, ------- watching each game and even crying when they lost.

    a. devout . . . diligently
    b. occasional . . . regularly
    c. apathetic . . . avidly
    d. unfaltering . . . dispassionately

36. In 1812, Napoleon's forces successfully ------- an attempted ------- by Claude François de Malet, a disgruntled general.

    a. foiled . . . subordination
    b. lost . . . rebellion
    c. halted . . . celebration
    d. quashed . . . coup

37. After careful -------, the school board decided to replace the wildly popular, yet ------- principal.

    a. consideration . . . brilliant
    b. deliberation . . . ineffective
    c. discussion . . . unpopular
    d. questioning . . . youthful

38. Though Kiana found her son's seemingly sudden decision to quit the basketball team to be -------, he had actually been ------- the change for months.

    a. alarming . . . disputing
    b. debatable . . . enjoying
    c. logical . . . pondering
    d. rash . . . contemplating

39. Giddy to be cast in a major film, Hassan knew he needed to ------- his ------- so that he could remain professional.

    a. increase . . . elation
    b. quell . . . anticipation
    c. temper . . . excitement
    d. understand . . . role

40. When James became ------- in a scandal, he was forced to resign as CEO to ------- the company's board of directors.

    a. embroiled . . . pacify
    b. interested . . . appease
    c. involved . . . outrage
    d. targeted . . . contradict

Section 2: Quantitative
37 Questions, 35 Minutes

The section is divided into two parts: problem solving and quantitative comparison. Directions for each part are provided.

Part 1 - Problem Solving

Instructions: Each question is followed by four possible answers. Select the best answer.

1. Find the cubed value of the lowest common factor of 25, 40, and 70.

    a. 5
    b. 25
    c. 125
    d. 150

2. The area of a circle is 64π. If the diameter of the circle is reduced by two, what is the area of the new circle?

    a. 36π
    b. 49π
    c. 81π
    d. 100π

3. If $\spadesuit k = k(k+1)$, what is the value of $\spadesuit 8$?

    a. 56
    b. 65
    c. 72
    d. 89

4. Randy is trying to figure out the age of one of his ten cousins. If the total age of his other nine cousins is 226 and the mean age of all of his cousins is 25, how old is the tenth cousin?

    a. 22
    b. 23
    c. 24
    d. 25

5. Based on the information in the graph below, it can be reasonably concluded that the average 45 year old's muscle strength will

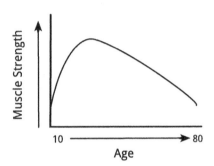

    a. gradually increase until it reaches a plateau.
    b. increase sharply, reach a plateau, and decline.
    c. gradually increase.
    d. gradually decline.

6. Which of the following is equal to a if $ayx = by + cy$?

    a. $\dfrac{b + c}{x}$
    b. $\dfrac{by + cy}{x}$
    c. $x(b + c)$
    d. $x(by + cy)$

7. The product of two consecutive negative integers must be

    a. negative and odd
    b. negative and even
    c. positive and odd
    d. positive and even

8. If $\dfrac{2}{x^{-4}} = 32$, what is the value of $3x^3$?

    a. 2
    b. 12
    c. 24
    d. 64

9. After going grocery shopping, Dan found a parking spot 45 feet away from his apartment door. If Dan's groceries weighed 150 pounds, what other piece of information is required to determine the total distance Dan travelled since parking his car in order to get all of his groceries to his apartment door?

    a. Dan's walking speed
    b. The amount of groceries, in pounds, that Dan can carry at once.
    c. The total volume of the groceries
    d. None of the above

10. Halle is selling cookies along the four blocks closest to her home. She wants to sell an average of 15 boxes per block. If she sold 18, 11, and 10 boxes of cookies in the first three blocks, respectively, how many cookies will she need to sell in the fourth block to meet her goal?

    a. 15
    b. 18
    c. 21
    d. 24

11. In the graph below, each dot represents a different date. What pattern does the graph show?

    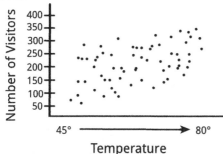

    Temperature

    a. There is a strong positive correlation between the number of park visitors and the temperature.
    b. There is a weak positive correlation between the number of park visitors and the temperature.
    c. There is a weak negative correlation between the number of park visitors and the temperature.
    d. There is no correlation between the number of park visitors and the temperature.

12. Krystal's cheer team is having a bake sale. They are selling cookies for $0.50 each and brownies for $0.75 each. The team sells twice as many cookies as brownies and makes a total of $175. How many brownies did they sell?

    a. 50
    b. 100
    c. 150
    d. 200

13. If $(x-10)^2 = x^2 + nx + 100$, what is the value of n?

    a. -20
    b. -10
    c. 10
    d. 20

14. A rectangle's width is 9 inches. If the area of the rectangle is smaller than 80 inches squared, and the height of the rectangle is an integer, what is the perimeter of the rectangle?

    a. 9 in
    b. 27 in
    c. 34 in
    d. 48 in

15. Lorraine has a collection of 6 black scarves and 8 white scarves. Of the black scarves, 1 is plain and 5 are patterned. Of the white scarves, 5 are plain and 3 are patterned. Lorraine randomly chooses one scarf to wear. Which of the following is greatest?

    a. If a black scarf is chosen, the probability that it is patterned
    b. If a black scarf is chosen, the probability that it is plain
    c. If a white scarf is chosen, the probability that it is patterned
    d. If a white scarf is chosen, the probability that it is plain

16. A swimming pool is being filled with water at a rate of 10,000 gallons of water every 2 hours. Which of the graphs below best represents this scenario?

Note: Each graph shows the volume of water (in tens of thousands of gallons) as a function of time.

a.

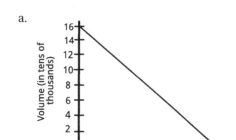

b.

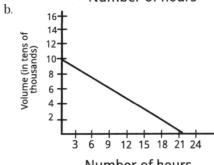

c.

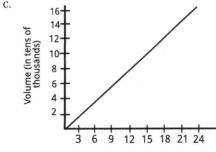

d.

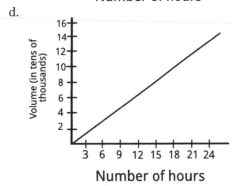

17. Which of the following could be a net of the cylinder shown below?

a.

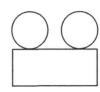

b.

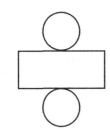

c.

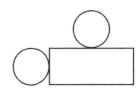

d.

18. Lines A and B lie in the same coordinate plane as point $(2, 5)$. If the equation of line A is $y = -2x - 6$ and the equation of line B is $y = \frac{1}{2}x + 4$, point $(2, 5)$ is on

   a. line A only.
   b. line B only.
   c. both line A and B.
   d. neither line A nor B.

19. An employee for a state tollway system tracks the number of vehicles that use the toll roads each day over the course of 30 days. The results are summarized in the histogram below. The employee realized that he accidentally put three days in the 1-2 million column that should have been in the 4-5 million column. Once he corrects his error, what would the new median of the data be?

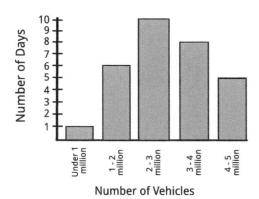

a.   1 - 2 million
b.   2 - 3 million
c.   3 - 4 million
d.   4 - 5 million

Part 2 - Quantitative Comparisons

Instructions: In each question, use the information provided to compare the quantity in Column A with the quantity in Column B. All quantitative comparison questions have the same answer choices:

    a. The quantity in column A is greater.
    b. The quantity in column B is greater.
    c. The two quantities are equal.
    d. The relationship cannot be determined from the information given.

20. | Column A | Column B |
|---|---|
| $6 - \dfrac{8}{2} + 3 \times 7 - 1$ | 34 |

21. | Column A | Column B |
|---|---|
| 15% of 70 | 10% of 85 |

$x \neq 0$

22. | Column A | Column B |
|---|---|
| $2x + 3$ | $3x - 5$ |

$y < z$

23. | Column A | Column B |
|---|---|
| $y^2 - z$ | $z^2 - y$ |

The base of a triangle is twice its height. The area of the triangle is 9 in².

24. | Column A | Column B |
|---|---|
| The base of the triangle. | 3 |

Nina rolls two 6-sided number cubes with sides labeled 1-6. She then adds the results together.

25. | Column A | Column B |
|---|---|
| If the sum is 2, the probability that the first roll was a 1 | If the sum is 3, the probability that the first roll was a 1 |

26. | Column A | Column B |
|---|---|
| 8 | The product of the distinct prime factors of 24. |

27. | Column A | Column B |
|---|---|
| $(x+y)(x^2 - xy + y^2)$ | $x^3 + y^3$ |

△ ABC is similar to triangle △ DEF.

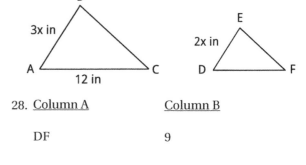

28. | Column A | Column B |
|---|---|
| DF | 9 |

Round each number to the nearest hundredth.

29. | Column A | Column B |
|---|---|
| 3.786 | 3.79421 |

Lines A and B are perpendicular and lie on the same coordinate plane. (3, 2) is a point on line A and (-6, 1) is a point on line B.

30. | Column A | Column B |
|---|---|
| The slope of line A. | The slope of line B. |

Triangle A

Triangle B

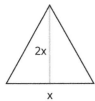
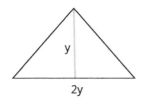

Note: The images are not drawn to scale.

31. Column A — The area of triangle A.

Column B — The area of triangle B.

The measure of an interior angle of a regular polygon is $\dfrac{180^\circ \, (n - 2)}{n}$.

32. Column A — The difference in the measure of an interior angle of a pentagon and a hexagon.

Column B — 12°

Emmanuel tosses two coins.

33. Column A — The probability that both coins land on heads.

Column B — The probability that only one coin lands on heads.

Let $f(x) = \sqrt{x}$ and $g(x) = x^2$ for all $x > 0$.

34. Column A — $f(g(x))$

Column B — $g(f(x))$

Two rectangular prisms are shown below. Prism X has one side that is shorter than the corresponding side on prism Y, one side that is longer, and one side that is equal in length.

35. Column A — The surface area of prism X

Column B — The surface area of prism Y

$y = 3x^2 - 6$

36. Column A — The minimum value of y when $-2 \le x \le 0$

Column B — The minimum value of y when $0 \le x \le 2$

ABCD is a rectangle. $\overline{BC}$ is the diameter of the circle pictured.

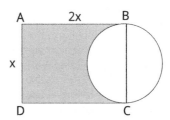

37. Column A — The area of the shaded region.

Column B — $2x^2 - \dfrac{1}{2}\left(\dfrac{1}{2}x\right)^2$

Section 3: Reading
36 Questions, 35 Minutes

Instructions: Carefully read each passage and answer the questions that follow it. For each question, decide which of the choices best answers the question based on the passage.

Questions 1 - 6

1 Generation Z, Gen Z, Post-Millenials,
2 iGen, Gen Wii: however you say it, there is no
3 argument that this generation of Americans is
4 going to be more educated and more diverse than
5 any preceding it. People born between 1997 and
6 2012 are included in the Gen Z moniker, and they
7 are defined not only by their diversity but also by
8 technology. Every member of Gen Z will have been
9 born into a world where the internet was widely
10 available, and this is a definitive characteristic of
11 their generation.
12 Before Gen Z, there was Y, colloquially
13 referred to as Millennials, born between 1981 and
14 1996. As of 2019, Millennials have overtaken Baby
15 Boomers as the largest generation in America.
16 Popularly portrayed in the media as narcissistic
17 and entitled, Millennials are critically referred to as
18 "Generation Me." This is a broad characterization of
19 an age group that grew up receiving participation
20 trophies and thinking they were bound for
21 greatness. A more accurate and less critical
22 understanding of Millenials is one that takes into
23 consideration the reality they faced in 2008. At a
24 time when many of them were graduating from
25 college and entering the job force, the American
26 economy entered a recession, leaving them saddled
27 with college loans without viable work options
28 to pay them off. Millennials themselves argue
29 that they will spend their lifetime cleaning up the
30 repercussions of failed fiscal and environmental
31 policies put in place by previous generations, above
32 all, the Baby Boomers.

33 "Ok, Boomer," a dismissive catchphrase
34 and meme that gained traction in late 2019
35 is perhaps the best insight into the strained
36 relationship between Boomers and Millennials. The
37 saying encapsulates the exasperation Millennials
38 (and Gen Z if we're keeping score) feel toward Baby
39 Boomers who condescend to their lifestyle choices.
40 Baby Boomers, born between 1946 and 1964, get
41 their name from the uptick in babies born following
42 World War II. In the same way Gen Z is defined
43 by technology, the Baby Boomers are defined by
44 wealth and the politics surrounding it. They are
45 particularly pessimistic; despite having higher
46 incomes than other generations, they worry about
47 money more. You would think a group of people
48 so exposed to social revolution and the cultural
49 renaissance of the mid-twentieth century could
50 find more enjoyment in life, especially with deeper
51 pockets, but in fact, it's the opposite.
52 Less reported on and scrutinized by the
53 media is Generation X whose members were born
54 between 1965 and 1980. Not only is Gen X largely
55 absent from the media landscape, but the United
56 States has never had a Gen X president and might
57 not have a chance of seeing one until 2028. The
58 Silent Generation, members born between 1928
59 and 1945, faces a problem similar to Gen X: being
60 sandwiched between two larger age groups who
61 are better known to the public. Although this is the
62 case, some of the most well-loved American heroes
63 are members of the Silent Generation, people like
64 Martin Luther King, Jr., Neil Armstrong, and Johnny
65 Cash.

1. Which word best describes the author's attitude toward Millennials?

    a. ambivalent
    b. sympathetic
    c. confused
    d. frustrated
    e.

2. According to the passage, Generation Z is best defined by

    a. their education.
    b. their diversity.
    c. the internet.
    d. their narcissism.

3. Which of the following best explains why some people view Millennials as narcissistic?

    a. They graduated college during a rough economic time.
    b. As children, they received awards for everything.
    c. They are left to take care of poor environmental policies.
    d. They are the second largest generation.

4. Based on lines 40 - 51, which of the following examples of Boomers is ironic?

    a. Boomers represent the largest population but had fewer children themselves.
    b. Boomers grew up during a time of social revolution but are not very tolerant of others.
    c. Boomers were born after World War II but are very pessimistic.
    d. Boomers have more income than any other generation but are less positive.

5. In line 26, "recession" most nearly means

    a. boom.
    b. downturn.
    c. impasse.
    d. problem.

6. In line 61 - 65, the author includes examples of famous people from the Silent Generation in order to

    a. show how they were representative of the sandwich generation.
    b. ensure readers they were not without worthy contributors.
    c. contrast them to Generation X.
    d. explain why we do not hear much about the silent generation.

Questions 7 - 12

1   Mary Louise walked toward the group in a leisurely
2   manner, her books under one arm. She wore a
3   dark skirt and a simple shirt, both quite becoming,
4   and her shoes were the envy of half the girls at the
5   school. Few people would describe Mary Louise
6   Burrows as beautiful, while all would agree that she
7   possessed elegance and charming manners.
8
9   "What do you think, Mary Louise," demanded
10 Jennie, "of this latest outrage?"
11
12 "What outrage, Jen?" with a whimsical smile at their
13 indignant faces.
14
15 "This latest decree of the tyrant Stearne. 'Young
16 ladies will refrain from leaving the school grounds
17 after the hour of six p.m., unless written permission
18 is first secured from the principal. Any infraction
19 of this rule will result in suspension or permanent
20 dismissal.' We're determined not to stand for this
21 rule a single minute."
22
23 "Well," said Mary Louise reflectively, "I'm not
24 surprised. The wonder is that Miss Stearne hasn't
25 stopped your evening parades before now. Did
26 you ever hear of any other private boarding
27 school where the girls were allowed to go to town
28 whenever they pleased?"
29
30 "Didn't I tell you?" snapped Mable, addressing the
31 group. "Mary Louise is always on the wrong side."
32 Mary Louise quietly seated herself upon the bench
33 beside them.
34
35 "You seem angry, Mable," she said with a smile,
36 "but I believe your parents sent you here because
37 Miss Stearne is known to be a very competent
38 teacher and her school has an excellent reputation
39 of long standing. It's evidence of good breeding
40 and respectability to have attended Miss Stearne's
41 school."
42
43 "Well, what's that got to do with this insulting
44 order to stay on school grounds in the evenings?"
45 demanded Sue Finley. "Miss Stearne has gone a
46 step too far in her tyranny. The only reason we go
47 to town is to see the picture show, which is our
48 one innocent recreation. I'm sure we've always
49 conducted ourselves properly."

50 "If Miss Stearne wishes to keep us away from the
51 pictures, she has a reason for it," observed Mary
52 Louise, "so let's discover what the reason is."
53
54 "To spoil any little fun we might have," asserted
55 Mable bitterly.
56
57 "No, I can't believe that," answered Mary Louise.
58 "She isn't unkind, nor is she too strict. I've heard
59 her remark that her boarders are young ladies who
60 can be trusted to conduct themselves properly, and
61 she's right about that. We must look for her reason
62 somewhere else, and I think it's in the pictures
63 themselves."
64
65 "I've seen Miss Stearne herself at the picture theatre
66 twice within the last week," said Jennie.
67
68 "Then that's it; she doesn't like the character of the
69 pictures shown. I think, myself, they've been rather
70 poor lately. Certainly, some of the pictures are
71 fine and dandy, but as long as the man who runs
72 the theatre mixes the horrid films with the decent
73 ones—and we can't know beforehand which is
74 which—it's really the safest plan to keep away from
75 the place altogether. I'm sure that's the position
76 Miss Stearne takes, and we can't blame her for it."
77
78 The girls received this statement sullenly, yet
79 they had no logical reply to controvert it. So Mary
80 Louise, feeling that her explanation of the edict
81 was not popular with her friends, quietly rose and
82 sauntered away.
83
84 "Pah!" sneered Mable, looking after the slim figure,
85 "I'm always suspicious of those goody-goody
86 creatures. Mark my words, girls: Mary Louise will
87 fall from her pedestal some day!"

7. Mary Louise can be described as

    a. agitated.
    b. boastful.
    c. composed.
    d. eager.

8. As it is used in line 18, "infraction" most nearly means

    a. conviction.
    b. disapproval.
    c. discussion.
    d. violation.

9. Which rhetorical device does Mary Louise use when she describes the girls' outing as a "parade" (line 25)?

    a. irony
    b. metaphor
    c. personification
    d. simile

10. Mary Louise believes that Miss Stearne wants the girls to stay on school grounds in the evenings because

    a. Miss Stearne believes that some of the pictures shown off school grounds are inappropriate.
    b. the girls have been misbehaving on their outings.
    c. the girls have been coming home after curfew.
    d. Miss Stearne has repeatedly told the girls not to go to the pictures while in town.

11. Mable speaks about Mary Louise with a tone of

    a. admiration.
    b. uncertainty.
    c. contempt.
    d. arrogance.

12. Lines 78 - 79 imply that

    a. Mary Louise feels superior to the girls.
    b. the girls disagree with Mary Louise's assessment but are hesitant to say so.
    c. Mary Louise believes that the girls are foolish to doubt Miss Stearne.
    d. the girls realize Mary Louise is probably right but are unhappy about it.

Questions 13 - 18

1　　　　One of the best ways to appreciate
2　Chicago's architecture is by boat. The guided
3　Chicago River cruise, popular with tourists and
4　locals alike, shows off some of the city's famous
5　buildings, like the Merchandise Mart and Tribune
6　Tower. As visitors look up at the skyscrapers from
7　the riverboat, it's hard for them to picture what the
8　city would have looked like more than a century
9　earlier after the Great Chicago Fire. In October of
10　1871, a monstrous blaze ripped through downtown
11　and spread north, damaging more than four square
12　miles of the city. Chicago was on fire for two days
13　until, finally, on October 10, it was extinguished,
14　and a population devastated by loss would begin to
15　rebuild.
16　　　　To understand what made the city so
17　susceptible to such a severe fire, it's important to
18　look back to 1850, when merely 30,000 people lived
19　in Chicago. By the time 1860 arrived, that number
20　had tripled, and by 1871, Chicago was a bustling
21　urban landscape with 324,000 residents. A city
22　unequipped to deal with such a population boom
23　left poor Chicagoans living in cramped conditions
24　downtown. Many of them lived and worked in
25　overcrowded, wooden buildings without much care
26　or regulation for safety. Additionally, the summer
27　and fall of 1871 had been particularly dry, and the
28　city was facing a drought. To make matters worse,
29　the night before the Great Chicago Fire started,
30　another serious fire broke out, exhausting the city's
31　firefighters and their equipment. This particular
32　combination of elements proved to be lethal to the
33　city.

34　　　　Historians espouse different theories of
35　the fire's cause. Some believe a comet or meteor hit
36　the city. Others say it was a lit cigarette or careless
37　thieves. The most popular explanation is that in
38　a barn on the southwest side, a cow kicked over
39　a lantern. Whatever the cause, the fire rapidly
40　spread east and north toward downtown and
41　the lake shore. There was more than 200 million
42　dollars (equivalent to four billion dollars in 2020)
43　in damage. Three hundred people were killed and
44　nearly 20,000 buildings destroyed. The fire left a
45　third of Chicago's resident's homeless. The city was
46　eager to repair and revive.
47　　　　The Great Chicago fire provided a unique
48　opportunity to rebuild the city and construct
49　even bigger buildings than were there previously.
50　Architects, attracted to the city by the opportunity,
51　began to shape the future of Chicago in the months
52　after the conflagration. By 1885, Chicago was
53　home to the world's first skyscraper. By 1889, when
54　New York celebrated its first, Chicago had already
55　built an additional four. As any passenger on the
56　architecture river cruise could tell you, Chicago
57　roared back to life following the destructive fire.

13. The author includes lines 9 - 12 in order to

    a. describe the aftermath of the fire.
    b. show the scope of the fire.
    c. detail the damage caused by the fire.
    d. explain the cause of the fire.

14. Which of the following would be an appropriate title for this passage?

    a. Reshaping Chicago: The Great Chicago Fire
    b. The History of Chicago's Architecture
    c. The Cow Kicked Over a Lantern: The Causes of the Great Chicago Fire
    d. Rebuilding After the Great Chicago Fire

15. All of the following are listed as contributing factors to the fire EXCEPT

    a. overpopulation.
    b. lack of regulation.
    c. inadequate training of firefighters.
    d. dry weather conditions.

16. What do all of the potential causes of the fire (lines 35 - 41) have in common?

    a. There is historical evidence for all of them.
    b. They are unavoidable.
    c. They are attributed to humans in some way.
    d. They are unintentional.

17. In line 34, "espouse" most nearly means

    a. admire.
    b. doubt.
    c. deny.
    d. support.

18. The author's tone in the final paragraph is best described as

    a. upbeat.
    b. inquisitive.
    c. cautionary.
    d. passionate.

Questions 19 - 24

1   Yellowstone National Park is one of the
2 most popular parks in the United States. Visitors
3 flock to the park to take in the surrounding nature,
4 view the geysers and springs, and, if they're lucky,
5 spot some wildlife. Interestingly, Yellowstone
6 is located right on top of a volcanic hot spot
7 and is considered not just an active volcano
8 but a supervolcano! A supervolcano has had an
9 explosion recorded at the highest level of the
10 volcanic explosivity index. The first explosion in
11 Yellowstone was recorded 2 million years ago, and
12 there was another explosion 1.3 million years ago.
13 The most recent eruption was about 630,000 years
14 ago, thus showing a pattern of explosive action
15 occurring roughly every 750,000 years. Although
16 it might initially seem like there is a level of risk
17 visiting a park with a supervolcano, geologists are
18 not too concerned over an eruption there any time
19 soon. If the pattern remains, the next explosion
20 won't occur in this lifetime.
21   Geologic activity in Yellowstone is
22 evident to the eye and the nose. Many visitors
23 remark on the way Yellowstone smells. The park,
24 especially near some of the famous geysers like
25 Mud Volcano, reeks of sulfur, like rotten eggs. To
26 understand why these geysers smell the way they
27 do, it helps to envision the underlying geology.
28 Geysers are holes in the earth that generally form
29 in volcanic areas. They serve as an escape for hot
30 water and steam when the pressure below the
31 crust becomes too much to contain. They erupt
32 on a regular basis, pushing that stinky, sulfuric
33 water and steam hundreds of feet into the air. The
34 water seeps back into the hole and back down
35 deep into Earth's hot crust, boiling and building
36 energy for another explosion, continuing the cycle.
37 Old Faithful, one of Yellowstone's most popular
38 destinations, is the most famous geyser in the
39 world, and it erupts about twenty times a day.
40 Though a visit to Yellowstone wouldn't have one
41 believing so, geysers are actually very rare. About
42 half of the geysers on planet Earth call Yellowstone
43 home; plenty more are located in Iceland and New
44 Zealand.

45   Another interesting geologic feature
46 and popular destination in Yellowstone is Grand
47 Prismatic Spring. It is the most photographed
48 feature of the park and is instantly recognizable
49 with its expansive size and bright, concentrated
50 colors. The outer ring of the pool is a burnt orange
51 that slowly fades into concentric circles of muted
52 yellow, emerald green, and a vibrant blue center.
53 Each of the distinct bands around the pool derives
54 its color from the heat-loving bacteria living
55 there. The spring itself is deeper than a ten-story
56 building and wider than a football field is long. It's
57 a stunning sight that leaves onlookers hypnotized.
58 If one were to take a dip in the 160°F spring, they
59 would suffer third degree burns in seconds and
60 likely death.

19. This passage is primarily concerned with

    a. Grand Prismatic Spring.
    b. Yellowstone's top tourist destinations.
    c. the geology of Yellowstone.
    d. supervolcanoes.

20. One of the reasons that geysers continually erupt rather than only erupting once is because they

    a. boil and release only a small portion of the water they contain.
    b. reabsorb the water they erupt.
    c. get new water from nearby hot springs.
    d. collect fresh rainwater.

21. Yellowstone's geologic features can be described as all of the following EXCEPT

    a. odorous.
    b. dangerous.
    c. colorful.
    d. commonplace.

22. Based on the information in the passage, it's likely that the geysers in New Zealand and Iceland

    a. erupt on a regular basis.
    b. are as numerous in each location as they are in Yellowstone.
    c. smell more strongly of sulfur than Yellowstone's geysers.
    d. are located in a volcanic area.

23. According to the passage, what causes the color variations found in Grand Prismatic Spring?

    a. the extreme heat
    b. bacteria
    c. sulfur
    d. geyser eruptions

24. The author uses the hyperbole "hypnotized" (line 57) to highlight the onlookers'

    a. astonishment.
    b. trance.
    c. joy.
    d. boredom.

Questions 25 - 30

1   By the time Hernán Cortés led his
2 expedition of Spanish conquistadors into the Aztec
3 capital of Tenōchtitlan, the Aztec Empire had
4 dominated the Mesoamerican landscape for nearly
5 two centuries. The invaders were awestruck by the
6 city's magnificence, which was unlike anything
7 they'd seen in Europe. One conquistador later
8 wrote that he and his companions were so stunned
9 by its beauty that they thought they were dreaming.
10   With an estimated population of over
11 250,000 people, Tenōchtitlan outsized other
12 metropolises like London, Paris, and Rome. Despite
13 its gargantuan proportions, the city was strikingly
14 clean and orderly. All of this was made more
15 impressive by the city's odd location: a swampy islet
16 in the middle of a lake.
17   A religious vision led the founders of the
18 Aztec Empire, the previously-nomadic Mexica
19 tribe, to build their settlement in Lake Texcoco.
20 Through careful construction, they gradually
21 enlarged and stabilized the island city. They built a
22 series of channels that were used for irrigation and
23 transport, and sidewalks replete with moveable
24 bridges for pedestrian traffic. They also employed
25 an extraordinary agricultural system of man-made
26 floating gardens, called chinampas, to increase
27 food production.
28   In stark contrast to the filth and chaos of
29 European cities, daily street sweepings and rigorous
30 waste management ensured that Tenōchtitlan's
31 dense grid of streets and canals remained tidy. The
32 people of Tenōchtitlan were also notably more
33 hygienic than their European counterparts. While
34 the Aztecs bathed on a daily basis, most Europeans
35 bathed once a month at most.

36   Ironically, Cortés' arrival in 1519 coincided
37 with the year that the Aztec calendar prophesied
38 the god Quetzalcoatl (whom Cortés is said to have
39 resembled) would return to Earth. The Aztecs had
40 never seen horses, guns, or steel swords before,
41 which they interpreted as further indicators of
42 Cortés' supernatural affiliations. So despite all
43 evidence to the contrary, the Aztecs welcomed
44 Cortés and his undoubtedly smelly companions as
45 divine beings.
46   It wasn't until Cortés' men massacred
47 unarmed citizens of Tenōchtitlan during a festival
48 in 1520 that the Aztec warriors turned on the
49 Spanish and launched a retaliatory attack. Even
50 with their superior weaponry, the Spanish were
51 forced to retreat. Unbeknownst to them (and
52 unfortunately for the Aztecs), they left their most
53 lethal weapon behind.
54   The Spanish were carriers of smallpox
55 disease, which was previously unknown to
56 Mesoamerica. Since the Aztecs had no immunity,
57 it absolutely decimated them. Some estimates hold
58 that up to 90% of the population died as a result of
59 the disease or the famine that ensued when sick
60 people were unable to tend to their crops. So when
61 Cortés attacked again in 1521 and laid siege to
62 Tenōchtitlan, much of his work had already been
63 done.

25. In line 57, "decimated" most nearly means

    a. angered.
    b. destroyed.
    c. lost.
    d. sickened.

26. The Aztecs welcomed Cortés to Tenōchtitlan because

    a. they feared his guns and horses.
    b. they thought he was a god.
    c. they wanted to learn about Europe.
    d. they desired the conquistadors' gold.

27. The author compares the Aztecs to Europeans in order to

    a. highlight the similarities between these two great civilizations.
    b. demean the Europeans.
    c. show that in many ways the Aztecs were far more advanced.
    d. cricize Cortés for destroying a beautiful city.

28. In lines 14 - 15, Tenōchtitlan is described as "strikingly clean and orderly". What is most surprising about this statement?

    a. Tenōchtitlan's size
    b. Tenōchtitlan's inhabitants
    c. Tenōchtitlan's location
    d. Tenōchtitlan's defeat

29. What does the author mean in lines 62 - 63, "much of his work had already been done"?

    a. Cortés had already killed many Aztecs at the festival.
    b. Someone else had already laid siege to Tenōchtitlan.
    c. Cortés did not need to capture Tenōchtitlan.
    d. Disease and famine had killed most of the inhabitants.

30. The primary purpose of this passage is to

    a. explain how Tenōchtitlan fell.
    b. describe the superiority of Spanish weapons.
    c. provide an overview of the history of Tenōchtitlan.
    d. detail the achievements of the Aztec people.

Questions 31 - 36

1　　　The concept of black holes is a little hard
2　to wrap one's head around. By definition, a black
3　hole is a "region of space having a gravitational field
4　so intense that no matter or radiation (including
5　light) can escape." It's hard to imagine what that
6　would even look like, and until recently, people
7　had only ever seen artistic interpretations of black
8　holes. Because they absorb light, black holes are
9　unable to be seen with a regular telescope. That
10　all changed in 2019 when a group of observatories
11　teamed up to photograph a black hole located
12　in the M87 galaxy, more than 53 million light
13　years from Earth. Although the photograph is a
14　scientific breakthrough, the image itself is rather
15　underwhelming. A blurry black dot sits in the
16　middle of a similarly blurry, but brightly colored,
17　orange ring of light. Sure, the image might be
18　lackluster, but it aids astronomy amateurs in
19　understanding the fuzzy concept of black holes.
20　　　The black hole in the photograph itself
21　is, well, a black hole. Because no light can escape
22　it, the image reflects a simple black dot. The term
23　"hole" is a little misleading because it is not really
24　a hole. Black holes are actually regions in space
25　that hold a huge amount of mass packed into a
26　very small area as a result of the death of a star or
27　multiple stars. When a star dies, it collapses in on
28　itself, and all of the matter it was once made of
29　shrinks into a smaller and smaller area. The mass
30　of all the dead star's matter is now compacted into
31　an exponentially smaller space, thus creating the
32　intense gravitational field. This is what is referred to
33　as a stellar (from Latin, meaning star) mass black
34　hole, and astronomers estimate that one is created
35　about once every second! Even larger than a stellar
36　mass black hole is the supermassive black hole. As
37　indicated by its name, these black holes are much
38　larger, containing the mass of millions and possibly
39　billions of dead stars in a single hole. Supermassive
40　black holes are some of the most extreme objects in
41　the universe.

42　　　The other important feature of the
43　groundbreaking 2019 photograph is the ring of
44　light encircling the black hole. This ring is called
45　an accretion disk, and it is made up of plasma, gas,
46　and celestial dust. It orbits an object, like a black
47　hole, and as a result of gravity pulling it inward,
48　spirals around the hole. Essentially, as gravity sucks
49　matter from the accretion disk inside the black
50　hole, it spins and spins around the hole, heating
51　up enough to glow and emit light. Most artistic
52　interpretations of black holes focus on illustrating
53　the colorful accretion disk, and now people can
54　see what one actually looks like thanks to the 2019
55　photograph.

31. The passage is primarily concerned with

    a. explaining why hole may not be the best way to describe this phenomenon.
    b. detailing what the 2019 photograph tells us about black holes.
    c. analyzing why it's so hard to comprehend black holes.
    d. describing how a black hole comes into existence.

32. As used in line 18, "lackluster" most nearly means

    a. modest.
    b. relevant.
    c. small.
    d. uninspiring.

33. According to the passage, why is the term black hole a bit of a misnomer?

    a. A black hole is difficult to see.
    b. A black hole is actually orange.
    c. A black hole holds a lot of mass.
    d. A black hole is very small.

34. The author uses the phrase, "wrap one's head around" (line 2) in order to

    a. alert the readers that what follows might be confusing.
    b. explain why scientists know so little about black holes.
    c. deter people from studying astronomy.
    d. demonstrate the enormous size of black holes.

35. What new information did the photograph of a black hole reveal?

    a. how often black holes are formed
    b. what black holes are comprised of
    c. the distance from earth a black hole is
    d. what the accretion disc looks like

36. All of the following are correct inferences about black holes EXCEPT

    a. they are large.
    b. they have a hot ring around them.
    c. they are very rare.
    d. they are far away from Earth.

Section 4: Math
47 Questions, 40 Minutes

Instructions: Each question is followed by four answer choices. Select the best answer.

1. In the xy coordinate plane, a line segment with endpoints N (4,-6) and B (2, 4) is reflected over the y-axis and then rotated 180° clockwise. What will be the resulting coordinates of point B after these transformations?

   a. (-2, -4)
   b. (2, -4)
   c. (2, 4)
   d. (6, 4)

2. What is the value of the expression 396,400 + 28,900?

   a. 4.253×10^5
   b. 6.854×10^5
   c. 4.253×10^6
   d. 6.854×10^6

3. Six apples at Jack's Grocery cost $4. If Andrew has $10, how many apples can he buy?

   a. 8
   b. 10
   c. 15
   d. 24

4. A nail salon is trying to determine which kind of coupon brings in the most customers. They mail out two different types of coupons and track how many customers use one of the coupons that month. The results are tracked in the circle graph below. What is the central angle of the portion of the circle represented by customers who use the $5 off coupon?

   a. 108°
   b. 120°
   c. 148°
   d. 172.8°

5. The diameter of the cylinder pictured below is three less than its height. What is the volume of the cylinder?

9 in.

   Note: The formula used to determine the volume of a cylinder is $V = r^2 \pi h$, where r is the cylinder's radius, h is the cylinder's height.

   a. 54π in^3
   b. 81π in^3
   c. 108π in^3
   d. 324π in^3

6. If 15 - 3y = 5x - xy, what is the value of x?

   a. -3
   b. 1
   c. 3
   d. 5

7. 170 is 85% of what number?

   a. 85
   b. 144.5
   c. 200
   d. 255

8. Which of the following describes all values for x for which |6x + 6| < 18?

   a. x < 2
   b. x < -4
   c. x < -4 or x < 2
   d. -4 < x < 2

9. (3, 7) and (-1, 6) are two points on line S. What is the slope of line S?

    a. $\frac{2}{13}$

    b. $\frac{1}{4}$

    c. 4

    d. $\frac{13}{2}$

10. Which expression is equivalent to $(x - 2)(x + 2)$?

    a. $x^2 - 4$
    b. $x^2 + 4$
    c. $x^2 - 2x - 4$
    d. $x^2 - 2x + 4$

11. Which of the following is equivalent to $.\overline{81}$?

    a. $\frac{10}{7}$

    b. $\frac{8}{7}$

    c. $\frac{2}{5}$

    d. $\frac{9}{11}$

12. What is the value of the numerical expression $\sqrt{3 \times 27}$?

    a. 5
    b. 6
    c. 9
    d. 14

13. A teacher is interested in how many hours of sleep her students get. She asked each of her students to record the number of hours they slept the previous night. The data is summarized in the table below. What is the mode of the data?

Hours slept	Numbers of Students Sleeping That Number of Hours
6	4
7	9
8	8
9	4
10	2

    a. 7
    b. 8
    c. 9
    d. 10

14. Britney rolls a standard 6-sided die two times. What is the probability that neither of her rolls lands on the number 1?

    a. $\frac{1}{6} \times \frac{1}{6}$

    b. $\frac{5}{6} \times \frac{5}{6}$

    c. $\frac{5}{6}$

    d. $\frac{11}{12}$

15. $\triangle DEF$ is similar to $\triangle GHI$. The length of $\overline{DE}$ is 4 inches and the length of $\overline{GH}$ is 3 inches. What is the length of $\overline{FD}$ if the length of $\overline{IG}$ is 12 inches?

    a. 9 inches
    b. 10 inches
    c. 14 inches
    d. 16 inches

16. What is the result of the expression?

$$2\begin{bmatrix} 6 & -5 & 8 \\ 4 & 0 & -4 \end{bmatrix}$$

a. $\begin{bmatrix} 8 & -10 & 16 \\ 4 & 0 & -4 \end{bmatrix}$

b. $\begin{bmatrix} 12 & -10 & 16 \\ 8 & 0 & -8 \end{bmatrix}$

c. $\begin{bmatrix} 12 & -5 & 8 \\ 8 & 0 & -4 \end{bmatrix}$

d. $\begin{bmatrix} 36 & 25 & -16 \\ 8 & 2 & 8 \end{bmatrix}$

17. Nicholson Kitchen Designs installs cabinets for a charge of $34 per hour plus a fixed charge of $150 per cabinet. Which of the following equations represents the total price (P) of installing c cabinets if the process takes h hours?

   a. P = 34h + 150c
   b. P = 150c - 34h
   c. P = 34c + 150h
   d. P = c(150 + 34h)

18. Three vertices of a rectangle are shown below. What are the coordinates of the fourth vertex?

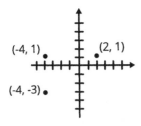

   a. (-4, -1)
   b. (-2, 3)
   c. (2, -3)
   d. (4, -1)

19. What is the third quartile of the data set below?

   3, 5, 6, 8, 10, 11, 13, 16, 18, 19, 20

   a. 13
   b. 16
   c. 17
   d. 18

20. Point (3, -1) is on a circle with center (8, -4). What is the radius of the circle?

   a. $\sqrt{34}$ grid units
   b. $\sqrt{41}$ grid units
   c. 8 grid units
   d. 9 grid units

21. Simplify: $\dfrac{9a^8b^2}{30a^4b^6}$.

   a. $\dfrac{a^4}{10b^4}$

   b. $\dfrac{3a^2}{10b^3}$

   c. $\dfrac{3a^4}{10b^4}$

   d. $\dfrac{3a^4b^4}{10}$

22. When measuring the length of a semi-truck, it would be most reasonable to use which of the following units?

   a. centimeters
   b. kilograms
   c. meters
   d. grams

23. Ali is making a friendship bracelet. He has 7 different colors but will only use 4 to make his bracelet. How many different color combinations could the bracelet have?

   a. 28
   b. 35
   c. 210
   d. 840

24. A circle is inscribed in the square below. What is the area of the shaded region?

8 in

   a. $(32 - 16\pi)$ in^2
   b. $(32 - 36\pi)$ in^2
   c. $(64 - 16\pi)$ in^2
   d. $(64 - 36\pi)$ in^2

25. Anisha interviews 23 of her classmates to find out how many books each student read over summer vacation. Five students reported reading 7 books, six students reported reading 3 books, four students reported reading 10 books, and the rest reported reading either 4 or 5 books. If Anisha calculates the mode of her data to be 5 books, and at least one student read 4 books, how many students read 5 books during summer vacation?

    a. 5
    b. 7
    c. 8
    d. It cannot be determined from the given information.

26. Which expression is equivalent to the expression $\dfrac{10y^3z + 8z^4 + 14yz^2}{2z^2}$?

    a. $\dfrac{5y^3 + 4z^3 + 7yz}{z}$

    b. $5y^3 + 4z^2 + 7y$

    c. $\dfrac{5y^3z + 4z^4 + 7yz^2}{z}$

    d. $\dfrac{5y^3 + 4z^4 + 7y^2}{2z}$

27. The graph below is the solution set for which inequality?

    a. $-5 < 2x - 9 \le 7$
    b. $-5 \le 2x - 9 < 7$
    c. $-5 \le 2x + 9 < 7$
    d. $-5 \le 2x + 9 \le 7$

28. Devon got a box of chocolate truffles as a birthday gift. Four of the truffles are white chocolate and the rest are either milk or dark chocolate. If the probability of randomly choosing a white chocolate truffle is 40%, how many total truffles are in the box?

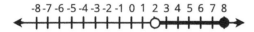

    a. 6
    b. 8
    c. 10
    d. 12

29. An art school wants to offer an introductory painting class on the weekends to attract new students. To determine what day and time to offer the class, the art school should survey

    a. the school's current students
    b. people who have previously expressed interest in classes, but not enrolled
    c. the school's teachers
    d. friends and family of the art school's staff

30. There are 1,760 yards in one mile and 1.196 meters in a yard. A cheetah is running at a speed of 12 meters per second. Which expression has a value equal to the cheetah's speed, in miles per hour?

    a. $\dfrac{1,760 \times 1.196}{12 \times 60 \times 60}$

    b. $\dfrac{12 \times 60 \times 60 \times 1,760}{1.196}$

    c. $\dfrac{12 \times 60}{1,760 \times 1.196 \times 60}$

    d. $\dfrac{12 \times 60 \times 60}{1,760 \times 1.196}$

31. Three members of a running club tracked the number of miles they each ran one Saturday. The number of miles they each ran is documented in the chart below. What is the mean number of miles run? Please round your answer to the nearest hundredth.

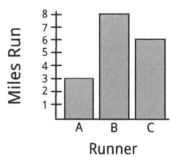

    a. 5.67
    b. 6
    c. 6.34
    d. 7

32. If f(x) = 10 - 2x, what is the value of f(-2) + f(3)?

    a. 8
    b. 10
    c. 18
    d. 26

33. Triangle XYZ is shown below. Which expression is equal to the length of side $\overline{XZ}$?

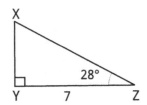

    a. $\dfrac{\cos 28°}{7}$

    b. $\dfrac{7}{\cos 28°}$

    c. $\dfrac{\tan 28°}{7}$

    d. $\dfrac{7}{\tan 28°}$

34. The first five terms of an algebraic sequence are shown below.

    5, 12, 19, 26, 33

    Which expression represents the nth term of this sequence?

    a. -2 + 7n
    b. 2 + 7n
    c. 5 + 7n
    d. 7 + n

35. Factory A manufactures 50 fewer cars each day than Factory B. If the total number of cars manufactured by both factories in one day is 650, how many cars did factory A manufacture?

    a. 250
    b. 300
    c. 350
    d. 600

36. What is the base of a triangle with an area of 100 cm² and height of 10 cm?

    a. 5 cm
    b. 10 cm
    c. 20 cm
    d. 25 cm

37. If 7(3a + 1) = 4a(9 - 2), what is the value of a?

    a. -7
    b. -1
    c. 1
    d. 7

38. What is the solution set for $x^2 + 121 = 0$?

    a. -11
    b. 11i
    c. ±11
    d. ±11i

39. A group of elementary school and middle school students were asked which flavor of candy they preferred. The results are summarized in the table below.

Candy Flavor	Elementary School Students	Middle School Students	Total Number of Students
Grape	14	18	32
Lemon	16	12	28
Orange	17	11	28
Strawberry	21	29	50
Total	68	70	138

What is the probability that if a student prefers grape that they are in middle school?

    a. $\dfrac{7}{34}$

    b. $\dfrac{9}{35}$

    c. $\dfrac{9}{16}$

    d. $\dfrac{7}{9}$

40. If a is a positive number, which expression is equivalent to $4a^3$?

   a. $\sqrt{4a^9}$

   b. $\sqrt{8a^6}$

   c. $\sqrt{16a^6}$

   d. $\sqrt{16a^9}$

41. What is the least common multiple of $6c^5d$, $14cd^3$, and $18c^2d$ if c and d are both prime?

   a. $2cd$
   b. $2c^5d^3$
   c. $126c^5d^3$
   d. $126c^7d^5$

42. What is the solution set to the inequality $-14 \leq 8x + 2 \leq 34$?

   a. $x \leq -4$ or $x \leq 2$
   b. $x \leq -4$ or $x \leq -2$
   c. $-4 \leq x \leq 2$
   d. $-2 \leq x \leq 4$

43. For what values(s) of x does

   $x^2 - 49 = 0$

   $(x + 5)(x - 2)$

   a. $x = 7$
   b. $x = 7, x = -7$
   c. $x = 5, x = 2$
   d. $x = -5, x = 2, x = 7, x = -7$

44. The formula for the surface area of a sphere is $4\pi r^2$, where r is the radius of the sphere. If a sphere has a circumference of 10π inches, what is the surface area of the sphere?

   a. 20π in^2
   b. 40π in^2
   c. 80π in^2
   d. 100π in^2

45. The expression below is an example of which property?

   $18 \times 1 = 18$

   a. commutative property
   b. associative property
   c. identity property
   d. distributive property

46. A quadrilateral is shown below. What is the measure of the missing angle?

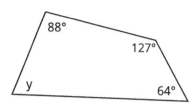

   a. 81°
   b. 82°
   c. 83°
   d. 84°

47. The box-and-whisker plot below shows Reece's English grades throughout the first semester. What is her median grade?

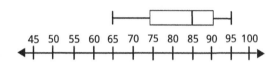

   a. 75
   b. 85
   c. 90
   d. 95

Essay

1 Question, 30 Minutes

Instructions: You have 30 minutes to write an essay on the topic below. It is not permitted to write an essay on a different topic. Your essay must be written in blue or black pen.

Please be aware that the schools you apply to will receive a copy of your essay. Your essay should be longer than a paragraph and use specific examples and details.

Write your response on this page and the next page.

Describe the qualities of a really good teacher. Why are these qualities important?

Test 5 Answer Key

Section 1: Verbal

1. A	9. A	17. A	25. D	33. B
2. B	10. B	18. B	26. C	34. C
3. B	11. A	19. C	27. A	35. A
4. C	12. C	20. D	28. D	36. D
5. D	13. D	21. A	29. B	37. B
6. A	14. D	22. B	30. D	38. D
7. B	15. C	23. B	31. C	39. C
8. C	16. D	24. A	32. D	40. A

Section 2: Quantitative

1. C	9. B	17. B	25. A	33. B
2. B	10. C	18. B	26. A	34. C
3. C	11. B	19. C	27. C	35. D
4. C	12. B	20. B	28. B	36. C
5. D	13. A	21. A	29. C	37. C
6. A	14. C	22. D	30. D	
7. D	15. A	23. D	31. D	
8. C	16. D	24. A	32. C	

Section 3: Reading

1. B	9. B	17. D	25. B	33. C
2. C	10. A	18. A	26. B	34. A
3. B	11. C	19. C	27. C	35. D
4. D	12. D	20. B	28. C	36. C
5. B	13. B	21. D	29. D	
6. B	14. A	22. D	30. A	
7. C	15. C	23. B	31. B	
8. D	16. D	24. A	32. D	

Section 4: Math

1. B	11. D	21. C	31. A	41. C
2. A	12. C	22. C	32. C	42. D
3. C	13. A	23. B	33. B	43. B
4. A	14. B	24. C	34. A	44. B
5. B	15. D	25. B	35. B	45. C
6. C	16. B	26. A	36. C	46. A
7. C	17. A	27. A	37. C	47. B
8. D	18. C	28. C	38. D	
9. B	19. D	29. B	39. C	
10. A	20. A	30. D	40. C	

ISEE Test 6

Section 1: Verbal
40 Questions, 20 Minutes

Synonyms

Instructions: Select the word whose meaning is closest to the word in capital letters.

1. DESCEND:

   a. decline
   b. finish
   c. intensify
   d. spin

2. PROVOKE:

   a. arouse
   b. jeer
   c. subdue
   d. upset

3. VERIFY:

   a. advance
   b. avow
   c. confirm
   d. guarantee

4. JOVIAL:

   a. amusing
   b. curious
   c. gleeful
   d. helpful

5. PECULIAR:

   a. errant
   b. picky
   c. specific
   d. unusual

6. JEER:

   a. dismiss
   b. oppress
   c. shout
   d. taunt

7. ACCLAIM:

   a. accolade
   b. assertion
   c. recommendation
   d. support

8. CACOPHONY:

   a. bellow
   b. din
   c. discussion
   d. shriek

9. VENERABLE:

   a. eager
   b. noble
   c. obliging
   d. revered

10. MOMENTUS:

   a. bold
   b. consequential
   c. negligible
   d. temporary

11. SERENITY:

   a. enmity
   b. scarcity
   c. tranquility
   d. tumult

12. VACUOUS:

   a. demure
   b. empty
   c. replete
   d. stark

13. MOROSE:

   a. demure
   b. dull
   c. irritable
   d. sullen

14. RECUPERATE:

   a. degenerate
   b. modify
   c. recover
   d. rescue

15. DEFERENCE:

    a. acquiescence
    b. elegance
    c. hostility
    d. motivation

16. PETULANT:

    a. bold
    b. overbearing
    c. peevish
    d. shrill

17. IGNOBLE:

    a. aristocratic
    b. civil
    c. dishonorable
    d. understanding

18. OBFUSCATE:

    a. awaken
    b. contemptuous
    c. insincere
    d. obscure

19. IMBUE:

    a. amplify
    b. permeate
    c. shrivel
    d. subdue

Sentence Completion

Instructions: Select the word or pair of words that best completes the sentence.

20. The actor ------- his income by teaching acting classes to children at his local park district once a week.

    a. collected
    b. depleted
    c. finalized
    d. supplemented

21. The snowstorm produced over a foot of snow, ------- the landscape in a blanket of white.

    a. absorbing
    b. camouflaging
    c. enveloping
    d. shielding

22. Carolyn couldn't ------- why anyone would choose to eat pineapple on their pizza.

    a. believe
    b. depict
    c. fathom
    d. question

23. The ------- puppy happily and obediently followed his owner's commands.
    a.
    b. docile
    c. excitable
    d. impulsive
    e. playful

24. Even though she felt quite nervous while giving her speech, Odina appeared to be confident and -------.

    a. anxious
    b. fervent
    c. nonchalant
    d. serious

25. The state government unanimously passed a(n) ------- bill to repair the aging bridges and roads.

    a. divisive
    b. infrastructure
    c. partisan
    d. quick

26. The dinner party was a -------: several guests got sick, the dessert was ruined, and the dog stole the roast off the table.

    a. bore
    b. fiasco
    c. phenomenon
    d. success

27. The factory emitted ------, pungent fumes that made residents of a local neighborhood sick.
    a.
    b. innocuous
    c. noxious
    d. pleasant
    e. unnoticeable

28. Hiking through the national park, Asad abruptly ------ in fear after a bear suddenly crossed his path.

    a. advanced
    b. attacked
    c. hesitated
    d. recoiled

29. After spending years carefully planning the design for the new skyscraper, the architects were surprised when the mayor ------ their proposal.

    a. finalized
    b. rebuffed
    c. recanted
    d. sanctioned

30. A surprising number of people have a strong ------ to the herb cilantro, claiming that it has a bitter, soap-like taste.

    a. aversion
    b. devotion
    c. propensity
    d. remediation

31. Amelia's brother wanted her to do his taxes for free, but Amelia insisted that she be ------ for her time.

    a. compensated
    b. disgraced
    c. dismissed
    d. thanked

32. Despite his initial ------, Anton found he was ------ by the production of Shakespeare's A Midsummer Night's Dream.

    a. enthusiasm . . . intrigued
    b. hesitation . . . captivated
    c. interest . . . absorbed
    d. reticence . . . disappointed

33. The desert's ------ landscape was completely ------ of plants, trees, and other wildlife.

    a. arid . . . full
    b. barren . . . devoid
    c. lush . . . bereft
    d. vibrant . . . bare

34. Kevin found most physics concepts to be quite ------; no matter how much he studied, he couldn't understand most of the underlying ------ of the science.

    a. accessible . . . fundamentals
    b. challenging . . . speculations
    c. elusive . . . principles
    d. fascinating . . . tenets

35. The president's ------ monologue on climate change was more eloquent and ------ than his carefully planned speeches.

    a. impromptu . . . compelling
    b. inarticulate . . . inspiring
    c. rehearsed . . . convincing
    d. unplanned . . . condescending

36. Even though cell phones have become ------, the small town ------ to remove its last phone booth.

    a. archaic . . . declined
    b. omnipresent . . . hoped
    c. sophisticated . . . decided
    d. ubiquitous . . . refused

37. Helena's rationale for cheating on the test didn't ------ her parents; in fact, it made them more ------.

    a. anger . . . guilty
    b. appease . . . livid
    c. placate . . . understanding
    d. trouble . . . irate

38. The ------ turnout at the candidate's final campaign rally ------ his poor performance in the election.
    a.
    b. expected . . . decided
    c. impressive . . . foretold
    d. lackluster . . . portended
    e. low . . . belied

39. Abstract art is a(n) ------- artform; some people
    find it ------- whereas others think it lacks
    meaning.

      a. appealing . . . offensive
      b. contentious . . . boring
      c. crude . . . transcendent
      d. divisive . . . inspiring

40. Martin was ------- that his sister truly believed
    that the earth was flat despite a(n) ------- of
    evidence that she was wrong.

      a. heartened . . . dearth
      b. incredulous . . . plethora
      c. outraged . . . lack
      d. relieved . . . abundance

Section 2: Quantitative
37 Questions, 35 Minutes

The section is divided into two parts: problem solving and quantitative comparison. Directions for each part are provided.

Part 1 - Problem Solving

Instructions: Each question is followed by four possible answers. Select the best answer.

1. The sum of the interior angles of a regular polygon with n sides is 180°(n - 2). If a regular polygon's interior angles add up to 540°, how many sides does the polygon have?

    a. 2
    b. 3
    c. 4
    d. 5

2. Which of the following is equivalent to $\frac{3}{x^4}$?

    a. $\frac{x^4}{3}$

    b. $3x^{-z4}$

    c. $3^4 x^{-4}$

    d. $(3x)^{-4}$

3. The area of a circle is 100π. If the diameter of the circle is reduced by 20%, what is the area of the new circle?

    a. 49π
    b. 64π
    c. 80π
    d. 81π

4. The formula for the volume of a cylinder is $V = \pi r^2 h$, where r represents the radius and h represents the height. If the volume of cylinder A is 4 times the volume of cylinder B, which of the following statements could be true?

    a. The radius of cylinder A is 2 times the radius of cylinder B, and the height of cylinder A is the same as the height of cylinder B.
    b. The radius of cylinder A is 2 times the radius of cylinder B, and the height of cylinder A is 2 times the height of cylinder B.
    c. The radius of cylinder A is 4 times the radius of cylinder B, and the height of cylinder A is the same as the height of cylinder B.
    d. The radius of cylinder A is the same as the radius of cylinder B, and the height of cylinder A is 2 times the height of cylinder B.

5. The local community center is offering guitar lessons for children ages 9 to 15. The average age of the first four children who signed up for lessons is 10 years old. If a fifth student who is 15 years old signs up for lessons, what will the new average age of the children be?

    a. 9
    b. 10
    c. 11
    d. 12

6. If $\frac{a}{c} = \frac{b}{d}$ which of the following is equal to c?

    a. $\frac{b}{ad}$

    b. $\frac{d}{ab}$

    c. $\frac{ab}{d}$

    d. $\frac{ad}{b}$

7. Andre and Maria are both climbing up ladders next to each other. There are 6 inches between each rung on Andre's ladder, while there are 10 inches between each rung on Maria's. Andre starts climbing up his ladder 10 seconds before Maria does. Assuming a constant climbing speed of one rung per second, how much time, rounded to the nearest second, will have passed since Andre started climbing before Maria surpasses Andre?

    a. 26 seconds
    b. 28 seconds
    c. 38 seconds
    d. 50 seconds

8. Two numbers have prime factorizations of $(2^x \times 3^{3y} \times 5^z)$ and $(2^{2x} \times 3^{2y} \times 7^z)$, respectively. Which of the following expressions represents the least common multiple of these two numbers?

    a. $(2^x \times 3^{3y} \times 5^z) + (2^{2x} \times 3^{2y} \times 7^z)$
    b. $(2^x \times 3^{3y} \times 5^z) \times (2^{2x} \times 3^{2y} \times 7^z)$
    c. $2^{3x} \times 3^{5y} \times 5^z \times 7^z$
    d. $2^{2x} \times 3^{3y} \times 5^z \times 7^z$

9. Rodger puts $200 into a savings account. His goal is to increase the amount of money in his account by 50% each year. If he meets his goal exactly, how much money will be in his account after 3 years?

    a. $375
    b. $450
    c. $525
    d. $675

10. The area of a square is 49 centimeters^2. The square is transformed into a rectangle by adding 2 centimeters to two of its sides. What is the area of the rectangle?

    a. 49 cm^2
    b. 56 cm^2
    c. 63 cm^2
    d. 81 cm^2

11. A fruit bowl contains 3 oranges and 5 apples. Two of the apples are red and the rest are green. Fiona chooses one piece of fruit at random. She then returns the fruit to the bowl and chooses another piece. Which of the following events has the lowest probability?

    a. Fiona chooses an orange first and an apple second.
    b. Fiona chooses a green apple followed by a red apple.
    c. At least one of the fruits Fiona chooses is an orange.
    d. Both of the fruits Fiona chooses are oranges.

12. Two different views of a triangular prism are shown below.

Which of the following figures could be a net for the prism?

a.

b.
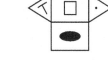

c.
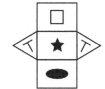

d.
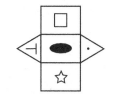

13. Lines C and D are parallel. The equation of line C is y = 3x - 4. Two points on line D are (x, 3) and (0, -6). What is x?

    a. -27
    b. -3
    c. 3
    d. 27

14. What is the maximum value for y if y is an integer and $y = \sqrt{2x + 8}$ and -4 < x < 5?

    a. 4
    b. 6
    c. 8
    d. 16

15. △ABC is similar to △GHI. Which of the following must be true?

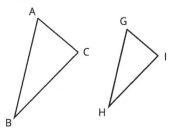

    a. AB = GH
    b. HI < BC
    c. ∠A + ∠C + ∠H = 180°
    d. ∠A ≅ ∠H

16. If n(x) = 2x and m(x) = $\frac{1}{x}$, which inequality is true?

    a. n(1) > n(-1) > m(1) > m(-1)
    b. n(1) > m(1) > m(-1) > n(-1)
    c. m(-1) > n(-1) > m(1) > n(1)
    d. m(1) > n(1) > m(-1) > n(-1)

17. If $5(x+y)^2 = 5x^2 + bxy + 5y^2$, what is the value of b?

    a. 5
    b. 10
    c. 25
    d. 50

18. The product of two consecutive odd integers is 63. What is the difference between the integers?

    a. 2
    b. 3
    c. 6
    d. 7

19. A high school history teacher graded her students' final and then calculated the mean, median, mode, and range of the data. That information is collected in the table below.

Measure	Value
Mean	84
Median	83
Mode	86
Range	44

The student with the lowest score had a score that was 10 points lower than any other student. If the teacher adds five points to that student's score, what would happen to the range of the data?

    a. It would decrease by 10 points.
    b. It would increase by 5 points.
    c. It would decrease by 5 points.
    d. It would stay the same.

20. ABCE is a square with side 4 inches and △ABD is an isosceles triangle with base $\overline{AB}$. What is the area of the shaded region?

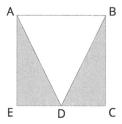

    a. 4 inches
    b. 6 inches
    c. 8 inches
    d. 12 inches

Part 2 - Quantitative Comparisons

Instructions: In each question, use the information provided to compare the quantity in Column A with the quantity in Column B. All quantitative comparison questions have the same answer choices:

- a. The quantity in column A is greater.
- b. The quantity in column B is greater.
- c. The two quantities are equal.
- d. The relationship cannot be determined from the information given.

21. Column A | Column B

x^2 x^3

22. Column A | Column B

The largest integer smaller than 6.98.

The smallest integer larger than $\frac{20}{3}$.

Let $m \lozenge n = 4m + \sqrt{n}$

23. Column A | Column B

$2 \lozenge 25$ $3 \lozenge 16$

A group of students is asked to randomly choose a number between one and ten. Their answers are summarized in the graph below.

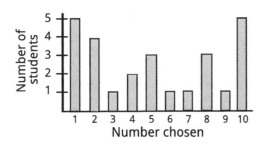

24. Column A | Column B

The number of students who chose even numbers.

The number of students who chose odd numbers.

25. Column A | Column B

$1 - 2^3 + 4 \times 5$ $1^2 - 3 \times 4 + 5$

The area of a parallelogram is 96 cm².

26. Column A | Column B

The height of the parallelogram.

The base of the parallelogram.

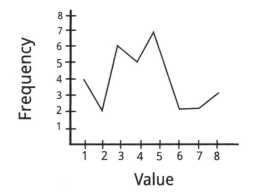

27. Column A | Column B

The range of the data.

The number of times the mode of the data occurs.

$s \neq 0$

28. Column A | Column B

$|2s - 5|$ $|\frac{1}{2}s - 5|$

Linda rolls two 6-sided number cubes with sides labeled 1- 6, then adds the results together.

29. Column A

If the first roll results in an odd number, the probability that the sum will also be an odd number

Column B

If the first roll results in an odd number, the probability that the sum will be an even number

Marco has a pile of nickels and dimes totaling $2.50. He has 20 more nickels than dimes.

30. Column A

The total value of the nickels

Column B

The total value of the dimes

10 - 2x

31. Column A

x > 0

Column B

x < 0

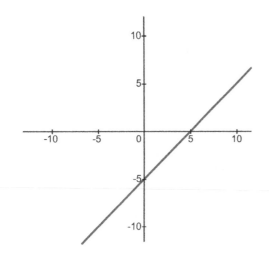

32. Column A

The y value of the y intercept.

Column B

The x value of the x intercept.

Consider the following dataset: 5, 4, 7, 8, 4, 4, 4

33. Column A

The median of the dataset

Column B

The mode of the dataset

x > 0 and y < 0

34. Column A

$(x + y)^2$

Column B

$(x - y)^2$

Rectangle A

Rectangle B

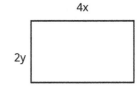

Note: The figures are not drawn to scale.

35. Column A

The area of rectangle A.

Column B

The area of rectangle B.

A bag contains a combination of pennies and nickels. Two random coins are removed from the bag without replacement.

36. Column A

The probability that both of the coins removed are pennies

Column B

The probability that one penny and one nickel are removed

A restaurant tracked how many patrons ordered a seafood entree each evening over the course of 26 days.

37. Column A

     Column B

     The mode of the data.

     The range of the data.

Section 3: Reading
36 Questions, 35 Minutes

Instructions: Carefully read each passage and answer the questions that follow it. For each question, decide which of the choices best answers the question based on the passage.

Questions 1 - 6

1　　　　When we picture the biggest culprits
2　of carbon dioxide emissions, we likely imagine
3　large factories, trucks, and automobiles. What we
4　probably do not envision is last week's leftover
5　lasagna sitting in our garbage. However, food waste
6　contributes up to 4.4 gigatons of carbon dioxide
7　equivalent. Carbon dioxide equivalent, or CO2-
8　eq is a measure used to compare the emissions
9　from various greenhouse gases on the basis of
10　their global-warming potential. Food waste is
11　roughly 8% of the total anthropogenic greenhouse
12　gas emissions, or greenhouse gas emissions that
13　originate from human activity. When ranked with
14　emissions from countries, food waste globally is
15　the third largest contributor of greenhouse gases
16　behind both the United States and China.
17　　　　One-third of food raised or prepared
18　never makes it to sale. This is astonishing when
19　we take into account that over 800 million people
20　worldwide suffer from hunger. Not only is food
21　not making it to people who need it most, but
22　this unused food is also heating up the planet.
23　Uneaten food wastes a ton of resources – seeds,
24　water, energy, land, fertilizer, hours of labor, capital
25　– and generates greenhouse gases at every stage of
26　production. Even sitting in a landfill, uneaten food
27　emits methane.
28　　　　The cause of this phenomenon varies
29　depending on where in the world one lives. In
30　low income nations, the cause is unintentional.
31　Poor infrastructure is the main reason. Bad roads,
32　poor packaging, lack of refrigeration and storage
33　facilities all contribute to food spoiling before it
34　can actually make it to market. In high income
35　nations, like the United States, the food waste is
36　often intentional. Retailers reject less than perfect
37　food, or they simply over-order and over-serve for
38　fear of consumer reprisal. Consumers, too, reject
39　food that doesn't meet a certain aesthetic. We also
40　overestimate how much food we can cook or eat in
41　a given week. Economics plays an important role
42　as well. If prices are too low, crops are left in fields
43　to rot; too high and they sit on store shelves and in
44　storerooms.

45　　　　There are many solutions to this problem.
46　The United Nations' Sustainable Development
47　goals aim to reduce food waste by 50 percent
48　at both the retail and consumer level by 2030.
49　In lower income countries, the UN looks to
50　improve infrastructure, storage, processing,
51　and transportation. Better communication and
52　coordination between producers and consumers
53　is also key. In higher income countries, major
54　intervention is needed on the part of legislators,
55　food businesses, environmental groups, anti-
56　hunger agencies, and consumers. For example,
57　labeling on food products like "sell by" and "use by"
58　dates needs to be standardized. Often the date has
59　nothing to do with food being expired but rather
60　with when it tastes best. While it is ideal to preempt
61　the food waste long before the products arrive
62　at stores, retailers need a plan for unused food,
63　such as distributing it to pantries, repurposing it
64　as animal feed, or composting. Consumers play a
65　major role in the solution, too. It is estimated that
66　35% of all food waste in high income countries
67　takes place in individual households. Consumers
68　need to buy less, use food more efficiently, and
69　compost whatever waste remains.

1. In lines 26 -27, one can infer that methane is

   a. harmful to the environment.
   b. something that is emitted from animals.
   c. a gas that must be conserved.
   d. used for food production.

2. According to the author, if high income countries want to reduce food waste it is important for

   a. distributors to improve refrigeration.
   b. consumers to buy less food.
   c. the government to facilitate coordination between producers and consumers.
   d. the food producers to create better packaging.

3. In line 39, "aesthetic" most nearly means

   a. attractiveness.
   b. health.
   c. spots.
   d. style.

4. The author includes the line "that over 800 million people worldwide suffer from hunger" (lines 19 - 20) in order to show

   a. that there is great suffering in the world.
   b. the irony of food waste.
   c. an effect of food waste.
   d. a solution to food waste.

5. In a low income country, which of the following is most likely the cause of food waste?

   a. The grocery store purchased too much produce.
   b. The railroad broke down.
   c. Food is blemished or bruised.
   d. Sell buy dates are not uniform.

6. The author views the issue of food waste as

   a. a serious issue that can be remedied.
   b. a hopeless scenario.
   c. the fault of wealthy countries.
   d. a minor climate issue.

Questions 7 - 12

1   Coal mining has historically been a
2 grueling and dangerous occupation, characterized
3 by inhumane hours of backbreaking toil at dismally
4 low wages amidst the constant threats of cave-ins,
5 explosions, and carbon monoxide poisoning. In
6 the late 19th and early 20th centuries, American
7 coal miners in most coal-producing states formed
8 labor unions. These unions allowed them to
9 leverage their collective bargaining power against
10 the unsafe, exploitative, and corrupt employment
11 practices of the coal companies.
12   When the United Mine Workers of America
13 (UMWA) organized a national strike in 1919, West
14 Virginia was the only major coal mining region in
15 the U.S. that had not yet unionized (and thus did
16 not participate). Union miners eventually received
17 a 27% pay raise from the coal companies in
18 exchange for ending the strike. The miners of West
19 Virginia requested a matching raise as a reward for
20 their loyalty, but their request was denied. Over
21 the next two years, the unrest and resentment
22 that ensued would boil into the largest conflict on
23 American soil since the Civil War.
24   Early attempts to unionize West Virginia
25 had been blocked with brutal efficiency, thanks
26 to the prevalence of the "company town" system.
27 Under this system, the coal companies literally
28 owned and operated entire towns – from the houses
29 to the stores to the schools. Miners were even paid
30 in company-printed money called "scrip" instead of
31 legal currency, which meant that they were unable
32 to make purchases anywhere else. Company town
33 miners suspected of union sympathies were fired,
34 which left them not only jobless but homeless and
35 penniless as well. As unions gained popularity
36 in other states, coal companies escalated their
37 control by hiring squads of private detectives to
38 harass, evict, beat, and even murder troublemaking
39 employees.
40   On May 19th, 1920, a team of Baldwin-
41 Felts Detectives hired by the Stone Mountain Coal
42 Company arrived in the town of Matewan in Mingo
43 County, WV to evict miners with UMWA ties. The
44 town mayor, Cabell Testerman, and chief of police,
45 Sid Hatfield, interceded. Armed miners gathered
46 in support, and a shootout erupted that left seven
47 detectives, the mayor, and two miners dead in
48 the streets in what would come to be called the
49 Matewan Massacre.

50   In retaliation, the coal companies and
51 state government staged a massive crackdown.
52 The governor declared a state of war in West
53 Virginia, and imposed martial law. State troopers
54 were brought in to enforce military rule as the coal
55 companies conducted mass firings and evictions.
56 Rather than subduing the miners, these tyrannical
57 measures only strengthened their resolve to free
58 themselves from their oppressors.
59   The summer after the Matewan Massacre
60 made Sid Hatfield a miners' hero; he was murdered
61 in broad daylight on the steps of a county
62 courthouse by Baldwin-Felts Detectives. It was the
63 last straw. Between 10,000-20,000 angry miners
64 poured out of the mountains within weeks. They
65 gathered weapons and formed an impressively
66 organized army, tying red bandanas around their
67 necks as makeshift uniforms (which later gave rise
68 to the pejorative term "redneck"). On August 24th,
69 1921, they marched to demand justice for their
70 fallen hero, an end to martial law and the right to
71 free speech, assembly, and unionization.
72   The miner army was intercepted at Blair
73 Mountain by a combined force of police, civilian
74 militia, and private detectives equipped with
75 machine guns, private planes, poison gas, and
76 explosives. Over the next week, an estimated 1
77 million rounds were fired as the battle raged. On
78 September 2nd, President Warren G. Harding
79 dispatched 2,000 federal troops and 12 military
80 aircraft to Blair Mountain. The overwhelmed
81 miners finally surrendered, and the Mine Wars
82 officially ended.

7. Why did the miners in West Virginia feel they deserved a raise?

    a. They had successfully won the strike.
    b. They had to live in company towns.
    c. They wanted to be rewarded for not striking.
    d. They worked a dangerous job.

8. As used in the passage, "resolve" (line 57) most nearly means

    a. determination.
    b. fear.
    c. fix.
    d. purpose.

9. Which best describes the organization of lines 72 - 82?

    a. A resolution occurred but the reader is left wondering.
    b. An event is analyzed for mistakes.
    c. A process is described.
    d. An opinion is presented with disappointment.

10. According to the passage the miners in West Virginia were unique from other miners in that they

    a. did not want to form a union.
    b. lived in "company towns".
    c. had a more dangerous job.
    d. used collective bargaining.

11. The primary purpose of this passage is to

    a. show the injustice suffered by the people of West Virginia.
    b. describe how the miners and coal mine owners felt about one another.
    c. promote the importance of labor unions.
    d. provide a history of the Mine Wars.

12. The author's tone in the passage is best described as

    a. hostile.
    b. matter of fact.
    c. optimistic.
    d. sympathetic.

Questions 13 - 18

1   Located in Northern California, Silicon
2   Valley is the area roughly between San Jose and
3   San Francisco. Silicon Valley is much more than
4   a geographical region, though. It's home of the
5   world's most well-known companies, where
6   technology has blossomed to meet the growing
7   demands of the digital universe. The seat of tech
8   wealth, Silicon Valley, might even be called a state
9   of mind.
10   Silicon Valley's history as the center of the
11 tech world stretches back to the 1940's at Stanford
12 University, located in the region's capital, Palo Alto.
13 Frederick Terman, a Stanford alumnus and the
14 dean of its School of Engineering, set his sights on
15 increasing the influence of its electrical engineering
16 department. His goal was to foster collaboration
17 between the university, the industry, and the
18 region. This mutually beneficial relationship gave
19 rise to Stanford Industrial Park, the archetype
20 of Silicon Valley. Stanford professors consulted
21 with local researchers and companies, and those
22 companies provided jobs to recent graduates. To a
23 great extent, Silicon Valley still functions this way
24 today.

25   Don Hoefler, a tech journalist, introduced
26 the term "Silicon Valley" in the 1970's. Since
27 then, the moniker is practically synonymous with
28 innovation. Intel, founded in 1968, spearheaded
29 the mid-20th century boom of Silicon Valley by
30 manufacturing the modern-day computer. This
31 resulted in the influx of other professionals to the
32 area; lawyers were needed to protect intellectual
33 property, software engineers to write code, and
34 venture capitalists to invest in start-ups. As Silicon
35 Valley moved from the 20th to 21st century, the
36 emphasis was no longer on manufacturing, but
37 instead on research and development.
38   Nowadays, Silicon Valley is well-known
39 for the companies that call it home as well as the
40 culture that exists in the region. Facebook, Google,
41 Netflix, and Apple are neighbors, and in an effort to
42 attract the best and the brightest of the talent pool,
43 they offer median annual salaries ranging from
44 $133,000 to $171,000. In addition, each provides its
45 own unique employee experience including perks
46 like extended maternity and paternity leaves, on-
47 site chiropractors and massage therapists, catered
48 meals, flexible work schedules, and the option to
49 purchase valuable company stock.

13. According to the passage, Stanford Industrial Park operated

    a. in partnership with the University.

    b. as a place for young entrepreneurs to start a business.

    c. as a business to help promote new ideas.

    d. in collaboration with Silicon Valley to find the best and brightest engineers.

14. In addition to engineers, why did other professionals move to Silicon Valley?

    a. They admired the state of mind.

    b. They came to provide support services to the tech businesses.

    c. They were sent there by Stanford University.

    d. They wanted to influence new start-ups.

15. The purpose of the passage is primarily to

    a. describe the link between Silicon Valley and Stanford University.

    b. explain why someone might want to move to Silicon Valley.

    c. provide a history of Silicon Valley.

    d. address the pros and cons of Silicon Valley in relation to other parts of California.

16. In line 27, "synonymous" most nearly means

    a. established.

    b. interchangeable.

    c. partial.

    d. similar.

17. Sentences 40 - 49 are included in order to

    a. provide examples of the benefits Silicon Valley companies offer.

    b. explain why the salaries are so high.

    c. show how innovative the tech companies are.

    d. illustrate the competition between companies.

18. Based on the passage, which of the following is a correct inference about people who live in Silicon Valley?

    a. They are educated.

    b. They are engineers.

    c. They are professors.

    d. They are from Stanford.

Questions 19 - 24

1 The evening before my departure for Blithedale, I
2 was returning to my bachelor apartments when an
3 elderly man of rather shabby appearance met me in
4 an obscure part of the street.
5
6 "Mr. Coverdale!—Mr. Coverdale!" said he, repeating
7 my name twice, in order to make up for the
8 hesitating and ineffectual way in which he uttered
9 it. "I ask your pardon, sir, but I hear you are going to
10 Blithedale tomorrow."
11
12 I knew the pale, elderly face, with the red-tipt
13 nose, and the patch over one eye. I likewise saw
14 something characteristic in the old fellow's way of
15 standing under the arch of a gate, only revealing
16 enough of himself to make me recognize him as an
17 acquaintance.
18
19 "Yes, Mr. Moodie," I answered, wondering what
20 interest he could take in the fact, "it is my intention
21 to go to Blithedale tomorrow. Can I be of any
22 service to you before my departure?"
23
24 "If you pleased, Mr. Coverdale," said he, "you might
25 do me a very great favor."
26
27 "A very great one?" repeated I, in a tone that must
28 have expressed but little alacrity of beneficence,
29 although I was ready to do the old man any amount
30 of kindness involving no special trouble to myself.
31 "My time is brief, Mr. Moodie, and I have many
32 preparations to make. But be good enough to tell
33 me what you wish."
34
35 "Ah, sir," replied Old Moodie, "I don't quite like to
36 do that, and, on further thoughts, Mr. Coverdale,
37 perhaps I had better apply to some older
38 gentleman, or to some lady, if you would have
39 the kindness to make me known to one, who may
40 happen to be going to Blithedale. You are a young
41 man, sir!"

42 "Does that fact lessen my availability for your
43 purpose?" asked I. "However, if an older man will
44 suit you better, there is Mr. Hollingsworth, who has
45 three or four years the advantage of me in age and
46 a philanthropist to boot. I am only a poet, and, so
47 the critics tell me, no great affair at that! But what
48 can this business be, Mr. Moodie? It begins to
49 interest me, especially since your hint that a lady's
50 influence might be found desirable. Come, I am
51 really anxious to be of service to you."
52
53 But the old fellow, in his civil and demure manner,
54 was both strange and obstinate; and he had now
55 taken some notion into his head that made him
56 hesitate in his former design.
57
58 "I wonder, sir," said he, "whether you know a lady
59 whom they call Zenobia?"
60
61 "Not personally," I answered, "although I expect
62 that pleasure tomorrow, as she is already a resident
63 at Blithedale. But have you a literary turn, Mr.
64 Moodie? Or have you taken up the advocacy of
65 women's rights? Or what else can have interested
66 you in this lady? But it is late. Will you tell me what I
67 can do for you?"
68
69 "Please excuse me to-night, Mr. Coverdale," said
70 Moodie. "You are very kind but I am afraid I have
71 troubled you, when, after all, there may be no need.
72 Perhaps, with your good leave, I will come to your
73 lodgings to-morrow morning, before you set out
74 for Blithedale. I wish you a good-night, sir, and beg
75 pardon for stopping you."
76
77 And so he slipt away; and, as he did not show
78 himself the next morning, it was only through
79 subsequent events that I ever arrived at a plausible
80 conjecture as to what his business could have been.

19. Prior to the events in this passage, Mr. Coverdale and Mr. Moodie

    a. were close friends.
    b. lived in the same apartment building.
    c. knew each other, but not very well.
    d. did not know each other.

20. Mr. Moodie's appearance can be described as

    a. unkempt.
    b. refined.
    c. youthful.
    d. tired.

21. It's likely that Mr. Moodie offers to ask another person for help (lines 35 - 41) because he

    a. is concerned that Mr. Coverdale won't relay his message accurately.
    b. realizes that his request is an imposition on Mr. Coverdale.
    c. needs a younger person to relay the message.
    d. is surprised that Mr. Coverdale is willing to help.

22. Throughout the passage, Mr. Moodie's attitude toward Mr. Coverdale can be described as

    a. demanding.
    b. encouraging.
    c. enthusiastic.
    d. respectful.

23. As it is used in line 80, "conjecture" most nearly means

    a. concern.
    b. decision.
    c. guess.
    d. stance.

24. During the course of the passage, Mr. Cloverdale's tone toward Mr. Moodie shifts from

    a. disinterested to encouraging.
    b. concerned to eager.
    c. insistent to worried.
    d. dismissive to curious.

Questions 25 - 30

1　　　A staple of American households for
2　over seventy years, Candyland has had a near
3　ubiquitous reach in 20th and 21st century America.
4　Today, over 95% of mothers are familiar with the
5　game, and over one million copies are sold every
6　year.
7　　　A game of chance, Candyland appeals
8　to young children because of its simplicity and
9　fantasy. The colorful board takes the players down
10　a path through a whimsical land of peppermint
11　stick forests, molasses swamps, and gumdrop
12　mountains. The players, whose goal is to reach
13　the candy castle first, simply select cards which
14　direct them to a new space on the path. There is
15　no strategy involved, making Candyland a perfect
16　introduction to board games for young children.
17　　　This light-hearted game was invented
18　in 1949 against the backdrop of one of the worst
19　epidemics in American history. Polio, a highly
20　contagious and life threatening viral disease, was
21　sweeping through America. Although people of
22　any age can get polio, it most commonly affects
23　children. The polio virus damages nerve cells in
24　the spinal cord, making it difficult for the body to
25　control its muscles. This leads to muscle weakness
26　and decay in the affected parts of the body. Often,
27　the leg muscles are affected, making many polio
28　survivors wheelchair-bound or dependent upon
29　leg braces. In the most serious cases, the function
30　of the diaphragm is impacted, making it nearly
31　impossible to breathe.

32　　　In the 1940's and 50's, patients who needed
33　breathing support were aided by mechanical iron
34　lungs. These huge metal machines encased the
35　patient and forced their body to breathe. Those
36　on iron lungs or with more serious cases of polio
37　ended up in polio wards of hospitals, sometimes for
38　months or years at a time.
39　　　It was in one of these wards that
40　Candyland was invented. A teacher named Eleanor
41　Abbott had contracted polio as an adult and
42　ended up in a ward filled with children. Most of
43　the children were bed-bound or using iron lungs,
44　making physical movement impossible. Abbott saw
45　how difficult this was for the children and set out
46　to create a game that would help them mentally
47　escape the confines of their beds. The first versions
48　of Candyland even featured a picture of a child in
49　a leg brace! Everything from the bright, fanciful
50　gameboard to the forward motion of the game play
51　was designed to help the children feel a sense of
52　liberation and joy.
53　　　Even though polio has been largely
54　eradicated from the United States today due to the
55　widely-used polio vaccine, the game of Candyland
56　still resonates with new generations of American
57　children.

25. As it is used in the passage, "ubiquitous" (line 3) most nearly means

    a. immeasurable
    b. intermittent
    c. popular
    d. universal

26. This passage is primarily concerned with

    a. the polio epidemic.
    b. the invention of Candyland.
    c. Eleanor Abbott's life.
    d. Candyland's popularity today.

27. Based on the information in the passage, those who needed iron lungs were experiencing muscle weakness in their

    a. legs.
    b. lungs.
    c. diaphragm.
    d. spinal cord.

28. The purpose of the second and third paragraph is to provide

    a. background which is relevant to the creation of Candyland.
    b. an overview of the average polio patient's experience.
    c. an explanation of the reasons polio spread so quickly.
    d. biographical information about the inventor of Candyland.

29. According to the passage, Eleanor Abbott invented the game of Candyland to

    a. overcome her own boredom when in the polio ward.
    b. teach important academic skills to kids in the polio ward.
    c. improve the lives of the children she taught in the classroom.
    d. distract and entertain children affected by polio.

30. As it is used in line 54, "eradicated" most nearly means

    a. discarded.
    b. eliminated.
    c. improved.
    d. spread.

Questions 31 - 36

1   Is listening to a book really the same as
2 reading it? Both scientists and readers agree: no.
3 One's preferred medium depends on the purpose
4 of the information being consumed. When reading
5 something for work or for study, most readers
6 prefer a written copy, be it digital or print. However,
7 if one is to read simply for leisure, an audiobook is a
8 suitable substitute.
9   The audiobook, although a recent
10 invention, is firmly rooted in anthropological
11 history. For tens of thousands of years, humans
12 have been engaged in sharing stories orally. In this
13 way, it should come as second nature to people
14 to listen and absorb information. Nevertheless,
15 audiobooks are a preferred medium only when it
16 comes to reading for pleasure. Audiobooks provide
17 opportunities for readers to multi-task: listen
18 while driving, doing dishes, or getting ready in the
19 morning. In this way, it is easier for readers to find
20 themselves distracted more often when listening
21 to a book rather than reading it. Additionally, there
22 are always the "mental sojourns" one is faced with
23 while listening to a narration. It is more difficult
24 to go back and find the time marking where one's
25 mind wandered than it is to locate the paragraphs
26 or pages when re-reading is necessary. While there
27 is greater flexibility with their consumption, studies
28 show that audiobooks do not allow their reader
29 to internalize as much information as traditional
30 written books do.

31   When it comes to the old-fashioned
32 way of reading – using one's eyes instead of
33 ears – audiences now have to choose between
34 two versions of a text: hard or digital copy. The
35 increased use of digital eReaders poses a challenge
36 to bibliophiles. An eReader provides convenience
37 and is environmentally friendly, but the fact
38 remains that it is not an exact substitute for a real,
39 tangible book. Psychologically speaking, books
40 provide spatial cues that readers find innately
41 pleasurable. Turning pages provides a reader with a
42 small break in which they can savor a book. It's also
43 simpler for a reader to visualize a story arc when
44 they can physically see the end of a book.
45   Although listening to a book, reading a
46 hard copy of a book, and reading an ebook are very
47 different experiences, there is one thing all readers
48 can agree on: storytelling is valuable. The more
49 accessible books are, the more benefit there is to
50 readers.

31. The passage is primarily concerned with

    a. encouraging different types of reading.
    b. explaining the benefits of audiobooks.
    c. exploring why people prefer hard copies of books.
    d. comparing and contrasting audiobooks and print books.

32. According to the passage, which of the following is true of audiobooks?

    a. They help listeners internalize information.
    b. They make it easy to figure out where you left off if your mind wanders.
    c. They can be enjoyed when doing other activities.
    d. They are environmentally friendly.

33. The phrase "mental sojourns" (line 22) refers to

    a. a listener's mind wandering.
    b. audiobooks.
    c. re-reading a written book.
    d. a listener's interest in the audiobook.

34. The phrase "challenge to bibliophiles" (line 35 - 36) refers to the

    a. fact that eReaders are becoming more popular.
    b. difficulties encountered when reading from an eReader.
    c. reasons many readers dislike eReaders.
    d. convenience of using an eReader.

35. As it is used in line 39, "tangible" most nearly means

    a. audio.
    b. non-fiction.
    c. new.
    d. physical.

36. The author of the passage would likely agree that

    a. listening to audiobooks is the same as reading print books.
    b. hard copies of books always provide the best reading experience.
    c. all types of reading experiences are valuable.
    d. eReaders are becoming more popular than hard copies of books.

Section 4: Math
47 Questions, 40 Minutes

Instructions: Each question is followed by four answer choices. Select the best answer.

1. Which value is NOT equal to $\frac{1}{6}$?

   a. .1666666667

   b. .16 (NOTE: repeating symbol over the 6)

   c. $\frac{.75}{4.5}$

   d. $\frac{4}{28}$

2. Which expression is equivalent to the expression $4x^3y - 2x^2y^3 - (-2x^2y^3 + x^3y)$?

   a. $3x^3y$
   b. $5x^3y$
   c. $4x^2y^3 + 3x^3y$
   d. $-4x^2y^3 + 3x^3y$

3. What is the slope of the line pictured below?

   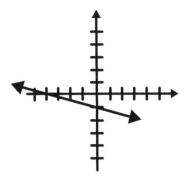

   a. 4

   b. $\frac{1}{4}$

   c. $-\frac{1}{4}$

   d. -4

4. A basketball coach records the number of baskets each of his 20 players makes over the course of a game. The data is summarized in the table below. What is the mean of the data?

   Note: Round to the nearest hundredth.

Baskets	Numbers of Players Making That Number of Baskets
1	7
2	6
3	4
4	3

   a. 1
   b. 1.45
   c. 2.15
   d. 5

5. A sphere has a diameter of 4 inches. What is the sphere's volume?

   Note: The formula used to determine the volume of a sphere is $V = \frac{4}{3}\pi r^3$, where r is the sphere's radius.

   a. $\frac{16}{3}\pi$ in^3

   b. $\frac{32}{3}\pi$ in^3

   c. $\frac{64}{3}\pi$ in^3

   d. $\frac{256}{3}\pi$ in^3

6. What is the value of .0001294 + .00000433?

   a. 1.3373×10^{-4}
   b. 1.727×10^{-4}
   c. 1.3373×10^{-5}
   d. 1.727×10^{-5}

7. The expression below is an example of which property?

    $z + y + z = y + x + z$

    a. commutative property
    b. identity property
    c. associative property
    d. distributive property

8. For what value(s) of x is the equation
    $\dfrac{x - 10}{10 - x} = 1$ true?

    a. -4
    b. 0
    c. all real numbers
    d. there are no values for x that make the equation true

9. If $h(x) = 2x + 4$, what is the value of $h(5) - h(1)$?

    a. 4
    b. 8
    c. 12
    d. 20

10. Martina has a box of colored paper clips that contains 10 blue clips, 6 green clips , 9 purple clips , and 5 yellow clips. Martina removes all of the yellow paper clips from the box and then selects one of the remaining paper clips at random. What is the probability that the paper clip Martina chooses is purple?

    a. 24%
    b. 30%
    c. 36%
    d. 40%

11. The owners of Sweet Treats Bakery count the total number of cupcakes sold each day during their first week in business. 64 cupcakes were sold on Monday, 47 were sold on Tuesday, 82 were sold on Wednesday, 64 were sold on Thursday, and 103 were sold on Friday. Which number represents the mode of the list?

    a. 56
    b. 64
    c. 72
    d. 82

12. A data set is represented in the box-and-whisker plot below. What is the third quartile of the data?

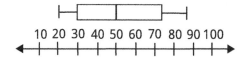

    a. 50
    b. 74
    c. 80
    d. 87

13. The first four terms of an algebraic sequence are shown below.

    4, -1, -6, -11

    Which expression represents the nth term of this sequence?

    a. 4 - 5n
    b. 4 + 5n
    c. 9 - 5n
    d. 9 + 5n

14. Solve: $x^2 + 6x - 40 = 0$

    a. x = -4, 10
    b. x = -5, 8
    c. x = -8, 5
    d. x = -10, 4

15. The radius of the cylinder below is 2 less than its height. What is the cylinder's surface area?

    Note: The formula used to determine the volume of a cylinder is $SA = 2r^2\pi + 2rh\pi$ where r is the cylinder's radius and h is the cylinder's height.

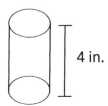

4 in.

    a. 16π in^2
    b. 20π in^2
    c. 24π in^2
    d. 48π in^2

16. There are 1,760 yards in a mile and 91.44 centimeters in a yard. Cassie cycles at a speed of 10 miles an hour. Which expression shows how many centimeters she cycles per second?

    a. $\dfrac{60 \times 60}{1,760 \times 91.44 \times 10}$

    b. $\dfrac{1,760 \times 91.44}{60 \times 60 \times 10}$

    c. $\dfrac{60 \times 60 \times 10}{1,760 \times 91.44}$

    d. $\dfrac{1,760 \times 91.44 \times 10}{60 \times 60}$

17. What is the measure of $\angle$ B in $\triangle$ ABC below?

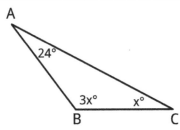

    a. 39°
    b. 78°
    c. 117°
    d. 135°

18. What is the greatest common factor of $4c^3d^2$, $14d^3$, and $16c^2d$ if c and d are both prime?

    a. 2
    b. 2d
    c. 112d
    d. $112c^3d^3$

19. What is the equation of a circle with center (5, -4) and radius 3?

    a. $(x - 4)^2 + (y + 5)^2 = 9$
    b. $(x + 5)^2 - (y - 4)^2 = 9$
    c. $(x - 4)^2 - (y + 5)^2 = 9$
    d. $(x - 5)^2 + (y + 4)^2 = 9$

20. What is the solution set to the inequality $-5 \leq -6x + 7 \leq 10$?

    a. $-2 \leq x \leq -\dfrac{1}{2}$

    b. $-2 \leq x \leq \dfrac{1}{2}$

    c. $-\dfrac{1}{2} \leq x \leq 2$

    d. $\dfrac{1}{2} \leq x \leq 2$

21. Krista earns $14 per hour for up to 40 hours of work per week. For each hour over 40 hours worked, she earns an additional $6 per hour on top of her regular rate. Which of the following equations represents the total amount of money (T) that Krista earned if she worked 40 + h hours last week?

    a. T = 14 + 20h
    b. T = 240 + 14h
    c. T = 560 + 6h
    d. T = 560 + 20h

22. What is the value of the numerical expression $\dfrac{\sqrt{100}}{\sqrt{4}}$?

    a. 5
    b. 8
    c. 16
    d. 25

23. The stem-and-leaf plot below represents the ages of the members of an extended family. What is the range of ages?

Stem	Leaf
0	2 4 6 8
1	4 5
2	3 3 5
3	5 9
4	7
5	6 9
6	3 7 9
7	2 8

    a. 70
    b. 72
    c. 76
    d. 78

24. Which of the following describes all values for x for which $|2x + 3| \geq 13$

    a. $x \leq -8$
    b. $x \geq 5$
    c. $-8 \geq x \geq 5$
    d. $x \leq -8$ or $x \geq 5$

25. How many lines of symmetry are in the square?

    a. 1
    b. 2
    c. 4
    d. 6

26. What is the solution set for $-3x^2 = 75$?

    a. $\pm5i$
    b. ±5
    c. ±25
    d. $\pm25i$

27. The parent teacher organization has 5 positions available. The applicant with the most votes will become president and the applicant with the second most votes will become co president. How many different combinations of president and co-president can there be?

    a. 20
    b. 60
    c. 120
    d. 200

28. Simplify: $6a^3b^2 \times 3a^4b^8$.

    a. $18a^3b^2$
    b. $18a^4b^8$
    c. $18a^7b^{10}$
    d. $18a^{12}b^{16}$

29. An ice cream store was interested in whether the temperature affected its daily ice cream cone sales. To determine this, the store tracked its sales, as well as the daily high temperature, and plotted the results on the scatterplot below. Which of the following conclusions can be drawn from the data?

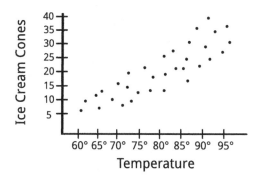

    a. The most ice cream cones are sold when it is between 80 and 85 degrees.
    b. The hotter it is, the fewer ice cream cones the store sells.
    c. The fewest ice cream cones are sold when it is between 70 and 75 degrees.
    d. The colder it is, the fewer ice cream cones the store sells.

30. A school principal sent a survey to his 300 students asking if the school day should start at a different time. Of the 55 students who responded, 36 indicated they wanted the school day to start later and 12 wanted the school day to start earlier. The principal can reasonably conclude that

    a. the majority of students want school to start later
    b. most students who responded to the survey want school to start earlier
    c. most students who responded to the survey want school to start later
    d. the majority of students don't want the school start time to change

31. A tree in Tim's backyard is 10 feet tall and casts a shadow that is 16 feet long, as shown below. A nearby building casts a shadow that is 40 feet long. How tall is the building?

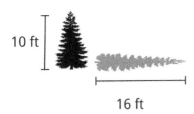

10 ft

16 ft

a. 14 ft
b. 25 ft
c. 46 ft
d. 64 ft

32. Two vertices of a triangle are shown below. Which of the following could NOT be the coordinates of the third vertex?

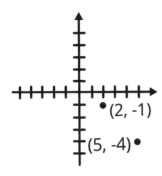

(2, -1)

(5, -4)

a. (-4, -2)
b. (-1, 2)
c. (0, 3)
d. (5, -8)

33. What is the result of the expression?

$$3\begin{bmatrix} 1 & 5 & -2 \\ 0 & -3 & 4 \end{bmatrix}$$

a. $\begin{bmatrix} 4 & 8 & 1 \\ 3 & 0 & 7 \end{bmatrix}$

b. $\begin{bmatrix} 3 & 15 & 6 \\ 3 & -6 & 12 \end{bmatrix}$

c. $\begin{bmatrix} 0 & -9 & 12 \\ 3 & 15 & -6 \end{bmatrix}$

d. $\begin{bmatrix} 3 & 15 & -6 \\ 0 & -9 & 12 \end{bmatrix}$

34. A rectangle has an area of 28 in². If the sides of the rectangles are integers, what could be the length of the longer side of the rectangle?

a. 2 in
b. 4 in
c. 7 in
d. 12 in

35. A group of high school students and their parents were asked which sport they most enjoyed watching. The results are summarized in the table below.

Favorite Sport	Students	Parents	Total Number of People
Baseball	17	9	26
Basketball	23	17	40
Football	24	32	56
Ice Hockey	20	22	42
Total	84	80	164

What is the probability that a parent's favorite sport is ice hockey?

a. $\frac{11}{40}$

b. $\frac{5}{21}$

c. $\frac{10}{21}$

d. $\frac{11}{21}$

36. If b is a positive number, which expression is equivalent to $b^2 \sqrt{b^7}$?

a. $\sqrt{b^9}$
b. $\sqrt{b^{11}}$
c. b^9
d. b^{11}

37. A circle is inscribed in the square below. What is the area of the shaded region?

6 in

a. $(24 - 9\pi)$ in^2
b. $(24 - 36\pi)$ in^2
c. $(36 - 9\pi)$ in^2
d. $(36 - 36\pi)$ in^2

38. Triangle DEF is shown below. Which expression is equal to the length of side $\overline{DF}$?

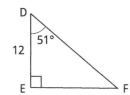

a. $\dfrac{12}{\cos 51°}$

b. $\dfrac{\cos 51°}{12}$

c. $\dfrac{12}{\sin 51°}$

d. $\dfrac{\sin 51°}{12}$

39. A teacher is interested in how much television her students watch on the weekends. She asks 10 of her students to track how many hours of television they watch on a Saturday. The results are summarized in the graph below. What is the median number of hours of television watched?

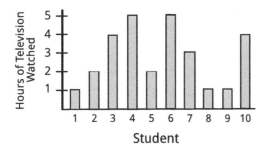

a. 2
b. 2.5
c. 3
d. 3.5

40. A spinner is made of equal sized wedges. There are 3 red wedges, 2 blue wedges, and 5 white wedges. If Kayla spins the spinner three times, what is the probability that all three spins will land on white?

a. $\dfrac{1}{6}$

b. $\dfrac{1}{2}$

c. $\dfrac{1}{2}^3$

d. $\dfrac{3}{2}$

41. $\triangle$ DEF is similar to $\triangle$ GHI. The length of $\overline{EF}$ is 4 inches and the length of $\overline{HI}$ is 6 inches. What is the length of $\overline{DE}$ if the length of $\overline{GH}$ is 12 inches?

a. 2 inches
b. 6 inches
c. 8 inches
d. 10 inches

42. When measuring the width of a picture frame, it would be most reasonable to use which of the following units?

a. grams
b. meters
c. kilograms
d. centimeters

43. The graph below is the solution set for which inequality?

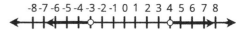

-8 -7 -6 -5 -4 -3 -2 -1 0 1 2 3 4 5 6 7 8

a. $|4x - 2| > 14$
b. $|4x - 2| < 14$
c. $|4x - 2| > 12$
d. $|4x - 2| < 12$

44. A 12% sales tax is applied to all purchases. If Carly wants to buy an item listed at $24.50, what will be her total cost including tax?

a. $21.56
b. $24.62
c. $27.44
d. $36.50

45. If $c^2 = 9c$ and $c \neq 0$, what is the value of c?

    a. -9
    b. -3
    c. 3
    d. 9

46. Josiah and Alina work together at a company. Josiah completes 2 fewer reports a day than Alina does. If 18 reports were completed in one day, how many reports did Josiah complete?

    a. 8
    b. 9
    c. 10
    d. 11

47. Which expression is equivalent to $(x + 9)(x - 2)$?

    a. $x^2 - 18$
    b. $x^2 + 7$
    c. $x^2 + 7x - 7$
    d. $x^2 + 7x - 18$

Essay

1 Question, 30 Minutes

Instructions: You have 30 minutes to write an essay on the topic below. It is not permitted to write an essay on a different topic. Your essay must be written in blue or black pen.

Please be aware that the schools you apply to will receive a copy of your essay. Your essay should be longer than a paragraph and use specific examples and details.

Write your response on this page and the next page.

If you could live anywhere in the world, where would you live and why?

Test 6 Answer Key

Section 1: Verbal

1. A	9. D	17. C	25. B	33. B
2. A	10. B	18. D	26. B	34. C
3. C	11. C	19. B	27. B	35. A
4. C	12. B	20. D	28. D	36. D
5. D	13. D	21. C	29. B	37. B
6. D	14. C	22. C	30. A	38. C
7. A	15. A	23. A	31. A	39. D
8. B	16. B	24. C	32. B	40. B

Section 2: Quantitative

1. D	9. D	17. B	25. A	33. C
2. B	10. C	18. A	26. D	34. B
3. B	11. B	19. C	27. C	35. A
4. A	12. A	20. C	28. D	36. D
5. C	13. C	21. D	29. C	37. B
6. D	14. A	22. B	30. A	
7. A	15. C	23. B	31. B	
8. D	16. B	24. A	32. B	

Section 3: Reading

1. A	9. A	17. A	25. D	33. A
2. B	10. B	18. A	26. B	34. B
3. A	11. D	19. C	27. C	35. D
4. B	12. B	20. A	28. A	36. C
5. B	13. A	21. B	29. D	
6. A	14. B	22. D	30. B	
7. C	15. C	23. C	31. D	
8. A	16. B	24. D	32. C	

Section 4: Math

1. D	11. B	21. D	31. B	41. C
2. A	12. B	22. A	32. B	42. D
3. C	13. C	23. C	33. D	43. A
4. C	14. D	24. D	34. C	44. C
5. B	15. C	25. C	35. A	45. D
6. A	16. D	26. A	36. B	46. A
7. A	17. C	27. A	37. C	47. D
8. D	18. B	28. C	38. A	
9. B	19. D	29. D	39. B	
10. C	20. C	30. C	40. C	

ISEE Test 7

Section 1: Verbal
40 Questions, 20 Minutes

Synonyms

Instructions: Select the word whose meaning is closest to the word in capital letters.

1. INTERROGATE:

    a. conspire
    b. harm
    c. question
    d. witness

2. FEASIBLE:

    a. enjoyable
    b. frustrating
    c. practical
    d. unlikely

3. ABHOR:

    a. appreciate
    b. enjoy
    c. loathe
    d. whine

4. EVOKE:

    a. conjure
    b. destroy
    c. incinerate
    d. lament

5. PERISH:

    a. arrive
    b. die
    c. justify
    d. wound

6. PREVALENT:

    a. applicable
    b. frugal
    c. victorious
    d. widespread

7. RESILIENT:

    a. delicate
    b. flexible
    c. reductive
    d. suspicious

8. ABSOLVE:

    a. describe
    b. forgive
    c. punish
    d. resolve

9. FEIGN:

    a. bluff
    b. earn
    c. rule
    d. take

10. INFAMOUS:

    a. average
    b. friendly
    c. notorious
    d. whimsical

11. LUCRATIVE:

    a. appealing
    b. bashful
    c. important
    d. profitable

12. MORTIFY:

    a. embarrass
    b. encourage
    c. grow
    d. shame

13. RAPPORT:

    a. coldness
    b. divulging
    c. fellowship
    d. warring

14. AUGMENT:

    a. debate
    b. enlarge
    c. judge
    d. silence

15. QUANTIFY:

    a. calculate
    b. deliberate
    c. fortify
    d. restore

16. REPUGNANT:

    a. appalling
    b. boisterous
    c. delectable
    d. lackadaisical

17. PANACEA:

    a. advocate
    b. cure
    c. toxin
    d. vitriol

18. METICULOUS:

    a. boorish
    b. humorous
    c. painstaking
    d. shiny

19. EMULATE:

    a. challenge
    b. design
    c. mimic
    d. strike

Sentence Completion

Instructions: Select the word or pair of words that best completes the sentence.

20. His rude and ------- behavior was off putting to everyone at the party.

    a. abrasive
    b. delightful
    c. obscure
    d. select

21. Finding her real name rather dull, the author used a(an) ------- for all the books she published.

    a. acronym
    b. homonym
    c. pseudonym
    d. synonym

22. The two smaller companies decided that it was in their mutual interest to ------- into one large entity.

    a. associate
    b. merge
    c. partner
    d. separate

23. David was ------- when his best friend had to move to another country.

    a. apologetic
    b. despondent
    c. frivolous
    d. overjoyed

24. Miguel is trying to ------- an end to hostilities between his two sisters after the giant fight they had yesterday.

    a. delay
    b. mediate
    c. obstruct
    d. provoke

25. The proposed new coffee shop is ------- since there are already four other coffee shops within a four block radius of it.

    a. appreciated
    b. lovely
    c. redundant
    d. reviled

26. By forgetting to do his math homework for the last two days, Dan has ------- his dream of a perfect report card.

    a. bolstered
    b. contributed
    c. emboldened
    d. jeopardized

27. Since she was not very interested in the topic, Sarah only gave the article a ------- glance before selecting something else to read.

    a. cursory
    b. measured
    c. thorough
    d. thoughtful

28. He was furious when he did not win reelection and tried his best to find ways to avoid ------- his power.

    a. destroying
    b. maintaining
    c. relinquishing
    d. usurping

29. It was most ------- that Rob stopped by Professor Smith's office since she had been meaning to talk to him about his excellent paper anyway.

    a. egregious
    b. opportune
    c. predictable
    d. unfortunate

30. Thinking about it -------, it probably wasn't a good idea for Evan to go out with his friends last night when he was still recovering from the flu.

    a. formulaically
    b. marvellously
    c. objectively
    d. retrospectively

31. Carmen was dismayed to learn that the autograph on her favorite player's jersey, which she believed to be -------, was actually a counterfeit.

    a. authentic
    b. ingenuine
    c. pristine
    d. robust

32. Because of his ------- and ------- attitude, Samuel was asked not to return to the study group until he could treat everyone else with respect.

    a. belligerent . . . deplorable
    b. friendly . . . odd
    c. neutral . . . confrontational
    d. recognizable . . . beneficial

33. The computer program Derek wrote kept ------- after the third step, but after several -------, it was working perfectly.

    a. accelerating . . . judgments
    b. deliberating . . . missteps
    c. malfunctioning . . . modifications
    d. performing . . . repetitions

34. Since she was only a ------ when it came to chess, Miriam sought out a true ------- of the game so that she could improve.

    a. champion . . . winner
    b. spectator . . . fan
    c. novice . . . master
    d. supporter . . . proponent

35. The cookie recipe called for ------- measurement of the ingredients, so it's no wonder that they didn't come out right when Chris only used ------- amounts of everything.

    a. exact . . . perfect
    b. futile . . . scant
    c. meaningful . . . useless
    d. precise . . . approximate

36. Although he knows that staying out three hours past curfew without calling home was -------, Kyle still thinks that being grounded for an entire month was excessively -------.

    a. disrespectful . . . equitable
    b. exciting . . . lenient
    c. reprehensible . . . punitive
    d. uncouth . . . troublesome

37. Although Seth was just trying to help, his ------- with a conflict he didn't fully understand only served to ------- the problem.

    a. assisting . . . relieve
    b. meddling . . . exacerbate
    c. operating . . . regulate
    d. trifling . . . solve

38. Although the alliance between the two rivals was -------, they agreed that it made sense to ------- their forces in order to achieve their mutual goal.

    a. agreeable . . . combine
    b. fortunate . . . destroy
    c. laughable . . . divide
    d. tenuous . . . unite

39. It was ------- when the volcano erupted last
    week since scientists estimated that it had been
    ------- for over 5000 years.

        a. certain . . . unpredictable
        b. glorious . . . extinct
        c. startling . . . dormant
        d. unexpected . . . active

40. The candidate had to do something to -------
    support from voters quickly, as his popularity
    in the polls was ------- while his opponents'
    numbers were climbing.

        a. bolster . . .waning
        b. contain . . . stagnant
        c. staunch . . . multiplying
        d. strengthen . . . surging

Section 2: Quantitative
37 Questions, 35 Minutes

The section is divided into two parts: problem solving and quantitative comparison. Directions for each part are provided.

Part 1 - Problem Solving

Instructions: Each question is followed by four possible answers. Select the best answer.

1. A coin is tossed 50 times and the results are tracked. Which of the following outcomes has the highest probability?

   a. At least 10 of the tosses will land on heads.
   b. Exactly 25 tosses will land on tails.
   c. More tosses will land on heads than on tails.
   d. There is not enough information given to determine the answer.

2. The manager of a car dealership has decided to hold a Memorial Day sale in which the price of all cars will be decreased by $2000. If the previous range of car prices was $40,000, what will be the range during the sale?

   a. $36,000
   b. $38,000
   c. $40,000
   d. Not enough information provided to solve the problem

3. An odd negative number plus an even negative number is squared. The result must be

   a. negative and even
   b. negative and odd
   c. positive and even
   d. positive and odd

4. In the graph below, each dot represents a different hiker. What pattern does the graph show?

   a. There is a weak negative correlation between the slope of a hill and walking speed.
   b. There is a strong negative correlation between the slope of a hill and walking speed.
   c. There is a weak positive correlation between the slope of a hill and walking speed.
   d. There is a strong positive correlation between the slope of a hill and walking speed.

5. Two perpendicular lines must have

   a. different y intercepts.
   b. the same y intercept
   c. the same slope.
   d. one set of intersecting points.

6. Which of the following figures could be a net of the cube shown below?

a.

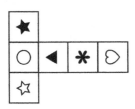

b.

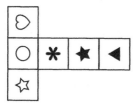

c.

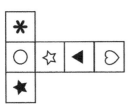

d.

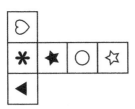

7. Which of the following is equivalent to $y^{\frac{4}{3}}$?

a. $\dfrac{1}{y^{\frac{3}{4}}}$

b. $\dfrac{y^4}{y^3}$

c. $\sqrt[3]{y^4}$

d. $\sqrt[4]{y^3}$

8. The graph below shows the sales for a toy manufacturer as a function of time. The manufacturer's sales were gradually increasing until they had to temporarily stop production due to a natural disaster. When they resumed production, their sales spiked and then went back to normal levels. In what year did the natural disaster occur?

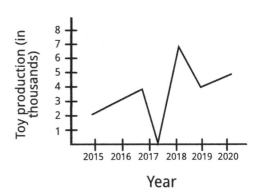

a. 2015
b. 2016
c. 2017
d. 2018

9. If $x^2 + y^2 = 29$ and $2xy = 20$, what is the value of $(x - y)^2$?

a. 9
b. 18
c. 36
d. 49

10. A researcher is compiling data in the chart below. After creating the chart, she realized that she accidentally left out data. Value 4 should have had a frequency of 4 and value 7 should have had a frequency of 1. With the new data added to values 4 and 7, what is the range of the data?

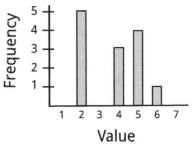

a. 4
b. 5
c. 6
d. 7

11. Which of the following is equal to d if
a(bc + d) = a - ab?

    a. 1 -b
    b. 1 -b - bc
    c. b
    d. b - bc

12. What is the value of the expression $\dfrac{(\sqrt{16})^3}{(\sqrt[3]{64})^1}$?

    a. 1
    b. 4
    c. 8
    d. 16

13. Let $h \clubsuit k = (h + k)^2$. What is the value of $3 \clubsuit 4$?

    a. 16
    b. 25
    c. 36
    d. 49

14. What is the range of possible values for y if
$y = x^2 - 3$ and $1 \le x \le 4$?

    a. $-2 \le y \le 13$
    b. $-2 \le y \le 1$
    c. $1 \le y \le 2$
    d. $2 \le y \le 13$

15. The average weight of the three cats at an
animal shelter is 8 pounds. If a fourth cat is
brought in that weighs 12 pounds, what is the
new average weight of the cats?

    a. 8 pounds
    b. 9 pounds
    c. 10 pounds
    d. 11 pounds

16. The formula for the surface area of a sphere is A
$A = 4\pi r^2 \, r^2$. If the surface area of sphere M is 4
times the surface area of sphere N, which of the
following statements must be true?

    a. The radius of sphere M is 2 times the
radius of sphere N.
    b. The radius of sphere M is 4 times the
radius of sphere N.
    c. The radius of sphere N is 2 times the
radius of sphere M.
    d. The radius of sphere N is 4 times the
radius of sphere M.

17. The area of a square is 49 inches². If the side of
the square is increased by 2, what is the new
perimeter of the square?

    a. 36 inches
    b. 48 inches
    c. 51 inches
    d. 81 inches

18. As a medicine's dosage is increased, the
medicine's effectiveness gradually, and then
sharply, increases until it reaches a plateau.
Which of the following graphs best represents
this scenario?

a.

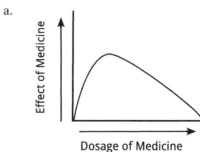

b.

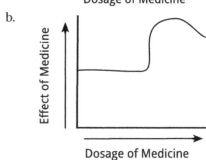

c.

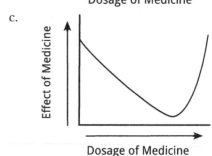

d.

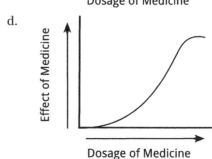

19. If the sum of all integers from 1 to 600, inclusive, is x, what is the sum of all integers from 1 to 599, inclusive?

    a. x - 601
    b. x - 600
    c. x - 599
    d. x - 1

20. A rectangle has an area of 50 in2. If the height and width of the rectangle are both integers, what is the smallest possible perimeter for the rectangle?

    a. 30 inches
    b. 35 inches
    c. 54 inches
    d. 68 inches

21. Jaida walks to and from school five days a week for four weeks. If Jaida's home is 1.5 miles from school, which of the following is the total distance that she walked?

    a. 7.5 miles
    b. 15 miles
    c. 30 miles
    d. 60 miles

Part 2 - Quantitative Comparisons

Instructions: In each question, use the information provided to compare the quantity in Column A with the quantity in Column B. All quantitative comparison questions have the same answer choices:

    a. The quantity in column A is greater.
    b. The quantity in column B is greater.
    c. The two quantities are equal.
    d. The relationship cannot be determined from the information given.

The base of an isosceles triangle is 7 inches and the perimeter of the triangle is 25 inches.

22. **Column A**   **Column B**

The measure of a leg of 9 inches.
the triangle.

Twice the value of an integer plus five times the value of another integer is 13. The difference between the first integer and three times the second integer is 1.

23. **Column A**   **Column B**

The product of the   The sum of the
integers   integers

24. **Column A**   **Column B**

The greatest   The least common
common factor   multiple of 2 and 3
of 18, 36, and 48

A new video game costs $60 at full price. Game Force puts the game on sale for 15% off, and a competitor store called Best Games offers a discount of $10 off.

25. **Column A**   **Column B**

The sale price at   The discounted price
Game Force   at Best Games

The measure of an exterior angle of a regular polygon with n sides is 360°/n.

26. **Column A**   **Column B**

The measure of an   The measure of an
exterior angle of a   exterior angle of a
regular hexagon.   regular polygon.

A jar contains 10 marbles. Some of the marbles are blue, some are green, and the rest are purple. If one marble is chosen at random, the probability that the marble will be blue is 20%.

27. **Column A**   **Column B**

The number of blue   The number of
marbles in the jar   purple marbles in
                the jar

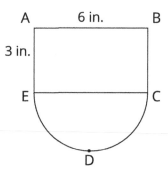

In the figure above, rectangle ABCE is connected to semicircle BDC.

28. **Column A**   **Column B**

The area of the   The area of the rect-
semi-circle.   angle.

x > 1

29. Column A

Column B

3x - (3 - 1)²

-2

_____

a, b, and c are consecutive integers (a < b < c)

30. Column A

Column B

c - a

b

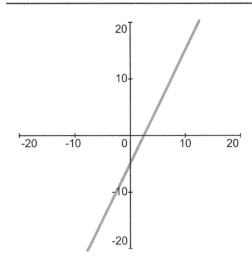

31. Column A

Column B

The x value of the
y intercept.

The y value of the x
intercept.

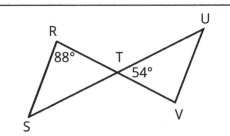

In the figure below, ∠ SRT is congruent to ∠ UVT.

32. Column A

Column B

The measure of
∠ RTS

The measure of
∠ TUV

33. Column A

Column B

(x+y)²

x² + y²

_____

A jar contains 50 quarters and 50 dimes.
Travis randomly removes 5 coins from the jar
and adds their values together.

34. Column A

Column B

The probability that
the 5 coins have a
combined value of
less than $1

The probability that
the 5 coins have a
combined value of $1
or more

_____

For any positive integer n, n! is the product of
all integers from 1 to n, inclusive.

35. Column A

Column B

4!

12

_____

Let f(x) = 1 – x for all values of x.

36. Column A

Column B

f(x+1)

f(x-1)

_____

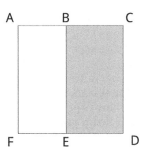

ACDF is a square with side 8

37. Column A

Column B

The area of the shaded
region

The perimeter of
ACDF

Section 3: Reading
36 Questions, 35 Minutes

Instructions: Carefully read each passage and answer the questions that follow it. For each question, decide which of the choices best answers the question based on the passage.

Questions 1 - 6

1 This was the first communication that had come
2 from her aunt in Rachel's lifetime.
3
4 "I think your aunt has forgiven me, at last," her
5 father said as he passed the letter across the table.
6 Rachel looked first at the signature. It seemed
7 strange to see her own name there. It was as if her
8 very identity was impugned by the fact that there
9 should be two Rachel Deanes. Moreover there
10 was a likeness between her aunt's autograph and
11 her own, a characteristic turn in the looping of
12 the letters, a hint of the same decisiveness and
13 precision. If Rachel had been educated fifty years
14 earlier, she might have written her name in just that
15 manner.
16
17 "You're very like her in some ways," her father said.
18
19 Rachel's eyelids drooped and her expression
20 indicated a faint, suppressed intolerance of her
21 father's remark. He said the same things so often,
22 and in so precisely the same tone, that she had
23 formed a habit of automatically rejecting the truth
24 of his statements. He had always appeared to her
25 as senile. He had been over fifty when she was
26 born, and ever since she could remember she had
27 doubted the correctness of his information. Yet she
28 was gentle in her answer. She condescended from
29 the heights of her youth to pity him.
30
31 "I should think you must almost have forgotten
32 what Aunt Rachel was like," she said. "How many
33 years is it since you've seen her?"
34
35 "More than forty," her father said, ruminating
36 profoundly. "We disagreed; we invariably
37 disagreed. Rachel always prided herself on being so
38 modern. She read Huxley and Darwin and things
39 like that. Altogether beyond me, I admit."
40
41 Rachel straightened her shoulders; there was
42 disdain in her face, but none in her voice as she
43 replied:"And so it seems that she wants to see me."

44 She was excited at the thought of meeting this
45 almost mythical aunt whom she had so often
46 heard about. Sometimes she had wondered if the
47 personality of this remarkable relative had not
48 been a figment of her father's imagination. But this
49 letter of hers that now lay on the breakfast table
50 was admirable in character. There was something
51 of condescension expressed in the very restraint
52 of its tone. She had written a kindly letter, but the
53 kindliness had an air of pity. It was all consistent
54 enough with what her father had told her.
55
56 Mr. Deane came out of his reminiscences with a
57 sigh.
58
59 "Yes, yes; she wants to see you, my dear," he said. "I
60 think you had better accept this invitation to stay
61 with her. She—she is rich and I, as you know, have
62 practically nothing to leave you. If she took a fancy
63 to you...."
64
65 He sighed again, and Rachel knew that for the
66 hundredth time he was regretting his own past
67 weakness. He had been foolish in money matters,
68 frittering away his once considerable capital in
69 aimless speculations.
70
71 "I'll certainly go," Rachel said. "I'm curious to see
72 this remarkable aunt. By the way, how old is she?"
73 "There were only fifteen months between us," Mr.
74 Deane said, "so she must be,—dear me, yes;—she
75 must be seventy-three. Fancy my sister Rachel
76 being seventy-three! It seems so absurd to think of
77 her as old...."
78
79 He continued his reflections, but Rachel was not
80 listening. He was asking for the understanding of
81 the young; reaching out over half a century to try
82 to touch the sympathy of his daughter. But she
83 was already bent on her own adventure, looking
84 forward eagerly to a visit to London that promised
85 delights other than the inspection of her mysterious
86 aunt.

1. Rachel and her aunt are similar in all of the following ways EXCEPT they both

   a. want to meet each other.
   b. have similar signatures.
   c. are rich.
   d. have the same name.

2. In lines 19 - 29, the author implies that Rachel

   a. admires her father.
   b. looks down on her father.
   c. feels inferior to her father.
   d. hates her father.

3. It can be inferred from lines 36 - 39 that Rachel's father

   a. views himself as very different than his sister.
   b. wishes that he read authors such as Huxley and Darwin.
   c. feels he was more modern than his sister.
   d. feels terrible that he argued with his sister.

4. Rachel's description of her aunt as "almost mythical" (line 45) indicates that

   a. she doesn't believe that her aunt actually exists.
   b. she wishes she had met her aunt sooner.
   c. her aunt hadn't seemed like a real person to her.
   d. her father definitely made up lies about her aunt.

5. As it is used in the passage, "capital" (line 68) most nearly means

   a. intelligence.
   b. metropolis.
   c. success.
   d. wealth.

6. Based on the last sentence of the passage, it can be concluded that Rachel

   a. is looking forward to meeting her aunt.
   b. is planning to do other things in London aside from seeing her aunt.
   c. is pretending she wants to visit her aunt so she can have a trip to London.
   d. plans to spend her entire time in London with her aunt.

Questions 7 - 12

1 In the United States veganism grew by
2 600% between 2014 and 2017, and it shows no
3 signs of decreasing. Vegans are people who refrain
4 from eating or using anything that involves animal
5 products, such as eggs and leather. Many adults
6 switch to a vegan diet for health, environmental,
7 and ethical reasons. Some people wonder if it's
8 safe for children to go vegan. According to both the
9 American Academy of Pediatrics and the Canadian
10 Paediatric Society, it is safe with careful planning.
11 The most important aspect of changing
12 to this type of diet is ensuring that children get
13 enough of the vitamins and minerals primarily
14 found in animal products. Those include but are
15 not limited to protein, iron, calcium, omega-3 fatty
16 acids, and vitamin B-12. Another concern is that
17 children ingest enough calories since plants tend to
18 offer lower overall calories.
19 Protein is relatively easy to find in plant-
20 based food. Nuts, seeds, beans, and 100% whole
21 grains are excellent sources. Iron can be found in
22 beans and leafy green vegetables, but vegans need
23 to eat an abundant amount. Studies have shown
24 that vegans require about 1.8 times more iron than
25 non-vegans. Leafy greens also contain calcium, as
26 do tofu and enriched orange juice. Omega-3 fatty
27 acids show up in walnuts, chia and flax seeds, and
28 brussel sprouts.

29 Vitamin B-12 presents a challenge because
30 it is naturally found only in animal products
31 like milk and meat. Children cannot skimp on
32 vitamin B-12 because it's essential for brain
33 development and blood cell function. However,
34 there are ways for vegans to incorporate B-12
35 into their diets without eating animal products.
36 Fortified foods like plant drinks, cereals, "veggie
37 meats," and nutritional yeast all contain B-12. It's
38 recommended that children ages nine to thirteen
39 get just 1.8 micrograms of the vitamin a day, which
40 is the equivalent to just two ounces of Swiss cheese.
41 Food labels indicate if a product has been fortified
42 with B-12.
43 Even though the advised amount of B-12 is
44 small, some authorities worry that a child following
45 a strict vegan diet will not meet it. For example,
46 the German Nutrition Society highly recommends
47 against a vegan diet for children and adolescents,
48 arguing that it is extremely difficult or impossible
49 to attain an adequate supply of some nutrients. In
50 Belgium and Italy, legislators have even proposed
51 laws making it a crime to feed a child a vegan diet.
52 These proposals have come under strong criticism
53 for fear of overreach.
54 Parents and children who want to make
55 the change to a vegan lifestyle should talk to their
56 pediatrician. It's vital that their decision is informed
57 and that they carefully follow nutritional guidelines.

7. The author's use of the word "just" in line 40 is to show

    a. how little vitamin B-12 is needed.
    b. only vitamin B-12 can be naturally found in animal products.
    c. that just vitamin B-12 is an issue for vegans.
    d. how important vitamin B-12 is.

8. All of the following are correct inferences from the passage EXCEPT

    a. both the American and Candian pediatric societies believe that a vegan diet can work for children.
    b. protein, iron, calcium, omega-3 fatty acids, and vitamin B-12 are the only nutrients not found in a plant-based diet.
    c. protein can easily be found in lots of vegetable products.
    d. going vegan can be a lot of work.

9. The primary purpose of the passage is to

    a. convince people to choose a vegan lifestyle.
    b. inform readers about the risk of feeding their children a plant-based diet.
    c. explain that a vegan lifestyle can be healthy for kids as long as certain guidelines are followed.
    d. dissuade readers from going vegan by addressing the risk of legal ramification.

10. According to the passage, what nutrients are found in leafy green vegetables?

    a. calcium
    b. iron
    c. vitamin B-12 and iron
    d. calcium and iron

11. In line 34, "incorporate" most nearly means

    a. consolidate.
    b. engulf.
    c. include.
    d. unite.

12. Which of the following best describes the author's attitude toward a vegan diet?

    a. alarming
    b. approving
    c. cautious
    d. skeptical

Questions 13 - 18

1   "Adopt, Don't Shop!" is a campaign started
2 by Last Chance for Animals (LCA), a nonprofit
3 organization that has worked to eradicate animal
4 cruelty since 1984. The campaign focuses on
5 highlighting the dangers of puppy mills while
6 advocating for pet adoption. Puppy mills, farms
7 where dogs are bred for commercial purposes, are
8 frequently unregulated and operate under unsafe
9 conditions. The goal of "Adopt, Don't Shop!" is to
10 educate the public about the value of adopting pets
11 rather than purchasing them from retail stores that
12 help sustain dangerous puppy mill practices.
13   In many cases, puppy mills rely on
14 hazardous breeding habits to keep their businesses
15 running. Female dogs are overbred to provide
16 a consistent supply of puppies to retailers. The
17 puppies, after being separated from their mothers,
18 live in horrible conditions, often without adequate
19 access to clean water, veterinary care, or healthy
20 food. Another problem with puppy mills is that
21 without regulation, puppies are inbred and risk
22 facing a lifetime of painful and complicated
23 medical problems.
24   The trouble is not just with the puppy
25 mills; responsibility lies with the retailers that sell
26 these puppies as well. The living conditions for the
27 puppies once they are at a store are also unsafe.
28 Their cages can be crowded, dirty, and noisy.
29 Additionally, stores have a hard time properly
30 socializing dogs, so pet owners may unknowingly
31 purchase puppies with behavior issues. Thanks
32 to animal advocacy groups like LCA, states like
33 California and Maryland have entirely outlawed
34 puppy mills.

35   The safest alternative to purchasing a
36 puppy from a store is to adopt one from a local
37 rescue center or shelter. There are many pros to
38 rescuing a dog. Most importantly, rescue dogs are
39 spayed or neutered which means they run no risk
40 of contributing to overpopulation. Rescue dogs
41 are usually vaccinated and still less expensive
42 than an intact, unvaccinated puppy from a store.
43 Many of the dogs that are available for adoption
44 have fully developed personalities, and adopters
45 can find a pet that is a perfect fit for their lifestyle.
46 Many adoptable dogs are already trained and
47 won't require the basic potty and crate training
48 that puppies do. However, if someone is looking for
49 a puppy, there are plenty of shelters that provide
50 puppies for adoption as well. An estimated 30% of
51 dogs in shelters are purebred, and there are breed-
52 specific rescue centers, so even for adopters looking
53 for something specific, pet adoption is the way to
54 go. Adopting a dog saves multiple lives. Not only
55 does a lucky dog find a family, but every adoption
56 frees up a space in the shelter for another dog to
57 find their chance at a forever home.

13. Which of the following is a correct inference regarding the author's intention in writing the passage?

    a. If customers knew about puppy mills, they would adopt rather than buy a dog.
    b. Breeders are the next alternative to adopting a dog.
    c. There may be some good puppy mills out there, but they lack regulation.
    d. Retailers are unaware that their dogs come from puppy mills.

14. All of the following are reasons as to why you should adopt a dog EXCEPT

    a. they are healthier.
    b. it is cheaper.
    c. they are still intact.
    d. they are trained.

15. As used in line 35, "alternative" most nearly means

    a. difference.
    b. option.
    c. relief.
    d. resort.

16. Which of the following best describes the author's attitude toward puppy mills?

    a. condemning
    b. hopeful
    c. indifferent
    d. skeptical

17. Lines 47 - 57 is included to show

    a. people have a lot of options when adopting a dog or puppy.
    b. the most important factor is the dog's health.
    c. it's mostly mixed breed dogs available at shelters.
    d. that knowing a dog's personality can help owners make a more informed decision.

18. The primary purpose of this passage is to

    a. inform readers about abuses in puppy mills.
    b. convince readers to adopt dogs not buy them.
    c. examine the benefits of dog ownership.
    d. pass legislation banning pet stores.

Questions 19 - 24

1   Until the early 1900s, the remote South
2 Australian town of Coober Pedy was simply another
3 barren landscape in the Australian outback. Then,
4 in 1915, an unlikely treasure was accidentally
5 discovered by the teenage son of a gold prospector:
6 opals.
7   Opal, a precious gemstone, is known for its
8 iridescent display of rainbow colors called play-
9 of-color. This phenomenon occurs because of the
10 interaction between light and the opal. Opals are
11 composed of sub-microscopic spheres of silica and
12 oxygen that are arranged in patterns within the
13 stone. As lightwaves move between these spheres,
14 the lightwaves bend and break into the colors of
15 the rainbow. This unique feature of precious opals
16 makes them extraordinarily valuable.
17   In Coober Pedy's early days, opal mining
18 was a painstaking and dangerous venture. Small
19 teams of miners worked together to dig mine shafts
20 by hand, typically using shovels or pickaxes. The
21 extremely dry, dusty soil was prone to collapse, so
22 the miners had to construct timber walls to hold
23 up the toppling soil. Even with this safeguard,
24 mine cave-ins occurred. Miners then lowered
25 themselves into the mine with a windlass and
26 manually hauled out buckets of waste soil, known
27 as mullock. Additional horizontal tunnels were
28 then dug to explore the mine further. These tunnels
29 had their own hazards, sometimes lacking oxygen
30 or becoming quickly flooded in heavy rain.

31   Miners would do all of this without any
32 guarantee opals would be found. Since opals are
33 hidden in the veins of rocks, there was no way to tell
34 which dig sites would produce precious opals. To
35 complicate matters further, some mines produced
36 only common opals, which do not contain the
37 desirable play-of-color, making them essentially
38 worthless.
39   By the 1970s, opal mining had become
40 mechanized. Today, miners use massive drills to
41 dig shafts, tunneling machines to dig horizontal
42 shafts underground, and pipe vacuums to move
43 the mullock out of the space. Modern-day miners
44 have to be extremely careful, as these vacuums can
45 pull out opals from the mine alongside the mullock,
46 damaging the opals.
47   In less than a hundred years, opal miners
48 dug over 250,000 mine shafts resulting in a surreal
49 landscape of gaping holes alongside massive hills of
50 mullock. Today, Coober Pedy produces more than
51 70% of the world's opals and is known as the opal
52 capital of the world.

19. As it is used in line 8, "iridescent" most nearly means

    a. commonplace.
    b. crude.
    c. pale.
    d. shimmering.

20. What causes a precious opal's play-of-colors?

    a. the interplay of light, silica, and oxygen
    b. the absorption of light by the opal
    c. the patterns of individual opals in a stone's vein
    d. the interaction of silica and chemicals found outside the opal

21. This passage is primarily concerned with

    a. the history of opal mining in Australia.
    b. opal mining in Coober Pedy.
    c. the first discovery of opals in Coober Pedy.
    d. modern day opal mining techniques.

22. According to the author, early opal miners faced all of the following dangers EXCEPT

    a. mine collapse.
    b. mine shaft flooding.
    c. falling from the windlass.
    d. lack of oxygen.

23. The purpose of the fourth paragraph is to

    a. show how easy it is to mistake common opals with precious opals.
    b. detail the opal mining process in Coober Pedy's early days.
    c. explain why an opal miner might not be successful in finding opals.
    d. clarify why an opal mine might not have precious opals.

24. What risk is posed when pipe vacuums are used when opal mining?

    a. They might pull mullock out of the mine.
    b. They often create unstable mine shafts.
    c. They might only uncover common opals.
    d. They can unintentionally damage the opals.

Questions 25 - 30

1   When Charlemagne established the Holy
2 Roman Empire, he sought to unite Western Europe
3 under Christian rule. In a demonstration of respect
4 and gratitude, Pope Leo III crowned him as Holy
5 Roman Emperor on Christmas Day in AD 800. So
6 in theory, the Catholic Church and the Holy Roman
7 Empire were supposed to be allies. In practice,
8 they were locked in a bitter rivalry for much of the
9 Middle Ages.
10   The strong political and religious influence
11 exerted by the Holy Roman Emperors threatened
12 the power of the church, and vice versa. One
13 major point of dispute was a practice called
14 "lay investiture," in which the emperor and his
15 government selected individuals to fill roles within
16 the church. Pope Gregory VII took a stand against
17 this practice in AD 1075 in the Dictatus Papae, a list
18 of what he considered to be his rights as pope. The
19 list extended far beyond addressing lay investiture.
20 Gregory claimed that not only did the emperor lack
21 the right to interfere in the appointments of church
22 officials, but that it was actually the other way
23 around and that the pope had the God-given right
24 to essentially fire the emperor.
25   Holy Roman Emperor Henry IV was
26 predictably irate at Gregory's obvious attempt to
27 turn the tables on him. He wrote Gregory a letter
28 warning him that he would no longer receive the
29 Holy Roman Empire's support and then appointed
30 a new bishop. Not to be outdone, Gregory
31 responded by excommunicating Henry. He then
32 decreed that Henry was no longer a legitimate
33 emperor and that all of his subjects were therefore
34 freed from their obligation to obey him.

35   As his subjects began to rebel, Henry
36 backed down. He attempted to apologize, but the
37 pope refused to acknowledge his apology or rescind
38 his exile from the church. In desperation, Henry
39 walked all the way from Germany to Canossa, Italy
40 in the winter of AD 1077 to confront Gregory and
41 beg for forgiveness. When the emperor arrived at
42 the castle where the pope was staying, Gregory
43 argued that he did not seem repentant enough and
44 refused to let him in. Henry had to wait outside in
45 the snow for three days before Gregory relented
46 and opened the castle doors. He then agreed to
47 restore Henry's status as a member of the Catholic
48 Church, but not as the ruler of the Holy Roman
49 Empire. As a result, the revolts continued.
50   Three years later, Gregory endorsed one
51 of the rebel leaders, Rudolf von Rheinfeld, as
52 emperor. For good measure, he kicked Henry out
53 of the church yet again. It was the last straw. Henry
54 marched his troops to Rome and attacked the
55 Vatican, forcing Gregory to flee. Henry announced
56 that Gregory was not the true pope and put a new
57 pope, Clement III, in Gregory's place. Clement
58 obligingly crowned Henry the Holy Roman
59 Emperor once more.

25. In lines 5 - 9 the author uses the phrases, "So in theory" and "In practice" in order to

    a. show the unique relationship between the Holy Roman Emperor and the Pope.
    b. explain there was a contradiction between what was supposed to happen and what actually occurred.
    c. describe that while the emperor should have been more powerful, the Pope actually was.
    d. criticize the link between church and state.

26. All of the following happened as a result of Henry's excommunication EXCEPT

    a. people revolted.
    b. Henry begged for forgiveness.
    c. Henry lost his title of Holy Roman Emperor.
    d. Henry attacked Rudolf von Rheinfeld.

27. The primary purpose of the passage is to

    a. provide a detailed history of the contentious relationship between the Catholic Church and the Holy Roman Empire.
    b. explain the difference between the Catholic Church and the Holy Roman Empire.
    c. describe the conflict that existed between Pope Greogory VII and Henry IV.
    d. show how Pope Gregory VII finally stood up to Henry IV.

28. In line 37, "rescind" more nearly means

    a. appeal.
    b. cancel.
    c. change.
    d. review.

29. It can be inferred from the passage that the Holy Roman Emperor used "lay investiture" to

    a. increase his own power.
    b. appoint the best person for the position.
    c. revolt against the Pope.
    d. recommend favored individuals for church leadership.

30. According to the passage, the Vatican was

    a. where the Holy Roman Emperor lived.
    b. where the Pope lived.
    c. a disputed territory between the Pope and Holy Roman Empire.
    d. the capital of the Holy Roman Empire.

Questions 31 - 36

1   If you made a list of common favorite
2   animals, it's safe to say that vultures would not
3   be near the top. They are notoriously ugly, with a
4   reputation that matches their appearance. Their
5   name has become synonymous with predatory
6   greed, and they are most commonly thought of as
7   morbid, squabbling, and dirty. Though they might
8   not be beloved, these highly efficient scavengers
9   play a vital role in ecosystems around the world.
10   Vultures, also known as buzzards, keep the
11   environment clean by removing animal carcasses
12   from their surroundings, which also helps prevent
13   disease from spreading. When buzzards make
14   a meal out of decaying carrion, they keep the
15   microbes in the dead animal from contaminating
16   the landscape. This is an especially important task
17   when their entrée died from a contagious illness
18   that could potentially spread to humans or other
19   animals.
20   As nature's sanitation workers, vultures
21   have de veloped remarkable adaptations that allow
22   them to safely consume meat that would poison
23   most other creatures. Even their notoriously bald
24   heads serve a clean purpose: the lack of feathers
25   makes it harder for potentially-hazardous leftovers
26   to stick to a vulture's face long enough to get them
27   sick. Once the food is ingested, buzzards' extremely
28   corrosive stomach acid takes over by breaking
29   down dangerous bacteria and viruses. Toxic threats
30   like anthrax, salmonella, tuberculosis, botulism,
31   cholera, and rabies don't stand a chance against
32   vultures' gastrointestinal tracts! In fact, vultures'
33   stomach acid is so powerful that it can even destroy
34   their prey's DNA.

35   Vultures are considered dominant, or
36   apex, scavengers. Groups of vultures (fittingly
37   referred to as "wakes" when feeding, and bizarrely
38   termed "kettles" when flying) will chase off
39   smaller competitors, such as rats. Since smaller,
40   opportunistic scavengers are often disease-carriers,
41   people actually benefit from buzzards' greedy
42   tendencies. Each vulture can eat up to 20% of its
43   body weight at a time, and large wakes of vultures
44   can devour a carcass in short order. After a meal,
45   they are often too fat to fly; they have to wait until
46   their meal is digested before they can become
47   airborne again. If they feel threatened, however,
48   they will vomit to reduce their weight. Vultures also
49   use their vomit as a weapon, since its acid content
50   can burn the skin of their enemies!

31. The primary purpose of the passage is to

    a. describe the adaptations that allow vultures to consume carrion.
    b. clarify the positive and negative ways birds impact ecosystems.
    c. passionately defend vultures against those who dislike them.
    d. explain the positive role that vultures have in nature.

32. The author's tone when discussing vultures can best be described as

    a. admiring.
    b. considerate.
    c. doubtful.
    d. reassuring.

33. The phrase "nature's sanitation workers" (line 20) is an example of what literary device?

    a. hyperbole
    b. irony
    c. metaphor
    d. simile

34. As it is used in line 28, "corrosive" most nearly means

    a. caustic.
    b. gentle.
    c. hot.
    d. ineffective.

35. The author's statement about the vultures' "greedy tendencies" (lines 41 - 42) refers to the

    a. small amount of food vultures eat at one time.
    b. method vultures use to steal food from other animals.
    c. fact that vultures must sometimes vomit their food.
    d. speed in which vultures chase away other scavengers.

36. According to the passage, it's preferable that a vulture consume a carcass rather than another scavenger because

    a. vultures will chase off other scavengers.
    b. other scavengers will fight over the carcass.
    c. vultures don't get sick from the carcass or carry disease.
    d. other scavengers will remove the carcass rather than leaving it in place.

Section 4: Math
47 Questions, 40 Minutes

Instructions: Each question is followed by four answer choices. Select the best answer.

1. Simplify: $5a^3b^4 \times 6a^5b^4$.

   a. $30a^3b^4$
   b. $30a^8b^4$
   c. $30a^8b^8$
   d. $30a^{15}b^{16}$

2. The triangle ABC shown in the xy-coordinate plane is rotated 90 degrees clockwise about the origin. Which of the following shows the new position of point A?

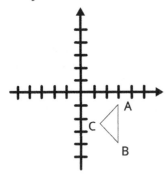

   a. (-3, 1)
   b. (-1, -3)
   c. (1, 3)
   d. (3, -1)

3. Point A is a point on a line L (not pictured), which is perpendicular to line S. What is another point on line L?

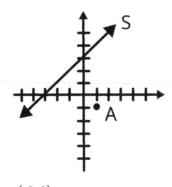

   a. (-3, 3)
   b. (0, -1)
   c. (2, 1)
   d. (4, -5)

4. Michael bought a new set of kitchen plates. If the circumference of the plates is 12π inches, what is the diameter of the plates?

   a. 6 inches
   b. 6π inches
   c. 12 inches
   d. 12π inches

5. A candy company surveyed a randomly selected sample of 12-18 year old Americans to determine what type of chocolate was their favorite. Of those surveyed, 40% chose milk chocolate, 30% chose dark chocolate, 20% chose white chocolate, and 10% indicated that they did not like chocolate. The company can reliably conclude that

   a. the majority of those surveyed prefer milk chocolate
   b. it's more likely that a 12-18 year old would prefer milk chocolate than white chocolate
   c. it's likely that most Americans enjoy chocolate
   d. white chocolate is disliked by most 12-18 year olds

6. Put the following numbers in order, from least to greatest: $5.6, -\frac{50}{9}, \frac{30}{6}, -8.7, \frac{25}{7}$.

   a. $-8.7, -\frac{50}{9}, \frac{25}{7}, \frac{30}{6}, 5.6$
   b. $-\frac{50}{9}, -8.7, \frac{25}{7}, \frac{30}{6}, 5.6$
   c. $-8.7, -\frac{50}{9}, \frac{25}{7}, 5.6, \frac{30}{6}$
   d. $-\frac{50}{9}, -8.7, \frac{25}{7}, 5.6, \frac{30}{6}$

7. A high school tracks its average daily student attendance each year. The school put all of this data into the graph below. If there are 2,000 students at the school, how many attended school on an average day in 2016?

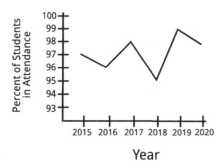

a. 960
b. 1,900
c. 1,920
d. 1,940

8. The function f is defined as f(x) = 3x + 15. What is the value of f(10)?

a. 25
b. 28
c. 35
d. 45

9. What is the solution set to the inequality -8 ≤ 2x + 12 ≤ 10?

a. -10 ≤ x ≤ -1
b. -10 ≤ x ≤ 1
c. x ≥ -10 or x ≤ -1
d. x ≤ -10 or x ≥ 1

10. If the diameter of the cone pictured below is 6 less than its height, what is the cone's volume?

Note: The formula used to determine the volume of a cone is $V = \frac{1}{3}\pi r^2 h$, where r is the cone's radius and h is the cone's height.

12 in.

a. 18 cm^3
b. 36 cm^3
c. 48 cm^3
d. 144π cm^3

11. What is the value of the expression $5.8 \times 10^6 - 3.4 \times 10^3$?

a. 2.4×10^3
b. 5.766×10^6
c. 5.7966×10^6
d. 5.89034×10^6

12. There were 560 students attending Cherry Hill School last year. This year, the total number of students increased by 5%. How many students are attending Cherry Hill School this year?

a. 532
b. 555
c. 565
d. 588

13. What is the solution set for $x^2 = -16$?

a. ±4
b. ±4i
c. ±8
d. ±8i

14. Celine can purchase 10 pencils from store A for $1.00, 14 pencils from store B for $2.50, or 24 pencils from Store C for $3.75 . What is the best price per pencil?

a. Store A
b. Store B
c. Store C
d. The price per pencil is the same at all three stores.

15. An art gallery tracked sales for four painters over the course of a week. The results are tracked in the chart below. What is the range of paintings sold?

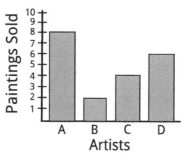

a. 2
b. 4
c. 6
d. 8

16. Which expression is equivalent to $(x - 6)(x - 3)$?

    a. $x^2 - 9x - 18$
    b. $x^2 - 9x - 9$
    c. $x^2 - 9x + 9$
    d. $x^2 - 9x + 18$

17. In the image below, $\angle X$ is congruent to $\angle Y$. What is the measure of $\angle Z$?

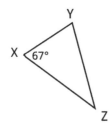

    a. $46°$
    b. $54°$
    c. $67°$
    d. $134°$

18. Arik is making a map of his town for a school project. He wants 2 inches on his map to represent 0.5 miles. If Arik's school is 3 miles away from his house, how far apart should his school and house be on the map?

    a. 3 in
    b. 6 in
    c. 9 in
    d. 12 in

19. Which expression is equivalent to the expression $-5a^4b - 8a^2b^3 + 3(3a^4b - 4a^2b^3)$?

    a. $14a^4b - 20a^2b^3$
    b. $4a^4b - 12a^2b^3$
    c. $-2a^4b - 12a^2b^3$
    d. $4a^4b - 20a^2b^3$

20. A data set is represented in the box-and-whisker plot below. What is the first quartile of the data?

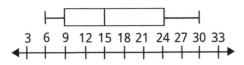

    a. 6
    b. 9
    c. 12
    d. 15

21. For what value(s) of k is the equation $\dfrac{k(k + 3)}{k + 4} = 0$ true?

    a. 0 only
    b. -3 only
    c. 0 and -3
    d. 0, -3, and -4

22. Sasha recorded the average daily temperature for each day of winter break. The temperatures she recorded ranged from 12 degrees to 36 degrees, and the median temperature recorded was 27 degrees. If the highest and lowest temperatures are both removed from the list, what will be the median temperature of the new list?

    a. 24 degrees
    b. 27 degrees
    c. 48 degrees
    d. It cannot be determined from the given information

23. A group of middle school students and their parents were asked which season they preferred. The results are summarized in the table below.

Favorite Season	Students	Parents	Total Number of People
Summer	35	15	50
Fall	17	22	39
Winter	12	15	27
Spring	19	28	47
Total	83	80	163

What is the probability that a student's favorite holiday is winter?

    a. $\dfrac{12}{83}$
    b. $\dfrac{15}{80}$
    c. $\dfrac{12}{27}$
    d. $\dfrac{15}{27}$

24. What is the surface area of the rectangular prism below?

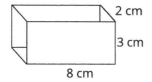

2 cm

3 cm

8 cm

    a. 60 cm^2
    b. 76 cm^2
    c. 80 cm^2
    d. 92 cm^2

25. Which expression is equivalent to $\frac{4x^{36}}{2}$?

    a. x^6
    b. x^{18}
    c. $2x^6$
    d. $2x^{18}$

26. If $(3.92 + 2.08)x = 18$, then what is the value of x?

    a. 2
    b. 3
    c. 4
    d. 5

27. What is the sixth number in this sequence?

   7, 10.5, 14, 17.5, 21

    a. 23
    b. 23.5
    c. 24
    d. 24.5

28. Which of the following describes all values for x for which $|6x - 3| > 15$?

    a. $-2 < x < 3$
    b. $-2 > x > 3$
    c. $x < -2$ or $x > 3$
    d. $x > -2$ or $x < 3$

29. A bookstore recorded the number of books purchased by each of its customers in the table shown. What is the mode of the data?

Number of Books	Numbers of Customers Purchasing That Number of Books
1	8
2	9
3	4
4	3
5	7

    a. 2
    b. 3
    c. 4
    d. 5

30. What is the result of the expression

$$\begin{bmatrix} -1 \\ 5 \\ 8 \\ 3 \end{bmatrix} + \begin{bmatrix} 6 \\ 5 \\ 0 \\ -2 \end{bmatrix}$$

    a. $\begin{bmatrix} -5 \\ 10 \\ 8 \\ 1 \end{bmatrix}$

    b. $\begin{bmatrix} 5 \\ 5 \\ 8 \\ 1 \end{bmatrix}$

    c. $\begin{bmatrix} -5 \\ 5 \\ 8 \\ -1 \end{bmatrix}$

    d. $\begin{bmatrix} 5 \\ 10 \\ 8 \\ 1 \end{bmatrix}$

31. Which is the most reasonable unit to use when measuring the weight of a flower?

    a. grams
    b. millimeters
    c. pounds
    d. inches

32. In the image below, the area of each grid square shown is 4 in². What is the area of the shaded area?

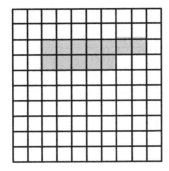

   a. 40 in²
   b. 42 in²
   c. 44 in²
   d. 48 in²

33. A cookie jar contains 6 chocolate chip cookies, 5 oatmeal raisin cookies, and 3 sugar cookies. Brendan randomly selects one cookie from the jar and eats it. Then Carly randomly selects one cookie. If the cookie that Brendan selected was oatmeal raisin, what is the probability that the cookie Carly selected was chocolate chip?

   a. $\dfrac{1}{3}$

   b. $\dfrac{2}{5}$

   c. $\dfrac{3}{7}$

   d. $\dfrac{6}{13}$

34. Triangle DEF is shown below. What is the sine of ∠D?

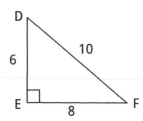

   a. $\dfrac{3}{5}$

   b. $\dfrac{4}{5}$

   c. $\dfrac{4}{3}$

   d. $\dfrac{5}{3}$

35. The equation for the area of a rhombus A=$\dfrac{1}{2}$pq, where p and q represent the diagonals. Which of the following shows the equation for p in terms of A and q?

   a. $p = \dfrac{2A}{q}$

   b. $p = \dfrac{A}{2q}$

   c. $p = 2Aq$

   d. $p = \dfrac{q}{2A}$

36. The solution to $x^2 = -3$ is which type of number?

   a. complex number
   b. natural number
   c. rational number
   d. real number

37. In the image below, what is the measure of ∠A in △ABC below?

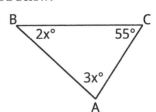

   a. 25°
   b. 50°
   c. 75°
   d. 100°

38. What is the area of the figure below?

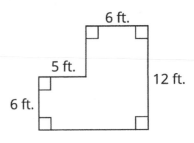

   a. 72 ft²
   b. 102 ft²
   c. 118 ft²
   d. 132 ft²

39. The graph below is the solution set for which inequality?

-8 -7 -6 -5 -4 -3 -2 -1 0 1 2 3 4 5 6 7 8

   a. $-10 \leq 3x + 4 \leq -8$
   b. $-10 \leq 3x + 4 \leq 8$
   c. $-10 \leq 3x - 4 \leq -8$
   d. $-10 \leq 3x - 4 \leq 8$

40. What is the prime factorization of $260a^2b$?

   a. $2 \times 5 \times 13 \times a \times b$
   b. $2^2 \times 5 \times 13 \times a^2 \times b$
   c. $2 \times 3 \times 5 \times 13 \times a \times b$
   d. $2^3 \times 3 \times 5 \times 13 \times a^2 \times b$

41. For what values(s) of x does

$$\frac{(x + 6)(x + 8)}{x^2 - 9} = 0$$

   a. $x = -8, x = -6$
   b. $x = 8, x = 6$
   c. $x = -8, x = -6, x = 3, x = -3$
   d. $x = 8, x = 6, x = 3, x = -3$

42. What is the value of the numerical expression $\sqrt{100} - \sqrt{36}$?

   a. 2
   b. 4
   c. 8
   d. 16

43. Four stores begin selling a new type of television. Their sales of that television on the first day it is available are depicted in the dot plot below. What is the mean of the first day's sales at the four stores? Note: Each dot on the plot represents one television sold.

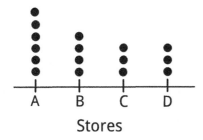

Stores

   a. 3
   b. 4
   c. 5
   d. 6

44. Sanjay is running out of time on his math test. He has 2 multiple choice questions left, each with 4 possible answer choices. If Sanjay randomly guesses on those remaining questions, what is the probability that he will get both of them correct? (Note: round to the nearest percent).

   a. 6%
   b. 13%
   c. 20%
   d. 25%

45. Daria is driving at a speed of 900 meters per minute. Which expression has a value equal to the car's speed, in miles per hour?

Note: There are 1760 yards in one mile and 1.196 meters in a yard.

   a. $\dfrac{900 \times 60}{1,760 \times 1.196}$
   b. $\dfrac{900 \times 60 \times 1.196}{1,760}$
   c. $\dfrac{900}{1,760 \times 1.196 \times 60}$
   d. $\dfrac{900 \times 1.196}{1,760 \times 60}$

46. Find the midpoint of the line segment defined by the points A (3, -1) and B (7, -5).

   a. (-2, 2)
   b. (-2, -3)
   c. (5, -3)
   d. (5, 2)

47. Central High School will vote for both a president and vice president. If 6 students are on the ballot, how many different combinations of president and vice president could you have?

   a. 10
   b. 30
   c. 60
   d. 120

Essay
1 Question, 30 Minutes

Instructions: You have 30 minutes to write an essay on the topic below. It is not permitted to write an essay on a different topic. Your essay must be written in blue or black pen.

Please be aware that the schools you apply to will receive a copy of your essay. Your essay should be longer than a paragraph and use specific examples and details.

Write your response on this page and the next page.

Describe a person who you admire and explain why you admire them.

Test 7 Answer Key

Section 1: Verbal

1.	C	9.	A	17.	B	25.	C	33.	C
2.	C	10.	C	18.	C	26.	D	34.	C
3.	C	11.	D	19.	C	27.	A	35.	D
4.	A	12.	A	20.	A	28.	C	36.	C
5.	B	13.	C	21.	C	29.	B	37.	B
6.	D	14.	B	22.	B	30.	D	38.	D
7.	B	15.	A	23.	B	31.	A	39.	C
8.	B	16.	A	24.	B	32.	A	40.	A

Section 2: Quantitative

1.	A	9.	A	17.	A	25.	A	33.	D
2.	C	10.	B	18.	D	26.	D	34.	A
3.	D	11.	B	19.	B	27.	D	35.	A
4.	A	12.	D	20.	A	28.	B	36.	B
5.	D	13.	D	21.	D	29.	A	37.	D
6.	B	14.	A	22.	C	30.	D		
7.	C	15.	B	23.	B	31.	C		
8.	C	16.	A	24.	C	32.	A		

Section 3: Reading

1.	C	9.	C	17.	A	25.	B	33.	C
2.	B	10.	D	18.	B	26.	D	34.	A
3.	A	11.	C	19.	D	27.	C	35.	B
4.	C	12.	C	20.	A	28.	B	36.	C
5.	D	13.	A	21.	B	29.	A		
6.	B	14.	C	22.	C	30.	B		
7.	A	15.	B	23.	C	31.	D		
8.	B	16.	A	24.	D	32.	A		

Section 4: Math

1.	C	11.	C	21.	C	31.	A	41.	A
2.	B	12.	D	22.	B	32.	D	42.	B
3.	A	13.	B	23.	A	33.	D	43.	B
4.	C	14.	A	24.	D	34.	B	44.	A
5.	B	15.	C	25.	B	35.	A	45.	A
6.	A	16.	D	26.	B	36.	A	46.	C
7.	C	17.	A	27.	D	37.	C	47.	B
8.	D	18.	D	28.	C	38.	B		
9.	A	19.	D	29.	A	39.	D		
10.	B	20.	B	30.	D	40.	B		

ISEE Test 8

Section 1: Verbal
40 Questions, 20 Minutes

Synonyms

Instructions: Select the word whose meaning is closest to the word in capital letters.

1. ADVOCATE:

    a. advance
    b. embrace
    c. regret
    d. support

2. EVOLVE:

    a. destroy
    b. develop
    c. reinforce
    d. spin

3. RECUR:

    a. reorganize
    b. represent
    c. reprise
    d. restrict

4. ENIGMA:

    a. celebrity
    b. mystery
    c. prodigy
    d. society

5. PITHY:

    a. brief
    b. laborious
    c. mature
    d. sour

6. FALLACY:

    a. compliment
    b. fact
    c. insult
    d. misconception

7. TREPIDATION:

    a. disgust
    b. fear
    c. joy
    d. whimsy

8. BOISTEROUS:

    a. masculine
    b. polite
    c. rowdy
    d. silent

9. FLOURISH:

    a. bake
    b. fail
    c. stand
    d. thrive

10. JAUNTY:

    a. energetic
    b. foamy
    c. lethargic
    d. terrifying

11. NEBULOUS:

    a. certain
    b. cryptic
    c. galactic
    d. revolutionary

12. PULVERIZE:

    a. chew
    b. form
    c. mold
    d. smash

13. EXALT:

    a. befriend
    b. degrade
    c. glorify
    d. season

14. JARGON:

    a. container
    b. exit
    c. terminology
    d. vehicle

15. SATIRICAL:

    a. abstract
    b. sardonic
    c. solemn
    d. unintelligible

16. DENOTE:

    a. calcify
    b. imply
    c. magnify
    d. signify

17. IDIOSYNCRATIC:

    a. eccentric
    b. formulaic
    c. grandiose
    d. tame

18. TUMULTUOUS:

    a. conclusive
    b. intellectual
    c. placid
    d. stormy

19. LAX:

    a. draining
    b. flexible
    c. supportive
    d. technical

Sentence Completion

Instructions: Select the word or pair of words that best completes the sentence.

20. Anika was asked to pick a(n) ------- of the book to write her report on since the entire book was over 2000 pages long.

    a. copy
    b. excerpt
    c. page
    d. reprint

21. Antonio knew that something was ------- when he showed up to the restaurant and his friends were not there waiting for him.

    a. alarming
    b. amiss
    c. corrupt
    d. delayed

22. It was ------- in Jamie's apartment since it was 101 degrees outside and her fan was broken.

    a. bitter
    b. calm
    c. frigid
    d. sweltering

23. Magda's delicious scones have been a long time ------- of her cafe for over thirty years.

    a. activity
    b. partner
    c. portion
    d. staple

24. There is always a(n) ------- amount of food served at the Smith's house on Thanksgiving, so they often live off the leftovers for a full week after the holiday!

    a. adequate
    b. copious
    c. fulfilling
    d. scant

25. Suzanne ------- a lovely music box from her great grandmother when she passed away.

    a. inherited
    b. invested
    c. judged
    d. lamented

26. Despite his tough demeanor and belief that he was ------- to insults, Nathan's feelings were definitely hurt by his friend's mean comments.

    a. allusive
    b. committed
    c. impervious
    d. virtuous

27. The flies trying to land on the beautiful picnic food were a constant ------.

    a. companion
    b. delight
    c. nuisance
    d. swarm

28. It was very ------ that Laverne didn't hit a single red light on her way to work because otherwise she would have been late for the big meeting.

    a. brief
    b. fortuitous
    c. untimely
    d. victorious

29. It ultimately wasn't a very ------ concert since the songs didn't really make sense when played together.

    a. adhesive
    b. cohesive
    c. disastrous
    d. hesitant

30. It was ------ of Jaren to leave the hot stove on unattended.

    a. frivolous
    b. negligent
    c. responsible
    d. wise

31. The ------ dog was very friendly and obedient to its owner's commands.

    a. amenable
    b. frantic
    c. lulling
    d. pushy

32. Hans ------ having to perform the ------ task because it was extremely boring to have to do the same thing over and over again.

    a. enjoyed . . . simple
    b. disliked . . . palatable
    c. resented . . . monotonous
    d. revelled . . . joyless

33. Sanjay ------ to increase his ------ so that he would have the endurance to run a marathon.

    a. aspired . . . stamina
    b. balked . . . strength
    c. sulked . . . speed
    d. trained . . . sluggishness

34. Ira looked ------ after his five day stomach flu and felt absolutely ------ when the symptoms finally started to dissipate.

    a. elated . . . nourished
    b. frustrated . . . satisfied
    c. gaunt . . . famished
    d. morose . . . numb

35. The houseguest was like a(n) ------ when he outstayed his welcome and refused to ------ to the cost of food.

    a. confidant . . . relent
    b. enemy . . . admit
    c. parasite . . . contribute
    d. pest . . . recede

36. A ------ was placed on the resort after a visitor was ------ with a highly contagious and potentially fatal disease.

    a. blockade . . . afflicted
    b. censure . . . struck
    c. colonnade . . . pilfered
    d. quarantine . . . diagnosed

37. Although Ali's loss at the track meet last month was ------, he was ------ when his team took first place in the relay race yesterday.

    a. disheartening . . . reinvigorated
    b. frustrating . . . crestfallen
    c. incredible . . . joyous
    d. unfortunate . . . sullen

38. Rosie is very determined to one day become a doctor, so she approaches her studies with great ------ and ------.

    a. belligerence . . . tactfulness
    b. indifference . . . devotion
    c. passion . . . zeal
    d. shock . . . reluctance

39. The swim meet and basketball game were happening -------, so Angelo would have to ------- which one he would attend.

     a.   concurrently . . . select
     b.   consecutively . . . debate
     c.   sequentially . . . resign
     d.   sporadically . . . relegate

40. Miles was already ------- with the software, so he didn't have to be ------- on how to use it.

     a.   comfortable . . . taught
     b.   efficient . . . orientated
     c.   magnificent . . . synchronized
     d.   proficient . . . educated

Section 2: Quantitative
37 Questions, 35 Minutes

The section is divided into two parts: problem solving and quantitative comparison. Directions for each part are provided.

Part 1 - Problem Solving

Instructions: Each question is followed by four possible answers. Select the best answer.

1. Anthony and Sophia decide to go on an hour long jog together. For the first half of the jog, Anthony and Sophia both jog at a constant speed of 350 feet per minute. Anthony maintains this speed for the entirety of the jog, but Sophia increases her jogging speed to 375 feet per minute for 15 minutes before slowing down to 330 feet per minute for the final 15 minutes of the jog. At the end of the jog, how far ahead of Anthony, in feet, is Sophia?

   a. 75 feet
   b. 150 feet
   c. 375 feet
   d. 675 feet

2. Let $a \star b = a^2 + b$ for all real numbers a and b. What is the value of $3 \star 5$?

   a. 11
   b. 14
   c. 22
   d. 28

3. Franco has a bag of 6 red and 9 green candies. Of the red candies, 4 are sweet and 2 are sour. Of the green candies, 6 are sweet and 3 are sour. Franco will choose one candy from the bag at random. Which of the following events has the lowest probability?

   a. Franco chooses a sweet green candy
   b. Franco chooses a sweet red candy
   c. Franco chooses a sour green candy
   d. Franco chooses a sour red candy

4. Four pairs of shoes are on sale for $55, $40, $68, and $63, respectively. What is the median price of the shoes?

   a. $55
   b. $59
   c. $63
   d. $68

5. If a is a positive integer and $(x - a)^2 = x^2 - 6x + 9$, what is the value of a?

   a. 3
   b. 4
   c. 5
   d. 6

6. What is the sum of the distinct prime factors of 56?

   a. 7
   b. 9
   c. 14
   d. 16

7. The length of the base of a rectangle is increased by 30% and the height is decreased by 20%. What is the percent increase in the area of the rectangle?

   a. 4%
   b. 8%
   c. 10%
   d. 20%

8. The formula for the volume of a cube is $V = s^3$, where s represents the side length. Cube X has side lengths that are 2 times the side lengths of cube Y. Which of the following statements regarding the volumes of the cubes is true?

   a. The volume of cube X is 2 times the volume of cube Y.
   b. The volume of cube X is 4 times the volume of cube Y.
   c. The volume of cube X is 6 times the volume of cube Y.
   d. The volume of cube X is 8 times the volume of cube Y.

9. A family drives several hours to reach their vacation destination. About halfway through their trip, they stop for lunch. Which graph best represents this scenario?

a.

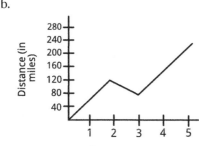

b.

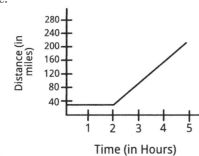

c.

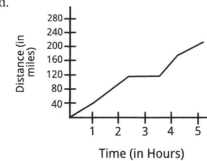

d.

10. The height of a rectangle is 9 and the area of the rectangle is 72 inches². If two inches are added to the rectangle's height and two inches are subtracted from the base, what is the area of the new rectangle?

    a. 66 inches
    b. 68 inches
    c. 70 inches
    d. 77 inches

11. Which graph's slope is zero?

a.

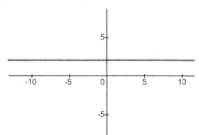

b.

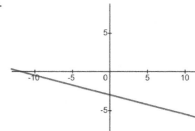

c.

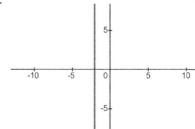

d.

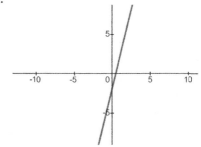

12. Ground floor tickets to the holiday concert cost $30 each, and balcony tickets cost $20 each. For Friday's performance, 200 tickets were sold for a total of $5,200. How many ground floor tickets were sold?

    a. 80
    b. 120
    c. 160
    d. 200

13. A gym manager calculates the number of days each of the gym's members comes in during a given month. He then calculated the mean, median, mode, and range of the data. That information is collected in the table below.

Measure	Value
Mean	9
Median	11
Mode	14
Range	23

If a person coming to the gym the median number of days came to the gym twice as often, the range would

    a. double.
    b. increase slightly.
    c. decrease slightly.
    d. stay the same.

14. The sum of two consecutive even integers is 34. What is the smaller of the two integers?

    a. 12
    b. 14
    c. 16
    d. 18

15. Which of the following expresses z in terms of x and y if $\dfrac{1}{x-y} = \dfrac{1}{y+z}$?

    a. x
    b. $x - y$
    c. $x - 2y$
    d. $x + 2y$

16. The pyramid below is made up of four equilateral triangles.

Which of the following could NOT be a net of the pyramid?

a.

b.

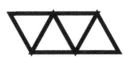

c.

    d. All of the figures above could be a net of the pyramid

17. A researcher collected data from an experiment. If a sixth value is added to the chart with a frequency of three, which of the following statistical measures would NOT change?

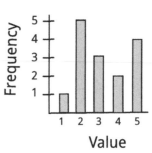

    a. median
    b. range
    c. mean
    d. mode

18. For any positive integer n, n! is the product of all integers from 1 to n, inclusive. What is the value of the expression below?

$$\frac{6!}{4!}$$

   a. 24
   b. 30
   c. 120
   d. 720

Part 2 - Quantitative Comparisons

Instructions: In each question, use the information provided to compare the quantity in Column A with the quantity in Column B. All quantitative comparison questions have the same answer choices:

    a. The quantity in column A is greater.
    b. The quantity in column B is greater.
    c. The two quantities are equal.
    d. The relationship cannot be determined from the information given.

19.   <u>Column A</u>   <u>Column B</u>

    $(5 - 3) \times 2 + 3^2 - (4 + 4)$ $2 \times 4^2 + 6(5 - 1)$

    $x < 0$

20. <u>Column A</u>   <u>Column B</u>

    $4(x - 2)$ $4x - 2$

Consider the number of letters in "January", "February", "March", and "April"

21. <u>Column A</u>   <u>Column B</u>

The median of the number of letters in a month name

The mode of the number of letters in a month name

Let $g(x) = x^2 - 5$.

22. <u>Column A</u>   <u>Column B</u>

    $g(3)$ $g(-3)$

---

23. <u>Column A</u>   <u>Column B</u>

The perimeter of an equilateral triangle with one side length of 4.

The perimeter of an isosceles triangle with one side length of 4.

---

24. <u>Column A</u>   <u>Column B</u>

    $\dfrac{1}{5}^{-3}$ $5 - 3$

Leonard tosses two coins.

25. <u>Column A</u>   <u>Column B</u>

The probability that the first coin toss lands on heads

If the first coin toss lands on heads, the probability that the second toss will land on tails

---

$\triangle$ RTS is similar to $\triangle$ UTV.

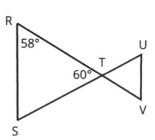

26. <u>Column A</u>   <u>Column B</u>

The measure of $\angle$ U

The measure of $\angle$ V

Lines A and B lie in the same coordinate plane and are perpendicular. The equation for line A is $y = 4x - 6$.

27. <u>Column A</u>   <u>Column B</u>

The slope of line B.

The y intercept of line B.

$y = -2(x - 2)$

28. <u>Column A</u>   <u>Column B</u>

The minimum value for y if $2 < x < 5$

The minimum value for y if $-3 < x < 1$

x < 0

29. Column A   Column B

$\sqrt{x^2}$ x^3

A researcher notices that data values are missing in the graph below. However, the researcher knows that the mean and median of the data are 4 and the data are symmetric about this value.

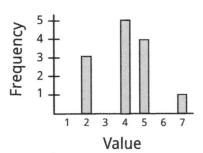

30. Column A   Column B

The frequency of value 3.   The frequency of value 6.

---

x > 0

31. Column A   Column B

$(x+2)(x^2-4x+4)$ $(x+2)^3$

Britney flips a coin and then rolls a 6-sided number cube with sides labeled 1-6.

32. Column A   Column B

If the coin lands on heads, the probability that Britney rolls an even number   If the coin lands on tails, the probability that Britney rolls an odd number.

---

33. Column A   Column B

70% of 20   35% of 40

Rectangle A   Rectangle B

 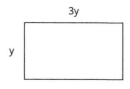

Note: The images are not drawn to scale.

34. Column A   Column B

The perimeter of rectangle A.   The perimeter of rectangle B.

---

35. Column A   Column B

The sum of the greatest common factor of 24, 32, and 64 and the greatest common factor of 12, 21, and 66   The difference between the least common multiple of 8 and 6 and the least common multiple of 9 and 6

The radius of the circle below is x.

36. Column A   Column B

The shaded portion of the circle. $\dfrac{x^2\pi}{3}$

The measure of an interior angle of a regular polygon is $\dfrac{180°\,(n-2)}{n}$. Polygons A and B are regular polygons.

Polygon A   Polygon B

37. Column A   Column B

The measure of an interior angle of polygon A.   The measure of an interior angle of polygon B.

Section 3: Reading
36 Questions, 35 Minutes

Instructions: Carefully read each passage and answer the questions that follow it. For each question, decide which of the choices best answers the question based on the passage.

Questions 1 - 6

1   On March 27, 1964, the strongest
2 earthquake ever recorded in North America
3 rocked much of Alaska. The record 9.2 magnitude
4 earthquake lasted for over four minutes – a lifetime
5 for an earthquake. According to eyewitnesses, the
6 earth shook so violently that asphalt streets rose
7 and fell like waves. In Anchorage, which was over
8 70 miles from the quake's epicenter, roads split
9 in half, entire buildings collapsed, and telephone
10 poles were toppled. Utilities such as water, gas,
11 electricity, and sewage were decimated. The quake
12 was so strong that in the span of these four minutes,
13 parts of the Alaskan coastline rose over 38 feet,
14 while other parts sank more than eight feet.
15   While the initial earthquake was
16 devastating, its aftermath was even more traumatic.
17 Tsunami waves triggered by the earthquake
18 traveled as far as Oregon, Washington, and
19 northern California. One 75 foot wave hit Crescent
20 City, California, causing over 23 million dollars in
21 damage and killing four people. In Valdez, Alaska,
22 a subterranean landslide brought about a tsunami
23 so massive that one of its waves measured over 200
24 feet. In Anchorage, the quake produced colossal
25 landslides, one of which sank the Anchorage
26 business district nine feet. In Turnagain, another
27 part of Anchorage, the earthquake led to soil
28 liquefaction, which basically means that the soil
29 lost its strength and stability, and behaved like a
30 liquid. This liquefaction caused a landslide which
31 sent 75 houses over 2,000 feet into the ocean.
32   After the earthquake, a team of sociologists
33 from Ohio State University traveled to Anchorage
34 to study the earthquake's effects on the city's
35 citizens. Expecting to see chaos, desperation, and
36 looting, they were shocked to find a city working
37 together in extraordinary ways to overcome
38 tragedy. Ordinary people combed through rubble,
39 searching for survivors. A boy scout troop helped
40 hospital patients down several flights of stairs
41 after their hospital started filling with natural gas.
42 A group of teenagers led by a local veterinarian
43 headed to Turnagain to retrieve any intact personal
44 belongings from destroyed houses.

45   Several individual volunteers sprang into
46 action, leading different elements of the city's
47 recovery effort. A radio reporter, Genie Chance,
48 spent the entire weekend disseminating emergency
49 information from authorities to the people of
50 Anchorage. Barely sleeping all weekend, she also
51 provided updates from local families over the air
52 so that people knew their loved ones were okay.
53 William Davis, a psychology professor, ended up
54 running Anchorage's search and rescue operations
55 after the city itself was unable to organize an
56 effort. Another man, an employee of the city's
57 public works department, coordinated a group
58 of volunteers to help keep the peace during the
59 cleanup operations.
60   In the months after the earthquake, the
61 sociologists endeavored to understand why the city
62 had come together so seamlessly in the aftermath
63 of this tragedy. The response from most citizens
64 was simple: they felt compelled to help.

1. The author of the passage included lines 5 - 14 in order to

   a. prove that the earthquake was less serious than originally expected.
   b. clarify why the earthquake wasn't the strongest ever in North America.
   c. explain why the city of Anchorage was unable to rebuild after the quake.
   d. show the immensity and destruction of the earthquake.

2. The mood of the passage goes from

   a. grim to hopeful.
   b. worried to unconcerned.
   c. serious to playful.
   d. pessimistic to earnest.

3. According to the passage, the aftereffects of the earthquake were felt in all of the following states EXCEPT

   a. Alaska.
   b. Ohio.
   c. California.
   d. Oregon.

4. Based on the information in the passage, it can be inferred that sociologists study

   a. the destruction of cities.
   b. the geological impact of earthquakes.
   c. people's behavior.
   d. natural disasters.

5. The houses referenced in lines 42 - 44 were destroyed during

   a. the initial moments of the earthquake.
   b. a tsunami wave.
   c. a landslide.
   d. an earthquake aftershock.

6. As it is used in line 61, "endeavored" most nearly means

   a. ceased.
   b. fought.
   c. refused.
   d. strived.

Questions 7 - 12

1   "Has the duchess returned?"

2

3   "No, your grace."

4

5   Knowles came farther into the room. He had a letter
6   on a salver. When the duke had taken it, Knowles
7   still lingered. The duke glanced at him.

8

9   "Is an answer required?"

10

11   "No, your grace." Still Knowles lingered. "Something
12   a little singular has happened. The carriage has
13   returned without the duchess, and the men say that
14   they thought her grace was in it."

15

16   "What do you mean?"

17

18   "I hardly understand it myself, your grace. Perhaps
19   you would like to see Barnes."

20

21   Barnes was the coachman.

22

23   "Send him up." When Knowles had gone, and he
24   was alone, his grace showed signs of being slightly
25   annoyed. He looked at his watch. "I told her she'd
26   better be in by four. She says that she's not feeling
27   well, and yet one would think that she was not
28   aware of the fatigue entailed in having the prince
29   come to dinner, and a mob of people to follow. I
30   particularly wished her to lie down for a couple of
31   hours."

32

33   Knowles ushered in not only Barnes, the
34   coachman, but Moysey, the footman, too. Both
35   these persons seemed to be ill at ease. The duke
36   glanced at them sharply. In his voice there was a
37   suggestion of impatience.

38

39   "What is the matter?"

40

41   Barnes explained as best he could. "If you please,
42   your grace, we waited for the duchess outside Cane
43   and Wilson's, the drapers. The duchess came out,
44   got into the carriage, and Moysey shut the door, and
45   her grace said, 'Home!' and yet when we got home
46   she wasn't there."

47   "She wasn't where?"

48

49   "Her grace wasn't in the carriage, your grace."

50

51   "What on earth do you mean? Her grace did get
52   into the carriage; you shut the door, didn't you?"

53

54   "Yes and she did get in. The duchess came out of
55   the shop. She seemed rather in a hurry, I thought.
56   She got into the carriage, and she said, 'Home,
57   Moysey!' I shut the door, and Barnes drove straight
58   home. We never stopped anywhere, and we never
59   noticed nothing happen on the way; and yet when
60   we got home the carriage was empty."

61

62   The duke started.

63

64   "Do you mean to tell me that the duchess got out of
65   the carriage while you were driving full pelt through
66   the streets without saying anything to you, and
67   without you noticing it?"

68

69   "The carriage was empty when we got home, your
70   grace."

71

72   "Was either of the doors open?"

73

74   "No, your grace."

75

76   "You fellows have been up to some infernal
77   mischief. You have made a mess of it. You never
78   picked up the duchess, and you're trying to palm
79   this tale off on me to save yourselves."

80

81   Barnes was moved to adjuration: "I'll take my Bible
82   oath, your grace, that the duchess got into the
83   carriage outside Cane and Wilson's."

84

85   Moysey seconded his colleague. "I will swear to
87   that, your grace. She got into that carriage, and I
88   shut the door, and she said, 'Home, Moysey!'"

89

90   The duke looked as if he did not know what to make
91   of the story and its tellers.

7. As it is used in the passage, "singular" (line 12) most nearly means

   a. boring.
   b. remarkable.
   c. routine.
   d. wonderful.

8. In line 9, the duke asks Knowles "Is an answer required?" because the duke

   a. is guessing why Knowles hasn't left the room.
   b. wants to reply to the letter privately.
   c. hopes Knowles will answer the letter for him.
   d. wants Knowles to understand that he will answer the letter if needed.

9. This conflict in this passage centers around the

   a. reason that the duchess went missing.
   b. duke learning that the duchess is missing.
   c. relationship between the duke and the duchess.
   d. ongoing search for the missing duchess.

10. According to the passage, it was important for the duchess to be home on time that evening because she

   a. was supposed to meet with the prince at the palace.
   b. and the duke were supposed to have a private dinner.
   c. needed to set up her draperies from Cane and Wilson.
   d. and the duke were hosting the prince for dinner.

11. The duke's tone toward Barnes and Moysey in lines 47 - 79 can best be described as

   a. furious.
   b. bitter.
   c. disappointed.
   d. suspicious.

12. Barnes says "I'll take my Bible oath" (line 81-82) in order to

   a. contradict the story that Moysey told the duke.
   b. show his devotion to the duke.
   c. convince the duke that he was telling the truth.
   d. appeal to the duke's religious beliefs.

Questions 13 - 18

1　　　What's the best way to get rid of hiccups?
2　Some popular "remedies" include holding one's
3　breath and swallowing three times, breathing into
4　a paper bag, eating a teaspoon of sugar, and even
5　drinking water upside down. The fact is, none of
6　these are scientifically proven. To best understand
7　how to get rid of hiccups, it's important to know
8　what hiccups are and why they happen.
9　　　First, what is a hiccup? Technically, it's a
10　muscle spasm of the diaphragm. The diaphragm,
11　a small, dome-shaped muscle that sits squarely
12　under the lungs and above the stomach, plays a
13　key role in a person's breathing. When breathing
14　normally, the diaphragm pulls the lungs down
15　while inhaling and then relaxes with each exhale.
16　Its essential function is to enlarge the size of the
17　lungs so that humans are able to take in more
18　air during normal breathing. Sometimes the
19　diaphragm will spasm between breaths, trapping a
20　small amount of air in the throat. That is a hiccup.
21　　　The cause of the diaphragm spasm
22　could be many things. Most commonly, people
23　experience hiccups after eating a big meal, drinking
24　carbonated beverages, or becoming suddenly
25　excited. Usually, the hiccups last a couple minutes
26　before the diaphragm settles back into a normal
27　breathing pattern. However, in rare cases, hiccups
28　may be long-lasting, persisting for days, weeks, and
29　even months. This is often a sign of an underlying
30　medical issue like nerve damage, encephalitis,
31　or meningitis. Long-term hiccups can also be
32　triggered by diabetes, anesthesia, or an electrolyte
33　imbalance.

34　　　Although many of the popular remedies
35　are unproven, some may provide relief. Breathing
36　into a paper bag helps decrease or stop the spasms
37　because the amount of carbon dioxide in the lungs
38　increases, relaxing the diaphragm. Small sips of
39　cold water stimulates the nose while also physically
40　exercising the throat. Being scared by a friend may
41　also provide relief, as it often triggers a large gasp
42　which may help realign the diaphragm to a normal
43　breathing pattern. Chronic hiccups may require
44　surgery, medicine, or, at least, a lifestyle change.

13. According to the author, what is a hiccup?

    a. a spasm of the diaphragm
    b. a shortage of oxygen in the lungs
    c. nerve damage
    d. enlargement of the lungs

14. It can be inferred from the passage that

    a. there is no relief for hiccups.
    b. hiccups lasting days are rare.
    c. the best way to avoid hiccups is to eat small meals.
    d. hiccups can be life threatening.

15. The passage is primarily concerned with

    a. the best remedies for hiccups.
    b. explaining what causes and provides relief for hiccups.
    c. laying bare popular myths about hiccup remedies.
    d. describing how to avoid getting hiccups.

16. According to the passage both encephalitis and meningitis are

    a. results of becoming overly excited.
    b. effects of long term hiccups.
    c. types of hiccups.
    d. medical conditions.

17. In line 33, "imbalance" most nearly means

    a. asymmetry.
    b. disparity.
    c. parity.
    d. problem.

18. Which best describes the organization of lines 34 - 44?

    a. The author compares and contrasts different remedies.
    b. The author refutes a common belief and then provides support for their ideas.
    c. The author makes an acknowledgment and describes remedies.
    d. The author gives medical advice for people who suffer from chronic hiccups.

Questions 19 - 24

1   In 2019, Americans consumed anywhere
2 from seven to thirteen hours of media a day from
3 the internet, television, film, newspapers, podcasts,
4 and radio. It's safe to say that for many of us, the
5 intake of media in all of its forms has become as
6 natural as breathing. But we don't often take the
7 time to think about it critically or consider the bias
8 inherent in it.
9   It's important to understand that all
10 media messages are constructed by people. The
11 advertisements you see on your favorite website,
12 the news articles you read in a trusted publication,
13 and the reporting you hear on a podcast were all
14 created by ordinary people who have their own
15 thoughts, opinions, and biases. All of us, including
16 those who produce media, have biases, or
17 inclinations for or against certain ideas, groups, or
18 people. Sometimes, as with implicit bias, we aren't
19 even aware that we have a preference! This means
20 that even when a media organization makes an
21 explicit effort to avoid bias, it's extremely difficult to
22 be totally objective.
23   Although bias can be found in all types of
24 media, detecting leanings in the news is especially
25 important when trying to acquire a nuanced
26 understanding of local, national, and international
27 events. For example, if a newspaper reported on a
28 new controversial law, these are the questions you
29 should ask. Were both proponents and opponents
30 of the law interviewed? Was equal attention given
31 to both? What types of words did the publication
32 use when describing the law and the reaction to
33 it? What photo accompanied the story? Did the
34 headline indicate favoritism?

35   Using the example above, a news
36 organization with an implicit bias against the new
37 law may have chosen a more negative headline
38 such as "Controversial New Law Passed Despite
39 Protests," and throughout the article used emotive
40 language like "disappointed" or "angered." They
41 may have run a picture that captured the defeated
42 facial expressions of people who were against the
43 law. The article might include more quotes from
44 the protesters than the politicians responsible
45 for creating the law. Conversely, another news
46 organization that favored the law may have written
47 a headline like "Supporters of New Law Celebrate
48 Its Passage" and used loaded words such as "hope"
49 and "enthusiasm." They may have interviewed only
50 the law's supporters and creators and picked a
51 photo showing the bill being signed into law.
52   It's easy to see how a consumer of either
53 publication could have their opinion influenced
54 by the way the information is presented. So what
55 are news media consumers to do? To begin,
56 it's important to carefully look for bias in news
57 stories. If you find yourself feeling overly upset or
58 enthusiastic after reading, watching, or listening
59 to what should have been unbiased reporting,
60 critically examine the way the story was told.
61 Look for other sources covering the same story,
62 especially those that may be showing it in a
63 different light. Make sure the facts in the story are
64 correct. By recognizing bias and actively educating
65 ourselves, we can all become more knowledgeable
66 news and media consumers.

19. In lines 5 - 6, the author uses the simile "as natural as breathing" to show

    a. why Americans must reduce their media consumption.

    b. how prevalent media has become in our lives.

    c. that people need to think more critically about the media they consume.

    d. that Americans don't realize that they are consuming media.

20. The purpose of this passage is to

    a. show how the media can avoid being biased.

    b. help media consumers understand why bias is helpful.

    c. explain how to detect bias in the media.

    d. critique the media.

21. As it is used in the passage, "proponents" (line 29) most nearly means

    a. advocates.

    b. critics.

    c. followers.

    d. interpreters.

22. The function of the fourth paragraph is to

    a. explain the purpose of the passage.

    b. illustrate how to detect bias in advertisements.

    c. clarify how bias could be shown in the news media.

    d. explain how a reader could avoid bias.

23. According to the author, it's sometimes difficult for people or organizations to be completely unbiased because they

    a. are unwilling to acknowledge that bias exists.

    b. may not realize that they have a bias.

    c. prefer to remain objective.

    d. don't focus on understanding the facts.

24. In the final paragraph, it can be inferred that the passage's author believes that

    a. it's easy for consumers to avoid bias in the news media they consume.

    b. the information presented in the news media is always correct.

    c. engaging with a variety of news media sources will only reinforce bias.

    d. media consumers are ultimately responsible for detecting bias.

Questions 25 - 30

1   Travel down south and you are likely
2   to find men named after Francis Marion. The
3   Revolutionary War hero, also known as the Swamp
4   Fox, hailed from South Carolina and is best known
5   for his guerilla warfare tactics and ability to evade
6   capture.
7   Francis Marion was born February 26,
8   1732, in Berkeley County, South Carolina. He was
9   a small boy with malformed legs, and, like many at
10 that time, he had little to no education and was only
11 semi-literate. At the age of fifteen, Marion joined
12 the crew of a ship and sailed to the West Indies.
13 Supposedly, the ship sank after a whale rammed
14 it, leaving Marion and his shipmates on a lifeboat
15 for seven days before they made it ashore. Not
16 surprisingly, Francis Marion never set sail again.
17 Secure on land, he operated his family's plantation
18 before joining the South Carolina militia at age 25
19 to fight in the French and Indian War. It is likely
20 during that experience that he learned the ambush
21 techniques he would later use against the British.
22   In 1775, Marion was elected to the South
23 Carolina Provincial Congress, an organization
24 established to support South Carolina's self-
25 determination. During the first three years of the
26 Revolutionary War, Marion saw little combat;
27 he commanded troops and guarded artillery at
28 Fort Sullivan. After an accident at a dinner party,
29 he spent several months recuperating in the
30 countryside. As luck would have it for both Marion
31 and the South, he was thus away from Charleston
32 when it was captured by the British.
33   With the Americans in retreat, the war
34 was not going well, especially in the South. Francis
35 Marion took control of a small militia and, knowing
36 he'd never be able to battle the British man-to-
37 man, reverted to tactics he'd learned fighting the
38 Cherokee Indians. Marion and his men embarked
39 upon harassment operations, such as hitting British
40 supply lines and cutting communications between
41 their posts. After one such attack, British Colonel
42 Tarleton spent seven hours traveling 26 miles by
43 foot attempting to apprehend Marion before he
44 escaped into a swamp. Tarleton swore, "As for this
45 ... old fox, the devil himself could not catch him."
46 The Swamp Fox continued to elude capture for the
47 duration of the war and even freed 150 captured
48 American soldiers along the way.

49   Legend has it that Marion was so
50 convincing and charming that upon meeting him
51 even Redcoats would change sides. However,
52 Francis Marion is not without controversy. He was
53 a slave owner, and many of his slaves ran away to
54 join the British in hopes of securing their freedom.
55 He used brutal tactics against the Cherokee
56 Indians in the French and Indian War. During the
57 Revolutionary War, he was notorious for destroying
58 property and lynching both British sympathizers
59 and enslaved African Americans who had been
60 forced to work for the British.
61   After the war, Marion returned to his
62 plantation as a gentleman farmer. He helped to
63 write the South Carolina Constitution and argued
64 passionately for peaceful reconciliation with
65 those who had supported the British. At 54, he
66 married his cousin Mary Esther Videau. He died
67 on February 27, 1795, leaving no heirs to take
68 his moniker, unless you count the thousands of
69 southerners who now bear his name.

25. Based on the passage, one can infer that a redcoat was

    a. a British soldier.
    b. a British sympathizer.
    c. a Native American
    d. a slave.

26. Which information contradicts the idea of Francis Marion as a war hero?

    a. He saw little action during the first three years of the war.
    b. He argued passionately for reconciliation with British sympathizers.
    c. He had an accident at a dinner party and was in the countryside recuperating.
    d. He lynched African Americans forced to work for the British.

27. The primary purpose of the passage is to

    a. vilify Francis Marion's behavior.
    b. show that Francis Marion was indeed a war hero.
    c. describe the life of Francis Marion.
    d. compare the tactics used by Franics Marion to the tactics used by the British.

28. In line 69, "bear" more nearly means

    a. carry.
    b. endure.
    c. support.
    d. yield.

29. Lines 44 - 45 provide an example of

    a. hyperbole.
    b. simile.
    c. onomatopoeia.
    d. pun.

30. What is the purpose of the first sentence of the passage?

    a. to show that Francis Marion is a popular name.
    b. to illustrate how important Francis Marion is to the South.
    c. to explain why people are named Francis Marion.
    d. to set the tone for the remainder of the passage.

Questions 31 - 36

1 "A penny for your thoughts," my
2 grandmother liked to say. I don't think she thought
3 they were worth very much. In the future, though,
4 she may have to spend more than a penny to learn
5 about what's floating around in my head. The
6 penny's days may be numbered.
7 Proponents of the penny argue that
8 eliminating it from our currency circulation would
9 increase prices of goods. Merchants are more apt
10 to round prices up than down. For example, if
11 pennies disappear, an ice cream shop owner would
12 likely increase the cost of an ice cream cone from
13 $2.97 to $3.00 rather than decrease it to $2.95. It is
14 worth noting that Canada got rid of their penny in
15 2012, and its citizens have seen no noticeable price
16 jumps. Supporters of the single cent also argue that
17 charities will be hurt if the coin is done away with
18 since many Americans may not be as generous
19 dropping larger coins in the donation bucket as
20 they are with pennies. Those pennies add up! In
21 2012 alone, McDonald's raised over 23 million
22 dollars through coin collection.
23 Opponents of the penny focus on how
24 inefficient it is. It is estimated that we spend 2.4
25 hours a year counting and sorting pennies for
26 change (or waiting for others to do so). With the
27 ubiquitousness of digital payments, one of the few
28 places Americans still use coins is the vending
29 machine, and even those don't accept pennies.
30 More importantly, manufacturing this particular
31 coin wastes valuable resources. Pennies are made
32 with zinc and copper, both of which are needed to
33 make laptops, batteries, washing machines, and
34 even sunscreen. Perhaps most surprisingly, it costs
35 more than a penny to actually produce a penny -
36 approximately 1.5 cents. Some analysts believe that
37 we could save millions of dollars each year if we
38 stopped minting pennies.

39 Of course there is a nostalgia factor where
40 pennies are concerned. We have memories of
41 scouring couch cushions for stray pennies or
42 buying penny candy. The penny also features
43 the face of one of our most beloved presidents,
44 Abraham Lincoln.
45 I'm not sure, given the costliness of making
46 pennies, that it makes sense to continue to produce
47 them. I'm sure just as many people would likely
48 toss a nickel into a donation jar as they would a
49 penny. Perhaps some of the savings the US reaps
50 from ceased production could even be donated
51 to charities. As far as Abraham Lincoln goes, he
52 graces the front of a five dollar bill, a far more useful
53 currency. A nickel for your thoughts doesn't sound
54 too bad given all that.

31. Which of the following is a correct inference from the passage?

    a. Pennies have no value.
    b. Resources used to make pennies are better spent elsewhere.
    c. It would be expensive to stop the production of pennies and make more nickels.
    d. People could no longer buy penny candies if the US got rid of the one cent.

32. Had the author chosen to replace the word "sense" with "cents" in line 46 they would have been using which literary device?

    a. irony
    b. metaphor
    c. pun
    d. simile

33. In line 39, "nostalgia" most nearly means

    a. homesickness.
    b. old.
    c. regret.
    d. reminiscence.

34. The primary purpose of the passage is to

    a. convince readers it's time to stop coining the penny.
    b. present both viewpoints on the topic of pennies equally.
    c. show that readers who want to keep making pennies are being wasteful.
    d. educate readers on the cost of making pennies.

35. The author addresses all of the ideas that the proponents put forward EXCEPT

    a. giving to charities.
    b. the image of Abraham Lincoln.
    c. the increase in prices.
    d. our feelings toward pennies.

36. What conclusion can best be drawn from the second paragraph?

    a. The price of American goods are likely to increase.
    b. The price of American goods are likely to decrease.
    c. The price of American goods will likely not change.
    d. The price of American goods cannot be compared to the price of Canadian goods.

Section 4: Math
47 Questions, 40 Minutes

Instructions: Each question is followed by four answer choices. Select the best answer.

1. Darnell is measuring the width of a bookcase he hopes to put in his office. Which of the following is the most reasonable unit of measure for him to use?

   a. kilogram
   b. millimeter
   c. liter
   d. centimeter

2. The first five terms of an algebraic sequence are shown below.

   5, 8, 11, 14, 17

   Which expression represents the nth term of this sequence?

   a. $2 + 3n$
   b. $3 + 2n$
   c. $5 + 2n$
   d. $5 + 3n$

3. A student tracks the cost of one-way flights from Chicago to San Francisco on a given day. He then makes a circle graph to represent the data. What is the central angle of the portion of the graph representing flights that cost $250-$300?

Cost of Flight	Number of Flights
$200 - $250	4
$250 - $300	5
$300 - $350	4
$350 - $400	2

   a. 30°
   b. 60°
   c. 120°
   d. 180°

4. The value of $\sqrt{75}$ falls between which of the following pairs of integers?

   a. 5 and 6
   b. 6 and 7
   c. 7 and 8
   d. 8 and 9

5. Find the first quartile of the following data set:

   29, 33, 38, 39, 45, 49, 60

   a. 29
   b. 33
   c. 38
   d. 39

6. 15 is what percent of 60?

   a. 10%
   b. 25%
   c. 30%
   d. 45%

7. Brayden subscribes to a grocery delivery service. There is a $7.00 fee for each delivery, plus an additional delivery charge of $0.05 per item delivered. If Brayden orders 45 items, how much is his total fee for the delivery?

   a. $2.25
   b. $7.00
   c. $9.25
   d. $29.50

8. Four musicians logged the number of hours they practiced over the course of a week. What was the mean number of hours practiced?

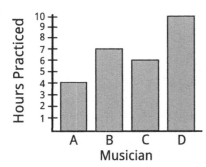

   a. 6
   b. 6.75
   c. 7
   d. 7.25

9. What is the least common multiple of 12 and 32?

   a. 32
   b. 96
   c. 144
   d. 192

10. If the image shown below is translated 6 units up and 2 units left. What is the new position of point A?

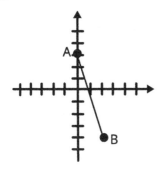

   a. (-2, 9)
   b. (-2, 6)
   c. (6, 1)
   d. (9, -2)

11. Fatima, Rachael, and Nolan are playing a board game. On his or her turn, each player rolls two 6-sided dice, with each die containing the numbers 1-6. Fatima needs to roll a sum of 12 to win the game on her next roll. What is the probability that she will win the game this round?

   a. $\frac{1}{36}$

   b. $\frac{1}{12}$

   c. $\frac{1}{11}$

   d. $\frac{1}{6}$

12. The area of each grid square shown is 3 cm². What is the area of the shaded area?

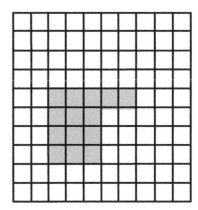

   a. 14 cm²
   b. 28 cm²
   c. 36 cm²
   d. 42 cm²

13. The Green Club at school is looking to choose new officers. If 6 of the 24 members apply but only 4 will be selected, how many groups of possible boards could there be?

   a. 9
   b. 15
   c. 144
   d. 4,320

14. If 2(a + ab) = 8 + 8b, what is the value of a?

   a. 2
   b. 4
   c. 8
   d. 16

15. Which of the following describes all values for x for which $|3x - 7| \leq 8$?

    a. $x \leq -\dfrac{1}{3}$

    b. $x \leq 5$

    c. $x \leq 5$ or $x \geq -\dfrac{1}{3}$

    d. $-\dfrac{1}{3} \leq x \leq 5$

16. What is the result of the expression

$$\begin{bmatrix} 3 & 5 \\ 4 & 9 \end{bmatrix} - \begin{bmatrix} 3 & 7 \\ 6 & 4 \end{bmatrix}?$$

    a. $\begin{bmatrix} 0 & -2 \\ -2 & 5 \end{bmatrix}$

    b. $\begin{bmatrix} 6 & 12 \\ 10 & 13 \end{bmatrix}$

    c. $\begin{bmatrix} 3 & 2 \\ -2 & 5 \end{bmatrix}$

    d. $\begin{bmatrix} 0 & 2 \\ 2 & 5 \end{bmatrix}$

17. One fifth of five cubed is equal to what number?

    a.   1
    b.   5
    c.   25
    d.   125

18. What is the distance between $(-2, 5)$ and $(3, -1)$?

    a.   3
    b. $\sqrt{17}$
    c. $\sqrt{41}$
    d. $\sqrt{61}$

19. If $10x + 4 = 30 - 3x$, what is the value of x?

    a.   -3
    b.   0
    c.   2
    d.   3

20. Which expression is equivalent to $\sqrt{144x^{16}}$?

    a. $12x^4$
    b. $12x^8$
    c. $72x^4$
    d. $72x^8$

21. The formula for the surface area of a square pyramid is $s^2 + 2sl$, where s is the length of a side of the base and l is the slant height. What is the surface area of a square pyramid where $s = 4$ inches and $l = 6$ inches?

    a. 24 in^2
    b. 40 in^2
    c. 50 in^2
    d. 64 in^2

22. The solution to $3 = -5x$ is a

    a.   irrational number
    b.   natural number
    c.   integer
    d.   real number

23. The table below shows the relationship between x and g(x). Which of the following could be the equation for the function?

x	g(x)
-1	8
0	7
1	6
2	5

    a. $g(x) = 7 - x$
    b. $g(x) = x + 7$
    c. $g(x) = x + 9$
    d. $g(x) = 2x + 10$

24. What is the solution set for $x^2 + 64 = 0$?

    a. ± 8
    b. $\pm 8i$
    c. ± 32
    d. $\pm 32i$

25. A university collected data on the number of hours of training and practice college athletes do each day. The results are summarized in the table below.

Number of hours of training	Probability
1	.10
2	.20
3	.30
4	.40

What is the expected number of hours of training per athlete?

    a. 2.5
    b. 3
    c. 3.5
    d. 4

26. In an attempt to win a free lunch, Tom put three of his business cards into the bowl at his favorite restaurant. If the probability of Tom's card being randomly selected is 5%, how many total cards are in the bowl?

    a. 30
    b. 45
    c. 60
    d. 75

27. The stem-and-leaf plot below represents the daily temperatures for a city over the course of a month. What is the mode of the data?

Stem	Leaf
4	6 7 7 7 9 9
5	4 5 5 6 6 6 8 8
6	2 2 2 2 3 7 9 9 9
7	1 2 2 3 3 3 4

    a. 47
    b. 56
    c. 62
    d. 73

28. The area of the rectangle below is 72 cm². If the sides of the rectangle are integers, what is the length of the longer side of the rectangle?

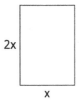

    a. 6 cm
    b. 12 cm
    c. 24 cm
    d. 36 cm

29. Triangle DEF is shown below. What is the cosine of $\angle$ F?

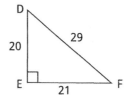

    a. 29
    b. $\frac{21}{29}$
    c. $\frac{29}{21}$
    d. $\frac{29}{20}$

30. Solve: $x^2 + 8x - 20 = 0$.

    a. $x = -10, 2$
    b. $x = -5, 4$
    c. $x = -4, 5$
    d. $x = -2, 10$

31. A researcher surveyed a random sample of 300 students at ABC High School to determine which movie genre they preferred. Of those surveyed, 70% indicated that comedies were their preferred genre. The researcher can reliably conclude that

    a. 30% of students surveyed dislike comedies
    b. 70% of American high school students prefer comedies
    c. the majority of students surveyed at ABC High School prefer comedies
    d. the majority of students surveyed at ABC High School only watch comedies

32. A cylinder has a height of 8 cm and volume of 128π cm³. What is the cylinder's radius?

Note: The formula used to determine the volume of a cylinder is $V = r^2h\pi$, where r is the cylinder's radius and h is the cylinder's height.

   a. 2 cm
   b. 4 cm
   c. 8 cm
   d. 16 cm

33. What is the solution set to the inequality $2 \leq -x + 3 \leq 5$?

   a. $x \leq -2$ or $x \leq -1$
   b. $x \leq -2$ or $x \leq 1$
   c. $-2 \leq x \leq -1$
   d. $-2 \leq x \leq 1$

34. Quadrilateral ABCD is similar to quadrilateral RSTU. The length of $\overline{BC}$ is 8 centimeters and the length of $\overline{TS}$ is 3 centimeters. What is the length of $\overline{DC}$ if the length of $\overline{TU}$ is 12 centimeters?

   a. 16 centimeters
   b. 24 centimeters
   c. 32 centimeters
   d. 36 centimeters

35. Kara goes on a run every Sunday morning. On Sundays in June, she ran 2.75 miles, 3.5 miles, 3.25 miles, and 2.5 miles. In July, Kara plans to run .25 miles further each Sunday than she ran that week the month before. If she is successful with her plan, what will Kara's median distance be for the month of July?

   a. 3 miles
   b. 3.25 miles
   c. 3.5 miles
   d. 3.75 miles

36. Which expression is equivalent to $x^2 + x - 42$?

   a. $(x - 6)(x - 7)$
   b. $(x - 6)(x + 7)$
   c. $(x - 3)(x - 14)$
   d. $(x - 3)(x + 14)$

37. A circle has a diameter of 22. What is the circle's area?

   a. 11
   b. 11π
   c. 22π
   d. 121π

38. There are 5,280 feet in a mile. Elise cycles at a speed of 12 feet per second. Which expression shows how many miles she cycles per hour?

   a. $\dfrac{12 \times 60 \times 60}{5,280}$

   b. $\dfrac{12 \times 5,280}{60 \times 60}$

   c. $\dfrac{60 \times 60}{12 \times 5,280}$

   d. $\dfrac{12 \times 60}{5,280}$

39. Point A is a point on line S (not pictured), which is parallel to line R. What is another point on line S?

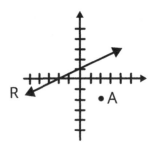

   a. $(0, -3)$
   b. $(1, -4)$
   c. $(2, 2)$
   d. $(4, 0)$

40. What is the value of the expression $\dfrac{2.8 \times 10^3}{4.0 \times 10^5}$?

   a. 7.0×10^8
   b. 7.0×10
   c. 7.0×10^{-1}
   d. 7.0×10^{-8}

41. The box-and-whisker plot below represents the weight, in pounds, of boxes on a delivery truck. What is the range of the data?

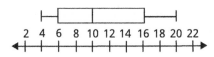

a. 10
b. 12
c. 16
d. 20

42. Aleya is painting the exterior of her house, which has a total surface area of 2,100 square feet. It takes 3 gallons of paint to cover 900 square feet. How many gallons of paint will Aleya need to paint the whole house?

a. 6
b. 7
c. 9
d. 15

43. Which expression is equivalent to the expression $\frac{6x^4y + 9x^2}{3x^4y - 6x^2}$?

a. $\frac{3x^4y + x^2}{x^4y^3x^2}$

b. $\frac{2x^4y + 3}{x^4y^2}$

c. $\frac{2x^2y}{x^2y}$

d. $\frac{2x^2y + 3}{x^2y^2}$

44. $\angle ABC$ measures $140°$ and $\overline{BD}$ bisects $\angle ABC$. What is the measure of $\angle ABD$?

a. $47°$
b. $65°$
c. $70°$
d. $80°$

45. The graph below is the solution set for which inequality?

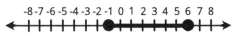

a. $|-2x+5| \leq 7$
b. $|2x+5| \leq 7$
c. $|-2x-5| \leq 7$
d. $|-2x+5| < 7$

46. For what value(s) of x is the equation $\frac{x-1}{x(x+7)} = 0$ true?

a. -7 only
b. 1 only
c. 0 and 1
d. -7, 0, and 1

47. Which of the following is larger than .87?

a. $\frac{8}{9}$

b. $\frac{9}{12}$

c. $\frac{14}{17}$

d. $\frac{4}{5}$

Essay

1 Question, 30 Minutes

Instructions: You have 30 minutes to write an essay on the topic below. It is not permitted to write an essay on a different topic. Your essay must be written in blue or black pen.

Please be aware that the schools you apply to will receive a copy of your essay. Your essay should be longer than a paragraph and use specific examples and details.

Write your response on this page and the next page.

What is your favorite movie, TV show, or book? Why do you enjoy it so much?

Test 8 Answer Key

Section 1: Verbal

1. D	9. D	17. A	25. A	33. A
2. B	10. A	18. D	26. C	34. C
3. C	11. B	19. B	27. C	35. C
4. B	12. D	20. B	28. B	36. D
5. A	13. C	21. B	29. B	37. A
6. D	14. C	22. D	30. B	38. C
7. B	15. B	23. D	31. A	39. A
8. C	16. D	24. B	32. C	40. D

Section 2: Quantitative

1. A	9. D	17. D	25. C	33. C
2. B	10. A	18. B	26. B	34. D
3. D	11. A	19. B	27. D	35. A
4. B	12. B	20. B	28. B	36. D
5. A	13. D	21. A	29. A	37. B
6. B	14. C	22. C	30. A	
7. A	15. C	23. D	31. B	
8. D	16. A	24. A	32. C	

Section 3: Reading

1. D	9. B	17. B	25. A	33. D
2. A	10. D	18. C	26. D	34. A
3. B	11. D	19. B	27. C	35. D
4. C	12. C	20. C	28. A	36. C
5. C	13. A	21. A	29. A	
6. D	14. B	22. C	30. B	
7. B	15. B	23. B	31. B	
8. A	16. D	24. D	32. C	

Section 4: Math

1. D	11. A	21. D	31. C	41. C
2. A	12. D	22. D	32. B	42. B
3. C	13. B	23. A	33. D	43. D
4. D	14. B	24. B	34. C	44. C
5. B	15. D	25. B	35. B	45. A
6. B	16. A	26. C	36. B	46. B
7. C	17. C	27. C	37. D	47. A
8. B	18. D	28. B	38. A	
9. B	19. C	29. B	39. A	
10. A	20. B	30. A	40. B	

ISEE Test 9

Section 1: Verbal
40 Questions, 20 Minutes

Synonyms

Instructions: Select the word whose meaning is closest to the word in capital letters.

1. SYNOPSIS:

   a. anthology
   b. dictionary
   c. story
   d. summary

2. DISCREET:

   a. distinct
   b. inconspicuous
   c. quiet
   d. small

3. ACCOLADE:

   a. epitome
   b. fame
   c. praise
   d. recommendation

4. ARTIFICE:

   a. candor
   b. facade
   c. intelligence
   d. ruse

5. SHUN:

   a. evade
   b. swindle
   c. thwart
   d. undermine

6. PROCLIVITY:

   a. advantage
   b. expertise
   c. inclination
   d. indifference

7. DAWDLE:

   a. appreciate
   b. linger
   c. outlast
   d. stop

8. EXUBERANT:

   a. ebullient
   b. irritated
   c. placid
   d. rushed

9. INCOHERENT:

   a. foolish
   b. irrational
   c. plausible
   d. unclear

10. CONJECTURE:

    a. faith
    b. idea
    c. guess
    d. validation

11. LIBERATION:

    a. emancipation
    b. incarceration
    c. justification
    d. subjugation

12. QUANDARY:

    a. decision
    b. dilemma
    c. hesitation
    d. judgment

13. PROTRACTED:
    a.
    b. endless
    c. intermittent
    d. measured
    e. prolonged

14. RUMINATE:

    a. coerce
    b. contemplate
    c. debate
    d. overlook

15. CAPITULATE:

    a. besiege
    b. contend
    c. propel
    d. relent

16. USURP:

    a. crush
    b. forge
    c. linger
    d. seize

17. TOME:

    a. almanac
    b. book
    c. letter
    d. paper

18. ELUCIDATE:

    a. clarify
    b. educate
    c. obfuscate
    d. repudiate

19. CONVALESCE:

    a. coalesce
    b. honor
    c. recover
    d. survive

Sentence Completion

Instructions: Select the word or pair of words that best completes the sentence.

20. Despite his teacher's instructions to stay on topic, Brayden often ------- when contributing to class discussions.

    a. digressed
    b. focused
    c. mumbled
    d. shouted

21. In early 2020, vandals ------- a mural by famed graffiti artist Banksy by writing over it with spray paint.

    a. constructed
    b. decorated
    c. defaced
    d. demolished

22. Furious that her boss made her work on a holiday with no notice, Ria made a(n) ------- decision to quit her job.

    a. earnest
    b. impetuous
    c. judicious
    d. studious

23. The ------- pickpocket stole three wallets the day after he was released from prison.

    a. cruel
    b. incorrigible
    c. reformed
    d. sullen

24. A curious and ------- child, Toya learned to read when she was just three years old.

    a. energetic
    b. garrulous
    c. precocious
    d. witty

25. After facing weeks of protests, the congress-man ------- his position that he was in favor of increasing taxes.

    a. concealed
    b. disputed
    c. mitigated
    d. recanted

26. Smallpox, a disease which killed 300 million people in the 20th century, was completely ------- by 1980 due to a highly effective and widely used vaccine.

    a. eradicated
    b. exposed
    c. hastened
    d. slowed

27. The referee ------- the basketball players for taunting each other during the game.

    a. admonished
    b. belittled
    c. extolled
    d. rankled

28. Since sickle cell anemia is a ------- condition, it can be diagnosed before or soon after a baby's birth.

    a. congenital
    b. environmental
    c. perious
    d. rare

29. The sudden closure of the library had a ------- impact on the community's senior citizens who frequently visited the building and used it as a meeting place.

    a. encouraging
    b. negligible
    c. profound
    d. unexpected

30. The typically ------- student was surprisingly compliant when he was gently asked to do something rather than firmly told.

    a. calm
    b. intrepid
    c. recalcitrant
    d. vivacious

31. The family's beach vacation had a(n) ------- beginning: the weather was beautiful, the water was crystal clear, and the beach wasn't crowded.

    a. auspicious
    b. intriguing
    c. stilted
    d. unpropitious

32. Since Javier was the most experienced and ------- teacher at the school, it seemed ------- that he'd get the promotion.

    a. controversial . . . doubtful
    b. lauded . . . inevitable
    c. loathed . . . logical
    d. respected . . . unlikely

33. New York City's ------- landscape provided a stark contrast to the ------- farming community Cassie grew up in.

    a. agrarian . . . suburban
    b. metropolitan . . . bustling
    c. provincial . . . rural
    d. urban . . . bucolic

34. Ashan ------- mushrooms; he couldn't ------- why anyone would eat a fungus!

    a. consumed . . . decipher
    b. despised . . . presume
    c. enjoyed . . . understand
    d. loathed . . . comprehend

35. The Bald Eagle Protection Act, passed by Congress in 1940, was the ------- for more ------- animal protection laws such as the Endangered Species Act of 1973.

    a. conclusion . . . extensive
    b. model . . . restricted
    c. precedent . . . comprehensive
    d. reason . . . focused

36. Marie Antoinette, an 18th century French queen, is best known for her luxurious and ------- lifestyle at a time when French ------- were starving.

    a. eccentric . . . royals
    b. lavish . . . subjects
    c. modest . . . citizens
    d. stoic . . . politicians

37. The ------- classical pianist was known for her technical skill, ------- timing, and heartfelt performances.

    a. adroit . . . rudimentary
    b. eminent . . . atrocious
    c. inept . . . flawless
    d. renowned . . . impeccable

38. Chandra was understandably ------- about her typically ------- husband's sudden plan to go bungee jumping.

    a. cavalier . . . adventurous
    b. confounded . . . prudent
    c. fascinated . . . reckless
    d. uneasy . . . experienced

39. Avyan was ------- by the ------- of the opposing
     team, who refused to shake hands after losing
     the game.

     a. astonished . . . apathy
     b. enraged . . . cordiality
     c. incensed . . . audacity
     d. surprised . . . cruelty

40. The manufacturer ------- that its production
     was ------- by an unavoidable shortage in
     supplies rather than any misstep in its part.

     a. claimed . . . amplified
     b. contended . . . encumbered
     c. purported . . . boosted
     d. scoffed . . . hindered

Section 2: Quantitative
37 Questions, 35 Minutes

The section is divided into two parts: problem solving and quantitative comparison. Directions for each part are provided.

Part 1 - Problem Solving

Instructions: Each question is followed by four possible answers. Select the best answer.

1. Which of the following solves for d if ab + ad = abc?

   a. bc - b
   b. bc + b
   c. abc - b
   d. abc + b

2. If the trend in the graph below continues, what will be the value of the graph in 2021?

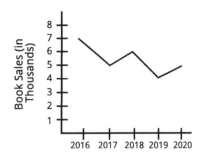

   a. 2,000
   b. 3,000
   c. 4,000
   d. 5,000

3. The area of a square is 81 inches². The square is transformed into a rectangle by subtracting 3 inches from two of its sides. What is the area of the rectangle?

   a. 54 in²
   b. 75 in²
   c. 81 in²
   d. 108 in²

4. What is the value of the expression $\dfrac{2\left(2^{3}+2^{4}\right)}{6\left(2+6\right)}$?

   a. 0
   b. 1
   c. 2
   d. 3

5. A hockey team hopes to score an average of greater than 4 goals per game in their 4 game tournament. If they scored 3, 5, and 0 goals respectively in the first three games, how many would the team need to score in the last game to achieve its goal?

   a. 6
   b. 7
   c. 8
   d. 9

6. The net for a triangular prism is shown below.

   Which of the following could NOT be a possible view of the prism?

   a.

   b.

   c.

   d.

7. If $(x + y)^2 = 81$ and $x^2 + 2xy = 56$, what is the value of y?

    a. 5
    b. 10
    c. 15
    d. 25

8. What number is the square root of the greatest common factor of 72, 108, and 144?

    a. 6
    b. 12
    c. 24
    d. 36

9. Quadrilateral ABCD is similar to quadrilateral EFGH. What must be true?

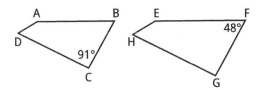

    a. 139° + BCD= 360°
    b. 139° + FEH = 360°
    c. 139° + BAD + ADC = 360°
    d. CBA + BDA + ADC = FEH + EHG + HGF

10. For any positive integer n, n! is the product of all integers from 1 to n, inclusive. What is the value of the expression below?

    3! + 2!

    a. 5
    b. 6
    c. 8
    d. 12

11. Karim has 30 math problems to solve for homework. He takes a break when he has completed 70% of the problems. How many more problems does Karim still need to complete?

    a. 6
    b. 9
    c. 12
    d. 21

12. Khalid and Jason are riding their bikes down the same trail, although they are travelling at different constant speeds. If they ride their bikes for 2 hours, what additional piece of information would be required in order to determine the total distance they both travelled?

    a. Khalid's speed
    b. Jason's speed
    c. The sum of Khalid and Jason's speeds
    d. The difference between Khalid and Jason's speeds

13. On any given day of his five-day Monday to Friday work week, Max always completes 3 more tasks than he did the previous day. If Max completed 5 tasks on Monday, what is the range of tasks he completed per day during this particular work week?

    a. 5
    b. 8
    c. 12
    d. 17

14. Let $r \triangledown s = r - 4s$. What is the value of $-5 \triangledown 5$?

    a. -25
    b. -20
    c. 20
    d. 25

15. In the graph below, each dot represents a different egg laying chicken. What pattern does the graph show?

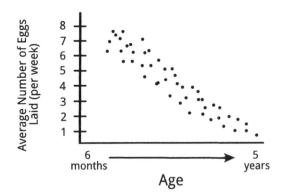

a. There is a weak positive correlation between the number of eggs laid and the chicken's age.
b. There is a weak negative correlation between the number of eggs laid and the chicken's age.
c. There is a strong positive correlation between the number of eggs laid and the chicken's age.
d. There is a strong negative correlation between the number of eggs laid and the chicken's age.

16. A bowl contains 15 red grapes and 20 green grapes. Two grapes are chosen from the bowl at random without replacement. Which of the following events has the highest probability?

a. Both of the grapes chosen are red.
b. The first grape chosen is red and the second chosen is green.
c. The first grape chosen is red or the second grape chosen is red.
d. The first grape chosen is red or the second grape chosen is green.

17. The area of a circle is 64π. If the radius of the circle is increased by 25%, what is the circumference of the new circle?

a. 10π
b. 20π
c. 81π
d. 100π

18. Lines C and D lie in the same coordinate plane as point (-1, 3). If the equation of line C is $y = 4x + 1$ and the equation of line D is $y = \frac{1}{3}x - 3$, point (-1, 3) is on

a. line C only.
b. line D only.
c. lines C and D.
d. neither line C nor D.

19. In the graph below, cost is shown as a function of pounds of apples sold.

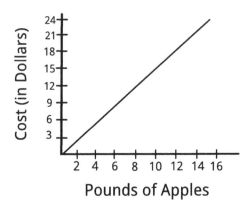

How much does one pound of apples cost?

a. $.50
b. $1.50
c. $3.00
d. $4.00

Part 2 - Quantitative Comparisons

Instructions: In each question, use the information provided to compare the quantity in Column A with the quantity in Column B. All quantitative comparison questions have the same answer choices:

    a. The quantity in column A is greater.
    b. The quantity in column B is greater.
    c. The two quantities are equal.
    d. The relationship cannot be determined from the information given.

The sum of the measures of the interior angles of a regular polygon is 180(n - 2). Both polygon A and B are regular polygons.

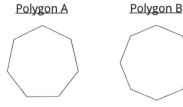

Polygon A   Polygon B

20. Column A

The sum of the measure of the interior angles in polygon A.

    Column B

The sum of the measure of the interior angles in polygon B.

21. Column A

$5 \times 5 + 5 - \dfrac{5}{5}$

    Column B

$5 - \dfrac{5}{5} + 5 \times 5$

Finley and Roberto had a competition to see who could read more books over the summer. Roberto read more books than Finley. The total number of books the boys read was 32.

22. Column A

The number of books that Finley read

    Column B

10 books

12,564.8091

23. Column A

The value of the digit in the thousandth place.

    Column B

The value of the digit in the tens place.

24. Column A

$\sqrt{a} \times \sqrt{b}$

    Column B

$\sqrt{ab}$

A group of students track the results of 100 coin tosses.

25. Column A

The probability that at least 30 tosses will land on tails

    Column B

The probability that exactly half of the tosses will land on tails

$z < 2$

26. Column A

$x - 4 = z$

    Column B

$x + 8 = z$

a, b, and c are consecutive even integers (a < b < c)

27. Column A

$c - a$

    Column B

4

A parallelogram has an area of 56 inches^2. The base is one inch longer than the height.

28. | Column A | Column B |
|---|---|
| The length of the height. | 8 inches |

ABCD is a square with side 2x.

29. | Column A | Column B |
|---|---|
| The area of the square. | $4x^2$ |

Let $^*a = -(a + 1)$

30. | Column A | Column B |
|---|---|
| $^*a$ for all a > 0 | $^*a$ for all a < 0 |

Hudson rolls two 6-sided number cubes with sides labeled 1-6. He then adds the results together.

31. | Column A | Column B |
|---|---|
| If the sum is 9, the probability that one of the rolls was a 6 | If the sum is 11, the probability that one of the rolls was a 6 |

The formula for the volume of a square pyramid is $V = \frac{1}{3}s^2h$, where s represents the side length of the base and h represents the height. Pyramid A has a side length that is 2 times the side length of pyramid B and a height that is $\frac{1}{4}$ the height of pyramid B.

32. | Column A | Column B |
|---|---|
| The volume of pyramid A | The volume of pyramid B |

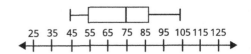

33. | Column A | Column B |
|---|---|
| The first quartile. | The range. |

x > 0

34. | Column A | Column B |
|---|---|
| $(x+7)^2$ | x^2+72 |

ABCD is a square with side x.

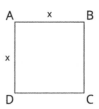

35. | Column A | Column B |
|---|---|
| The area of ABCD. | The perimeter of ABCD. |

Lines X and Y are parallel and are graphed on the same coordinate plane. The slope of the lines is 2.

36. | Column A | Column B |
|---|---|
| The y value of the y intercept of line X. | The y value of the y intercept of line Y. |

y = -2x - 1

37. | Column A | Column B |
|---|---|
| The maximum value of y when x = 0 | The maximum value of y when x > 0 |

Section 3: Reading
36 Questions, 35 Minutes

Instructions: Carefully read each passage and answer the questions that follow it. For each question, decide which of the choices best answers the question based on the passage.

<u>Questions 1 - 6</u>

1   Rhinella marina, more commonly known
2   as the cane toad, was deliberately introduced
3   to Australia's Northern Territory in 1935. At the
4   time, the larvae of French's cane beetle and the
5   greyback cane beetle were devastating the local
6   sugar cane crops. The Australian Bureau of Sugar
7   Experimental Stations released a few thousand
8   toads in hopes that they would eat the invasive
9   beetles. Unfortunately, the cane toads were largely
10 ineffective at ridding the area of either species of
11 beetle. And as with many purposely introduced
12 species, the cane toad ultimately became more of
13 a nuisance than the pest that it was intended to
14 destroy.
15   Native to South and Central America, cane
16 toads are amphibians with stocky bodies, bony
17 heads, and brownish, warty skin. Typically ranging
18 from nine to fifteen centimeters long, cane toads
19 can grow as long as 24 centimeters. Notoriously
20 voracious eaters, cane toads eat nearly anything
21 they can swallow. Although their diet primarily
22 consists of living insects, they also are known to
23 eat frogs, other toads, honey bees, and even small
24 mammals. Cane toads breed prolifically; one
25 female cane toad can lay up to 35,000 eggs twice a
26 year.
27   Since cane toads are not native to
28 Australia, they have no natural predators. If native
29 animals do try to eat cane toads, they're in for a
30 nasty surprise. Even as tadpoles, cane toads are
31 extremely poisonous. Behind their eardrums, cane
32 toads have large swellings called parotoid glands
33 which produce bufotoxin, a deadly poison. This
34 toxin is also found on their skin and in other glands.
35 A single lick of a cane toad by a native animal or
36 domesticated pet can cause convulsions, paralysis,
37 and even death.

38   This combination of factors has led to the
39 proliferation of cane toads throughout northern
40 Australia. Although only 3,000 toads were released
41 in 1935, more than 200 million exist today. This
42 abundance of cane toads has wreaked havoc on
43 indigenous animals, many of whom have become
44 endangered. A few species have even become
45 extinct. In some cases, predators die attempting
46 to eat the cane toad, and in others, the cane toad
47 has wiped out the prey of native species, leaving it
48 without food.
49   Today, the cane toad continues to spread
50 throughout Australia, despite the efforts of
51 Australian wildlife conservationists. Biodiversity
52 in places like the Northern Territory's Kakadu
53 National Park has been decimated. The cane toads
54 are now encroaching upon other regions with
55 profuse native wildlife such as the Kimberly in
56 Western Australia. Despite these setbacks, some
57 mitigation efforts have proven successful, such as
58 aversion training, which helps native predators
59 recognize and avoid the taste of cane toads.
60 Other researchers are experimenting with ways to
61 interrupt the breeding cycle of cane toads using
62 pheromones or gene technology.

1. This passage is primarily concerned with

   a. the reasons for the introduction of the cane toad to Australia.
   b. the spread of the cane toad in Australia.
   c. the Australian response to the cane toad.
   d. the dangers of introduced species.

2. Lines 11 - 14 provides an example of

   a. hyperbole.
   b. imagery.
   c. irony.
   d. personification.

3. The cane toad population has grown significantly for all of the reasons EXCEPT

   a. they have made native animals go extinct.
   b. they have no natural predators in Australia.
   c. female cane toads lay up to 35,000 eggs at a time.
   d. they excrete a toxin that can harm native animals.

4. The phrase "nasty surprise" (line 30) refers to the

   a. vast number of cane toads.
   b. bitter taste of the cane toad.
   c. cane toad's poison.
   d. cane toad's lack of natural predators.

5. In line 39, "proliferation" most nearly means

   a. depletion.
   b. experimentation.
   c. popularity.
   d. spread.

6. Based on the passage, scientists are hoping aversion training will

   a. help native animals hunt cane toads.
   b. stop cane toads from eating native wildlife.
   c. halt the spread of cane toads in the Kimberly.
   d. stop native animals from eating cane toads.

Questions 7 - 12

1   Arguably one of the best known and most
2 revered authors of all time, William Shakespeare is
3 not without controversy. Born in Stratford-upon-
4 Avon, England in 1564, Shakespeare eventually
5 moved to London where he worked as an actor. He
6 later moved back to Stratford-upon-Avon before his
7 death in 1616. This small set of facts is agreed upon
8 by all historians who study Shakespeare. What's up
9 for debate is this: Did William Shakespeare actually
10 write the plays attributed to him?
11   This "authorship question" has been
12 addressed in thousands of scholarly articles and
13 books. Most scholars, known as Stratfordians,
14 believe that Shakespeare was correctly credited for
15 his work. They point out that there are numerous
16 historical references to Shakespeare the playwright,
17 that his name was found on records from
18 Elizabethan theatres, and, most importantly, that
19 Shakespeare's name was written on all of his plays.
20   Other scholars, however, are more
21 skeptical. Many believe that it would have been
22 impossible for a man like Shakespeare, who had
23 little formal education or wealth, to write the
24 plays he is credited for. These cynics argue that
25 Shakespeare wouldn't have had the knowledge or
26 experience to write about the topics covered in his
27 plays. Some of them, for example, are set in royal
28 courts. Skeptics believe that it would have been
29 entirely unlikely for a non-aristocrat to successfully
30 write about court customs. Others point to the
31 fact that there are no letters, manuscripts, or other
32 items written in Shakespeare's hand in existence.
33 They find this dearth of material incongruous with
34 such a prolific writer.
35   Over the past few centuries, skeptics
36 have posited that either playwright Christopher
37 Marlowe or essayist Francis Bacon was responsible
38 for Shakespeare's plays. These alternatives have
39 fallen out of favor, though. Today, modern-day
40 Shakespeare disbelievers suggest that aristocrat
41 Edward de Vere, the 17th Earl of Oxford, actually
42 wrote the plays credited to Shakespeare. De Vere
43 was a highly educated lawyer who travelled to many
44 of the places written about by Shakespeare. As an
45 earl, he was also very familiar with royal courts.
46 Scholars known as Oxfordians believe that De Vere
47 would have purposely hidden his involvement
48 in playwriting because it was considered a lower
49 class profession. However, Stratfordians argue that
50 De Vere could not possibly have been the author
51 of the plays. Not only was there no proof of such
52 authorship, but also De Vere died in 1604, after
53 which some of Shakespeare's most famous plays
54 were written.

55   Today, Stratfordians stand firm in their
56 belief that Shakespeare did indeed write the plays
57 he is credited for. They contend that some of the
58 cynics' doubts come from a misunderstanding of
59 Elizabethan England. For example, Stratfordians
60 point out that even though Shakespeare was not
61 educated at a prestigious university, he did attend
62 a grammar school where he learned the classics,
63 history, and other subjects included in his plays.
64 And although Shakespeare did commonly write
65 about royal courts, he was actually criticized during
66 his lifetime for his somewhat inaccurate depiction
67 of courts. These Stratfordians find Shakespeare's
68 unremarkable background and education
69 compelling, relishing the idea that an ordinary man
70 could produce such extraordinary, enduring, and
71 beautifully written plays.

7. According to the passage, Stratfordians believe that

   a. Shakespeare did not write the plays he is credited for.
   b. it's uncertain whether Shakespeare wrote the plays he is credited for.
   c. Shakespeare did write the plays he is credited for.
   d. De Vere wrote the plays Shakespeare is credited for.

8. The purpose of this passage is to

   a. defend the Oxfordians' viewpoints about Shakespeare.
   b. explain why some people believe that Shakespeare did not write his plays.
   c. give an overview of Shakespeare's life and plays.
   d. explore the Shakespearean authorship question.

9. Which of the following best describes the organization of paragraph 3?

   a. A statistic is cited and then debated.
   b. A belief is followed by evidence in support of that belief.
   c. Two ideas are contrasted.
   d. An idea is followed by the history of the belief.

10. In line 33, "dearth" most nearly means

    a. abundance.
    b. complexity.
    c. lack.
    d. necessity.

11. Some believe that it's unlikely that De Vere wrote Shakespeare's plays because De Vere

    a. was an aristocrat and very familiar with royal courts.
    b. died before some of Shakespeare's plays were written.
    c. traveled widely, but not to locations where Shakespeare's plays were set.
    d. stated that he did not write the plays.

12. The critiques of Shakespeare's "depiction of the courts" (lines 66 -67) indicate that

    a. Shakespeare probably did not frequent royal courts.
    b. Shakespeare was likely an aristocrat.
    c. his critics did not understand court customs.
    d. his writing was of a lower quality than previously believed.

Questions 13 - 18

1   "Fast fashion" is a phrase used to describe
2 a wasteful and dangerous cycle of expeditious
3 clothing production and consumption. This part
4 of the fashion world developed out of consumer
5 demand for high fashion at low cost. The
6 destructive course continues in large part because
7 companies are making multi-billion dollar profits.
8   Where once there were biannual seasonal
9 trends - fall/winter and spring/summer - popular
10 retailers like H&M, Zara, and Forever21 now
11 quickly cycle through various trends by replacing
12 old products with new in just a week's time.
13 Companies market to consumers through social
14 media, often using celebrity spokespeople and
15 influencers. These "models" are never seen wearing
16 the same outfit twice, so the shoppers who emulate
17 them demand new clothing choices (and toss
18 their recently purchased items) in order to stay
19 fashionably relevant. In turn, stores are always
20 stocked with new, desirable products.
21   The resulting waste makes fast fashion one
22 of the most environmentally damaging industries
23 in the world. In 2017 alone, more than 11,000 tons
24 of textile waste wound up in landfills. To make
25 matters worse, sixty percent of the material used
26 to make clothing is synthetic, meaning it is derived
27 from fossil fuels. It will never decay. Instead, the
28 thousands of pairs of Old Navy flip flops discovered
29 by archaeologists hundreds of thousands of years
30 from now will remain evidence of tremendously
31 wasteful manufacturing and use.

32   The environment is not the only victim
33 of this throwaway approach to style. Nearly all
34 of the most popular fast fashion brands utilize
35 cheap labor, like sweatshops, that puts workers'
36 lives at risk. Poor conditions in factories expose
37 workers to harmful chemicals and carcinogens.
38 Many of the factory workers are women who
39 receive substandard wages and experience sexual
40 harassment and unfair maternity leave policies.
41   Fast fashion is ugly. The industry needs to
42 clean up its operations and establish sustainable
43 trends for consumers. Fashionistas and their
44 followers must understand the consequences
45 of their purchasing habits and commit to more
46 thoughtful shopping.

13. In line 42, "sustainable" most nearly means

    a. enduring.
    b. helpful.
    c. temporary.
    d. useful.

14. The primary purpose of the passage is to

    a. explain the history of fast fashion.
    b. illustrate the problems associated with fast fashion.
    c. describe the desire for consumers to have fast fashion.
    d. convince factories to improve their working conditions.

15. The author's tone toward fast fashion can best be described as

    a. antagonising.
    b. condemning.
    c. distrusting.
    d. questioning.

16. All of the following are problems of fast fashion EXCEPT

    a. low cost.
    b. substandard wages.
    c. synthetic fabrics.
    d. textile waste.

17. It can be inferred that prior to fast fashion new styles only came out at the stores

    a. once a year.
    b. twice a year.
    c. monthly.
    d. weekly.

18. Which best describes the organization of lines 41 - 46?

    a. Readers are asked to reconsider their habits and are provided with alternatives.
    b. An opinion is stated and requests are made.
    c. A problem is defined in detail.
    d. Different alternatives for fast fashion are explained.

Questions 19 - 24

1   Beth De Graf was a puzzle to all who knew her.
2   She was a puzzle even to herself, and was wont to
3   say, indifferently, that the problem was not worth
4   a solution. For this beautiful girl of fifteen was
5   somewhat bitter and misanthropic, a condition
6   perhaps due to the uncongenial atmosphere in
7   which she had been reared. Her big brown eyes
8   held a sombre and unfathomable expression. Once
9   she had secretly studied their reflection in a mirror,
10 and the eyes frightened her and made her uneasy.
11 She had analyzed them much as if they belonged to
12 someone else and wondered what lay behind their
13 mask.
14
15 But this morbid condition mostly affected her
16 when she was at home, listening to the unpleasant
17 bickerings of her father and mother, who quarrelled
18 constantly over trifles that Beth completely ignored.
19 Her parents seemed like two ill tempered animals
20 confined in the same cage and their snarls had long
21 since ceased to interest her.
22
23 This condition had, of course, been infinitely worse
24 in all those years when they were poverty stricken.
25 But now her father, the professor, no longer
26 harassed by debts, devoted less time to teaching
27 and began composing an oratorio that he firmly
28 believed would render his name famous. So, there
29 being less to quarrel about, Beth's parents indulged
30 more moderately in that pastime. But their natures
31 were discordant, and harmony in the De Graf
32 household was impossible.
33
34 When away from home Beth's disposition softened.
35 Some of her friends had seen her smile—a
36 wonderful and charming phenomenon, during
37 which her expression grew sweet and her eyes
38 radiant with mirthful light. At such times the
39 gentleness of Beth, her almost passionate desire to
40 be loved, completely transformed her. It was not
41 the same Beth at all.
42
43 Beth's trained indifference while at home was
44 demonstrated by her reception of Uncle John's
45 telegram. She quietly handed it to her mother and
46 said, as calmly as if it were an invitation to a church
47 picnic:
48
49 "I think I shall go."
50
51 "Nothing like that ever happened to me," remarked
52 Mrs. De Graf, enviously. "If John Merrick had an
53 atom of common sense he'd take me to Europe
54 instead of a troop of stupid school girls. But John
55 always was a fool. When will you start, Beth?"

56 "Tomorrow morning. I'll go to Patsy and stay with
57 her until we sail."
58
59 "Are you glad?" asked her mother, looking into the
60 expressionless face half curiously.
61
62 "Yes," returned Beth, as if considering her reply;
63 "a change is always interesting, and I have never
64 travelled except to visit Aunt Jane at Elmhurst. So I
65 think I am pleased to go to Europe."
66
67 Mrs. De Graf sighed. There was little in common
68 between mother and daughter; but that, to a grave
69 extent, was the woman's fault. She had never
70 tried to understand her child's complex nature,
71 and somewhat resented Beth's youth and good
72 looks, which contrasted unfavorably with her own
73 deepening wrinkles and graying hair. For Mrs. De
74 Graf was vain and self-important, and still thought
75 herself attractive and even girlish.
76
77 Beth packed her own trunk and arranged for it to
78 be taken to the station. In the morning she entered
79 the music room to bid the Professor good-bye. He
80 frowned at the interruption, for the oratorio was
81 especially engrossing at the time.
82
83 Mrs. De Graf kissed her daughter lightly and said in
84 a perfunctory way that she hoped Beth would have
85 a good time. The girl had no thought of resenting
86 the lack of affection displayed by her parents for
87 she had no reason to expect anything different.

19. The phrase "that the problem was not worth a solution" (lines 3 - 4) refers to

    a. Beth's belief that her condition is so confusing it can be solved.
    b. Beth's acceptance of her condition.
    c. Beth's concern that solving her condition would be impossible.
    d. Beth's desire to blame her parents.

20. In line 5, "misanthropic" most nearly means

    a. aloof.
    b. fortunate.
    c. funny.
    d. unsocial.

21. Which word best describes the relationship between Beth and her parents?

    a. disappointing.
    b. distant.
    c. resentful.
    d. temperamental.

22. The phrase "like two ill tempered animals confined in the same cage" in lines 19 - 20 is an example of

    a. irony.
    b. pun.
    c. personification.
    d. simile.

23. The primary purpose of the passage is to

    a. describe the trip to Europe Beth is about to take.
    b. explain Beth's peculiar behavior.
    c. demonstrate the difficult marriage of Beth's parents.
    d. portray the resentment between a mother and daughter.

24. Beth's reception of the telegram was

    a. a moment of jubilation.
    b. consistent with her earlier interactions.
    c. remarkable.
    d. tempered by her mother's envy.

Questions 25 - 30

1 Prior to the 20th century, a simple
2 infection could be deadly. Then, in 1928, chemist
3 Alexander Fleming discovered penicillin, the
4 first antibiotic. By the mid 1940s, antibiotics had
5 become widely available, and today they are an
6 integral part of modern medicine.
7 Antibiotics are a type of antimicrobial that
8 works by either inhibiting the growth of bacteria
9 or killing bacteria. Different families of antibiotics
10 work in different ways. For example, beta-lactam
11 antibiotics, like penicillin, damage the bacteria's
12 cell walls. More specifically, they stop the bacteria
13 from synthesizing a molecule called peptidoglycan
14 which allows the cell wall to survive in the human
15 body. Macrolide antibiotics like erythromycin
16 stop bacterial ribosomes from building proteins
17 that the bacteria need to survive. And quinolone
18 antibiotics, such as ciprofloxacin, stop bacterial
19 DNA replication by targeting an enzyme called
20 DNA gyrase. By damaging the DNA gyrase, strands
21 of replicated DNA permanently break.
22 Regardless of how they work, antibiotics
23 are extremely effective at damaging bacterial cells
24 without harming human cells. However, they can
25 sometimes inadvertently kill good bacteria which
26 are naturally found in the human body. Good
27 bacteria, like bifidobacteria, help humans stay
28 healthy by supporting biological processes such
29 as digestion. When a person loses a significant
30 amount of good bacteria, it becomes easier for
31 other types of bacteria to multiply. This can lead to
32 an opportunistic infection, in which a potentially
33 harmful bacteria is able to multiply quickly since
34 there are no good bacteria to keep it under control.
35 The unchecked proliferation of an opportunistic
36 bacteria, such as clostridium difficile, can cause
37 nausea, inflammation, and fever.
38 Overall though, antibiotics are a safe and
39 important part of modern medical treatments. They
40 treat life-threatening infections such as sepsis, are
41 used to prevent infections after surgery, and treat
42 many common ailments such as ear infections.
43 In fact, one of the greatest concerns of modern
44 medicine is antibiotic resistance, which occurs
45 when bacteria develop defences against antibiotics,
46 making them less effective or completely
47 ineffective. Bacteria can develop these resistance
48 mechanisms relatively quickly, making it difficult
49 to continually find new antibiotics to treat these
50 stubborn bacterial infections.

51 Antibiotic resistance has developed
52 because of the misuse and overuse of antibiotics.
53 Antibiotics are sometimes improperly used to treat
54 viral or fungal infections, neither of which respond
55 to antibiotics. Additionally, patients prescribed
56 antibiotics sometimes don't take the entire course
57 of the prescription, leaving some bacteria still
58 alive. When that happens, the remaining bacteria
59 learn how to better defend themselves when
60 they next encounter that same antibiotic. Even
61 when antibiotics are used correctly, they don't
62 necessarily kill every single bacteria and this same
63 phenomenon can occur.
64 A noteworthy example of a bacteria
65 developing antibiotic resistance is a staph infection
66 called Methicillin-resistant Staphylococcus
67 aureus (MRSA). MRSA is a relatively common skin
68 infection which is often contracted in hospitals
69 or nursing homes. In some individuals, especially
70 those who are elderly or who have compromised
71 immune systems, MRSA can cause a more serious
72 infection that affects the heart, bloodstream, bones,
73 and lungs. Since MRSA is resistant to antibiotics, it
74 can take a long time to effectively treat an infected
75 individual. Today, scientists and other researchers
76 are working hard to develop new and innovative
77 antibiotics that are effective against antibiotic
78 resistant bacteria like MRSA.

25. According to the passage, beta-lactam antibiotics negatively affect

    a. bacterial ribosomes.
    b. peptidoglycan.
    c. ciprofloxacin
    d. penicillin.

26. The author includes lines 40 - 42 to show

    a. why antibiotics are necessary.
    b. why antibiotics were invented.
    c. how antibiotics can be harmful.
    d. how antibiotics stop bacterial infections.

27. Based on the information in the passage, opportunistic infections occur because an antibiotic

    a. kills a human's good bacteria.
    b. is overused.
    c. kills human cells.
    d. only partially damages the bad bacteria.

28. As it is used in the passage, "phenomenon" (line 63) most nearly means

    a. mistake.
    b. prodigy.
    c. rarity.
    d. situation.

29. It can be concluded that antibiotics that are "used correctly"(line 61) are

    a. used only for viral or fungal infections.
    b. taken until the symptoms of the bacterial infection clear up.
    c. taken for the prescribed length of time for bacterial infections.
    d. prescribed by a doctor.

30. It can be concluded that in young and healthy individuals, MRSA is primarily an infection of the

    a. bones.
    b. heart.
    c. lungs.
    d. skin.

Questions 31 - 36

1   Although there were loosely formed
2 concepts of stocks and bonds as early as the 12th
3 century, the first formal stock trading is believed
4 to have originated with the formation of the East
5 Indian Trading Companies in 1602. Prior to 1602,
6 chartered ships from Holland, England, France, and
7 other European nations transported goods from the
8 East Indies and Asia to Europe. These voyages were
9 quite dangerous and were often impeded by pirates
10 or storms. To reduce the financial risk of sailing,
11 ship owners would seek investors to pay for the
12 voyage. In return, if the voyage was successful, the
13 investors received part of the profit from the sale of
14 the goods. After the voyage was completed, either
15 successfully or unsuccessfully, the agreement
16 between the ship owners and investors ended.
17   When the East Indian Trading Companies
18 were officially formed in 1602, they modified
19 this investment process. Instead of securing new
20 investors for each voyage, they had backers invest
21 in the company itself and all of its voyages. Each
22 company issued stock, which essentially made
23 the investors part-owners of the company. If
24 the company made money, the stock would pay
25 dividends, which are a portion of the company's
26 profits. The money generated through the sale of
27 stock gave the company a significant amount of
28 funding with which to purchase new ships and
29 goods. In return, the investors made a hefty profit
30 if the voyages went well. Additionally, because the
31 stock was issued on paper, the investors could sell
32 their stock to other financiers if they chose.

33   Over time, this concept of buying and
34 selling stocks led to the formation of the London
35 Stock Exchange in 1773, which was the first
36 regulated stock exchange. In 1790, the first stock
37 exchange was formed in the United States, and in
38 1792 the New York Stock Exchange (NYSE) was
39 established. The NYSE quickly became the most
40 powerful stock exchange in the world, mainly due
41 its fortuitous location. The exchange was positioned
42 at the epicenter of U.S. banks, business, and trade.
43 The NYSE also established more requirements for
44 trading, including significant fees, which helped
45 it gain wealth and long-term stability. Today,
46 the NYSE is still considered the largest and most
47 influential stock exchange in the world.

31. All of the following are ways companies benefit from issuing stock EXCEPT

   a. increased funding.
   b. reduced risk.
   c. less power.
   d. more profits.

32. In line 41, "fortuitous" most nearly means

   a. advantageous.
   b. expensive.
   c. haphazard.
   d. timely.

33. The primary purpose of this passage is to

   a. provide a history of stock trading.
   b. tell the origin story of the NYSE stock exchange.
   c. compare stock trading in the 1600s to the 1700s.
   d. explain how stocks work.

34. The author uses the phrase "Although there were loosely formed concepts of stocks and bonds as early as the 12th century," in lines 1 - 3 to

   a. let readers know the stock market has been around for a long time.
   b. to acknowledge the existence of stocks were around before the documented trading of stocks.
   c. to compare and contrast early stock to the stocks of the East Indian Trading Companies.
   d. to show that these stocks did not actually succeed.

35. Which best describes the organization of lines 1 - 16?

   a. An overview of the stock market is given.
   b. A rationale for stocks is described.
   c. The drawbacks to issuing stocks is examined.
   d. A description of risk is provided.

36. Which of the following is a correct inference?

   a. The New York Stock Exchange was not the first stock exchange in the US.
   b. The investors in the East India Trading Companies rarely lost money.
   c. Stocks could not be sold until the voyage had been completed.
   d. The companies did not have to give up any ownership in order to issue stock.

Section 4: Math
47 Questions, 40 Minutes

Instructions: Each question is followed by four answer choices. Select the best answer.

1. What is the value of the numerical expression $\sqrt{16+9}$?

    a. 1
    b. 5
    c. 7
    d. 12

2. Three vertices of a parallelogram are shown below. What are the coordinates of the fourth vertex?

    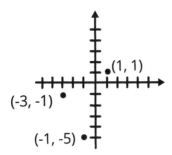

    a. (3, -3)
    b. (3, -2)
    c. (-3, -2)
    d. (-3, -3)

3. What is the solution set to the inequality $-4 \le -2x + 2 \le 18$?

    a. $-8 \le x \le 3$
    b. $x \le -8$ or $x \le 3$
    c. $x \le 3$ or $x \le 8$
    d. $8 \le x \le 3$

4. Which of the options below consists of both a complex number and irrational number?

    a. $\sqrt{8}$

    b. $\sqrt{-7}$

    c. π

    d. $-\dfrac{4589}{781}$

5. For what value(s) of p is the equation $\dfrac{p-5}{5-p} = 1$ true?

    a. -5 only
    b. 0 only
    c. all real numbers except 5
    d. there are no values for p that make the equation true

6. Janet brings a selection of juice boxes to share with her team after their soccer game. 7 boxes contain apple juice, 5 boxes contain grape juice, and 9 boxes contain fruit punch. The first three players take fruit punch. Janet chooses fourth and decides to pick a box at random. What is the probability that Janet will NOT pick fruit punch?

    Note: round to the nearest percent.

    a. 25%
    b. 33%
    c. 50%
    d. 67%

7. How many unique prime factors does the number 210 have?

    a. 1
    b. 2
    c. 3
    d. 4

8. What is the result of the expression below.

$$4 \begin{bmatrix} -1 \\ 3 \\ 6 \\ -5 \end{bmatrix}$$

a. $\begin{bmatrix} 3 \\ 7 \\ 10 \\ -1 \end{bmatrix}$

b. $\begin{bmatrix} -4 \\ 12 \\ 24 \\ -20 \end{bmatrix}$

c. $\begin{bmatrix} -4 \\ 12 \\ 24 \\ -5 \end{bmatrix}$

d. $\begin{bmatrix} 4 \\ 12 \\ 24 \\ 5 \end{bmatrix}$

9. The stem-and-leaf plot below represents the number of cars that go through a car wash on each day of a month. What is the range of the data?

Stem	Leaf
1	2 2 3 5 5 6
2	0 0 1 2 2 3 5
3	4 5 5 6 7 7 8
4	2 7 7 7 9 9
5	0 2 2 3

a. 34
b. 38
c. 41
d. 51

10. There are 5,280 feet in a mile. Vikram walks at a speed of 3 miles an hour. Which expression shows how many feet he walks per minute?

a. $\dfrac{5,280 \times 3}{60 \times 60}$

b. $\dfrac{60}{5,280 \times 3}$

c. $\dfrac{5,280 \times 3}{60}$

d. $\dfrac{3 \times 60}{5,280}$

11. Sasha has a photograph that is 3 inches tall and 5 inches wide. She wants to enlarge the picture so that the new width is 20 inches. How tall will the enlarged photograph be?

a. 8 inches
b. 12 inches
c. 15 inches
d. 22 inches

12. Which expression is equivalent to the expression $3x^2(5x^4y + 2x^3 + 7)$?

a. $15x^6y + 6x^5 + 21x^2$
b. $15x^6y + 6x^3 + 21$
c. $15x^8y + 6x^6 + 21x^2$
d. $15x^4y + 6x^3 + 21x^2$

13. Maria is trying to determine which new lunch options at her school's cafeteria are most popular with students. Which group would give her the most reliable information about the students' preferences?

a. her classmates' parents
b. all of the students in her homeroom
c. a random sample from her group of friends
d. a random sample of students at the school

14. Find the midpoint of the line segment defined by the points A (2, -4) and B (4, -8).

a. (1, 2)
b. (1, -6)
c. (3, -6)
d. (3, 2)

15. In a standard xy coordinate plane if point (7, -2) is reflected over the x axis, what is the location of the new point?

    a. (-7, -2)
    b. (-2, 7)
    c. (2, -7)
    d. (7, 2)

16. A library tracks the number of books checked out by its first 10 library patrons. The data is summarized in the graph below. What is the mode of the data?

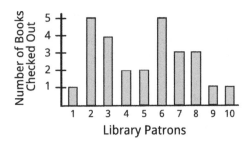

    a. 1
    b. 2
    c. 3
    d. 4

17. The difference of two numbers is 6. The larger number is three times the value of the smaller number. What is the larger number?

    a. 3
    b. 6
    c. 9
    d. 12

18. Convert 15% to a fraction.

    a. $\frac{3}{20}$

    b. $\frac{7}{25}$

    c. $\frac{6}{20}$

    d. $\frac{1}{2}$

19. Solve: $x^2 - 49 = 0$.

    a. $x = -7$
    b. $x = 0$
    c. $x = 7$
    d. $x = -7, 7$

20. Mark is planning a kitchen remodel. His contractor has allowed him to choose from 3 different kinds of cabinets, 2 types of countertops, and 4 styles of flooring. How many different kitchen combinations can Mark create?

    a. 10
    b. 24
    c. 62
    d. 144

21. Which of the following describes all values for x for which $|9x + 1| \geq 17$?

    a. $x \geq -2$ or $x \leq \frac{16}{9}$

    b. $x \leq -2$ or $x \geq \frac{16}{9}$

    c. $\frac{16}{9} \geq x \geq -2$

    d. $-2 \geq x \geq \frac{16}{9}$

22. What is the measure of the smaller angle?

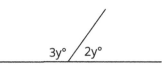

    a. 36°
    b. 60°
    c. 72°
    d. 108°

23. What is the value of the expression $\frac{6.4 \times 10^2}{8.0 \times 10^4}$?

    a. 8.0×10^8
    b. 8.0×10^6
    c. 8.0×10^5
    d. 8.0×10^2

24. A local theater has 1,500 seats. If 870 tickets have been purchased for an upcoming show, what percent of the seats are still available?

    a. 42%
    b. 50%
    c. 58%
    d. 63%

25. The equation for a given line is $3y - 8x = 12$. Which of the following expresses the equation in slope-intercept form?

    a. $y = 2x + 4$

    b. $y = \frac{8}{3}x + 4$

    c. $y = \frac{8}{3}x + 12$

    d. $y = 8x + 4$

26. Triangle PQR is shown below. Which expression is equal to the length of side $\overline{QR}$?

    a. $\dfrac{\cos 63°}{18}$

    b. $18 \cos 63°$

    c. $\dfrac{\sin 63°}{18}$

    d. $18 \sin 63°$

27. Brianna earned test scores of 86%, 91%, 88%, and 83% in her history class. On the final exam, she earned a score of 81%. If the final exam score was counted as two tests when calculating final grades, what was Brianna's mean score?

    a. 80%
    b. 84%
    c. 85%
    d. 88%

28. Which graph represents the solution set of the inequality $-8 \leq 3x - 2 \leq 13$?

    a.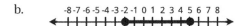

    b.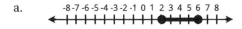

    c.

    d.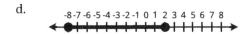

29. The height and base of the triangular prism pictured below are both 2 centimeters less than its length. What is the volume of the prism?

Note: The formula used to determine the volume of a triangular is $V = \frac{1}{2}lbh$, where l is the prism's length, b is the prism's base and h is the prism's height.

    a. 24
    b. 36
    c. 48
    d. 96

30. What is the solution set for $x^2 + 144 = 0$?

    a. 0
    b. 12i
    c. ±12
    d. ±12i

31. A local band is trying to determine if the attendance at their concerts affects the number of band t-shirts they sell at the concert. They track both attendance and shirt sales and plot them in a scatterplot. Based on the data, if they want to sell at least 40 t-shirts a show, at least how many people must attend their show?

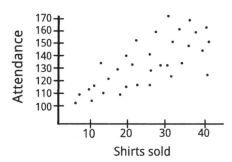

    a. 120
    b. 140
    c. 150
    d. 170

32. The difference of seven squared and two cubed is what number?

    a. 41
    b. 49
    c. 53
    d. 57

33. Lee wants to measure the volume of liquid in a can of soda. What is the most reasonable unit of measure for him to use?

    a. grams
    b. meters
    c. milliliters
    d. gallons

34. Mr. Williams is dividing his students into 5 groups labeled A-E for an upcoming science project. Tina and Marianne are really hoping to work together. If students are assigned to groups randomly and all groups are equal in size, what is the probability that Tina and Marianne will both end up in group A?

    a. 0%
    b. 4%
    c. 20%
    d. 40%

35. A rectangle has an area of 32 in^2. If the sides of the rectangle are integers, what could be the length of the longer side of the rectangle?

    a. 4 in
    b. 6 in
    c. 8 in
    d. 12 in

36. Which expression is equivalent to $\sqrt{49a^8b^2}$?

    a. $7a^4b$
    b. $7a^4b^2$
    c. $7a^8b$
    d. $7a^8b^2$

37. The graph of the function f is shown below. Which of the following could be the equation for f(x)?

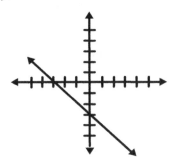

    a. $f(x) = -x + 3$
    b. $f(x) = -x - 3$
    c. $f(x) = x + 3$
    d. $f(x) = x - 3$

38. What is the surface area of the rectangular prism below?

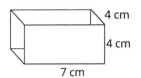

    a. 92 cm^2
    b. 112 cm^2
    c. 128 cm^2
    d. 144 cm^2

39. A nature preserve collected data on the number of hummingbirds spotted in a 100 square meter portion of their preserve. The results are summarized in the table below.

Number of hummingbirds	Probability
1	.5
2	.2
3	.1
4	.2

What is the expected number of hummingbirds in each 100 square meters of the nature preserve?

    a. 1
    b. 2
    c. 3
    d. 4

40. If $\frac{1}{3}x = -\frac{2}{3}(x + 12)$, then what is the value of x?

   a. -24
   b. -8
   c. 4
   d. 8

41. A baseball coach recorded the number of home runs each of its players hit over the course of a season. What is the median number of homeruns?

Homeruns	Numbers of Players Hitting That Number of Home Runs
0	5
1	4
2	3
3	1
4	0

   a. 0
   b. 1
   c. 2
   d. 3

42. Point (-7, 8) is on a circle with center (-5, 10). What is the radius of the circle?

   a. $\sqrt{8}$ grid units
   b. 4 grid units
   c. 8 grid units
   d. 16 grid units

43. What is the seventh number in this sequence?

   11, 6, 1, -4, -9

   a. -14
   b. -15
   c. -19
   d. -20x

44. What is the area of the figure below?

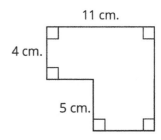

   a. 74 cm²
   b. 82 cm²
   c. 87 cm²
   d. 99 cm²

45. In the figure below, ∠X is congruent to ∠Y. What is the measure of ∠X?

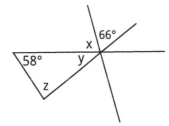

   a. 48°
   b. 54°
   c. 57°
   d. 114°

46. Which expression is equivalent to $x^2 - 12x + 32$?

   a. $(x - 4)(x + 8)$
   b. $(x - 4)(x - 8)$
   c. $(x - 2)(x + 16)$
   d. $(x - 2)(x - 16)$

47. A data set is represented in the box-and-whisker plot below. What is the first quartile of the data?

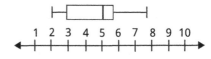

   a. 2
   b. 3
   c. 5
   d. 5.75

Essay
1 Question, 30 Minutes

Instructions: You have 30 minutes to write an essay on the topic below. It is not permitted to write an essay on a different topic. Your essay must be written in blue or black pen.

Please be aware that the schools you apply to will receive a copy of your essay. Your essay should be longer than a paragraph and use specific examples and details.

Write your response on this page and the next page.

Describe your favorite things about your school, neighborhood, or community.

Test 9 Answer Key

Section 1: Verbal

1. D	9. D	17. B	25. D	33. D
2. B	10. C	18. A	26. A	34. D
3. C	11. A	19. C	27. A	35. C
4. D	12. B	20. A	28. A	36. B
5. A	13. D	21. C	29. C	37. D
6. C	14. B	22. B	30. C	38. B
7. B	15. D	23. B	31. A	39. C
8. A	16. D	24. C	32. B	40. B

Section 2: Quantitative

1. A	9. C	17. B	25. A	33. B
2. B	10. C	18. D	26. A	34. A
3. A	11. B	19. B	27. C	35. D
4. B	12. C	20. B	28. B	36. D
5. D	13. C	21. C	29. C	37. D
6. C	14. A	22. D	30. B	
7. A	15. D	23. A	31. B	
8. A	16. D	24. C	32. C	

Section 3: Reading

1. B	9. B	17. B	25. B	33. A
2. C	10. C	18. B	26. A	34. B
3. A	11. B	19. B	27. A	35. B
4. C	12. A	20. D	28. D	36. A
5. D	13. A	21. B	29. C	
6. D	14. B	22. D	30. D	
7. C	15. B	23. B	31. C	
8. D	16. A	24. B	32. A	

Section 4: Math

1. B	11. B	21. B	31. A	41. B
2. A	12. A	22. C	32. A	42. A
3. A	13. D	23. C	33. C	43. C
4. B	14. C	24. A	34. B	44. A
5. C	15. D	25. B	35. C	45. C
6. D	16. A	26. D	36. A	46. B
7. D	17. C	27. C	37. B	47. B
8. B	18. A	28. B	38. D	
9. C	19. D	29. C	39. B	
10. C	20. B	30. D	40. B	

ISEE Test 10

Section 1: Verbal
40 Questions, 20 Minutes

Synonyms
Instructions: Select the word whose meaning is closest to the word in capital letters.

1. ADAPT:

   a. certain
   b. modify
   c. please
   d. quick

2. ENTICE:

   a. allure
   b. enjoy
   c. entertain
   d. enry

3. VETO:

   a. avoid
   b. meet
   c. reject
   d. vote

4. SPITE:

   a. bad
   b. fairy
   c. malice
   d. saliva

5. SCOFF:

   a. manipulate
   b. mock
   c. slander
   d. trouble

6. TEMPESTUOUS:

   a. attitude
   b. temperament
   c. tornado
   d. violent

7. PROVIDENTIAL:

   a. bank
   b. gift
   c. kind
   d. opportune

8. QUERY:

   a. anomaly
   b. inquiry
   c. puzzle
   d. quest

9. ODIOUS:

   a. livid
   b. musical
   c. smelly
   d. revolting

10. MOTIF:

    a. detail
    b. motion
    c. motive
    d. pattern

11. IRE:

    a. iron
    b. irritant
    c. rage
    d. revolt

12. TOTTER:

    a. lengthen
    b. manipulate
    c. turn
    d. wobble

13. PETITE:

    a. childish
    b. French
    c. microscopic
    d. slight

14. GLUTTON:

    a. abstain
    b. food
    c. greed
    d. gully

15. EXTENSIVE:

    a. expand
    b. intense
    c. substantial
    d. existential

16. CONCUR:

    a. agree
    b. concise
    c. disjoint
    d. head

17. CIRCUMSPECT:

    a. appalled
    b. confused
    c. suspect
    d. wary

18. BRAZEN:

    a. bashful
    b. bold
    c. rancid
    d. rash

19. AGILE:

    a. articulate
    b. dull
    c. spry
    d. wistful

Sentence Completion

Instructions: Select the word or pair of words that best completes the sentence.

20. The former president refused to ------- a particular candidate citing he had too many friends in the race.

    a. acknowledge
    b. alienate
    c. endorse
    d. pay

21. Her support for her daughter never ------- even after she found out that she cheated on her exam.

    a. began
    b. improved
    c. questioned
    d. waned

22. The tattered, worn couch did not create the luxurious ------- the realtor hoped would quickly sell the house.

    a. ambiance
    b. artifact
    c. facility
    d. tempo

23. People can still spread a disease even when they have no symptoms and should be considered -------.

    a. asymptomatic
    b. contagious
    c. dangerous
    d. ill

24. It is well known that trees benefit our ------- health, making it easier for everyone to breathe.

    a. atmospheric
    b. communal
    c. immediate
    d. respiratory

25. Contrary to popular belief, poinsettia plants are not actually poisonous to cats; they are not ------- and may only cause mild stomach irritation.

    a. acute
    b. contaminated
    c. fatal
    d. terminal

26. Never believing in extremes, my mother's favorite saying is "Everything in ------- ."

    a. adequation
    b. moderation
    c. purpose
    d. time

27. The student looked ------- when the principal accused her of cheating on the test; she hadn't even been to class that day.

    a. bewildered
    b. elated
    c. rambunctious
    d. stoic

28. After her dog passed away, the warmth and ------- expressed by her peers was almost overwhelming.

    a. compassion
    b. congenialness
    c. timidity
    d. withdrawal

29. After Alma won the modeling contest it was impossible to ignore her -------; she exuded confidence and vivaciousness.

    a. adjustment
    b. flamboyance
    c. personally
    d. temper

30. The new city council was unanimously voted in by the community, giving them a(n) ------- to make the necessary changes.

    a. choice
    b. explanation
    c. link
    d. mandate

31. Alternative energy sources use ------- to move things like air or water around.

    a. animals
    b. hydraulics
    c. turbines
    d. wheels

32. The kitchen remodel progressed ------- despite lots of ------- to speed the process up.

    a. haltingly . . . predicaments
    b. quickly . . . reasons
    c. rapidly . . . benefits
    d. slowly . . . incentives

33. Loneliness affects all of us at some point even when we don't live ------- or in -------.

    a. alone . . . seclusion
    b. reclusion . . . isolation
    c. solitary . . . homes
    d. solo . . . groups

34. Many Americans have a(n) ------- to dairy and will often become ill if they ------- too much.

    a. adoration . . . consume
    b. allergy . . . tolerate
    c. aversion . . . eat
    d. intolerance . . . ingest

35. The library will ------- close their doors at least until the ------- weather passes, and it's safe for people to travel.

    a. eventually . . . temperate
    b. permanently . . . stormy
    c. temporarily . . . inclimate
    d. ultimately . . . benign

36. Miniature pinschers are a dog breed that ------- doberman pinschers; they are several centuries older and despite looking like a miniature doberman, they are a(n) ------- between Italian greyhounds and dachshunds.

    a. dominate . . . hybrid
    b. mimic . . . mix
    c. predate . . . cross
    d. resemble . . . alliance

37. Traffic ------- has/have been greatly -------now that department of transportation has turned the one lane highway into two lanes.

    a. accidents . . . aggravated
    b. congestion . . . reduced
    c. patterns . . . curtailed
    d. zones . . . impacted

38. Despite high levels of security, a surprisingly ------- amount of artwork has been stolen from ------- art museums throughout the world that welcome millions of visitors a year.

    a. abundant . . . obscure
    b. large . . . prominent
    c. miniscule . . . infamous
    d. small . . . diminutive

39. The school year will not be ------- even though the district has not met the ------- days of attendance.

    a. changed . . . additional
    b. extended . . . mandatory
    c. lengthened . . . maximum
    d. shortened . . . required

40. ------- in the weather are normal during the spring and fall when temperatures ------- change as much as twenty degrees in a 24 hour period.

    a. Disruptions . . . placidly
    b. Fluctuations . . . drastically
    c. Templates . . . ordinarily
    d. Variations . . . mildly

Section 2: Quantitative
37 Questions, 35 Minutes

The section is divided into two parts: problem solving and quantitative comparison. Directions for each part are provided.

Part 1 - Problem Solving

Instructions: Each question is followed by four possible answers. Select the best answer.

1. What is the minimum value for y if y = -2x - 4 and -4 < x < 0?

   a. -12
   b. -6
   c. -4
   d. 0

2. The net for a cube is shown below.

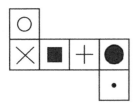

   Which of the following is a possible view of the folded cube?

   a.

   b.

   c.

   d.

3. The average of 4 values is 4. If the smallest value is increased by 8 and the largest value is decreased by 2, what is the new average?

   a. 4
   b. 4.5
   c. 5
   d. 5.5

4. If $\dfrac{ab}{d} = \dfrac{ad}{c}$ which of the following is equal to b?

   a. $\dfrac{ad}{c}$
   b. $\dfrac{d}{c}$
   c. $\dfrac{d^2}{c}$
   d. $\dfrac{d^2}{ac}$

5. A florist surveyed his customers about their favorite type of flowers and put the data in the pie chart below. The most popular flower is roses and least popular is carnations. If lilies and peonies are equally popular, what part of the pie chart represents orchids?

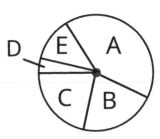

   a. B
   b. C
   c. D
   d. E

6. If $(x+6)(x+y) = x^2 + 2x - 24$, what is the value of y?

   a. -8
   b. -4
   c. 4
   d. 8

7. The graph below represents the temperature changes experienced by a North American city throughout the course of the year.

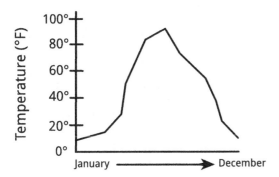

The graph shows that in this city temperatures

   a. peak at several times throughout the year.
   b. hit one peak and one valley throughout a year.
   c. experience several peaks and valleys throughout the year.
   d. peak very late in the year.

8. If the area of triangle ADC is 72 inches², what is the perimeter of square ABCD?

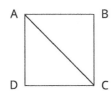

   a. 24 inches
   b. 32 inches
   c. 48 inches
   d. 144 inches

9. What number is half of the least common multiple of 4, 8, and 20?

   a. 4
   b. 16
   c. 20
   d. 40

10. Jaime is instructed to run to the end of a field and then back to where he started as many times as he can in 15 minutes. If Jaime can run 8 feet per second, what other additional piece of information would be required to determine the number of times he crossed the field and returned to the starting point?

    a. The direction and speed of the wind that day
    b. The length of the field, in feet
    c. The speed of those also running across the field
    d. None of the above

11. If the two triangles pictured below are congruent, which of the following must be true?

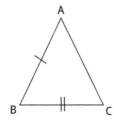 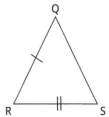

    a. $\angle BAC \cong \angle QRS$
    b. $\angle ABC \cong \angle QSR$
    c. $\overline{AB} \cong \overline{QS}$
    d. $\overline{AC} \cong \overline{QS}$

12. Lines C and D are perpendicular. The equation of line C is $y = \frac{1}{2}x + 5$. Two points on line D are $(3, -1)$ and $(x, -7)$. What is x?

    a. -6
    b. 0
    c. 6
    d. 8

13. On the graph below, each dot represents a different date. What pattern does the graph show?

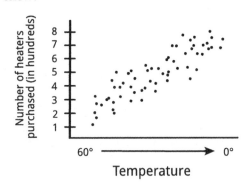

a. There is a strong positive correlation between the temperature and the number of heaters purchased.
b. There is a weak positive correlation between the temperature and the number of heaters purchased.
c. There is a weak negative correlation between the temperature and the number of heaters purchased.
d. There is a strong negative correlation between the temperature and the number of heaters purchased.

14. Nico is sewing a tablecloth for his round patio table. His table has a diameter of 24 inches. If he wants the tablecloth to hang over all edges of the table by four inches, what will be the area of the resulting tablecloth?

a. 28π
b. 32π
c. 142π
d. 162π

15. Which equation represents the statement below?

The square of a number is equal to the quotient of the number and five.

a. $x^2 = x - 5$

b. $x^2 = \dfrac{x}{5}$

c. $2^x = x - 5$

d. $2^x = \dfrac{x}{5}$

16. A bookstore had a huge end of year sale. The bookstore's owner tracked the number of books purchased by 20 different customers during the sale and put it in the histogram below. She then realized that she accidentally marked two customers as having purchased eight books each when they only purchased seven books each. Once she corrects her error, what would the new median of the data be?

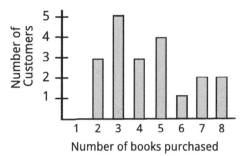

a. 3
b. 4
c. 5
d. 6

17. The formula for the volume of a cone is $V = \dfrac{1}{3}r^2h$, where r represents the radius of the cone's base and h represents the height of the cone. If the radius of a given cone is doubled and the height remains the same, which of the following will be the effect on the cone's volume?

a. The volume of the cone will be cut in half.
b. The volume of the cone will be doubled.
c. The volume of the cone will be tripled.
d. The volume of the cone will be quadrupled.

18. If $d(x) = 10x$, which inequality is true?

a. $d(0) > d(2) > d(4)$
b. $d(0) > d(4) > d(2)$
c. $d(4) > d(2) > d(0)$
d. $d(2) > d(0) > d(4)$

19. The measure of an interior angle of a regular polygon is $\frac{180° \, (n - 2)}{n}$. What is the difference in the measure of an interior angle of a quadrilateral and a pentagon?

    a. 18°
    b. 24°
    c. 30°
    d. 38°

20. A cookie jar contains a mixture of chocolate chip cookies, oatmeal raisin cookies, and sugar cookies. If someone were to reach into the jar and remove one cookie at random, the probability that they would choose a chocolate chip cookie is $\frac{1}{3}$. The probability that they would choose a sugar cookie is $\frac{2}{9}$. Which of the following is greatest?

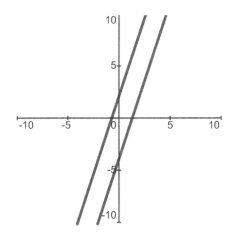

Part 2 - Quantitative Comparisons

Instructions: In each question, use the information provided to compare the quantity in Column A with the quantity in Column B. All quantitative comparison questions have the same answer choices:

    a. The quantity in column A is greater.
    b. The quantity in column B is greater.
    c. The two quantities are equal.
    d. The relationship cannot be determined from the information given.

a. The number of chocolate chip cookies in the jar
b. The number of oatmeal raisin cookies in the jar

c. cookies in the jar
d. There is not enough information given to determine the answer.

21.

Column A	Column B
$(x+3)(x^2 - 3x + 9)$	$x^3 + 33$

$x < 0$

22.

Column A	Column B
$|-2x - 4|$	$|2x + 4|$

The sum of two positive integers is 36. The larger integer is 9 less than two times the smaller integer.

23.

Column A

27

Column B

x is a positive, even integer and y is a negative odd integer.

24.

The larger of the two integers

Column A

x + y Column B

x - y

25.

Column A

The mode of 3, 8, 4, 2, 3

Column B

The mean of 2, 2, 8, 1, 12

26.

Column A

The difference between the slope of lines R and S.

Column B

The y value of the x intercept of line R.

A jar contains 8 marbles: 5 pink marbles and 3 orange marbles. A random marble is removed from the jar and then replaced. Then a second marble is

27. removed.

The probability that both marbles removed are pink

Column A

Column B

The probability that neither of the marbles removed is pink

x < 1

Column A

$10 - \frac{4}{2} + 5x$

28.

Column B

0

29.

$\left(\frac{1}{3}\right)^{-2}$

Column A

Column B

32

z is a

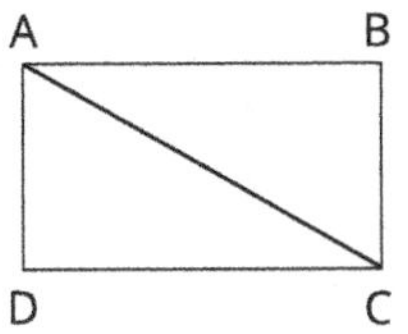

30.

Column A Column B

$\frac{1}{z}$ $\frac{1}{z^2}$

x, y, and z are consecutive integers (x < y < z)

31.

Colur

x - y -

Colur

z - y -

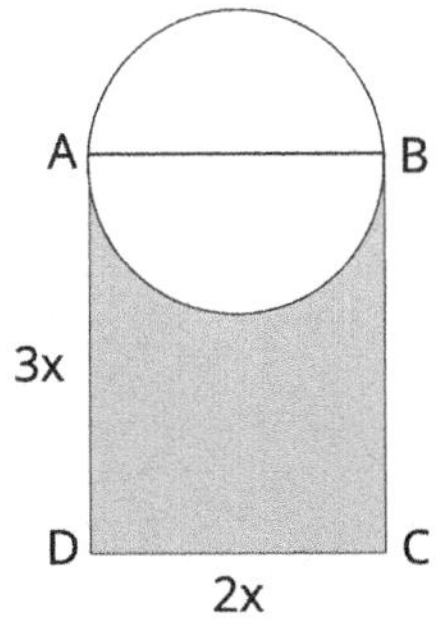

is 4 inches and the area of the rectangle is 20 inches².

32.

Column A

The area of △ABC

Column B The perimeter of the rectangle

ABCD is a rectangle. $\overline{AB}$ is the diameter of the circle pictured.

Column A

The perimeter of ABCD

33.

Column B

The perimeter of the shaded region

Let $p(x) = (x + 1)^2$ and $q(x) = x^2 + 10$.

34.

Column A

p(5)

Column B

q(5)

Leah put $300 into a savings account. The account earns 1% compound interest each month, and

Section 3: Reading
36 Questions, 35 Minutes

Instructions: Carefully read each passage and answer the questions that follow it. For each question, decide which of the choices best answers the question based on the passage.

Questions 1 - 6

1 Throughout human history, the beauty
2 and ethereal quality of rainbows have made them
3 the source of legends. These myths, many of
4 which involve leprechauns and pots of gold, have
5 attempted to explain what rainbows are and why
6 they occur. Today we know that while rainbows
7 may seem tangible, they are actually optical
8 illusions that appear when specific meteorological
9 conditions are met.
10 For a rainbow to materialize, water
11 droplets must be suspended in the air, which is
12 why rainbows so often appear after a rainstorm.
13 Sunlight must also be present and has to shine on
14 droplets of water from a slightly upward angle. The
15 water slows the light down, causing it to refract,
16 or bend. The refracted light then reflects within
17 the water droplet in what is known as internal
18 reflection. Then, as the light exits the water
19 droplet, the sunlight reenters the air, speeding
20 up and refracting into wavelengths of light. Each
21 wavelength appears as a different color depending
22 on the angle at which the light bends. Since violet
23 has the shortest wavelength, it bends the most.
24 Red, which has the longest wavelength, bends the
25 least. This is why violet is always at the bottom of a
26 rainbow and red is always at the top.
27 Even after these conditions are present,
28 a person must be in precisely the right place to
29 actually see the rainbow. Rainbows always occur
30 in the opposite direction of the sun, so a viewer
31 must have their back to the sun. They must also be
32 viewing the rainbow at a 42-degree angle for the
33 wavelengths of light to reach them.

34 An even more rare phenomenon is the
35 double rainbow in which one rainbow appears
36 on top of another. In double rainbows, the lower,
37 primary rainbow is brighter and the higher,
38 secondary rainbow is fainter. The secondary
39 rainbow occurs when the light within the rainbow
40 is reflected a second time. This re-reflected light
41 leaves the rainbow at a higher angle, which is
42 why the secondary rainbow appears above the
43 primary rainbow. The double reflection also causes
44 a reversal of the secondary rainbow's colors with
45 violet at the top and red at the bottom.
46 Sometimes, a similar illusion called a
47 white rainbow, or fogbow, occurs. White rainbows
48 often appear on foggy days and are created by the
49 same optical phenomena that produce their more
50 colorful counterparts. However, the water droplets
51 present in fog are much smaller than those in
52 traditional rainbows, so instead of being refracted
53 into different wavelengths, the light is diffused.
54 Essentially, the light gets scattered, resulting in
55 a fuzzy white light in the shape of a rainbow.
56 Interestingly, white rainbows can also be caused by
57 moonlight!

1. This passage is primarily concerned with

   a. clarifying how fogbows are different than regular rainbows.
   b. debunking myths about rainbows.
   c. explaining how different types of rainbows form.
   d. describing the best way to see a rainbow.

2. Based on the information in the passage, it can be concluded that colorful rainbows refract light

   a. into only red and violet wavelengths.
   b. only after the light leaves the water droplet.
   c. once the lightwave slows down.
   d. into different wavelengths.

3. When a colorful rainbow occurs, which of the following happens to the sunlight within a water droplet?

   a. It diffuses.
   b. It refracts.
   c. It reflects.
   d. It speeds up.

4. The author includes the third paragraph to explain

   a. where rainbows occur.
   b. why it is so hard to see a rainbow.
   c. why rainbows appear in the opposite direction of the sun.
   d. how to see a double rainbow.

5. White rainbows scatter light rather than refract light because

   a. the water droplets are too small to refract light.
   b. there is more intense sunlight present.
   c. the light is re-refracted.
   d. the light is reflected within the water droplet.

6. It can be inferred that white rainbows were given the nickname fogbows because they

   a. occur when there is no fog.
   b. are difficult to see when there is fog.
   c. look like fog.
   d. often occur on foggy days.

Questions 7 - 12

1   Constitutional amendments, which modify
2 the Constitution in some way, are notoriously
3 difficult to pass. Throughout the history of
4 the United States, over 11,600 constitutional
5 amendments have been presented to Congress but
6 only 27 have ever been ratified.
7   Ratifying an amendment is a long and
8 complicated process. An amendment must first
9 be proposed, which requires either a two-thirds
10 vote in Congress or approval through a national
11 convention made up of two-thirds of the states.
12 Interestingly, as of 2020, all ratified constitutional
13 amendments had been proposed by Congress,
14 not the states. Once the amendment is officially
15 proposed, it must be ratified, which occurs at
16 the state level. Most commonly, three-fourths of
17 state legislatures must approve the amendment.
18 However, it's also possible for states to set up
19 conventions for ratification, which is the way that
20 the 21st Amendment was ratified.
21   This process can take quite a long time
22 and is best illustrated by the 27th Amendment's
23 200 year long road to ratification. This amendment
24 simply states that any raise that Congress gives
25 itself will take effect in the next congressional
26 term. James Madison, who proposed the original
27 amendment, hoped it would stop members of
28 Congress from giving themselves exorbitant raises.
29 And if members did abuse their power, it would
30 give voters the ability to remove them from office
31 before the raise would take effect. Although this
32 amendment was proposed in 1789 as part of the
33 original Bill of Rights, it did not pass in enough
34 states to be ratified.

35   Fast forward to 1982 when a college
36 sophomore named Gregory Watson was doing
37 research for his government class at the University
38 of Texas at Austin. Watson pulled out a book that
39 listed proposed, but unratified, amendments.
40 One stuck out to him immediately - Madison's
41 amendment about congressional pay. He was
42 shocked to find that only nine states had passed
43 what seemed to be such a logical modification to
44 the Constitution. Watson immediately decided to
45 write a paper for his class arguing that the proposed
46 amendment was still viable and could be ratified.
47 His essay earned a C.
48   Surprised by the mediocre grade, Watson
49 appealed to his professor for a higher grade, but she
50 remained unimpressed and refused to acquiesce.
51 In a moment of history-changing stubbornness,
52 Watson decided that he would prove his teacher
53 wrong and get the amendment ratified. Since
54 nine states had already passed the amendment,
55 he needed only 29 more for it to be added to the
56 Constitution. He got to work, contacting members
57 of Congress to see if they could help him get the
58 amendment introduced in their states. After
59 receiving mostly negative responses, he finally
60 convinced a senator from Maine to take the
61 amendment to state officials. Maine passed the
62 amendment in 1983. Throughout the rest of the
63 1980s and early 1990s, more states followed. In
64 1992, Michigan became the 38th state to pass the
65 amendment, the final step in getting it ratified.
66   After 10 years of work, Watson was able
67 to get the 27th Amendment added to the U.S.
68 Constitution. Word got back to his old professor,
69 and, in 2017, more than 35 years after he wrote his
70 C paper, she happily changed his grade to an A.

7. Historically, most amendments were proposed by

    a. congress and ratified by state legislatures.
    b. congress and ratified by state convention.
    c. state legislatures and ratified by state legislatures.
    d. state legislatures and ratified by state convention.

8. The phrase "abuse their power" (line 29) refers to congressmen

    a. getting raises in their current term.
    b. getting voted out of office.
    c. being dishonest and corrupt.
    d. giving themselves unreasonable raises.

9. This excerpt is primarily about

    a. the reason Watson wanted to pass the 27th amendment.
    b. the passage of the 27th amendment.
    c. constitutional amendments that never were passed.
    d. the history of constitutional amendments.

10. As it is used in the passage, "acquiesce" (line 50) most nearly means

    a. improve.
    b. protest.
    c. stop.
    d. yield.

11. It can be inferred that James Madison believed that

    a. members of congress should not be given raises.
    b. the amount of congressional raises should be determined by the public.
    c. members of congress may act immorally if there is no rule in place to stop them.
    d. all congressmen have the right to yearly raises.

12. The author included lines 56 - 65 to show

    a. why Watson thought passing the amendment was important.
    b. Watson's persistence.
    c. that Watson was overly optimistic.
    d. Watson's frustration.

Questions 13 - 18

1   Across the United States, Americans
2 are turning their gardens into habitats for
3 butterflies and bees. As we become more aware
4 of how important both bees and butterflies are
5 to pollination, even novice gardeners and those
6 with small spaces are attempting to attract these
7 precious creatures. It's actually quite easy to draw
8 bees and butterflies to your yard, little garden, or
9 even a carefully curated flower pot.
10   There are a few must-haves when it comes
11 to setting up an enticing destination for bees and
12 butterflies. First, locate the part of your garden
13 that gets the most sunlight. Next, consider what
14 shelter you can provide to help the insects hide
15 from predators. Caterpillars, especially, require a
16 secluded spot where they can safely form a pupa or
17 chrysalis. Most garden centers sell butterfly and bee
18 houses, but old logs, dead trees, and tall grass also
19 do the trick. Simply neglecting a portion of your
20 yard and letting it go wild can provide butterflies,
21 bees, and other pollinators a place to live.
22   As for what to plant, think bright, colorful
23 flowers. Just make sure to pick flowers that are
24 nectar and pollen-rich. The best types of flowers for
25 your garden depend on the part of the country you
26 live in. In general, try to pick plants that bloom at
27 various times throughout the spring, summer, and
28 fall. Nectar-rich tubular plants like hollyhocks and
29 petunias are excellent choices. Pollen-rich flowers
30 include sunflowers and marigolds.

31   Milkweed is one of the most important
32 plants butterfly enthusiasts can grow. Essential for
33 monarch butterflies, milkweed is the only plant that
34 they'll lay their eggs on. Often considered a weed,
35 this plant has been disappearing because of land
36 development and pesticides. Many organizations
37 across the country will happily send you milkweed
38 seeds for a small donation.
39   Like all living things, bees and butterflies
40 need access to water. A bird bath or shallow area of
41 water gives them the nutrients they need to survive.
42 It's important to change the water frequently,
43 especially during mosquito season. Creating a bee
44 or butterfly habitat not only helps these dwindling
45 populations, but also provides you with enjoyment
46 in your own space.

13. In order to help monarch butterflies, what is the most important thing gardeners can do?

    a. Provide shelter.
    b. Plant milkweed.
    c. Locate a sunny spot.
    d. Neglect your yard.

14. The main purpose of this passage is to

    a. convince people of the importance in saving bee and butterfly populations.
    b. explain how to attract bees and butter-flies.
    c. analyze why so many Americans are creating bee and butterfly gardens.
    d. alter our viewpoints on pollination.

15. You can infer from the passage that during the summer months water must be changed frequently in order to

    a. prevent mold from spreading.
    b. keep mosquitoes from laying eggs.
    c. save mosquitoes from drowning.
    d. keep the water temperature cool.

16. In line 19 "neglecting" most nearly means

    a. abandoning.
    b. cultivating.
    c. disturbing.
    d. ignoring.

17. The passage is organized

    a. by sequential steps one must take to start a bee or butterfly garden.
    b. by putting in order of importance those things needed for a bee or butterfly garden.
    c. by the different components needed to make a bee or butterfly garden.
    d. by examples of what other gardeners have done in their bee or butterfly gardens.

18. The passage's tone can best be described as

    a. alarming.
    b. critical.
    c. entertaining.
    d. informative.

Questions 19 - 24

1   Twenty-eight years after the death of
2 Russian ruler Ivan III, his grandson and namesake
3 assumed the throne. Ivan IV was crowned at merely
4 three years old due to the untimely death of his
5 father. For the next five years, Ivan's mother acted
6 as his regent and maintained stability by continuing
7 the policies of her son's predecessors. However,
8 she died under suspicious circumstances in 1538.
9 Young Ivan was left orphaned and at the mercy
10 of the Russian aristocrats known as Boyars, who
11 attempted to manipulate him for their own gains
12 as they jostled for power. Despite his youth, Ivan
13 was far from naïve. He grew up with a deep-rooted
14 distrust of the nobility—a sentiment that would
15 later shape his infamous reign.
16   When Ivan came of age in 1547, he was
17 officially crowned Czar of Russia in another
18 homage to his deceased grandfather. Though Ivan
19 IV was technically the first to bear the title, Ivan III
20 had sometimes referred to himself as a Czar (a title
21 which is a reference to the great Julius Caesar of the
22 Roman Empire). For all the seeming similarities
23 between Ivans III and IV, the elder Ivan was revered
24 as a glorious and just ruler who united Russia
25 and drove out the oppressive Mongol Empire. His
26 grandson, on the other hand, became a notoriously
27 paranoid despot who massacred his own people.
28 Ivan III was known as Ivan the Great, while Ivan IV
29 was known as Ivan the Terrible.
30   The coronation as Czar allowed Ivan to lay
31 full claim to the throne he'd sat on for more than
32 a decade. He took full advantage of his newfound
33 autonomy as an adult monarch and immediately
34 set to work consolidating and exercising his power
35 with some initially positive results. He brought
36 the first printing press to Russia, ordered the
37 construction of St. Basil's Cathedral, and opened
38 important new trade routes.

39   It wasn't until after the death of his first
40 wife, Anastasia, in 1560 that Ivan the Terrible began
41 to truly live up to his name. As Russia suffered
42 under a slew of famines and droughts, Ivan became
43 obsessively suspicious that Anastasia had been
44 poisoned by the ever-treasonous Boyars, whom he
45 also deemed responsible for his frequent military
46 losses. In 1564, he ran off and abandoned his role
47 as Czar and sent a letter indicating that he was
48 abdicating in protest to the Boyars' treachery. With
49 Russia in chaos, the Boyars could not rule on their
50 own and begged Ivan to come back. He agreed,
51 under the condition that he be granted absolute
52 power.
53   Upon Ivan's return, Boyar land was
54 confiscated and claimed as government property.
55 The Boyars themselves were persecuted, tortured,
56 and killed with impunity by Ivan's brutal political
57 police force, the Oprichniki. When peasants began
58 fleeing due to the constant war and civil unrest,
59 Ivan instituted new laws that forbade them from
60 moving off the land they were born on. Towards the
61 end of his life, he married five wives in nine years.
62 He even murdered his own son. By the time Ivan
63 finally died in 1584, Russia was in tatters.

19. Based on the passage, all of the following are reasons Ivan IV distrusted nobility EXCEPT

    a. he thought they poisoned his wife.
    b. as a child he was manipulated by them.
    c. he was convinced that they had something to do with his military defeats.
    d. he believed they were the reason that the peasants fled.

20. In line 13, "naïve" most nearly means

    a. auspicious.
    b. cynical.
    c. guilty.
    d. ignorant.

21. Which best expresses the main idea of the passage?

    a. Ivan IV did not really deserve the nickname Ivan the Terrible.
    b. Ivan IV had much in common with his grandfather Ivan IV.
    c. Ivan IV's reign started off well but quickly changed after the death of his first wife.
    d. Ivan IV created serfdom which bonded peasants to the land.

22. Which of the following is a correct inference from the passage?

    a. The Mongols had taken over Russia.
    b. Russia was comprised mostly of peasants.
    c. The Boyars killed Ivan's father.
    d. If Ivan's parents had lived he would have been a great leader.

23. What conclusion can be drawn about the Boyars?

    a. They caused the famines in Russia.
    b. They were nobles.
    c. They had more power than Ivan IV.
    d. They did little to stop Ivan's treachery.

24. The purpose of the third paragraph (lines 30 - 38) is to

    a. prove Ivan IV was not all terrible.
    b. show how Ivan IV got his name.
    c. contrast Ivan the Great from Ivan the Terrible.
    d. ilustrate Ivan the Great's achievements.

Questions 25 - 30

1 Like many other snug little harbors on the coast of
2 Newfoundland, Ruddy Cove is confronted by the
3 sea and flanked by a vast wilderness, abd all the
4 folk take their living from the sea as they have done
5 for generations.
6
7 It takes courage and a will for work to sweeten the
8 hard life of those parts, which otherwise would be
9 filled with an intolerable weariness, and Donald
10 North of Ruddy Cove was brave enough till he
11 was eight years old. But after that he was so timid
12 that he shrank from the edge of the cliffs when the
13 breakers were beating the rocks below. He was a
14 fisherman's son; thus the mishap which gave him
15 that great fear of the sea cast a dark shadow over
16 him.
17
18 "Billy," he said to his friend on the unfortunate day,
19 "leave us go sail my new miniature boat. I've rigged
20 her out with a grand new sail."
21
22 "Sure!" said Billy. "Where to?"
23
24 "Uncle George's wharf. 'Tis a place as good as any."
25
26 Off Uncle George's wharf the water was deep and
27 cold. Its clear waters covered a rocky bottom, upon
28 which a multitude of starfish laid in clusters and
29 purple-shelled mussels gripped the rocks.
30
31 The tide had fallen and was still on the ebb. Donald
32 found it a long reach from the wharf to the water.
33 The most he could do was to touch the mast tip of
34 the miniature ship with his fingers. Then a little
35 gust of wind crept round the corner of the wharf,
36 catching the sails of the tiny vessel, and the little
37 craft shot away.
38
39 "Come back, will you?" Donald cried.
40
41 He reached for the mast. His fingers touched it, but
42 the boat escaped before they closed. He laughed,
43 hitched nearer to the wharf's edge, and reached
44 again. The little boat was tossing in the ripples,
45 below and just beyond his grasp.

46 "I can't catch her!" he called to Billy, who was
47 farther back, looking for squids.
48
49 Billy looked up, and laughed to see Donald's
50 awkward position—to see him hanging over the
51 water, red-faced and straining. Donald laughed,
52 too. At once he lost his balance and fell forward.
53
54 This was in the days before he could swim, so he
55 floundered about in the water, beating it wildly.
56 When he came to the surface, Billy was leaning
57 over to catch him. Donald lifted his arm. His fingers
58 touched Billy's; that was all. Then he sank, and
59 when he came up again and lifted his arm, there
60 was half a foot of space between his hand and
61 Billy's. Some measure of self-possession returned.
62 He took a breath, and let himself sink.
63
64 Those moments were full of the terror of which,
65 later, Donald could not rid himself. But when his
66 feet touched bottom, he was deliberate in all that
67 he did.
68
69 For a moment he let them rest on the rock. Then
70 he gave himself a strong upward push. It took little
71 effort to bring him within reach of Billy's hand. He
72 easily was pulled out of the water and was soon safe
73 on the wharf.
74
75 But Donald was haunted by what might have
76 happened. Soon he became a timid lad, utterly
77 lacking confidence. He was afraid to go out to the
78 fishing grounds, where he must go every day with
79 his father, and he had a great fear of the wind and
80 the breakers.
81
82 But he was not a coward. On the contrary, although
83 he was circumspect in all his dealings with the sea,
84 he never failed in his duty.

25. The primary purpose of the passage is to

    a. explain why Donald is afraid of the sea.
    b. clarify how Donald fell into the sea.
    c. show a typical day in Ruddy Cove.
    d. demonstrate why it's important to know how to swim.

26. Billy and Donald went to the wharf to

    a. go sailing in their boat.
    b. go fishing.
    c. sail a toy boat.
    d. look for mussels.

27. What figure of speech does the author use in lines 34 - 37?

    a. personification
    b. simile
    c. hyperbole
    d. irony

28. All of the following factors contributed to Donald's fall into the water EXCEPT

    a. he was distracted.
    b. the water was far below the wharf.
    c. he was leaning over the edge of the wharf.
    d. he tried to jump in.

29. In line 62, Donald "let himself sink" because he

    a. had given up.
    b. was trying to swim away.
    c. wanted to reach the bottom so he could push back up.
    d. didn't know what to do.

30. As it is used in the passage, "circumspect" (line 83) most nearly means

    a. aggressive.
    b. cautious.
    c. firm.
    d. wild.

Questions 31 - 36

1   The human brain is incredibly complex,
2 and there are countless approaches to addressing
3 mental health challenges. Many of the most
4 common methods recommended by mental health
5 professionals, however, can be classified using
6 three categories: therapy, medication, and social
7 support. It is important to remember that each of
8 these categories encompasses numerous, distinct
9 forms of treatment. Though certain approaches
10 may be recommended for specific conditions, most
11 are more widely applicable. Furthermore, many
12 people find that a combination of treatments best
13 meets their needs.
14   Psychotherapy, also known as "talk
15 therapy", is one of the most popular and well-
16 known approaches to mental health treatment.
17 There are multiple kinds of talk therapy, including
18 client-centered therapy (CCT) and cognitive
19 behavioral therapy (CBT). Experiential therapy
20 (such as art therapy, music therapy, and animal-
21 assisted therapy) is another widely recognized
22 option.
23   Pharmacological interventions in the
24 form of psychiatric medication can be another
25 effective way to treat mental illness. When carefully
26 diagnosed, prescribed, and monitored, medication
27 can have very high success rates.

28   Social support may be the least formalized
29 of the treatment categories, but is no less
30 important. Social relationships play a key role in
31 establishing and protecting wellbeing, and leaning
32 on a strong support network can demonstrably
33 lower negative outcomes in times of crisis.
34 Structured peer support groups allow people who
35 are coping with specific life scenarios (such as grief,
36 trauma, or addiction) to gain emotional support
37 and coping tools through discussing the issue with
38 those who have similar experiences.
39   Studies show that between 20-25% of
40 Americans experience some form of mental
41 illness every year. Fortunately, most mental health
42 conditions are treatable, and available treatment
43 options have dramatically expanded and improved
44 in recent years thanks to research, outreach,
45 and advocacy efforts. These efforts have also
46 increased public awareness around the prevalence
47 of mental health issues and helped promote the
48 normalization of seeking treatment. Evidence
49 suggests that the increased visibility and reduced
50 stigma associated with mental illness has led more
51 Americans to seek support than ever before, though
52 many barriers still exist that can prevent people
53 from accessing care.

31. Which best describes the organization of the passage?

    a. Different types of mental health treatments are compared.
    b. The process of treating someone with mental health issues is explained.
    c. An opinion about mental health is given and supported by facts.
    d. The history of mental health is traced from past to present.

32. According to the author, in most cases _____ is the best approach to addressing mental health.

    a. medication
    b. talk therapy
    c. social support
    d. a combination of treatments

33. The article answers all of the following EXCEPT

    a. why treatment for mental health has improved.
    b. what the barriers are for getting treatment.
    c. who benefits most from social support.
    d. what the different types of talk therapy are.

34. The author's tone is best described as

    a. direct.
    b. informal.
    c. inspirational.
    d. urgent.

35. In line 8, "distinct" most nearly means

    a. ambiguous.
    b. concise.
    c. similar.
    d. unique.

36. Which conclusion can be drawn from the third paragraph (lines 23 - 27)?

    a. If not carefully monitored, pharmacological interventions can be dangerous.
    b. People should not rely on medication alone.
    c. Medication should only be used as a last resort.
    d. Medication should be part of all mental health treatment plans.

Section 4: Math
47 Questions, 40 Minutes

Instructions: Each question is followed by four answer choices. Select the best answer.

1. What is the measure of ∠ x?

    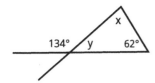

    a. 46°
    b. 56°
    c. 62°
    d. 72°

2. Convert 36% to a fraction.

    a. $\frac{9}{25}$

    b. $\frac{19}{50}$

    c. $\frac{12}{25}$

    d. $\frac{18}{5}$

3. In the xy coordinate plane, a line segment with endpoints R (2,-6) and S (2, 3) is rotated 180° clockwise about the origin. What will be the resulting coordinates of point S after these transformations?

    a. (-3, 2)
    b. (-2, 6)
    c. (-2, -3)
    d. (2, -3)

4. In the figure below, ∠ X is congruent to ∠ Y. What is the measure of ∠ Z?

    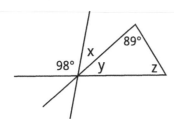

    a. 41°
    b. 47°
    c. 50°
    d. 82°

5. Lincoln Middle School requires 3 adult chaperones for every 15 students on field trips. If 75 students are going on a trip to the museum, how many chaperones are needed?

    a. 15
    b. 18
    c. 20
    d. 25

6. A snow removal company plows the driveways of homeowners in five different neighborhoods. The number of driveways plowed in each neighborhood is represented in the chart below. If each dot represents one driveway, what is the mode of the data?

    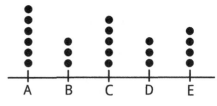

    Neighborhoods

    a. 2
    b. 3
    c. 4
    d. 6

7. Jonas wants to determine the average time 9th grade students in his high school wake up each morning. Which sample of students will give him the most reliable information?

    a. a random sample of 9th grade students at his school
    b. all of the 9th grade students in his honors English class
    c. a random sample of students from all grades at his school
    d. all of the 9th grade students who arrive to school late on a given day

8. The formula for the surface area of a sphere is $4\pi r^2$, where r is the radius of the sphere. If a sphere has a diameter of 6 cm, what is the surface area of the sphere?

    a. 12π cm^2
    b. 24π cm^2
    c. 36π cm^2
    d. 144π cm^2

9. In the image below, a smaller rectangle is inscribed in a larger rectangle. The side lengths of the smaller rectangle are one-quarter of the side lengths of the larger rectangle. What is the area of the shaded region?

    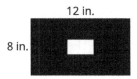

    12 in.

    8 in.

    a. 6 in^2
    b. 88 in^2
    c. 90 in^2
    d. 96 in^2

10. Ankit earned scores of 78, 84, 72, and 81 on his first four chemistry tests. What is the minimum score Ankit needs on his next test in order to increase his mean score to at least 80?

    a. 75
    b. 80
    c. 85
    d. 90

11. The equation for distance is d = rt, where r represents the rate of travel and t represents time. Which of the following shows the equation for t in terms of d and r?

    a. $t = dr$
    b. $t = \dfrac{d}{r}$
    c. $t = \dfrac{r}{d}$
    d. $t = \dfrac{1}{dr}$

12. What is the value of the expression $2.9 \times 10^5 + 7.2 \times 10^4$?

    a. 2.972×10^5
    b. 3.62×10^5
    c. 10.1×10^5
    d. 10.1×10^9

13. Which numerical expression represents a positive integer?

    a. $\sqrt{25 - 9}$
    b. $\sqrt{25 + 9}$
    c. $\sqrt{9} - \sqrt{25}$
    d. $\dfrac{\sqrt{9}}{\sqrt{25}}$

14. There are 5,280 feet in a mile. Juan runs at a speed of 6 feet per second. Which expression shows how many miles he runs per hour?

    a. $\dfrac{6 \times 60}{5,280 \times 60}$
    b. $\dfrac{5,280}{6 \times 60 \times 60}$
    c. $\dfrac{5,280 \times 6}{60 \times 60}$
    d. $\dfrac{6 \times 60 \times 60}{5,280}$

15. The product of two irrational numbers can result in

    a. an irrational number only
    b. a rational number only
    c. a rational or irrational number
    d. an irrational and complex number

16. Which graph represents the solution set of the inequality $4 \le 2x - 8 \le 6$?

    a. -8 -7 -6 -5 -4 -3 -2 -1 0 1 2 3 4 5 6 7 8

    b. -8 -7 -6 -5 -4 -3 -2 -1 0 1 2 3 4 5 6 7 8

    c. -8 -7 -6 -5 -4 -3 -2 -1 0 1 2 3 4 5 6 7 8

    d. -8 -7 -6 -5 -4 -3 -2 -1 0 1 2 3 4 5 6 7 8

17. The graph of the function g is shown below. Which of the following could be the equation for g(x)?

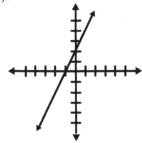

  a. g(x) = -2x + 2
  b. g(x) = -2x - 1
  c. g(x) = 2x - 1
  d. g(x) = 2x + 2

18. Jasmine sorts her bag of colored chocolate candies and counts 4 red candies, 3 blue candies, 3 yellow candies, and 2 orange candies. Her brother comes in and eats some of the red candies. If the probability of selecting a red candy from the candies remaining after her brother eats some is $\frac{1}{5}$, how many red candies did Jasmine's brother eat?

  a. 1
  b. 2
  c. 3
  d. 4

19. Solve: $x^2 - 10x - 24 = 0$.

  a. x = 6, -4
  b. x = -6, -4
  c. x = 12, -2
  d. x = 12, 2

20. 72 is 20% of what number?

  a. 92
  b. 144
  c. 216
  d. 360

21. A car's tire has a circumference of 26π inches. What is the tire's diameter?

  a. 13 inches
  b. 26 inches
  c. 13π inches
  d. 169π inches

22. The first four terms of a geometric sequence are shown below.

   1000, 200, 40, 8

   Which term represents the 6th term of this sequence?

  a. $\frac{8}{25}$
  b. $\frac{8}{5}$
  c. 2
  d. 4

23. The stem-and-leaf plot below represents a high school basketball team scored in all of their games over the course of a season. What is the median of the data?

Stem	Leaf
4	6 7 7 7 9 9
5	3 4 5 5 6 6 8
6	1 2 2 3 7 9 9 9
7	1 2 2 3

  a. 56
  b. 58
  c. 61
  d. 62

24. What is the result of the expression

$$\begin{bmatrix} 6 & -4 \\ 1 & 3 \end{bmatrix} + \begin{bmatrix} -2 & 5 \\ 0 & 7 \end{bmatrix}?$$

  a. $\begin{bmatrix} 8 & 9 \\ 1 & 10 \end{bmatrix}$
  b. $\begin{bmatrix} 8 & 9 \\ 1 & 3 \end{bmatrix}$
  c. $\begin{bmatrix} 4 & 1 \\ 1 & 3 \end{bmatrix}$
  d. $\begin{bmatrix} 4 & 1 \\ 1 & 10 \end{bmatrix}$

25. What is the area of the triangle below?

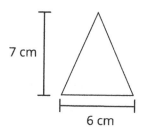

7 cm

6 cm

   a.   13 cm²
   b.   18 cm²
   c.   21 cm²
   d.   42 cm²

26. Triangle XYZ is shown below. Which expression is equal to the length of side $\overline{XZ}$?

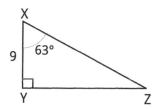

   a. $\dfrac{9}{\cos 63°}$

   b. $\dfrac{\cos 63°}{9}$

   c. $\dfrac{9}{\sin 63°}$

   d. $\dfrac{\sin 63°}{9}$

27. If $ab + b = 5a + 5$, what is the value of b?

   a.   1
   b.   5
   c.   10
   d.   15

28. What is the most reasonable unit of measure to use when measuring the height of a house?

   a.   kilometers
   b.   meters
   c.   kilograms
   d.   grams

29. What is the distance between the points pictured below?

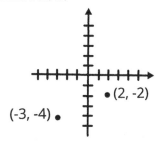

   a. $\sqrt{29}$
   b. $\sqrt{32}$
   c.   7
   d.   29

30. Which of the following describes all values for x for which $|2x + 5| \leq 11$?

   a. $x \leq -8$
   b. $x \leq 3$
   c. $-8 \leq x \leq 3$
   d. $3 \leq x \leq -8$

31. After collecting data from its factories, a manufacturer determined the probability of employees making errors in the manufacturing process. The results are summarized in the table below.

Number of errors per employee per day	Probability
0	$\dfrac{2}{8}$
1	$\dfrac{1}{8}$
2	$\dfrac{1}{8}$
3	$\dfrac{3}{8}$
4	$\dfrac{1}{8}$

What is the expected number of errors per worker?

   a. $1\dfrac{5}{6}$

   b.   2

   c. $2\dfrac{1}{6}$

   d.   3

32. Which expression is equivalent to $x^2 - 25$?

    a. $(x + 25)(x - 1)$
    b. $(x + 5)(x + 5)$
    c. $(x + 5)(x - 5)$
    d. $(x - 25)(x + 1)$

33. What is the first quartile of this data set:

    78, 82, 91, 95, 100, 101

    a. 78
    b. 82
    c. 91
    d. 95

34. Simplify: $\dfrac{8a^4b^9c}{32a^4b^6}$.

    a. $\dfrac{abc}{4}$

    b. $\dfrac{b^3c}{4}$

    c. $\dfrac{ab^3c}{4}$

    d. $4b^3c$

35. The radius of the cylinder pictured below is one-fourth of its height. What is the volume of the cylinder?

12 in.

Note: The formula used to determine the volume of a cylinder is $V = r^2\pi h$, where r is the cylinder's radius, h is the cylinder's height.

    a. 72π in^3
    b. 96π in^3
    c. 108π in^3
    d. 192π in^3

36. A student tracks the local weather over the course of a 30 day month and records the data below. He then makes a circle graph to represent the data. What is the central angle of the portion of the graph representing sunny days?

Type of Weather	Numbers of Days
Sunny	5
Partly Cloudy	9
Cloudy	9
Rainy	7

    a. 30°
    b. 60°
    c. 90°
    d. 120°

37. Tomás and Courtney have a set of 100 index cards numbered 1-100. Tomás picks a card at random and keeps it. Then, Courtney picks a card. If the card that Tomás picked is an even number, what is the probability that the card Courtney chose is an odd number?

    a. $\dfrac{49}{100}$

    b. $\dfrac{49}{99}$

    c. $\dfrac{1}{2}$

    d. $\dfrac{50}{99}$

38. If $\dfrac{y}{100} = 0.54 - 0.26$, what is the value of y?

    a. 2.8
    b. 8
    c. 28
    d. 80

39. Which expression is equivalent to the expression $2z^2(4y^4z + 6z^3 + 5y)$?

    a. $8y^4z + 12z^3 + 10y$
    b. $8y^4z + 12z^3 + 10yz^2$
    c. $8y^4z^2 + 12z^6 + 10yz^2$
    d. $8y^4z^3 + 12z^5 + 10yz^2$

40. The difference of two numbers is 5. The larger number is twice as large as the smaller number. What is the smaller number?

    a. 5
    b. 10
    c. 15
    d. 20

41. A teacher was interested in how much each of her students contributed while doing small group work. She decided to track how many minutes each of the four students in one of her class's groups spoke. The data is summarized in the chart below. What is the range of minutes spoken?

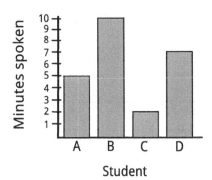

    a. 5
    b. 6
    c. 7
    d. 8

42. Three vertices of a parallelogram are shown below. What are the coordinates of the fourth vertex?

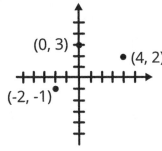

    a. (-3, -6)
    b. (-2, -2)
    c. (1, -2)
    d. (2, -2)

43. Which expression is equivalent to $\frac{\sqrt{64x^2}}{8x}$?

    a. 0
    b. 1
    c. $\frac{x}{8}$
    d. x

44. What is the greatest common factor of 84 and 120?

    a. 2
    b. 4
    c. 12
    d. 24

45. As a freshman in high school Terrell is taking five classes. If he will be able to create his own schedule, how many different schedules could he have?

    a. 50
    b. 120
    c. 230
    d. 700

46. What is the solution set for $x^2 + 81 = 0$?

    a. ±3i
    b. 9i
    c. ±9
    d. ±9i

47. What is the solution set to the inequality $-7 \le 3x + 4 \le 9$?

    a. $1 \le x \le \frac{5}{3}$
    b. $1 \le x \le \frac{13}{3}$
    c. $-\frac{11}{3} \le x \le \frac{5}{3}$
    d. $-\frac{11}{3} \le x \le \frac{13}{3}$

Essay
1 Question, 30 Minutes

Instructions: You have 30 minutes to write an essay on the topic below. It is not permitted to write an essay on a different topic. Your essay must be written in blue or black pen.

Please be aware that the schools you apply to will receive a copy of your essay. Your essay should be longer than a paragraph and use specific examples and details.

Write your response on this page and the next page.

Describe the qualities of a good friend. Why are these qualities important?

Test 10 Answer Key

Section 1: Verbal

1. B	9. D	17. D	25. C	33. A
2. A	10. D	18. B	26. B	34. D
3. C	11. C	19. C	27. A	35. C
4. C	12. D	20. C	28. A	36. C
5. B	13. D	21. D	29. B	37. B
6. D	14. C	22. A	30. D	38. B
7. D	15. C	23. B	31. C	39. B
8. B	16. A	24. D	32. D	40. B

Section 2: Quantitative

1. C	9. C	17. D	25. B	33. B
2. A	10. B	18. C	26. C	34. A
3. D	11. D	19. A	27. A	35. A
4. C	12. C	20. B	28. D	36. D
5. D	13. A	21. C	29. C	37. C
6. B	14. D	22. C	30. A	
7. B	15. B	23. A	31. B	
8. C	16. B	24. B	32. B	

Section 3: Reading

1. C	9. B	17. C	25. A	33. B
2. D	10. D	18. D	26. C	34. A
3. C	11. C	19. D	27. A	35. D
4. B	12. B	20. D	28. D	36. A
5. A	13. B	21. C	29. C	
6. D	14. B	22. A	30. B	
7. A	15. B	23. B	31. A	
8. D	16. D	24. A	32. D	

Section 4: Math

1. D	11. B	21. B	31. B	41. D
2. A	12. B	22. A	32. C	42. D
3. C	13. A	23. B	33. B	43. B
4. C	14. D	24. D	34. B	44. C
5. A	15. C	25. C	35. C	45. B
6. B	16. D	26. A	36. B	46. D
7. A	17. D	27. B	37. D	47. C
8. C	18. B	28. B	38. C	
9. C	19. C	29. A	39. D	
10. C	20. D	30. C	40. A	

Answer Sheets

Test 1 Answer Sheet

Verbal

1. Ⓐ Ⓑ Ⓒ Ⓓ	9. Ⓐ Ⓑ Ⓒ Ⓓ	17. Ⓐ Ⓑ Ⓒ Ⓓ	25. Ⓐ Ⓑ Ⓒ Ⓓ	33. Ⓐ Ⓑ Ⓒ Ⓓ
2. Ⓐ Ⓑ Ⓒ Ⓓ	10. Ⓐ Ⓑ Ⓒ Ⓓ	18. Ⓐ Ⓑ Ⓒ Ⓓ	26. Ⓐ Ⓑ Ⓒ Ⓓ	34. Ⓐ Ⓑ Ⓒ Ⓓ
3. Ⓐ Ⓑ Ⓒ Ⓓ	11. Ⓐ Ⓑ Ⓒ Ⓓ	19. Ⓐ Ⓑ Ⓒ Ⓓ	27. Ⓐ Ⓑ Ⓒ Ⓓ	35. Ⓐ Ⓑ Ⓒ Ⓓ
4. Ⓐ Ⓑ Ⓒ Ⓓ	12. Ⓐ Ⓑ Ⓒ Ⓓ	20. Ⓐ Ⓑ Ⓒ Ⓓ	28. Ⓐ Ⓑ Ⓒ Ⓓ	36. Ⓐ Ⓑ Ⓒ Ⓓ
5. Ⓐ Ⓑ Ⓒ Ⓓ	13. Ⓐ Ⓑ Ⓒ Ⓓ	21. Ⓐ Ⓑ Ⓒ Ⓓ	29. Ⓐ Ⓑ Ⓒ Ⓓ	37. Ⓐ Ⓑ Ⓒ Ⓓ
6. Ⓐ Ⓑ Ⓒ Ⓓ	14. Ⓐ Ⓑ Ⓒ Ⓓ	22. Ⓐ Ⓑ Ⓒ Ⓓ	30. Ⓐ Ⓑ Ⓒ Ⓓ	38. Ⓐ Ⓑ Ⓒ Ⓓ
7. Ⓐ Ⓑ Ⓒ Ⓓ	15. Ⓐ Ⓑ Ⓒ Ⓓ	23. Ⓐ Ⓑ Ⓒ Ⓓ	31. Ⓐ Ⓑ Ⓒ Ⓓ	39. Ⓐ Ⓑ Ⓒ Ⓓ
8. Ⓐ Ⓑ Ⓒ Ⓓ	16. Ⓐ Ⓑ Ⓒ Ⓓ	24. Ⓐ Ⓑ Ⓒ Ⓓ	32. Ⓐ Ⓑ Ⓒ Ⓓ	40. Ⓐ Ⓑ Ⓒ Ⓓ

Quantitative

1. Ⓐ Ⓑ Ⓒ Ⓓ	9. Ⓐ Ⓑ Ⓒ Ⓓ	17. Ⓐ Ⓑ Ⓒ Ⓓ	25. Ⓐ Ⓑ Ⓒ Ⓓ	33. Ⓐ Ⓑ Ⓒ Ⓓ
2. Ⓐ Ⓑ Ⓒ Ⓓ	10. Ⓐ Ⓑ Ⓒ Ⓓ	18. Ⓐ Ⓑ Ⓒ Ⓓ	26. Ⓐ Ⓑ Ⓒ Ⓓ	34. Ⓐ Ⓑ Ⓒ Ⓓ
3. Ⓐ Ⓑ Ⓒ Ⓓ	11. Ⓐ Ⓑ Ⓒ Ⓓ	19. Ⓐ Ⓑ Ⓒ Ⓓ	27. Ⓐ Ⓑ Ⓒ Ⓓ	35. Ⓐ Ⓑ Ⓒ Ⓓ
4. Ⓐ Ⓑ Ⓒ Ⓓ	12. Ⓐ Ⓑ Ⓒ Ⓓ	20. Ⓐ Ⓑ Ⓒ Ⓓ	28. Ⓐ Ⓑ Ⓒ Ⓓ	36. Ⓐ Ⓑ Ⓒ Ⓓ
5. Ⓐ Ⓑ Ⓒ Ⓓ	13. Ⓐ Ⓑ Ⓒ Ⓓ	21. Ⓐ Ⓑ Ⓒ Ⓓ	29. Ⓐ Ⓑ Ⓒ Ⓓ	37. Ⓐ Ⓑ Ⓒ Ⓓ
6. Ⓐ Ⓑ Ⓒ Ⓓ	14. Ⓐ Ⓑ Ⓒ Ⓓ	22. Ⓐ Ⓑ Ⓒ Ⓓ	30. Ⓐ Ⓑ Ⓒ Ⓓ	
7. Ⓐ Ⓑ Ⓒ Ⓓ	15. Ⓐ Ⓑ Ⓒ Ⓓ	23. Ⓐ Ⓑ Ⓒ Ⓓ	31. Ⓐ Ⓑ Ⓒ Ⓓ	
8. Ⓐ Ⓑ Ⓒ Ⓓ	16. Ⓐ Ⓑ Ⓒ Ⓓ	24. Ⓐ Ⓑ Ⓒ Ⓓ	32. Ⓐ Ⓑ Ⓒ Ⓓ	

Reading

1. Ⓐ Ⓑ Ⓒ Ⓓ
2. Ⓐ Ⓑ Ⓒ Ⓓ
3. Ⓐ Ⓑ Ⓒ Ⓓ
4. Ⓐ Ⓑ Ⓒ Ⓓ
5. Ⓐ Ⓑ Ⓒ Ⓓ
6. Ⓐ Ⓑ Ⓒ Ⓓ
7. Ⓐ Ⓑ Ⓒ Ⓓ
8. Ⓐ Ⓑ Ⓒ Ⓓ

9. Ⓐ Ⓑ Ⓒ Ⓓ
10. Ⓐ Ⓑ Ⓒ Ⓓ
11. Ⓐ Ⓑ Ⓒ Ⓓ
12. Ⓐ Ⓑ Ⓒ Ⓓ
13. Ⓐ Ⓑ Ⓒ Ⓓ
14. Ⓐ Ⓑ Ⓒ Ⓓ
15. Ⓐ Ⓑ Ⓒ Ⓓ
16. Ⓐ Ⓑ Ⓒ Ⓓ

17. Ⓐ Ⓑ Ⓒ Ⓓ
18. Ⓐ Ⓑ Ⓒ Ⓓ
19. Ⓐ Ⓑ Ⓒ Ⓓ
20. Ⓐ Ⓑ Ⓒ Ⓓ
21. Ⓐ Ⓑ Ⓒ Ⓓ
22. Ⓐ Ⓑ Ⓒ Ⓓ
23. Ⓐ Ⓑ Ⓒ Ⓓ
24. Ⓐ Ⓑ Ⓒ Ⓓ

25. Ⓐ Ⓑ Ⓒ Ⓓ
26. Ⓐ Ⓑ Ⓒ Ⓓ
27. Ⓐ Ⓑ Ⓒ Ⓓ
28. Ⓐ Ⓑ Ⓒ Ⓓ
29. Ⓐ Ⓑ Ⓒ Ⓓ
30. Ⓐ Ⓑ Ⓒ Ⓓ
31. Ⓐ Ⓑ Ⓒ Ⓓ
32. Ⓐ Ⓑ Ⓒ Ⓓ

33. Ⓐ Ⓑ Ⓒ Ⓓ
34. Ⓐ Ⓑ Ⓒ Ⓓ
35. Ⓐ Ⓑ Ⓒ Ⓓ
36. Ⓐ Ⓑ Ⓒ Ⓓ

Math

1. Ⓐ Ⓑ Ⓒ Ⓓ
2. Ⓐ Ⓑ Ⓒ Ⓓ
3. Ⓐ Ⓑ Ⓒ Ⓓ
4. Ⓐ Ⓑ Ⓒ Ⓓ
5. Ⓐ Ⓑ Ⓒ Ⓓ
6. Ⓐ Ⓑ Ⓒ Ⓓ
7. Ⓐ Ⓑ Ⓒ Ⓓ
8. Ⓐ Ⓑ Ⓒ Ⓓ
9. Ⓐ Ⓑ Ⓒ Ⓓ
10. Ⓐ Ⓑ Ⓒ Ⓓ

11. Ⓐ Ⓑ Ⓒ Ⓓ
12. Ⓐ Ⓑ Ⓒ Ⓓ
13. Ⓐ Ⓑ Ⓒ Ⓓ
14. Ⓐ Ⓑ Ⓒ Ⓓ
15. Ⓐ Ⓑ Ⓒ Ⓓ
16. Ⓐ Ⓑ Ⓒ Ⓓ
17. Ⓐ Ⓑ Ⓒ Ⓓ
18. Ⓐ Ⓑ Ⓒ Ⓓ
19. Ⓐ Ⓑ Ⓒ Ⓓ
20. Ⓐ Ⓑ Ⓒ Ⓓ

21. Ⓐ Ⓑ Ⓒ Ⓓ
22. Ⓐ Ⓑ Ⓒ Ⓓ
23. Ⓐ Ⓑ Ⓒ Ⓓ
24. Ⓐ Ⓑ Ⓒ Ⓓ
25. Ⓐ Ⓑ Ⓒ Ⓓ
26. Ⓐ Ⓑ Ⓒ Ⓓ
27. Ⓐ Ⓑ Ⓒ Ⓓ
28. Ⓐ Ⓑ Ⓒ Ⓓ
29. Ⓐ Ⓑ Ⓒ Ⓓ
30. Ⓐ Ⓑ Ⓒ Ⓓ

31. Ⓐ Ⓑ Ⓒ Ⓓ
32. Ⓐ Ⓑ Ⓒ Ⓓ
33. Ⓐ Ⓑ Ⓒ Ⓓ
34. Ⓐ Ⓑ Ⓒ Ⓓ
35. Ⓐ Ⓑ Ⓒ Ⓓ
36. Ⓐ Ⓑ Ⓒ Ⓓ
37. Ⓐ Ⓑ Ⓒ Ⓓ
38. Ⓐ Ⓑ Ⓒ Ⓓ
39. Ⓐ Ⓑ Ⓒ Ⓓ
40. Ⓐ Ⓑ Ⓒ Ⓓ

41. Ⓐ Ⓑ Ⓒ Ⓓ
42. Ⓐ Ⓑ Ⓒ Ⓓ
43. Ⓐ Ⓑ Ⓒ Ⓓ
44. Ⓐ Ⓑ Ⓒ Ⓓ
45. Ⓐ Ⓑ Ⓒ Ⓓ
46. Ⓐ Ⓑ Ⓒ Ⓓ
47. Ⓐ Ⓑ Ⓒ Ⓓ

Test 2 Answer Sheet

Verbal

1. Ⓐ Ⓑ Ⓒ Ⓓ	9. Ⓐ Ⓑ Ⓒ Ⓓ	17. Ⓐ Ⓑ Ⓒ Ⓓ	25. Ⓐ Ⓑ Ⓒ Ⓓ	33. Ⓐ Ⓑ Ⓒ Ⓓ
2. Ⓐ Ⓑ Ⓒ Ⓓ	10. Ⓐ Ⓑ Ⓒ Ⓓ	18. Ⓐ Ⓑ Ⓒ Ⓓ	26. Ⓐ Ⓑ Ⓒ Ⓓ	34. Ⓐ Ⓑ Ⓒ Ⓓ
3. Ⓐ Ⓑ Ⓒ Ⓓ	11. Ⓐ Ⓑ Ⓒ Ⓓ	19. Ⓐ Ⓑ Ⓒ Ⓓ	27. Ⓐ Ⓑ Ⓒ Ⓓ	35. Ⓐ Ⓑ Ⓒ Ⓓ
4. Ⓐ Ⓑ Ⓒ Ⓓ	12. Ⓐ Ⓑ Ⓒ Ⓓ	20. Ⓐ Ⓑ Ⓒ Ⓓ	28. Ⓐ Ⓑ Ⓒ Ⓓ	36. Ⓐ Ⓑ Ⓒ Ⓓ
5. Ⓐ Ⓑ Ⓒ Ⓓ	13. Ⓐ Ⓑ Ⓒ Ⓓ	21. Ⓐ Ⓑ Ⓒ Ⓓ	29. Ⓐ Ⓑ Ⓒ Ⓓ	37. Ⓐ Ⓑ Ⓒ Ⓓ
6. Ⓐ Ⓑ Ⓒ Ⓓ	14. Ⓐ Ⓑ Ⓒ Ⓓ	22. Ⓐ Ⓑ Ⓒ Ⓓ	30. Ⓐ Ⓑ Ⓒ Ⓓ	38. Ⓐ Ⓑ Ⓒ Ⓓ
7. Ⓐ Ⓑ Ⓒ Ⓓ	15. Ⓐ Ⓑ Ⓒ Ⓓ	23. Ⓐ Ⓑ Ⓒ Ⓓ	31. Ⓐ Ⓑ Ⓒ Ⓓ	39. Ⓐ Ⓑ Ⓒ Ⓓ
8. Ⓐ Ⓑ Ⓒ Ⓓ	16. Ⓐ Ⓑ Ⓒ Ⓓ	24. Ⓐ Ⓑ Ⓒ Ⓓ	32. Ⓐ Ⓑ Ⓒ Ⓓ	40. Ⓐ Ⓑ Ⓒ Ⓓ

Quantitative

1. Ⓐ Ⓑ Ⓒ Ⓓ	9. Ⓐ Ⓑ Ⓒ Ⓓ	17. Ⓐ Ⓑ Ⓒ Ⓓ	25. Ⓐ Ⓑ Ⓒ Ⓓ	33. Ⓐ Ⓑ Ⓒ Ⓓ
2. Ⓐ Ⓑ Ⓒ Ⓓ	10. Ⓐ Ⓑ Ⓒ Ⓓ	18. Ⓐ Ⓑ Ⓒ Ⓓ	26. Ⓐ Ⓑ Ⓒ Ⓓ	34. Ⓐ Ⓑ Ⓒ Ⓓ
3. Ⓐ Ⓑ Ⓒ Ⓓ	11. Ⓐ Ⓑ Ⓒ Ⓓ	19. Ⓐ Ⓑ Ⓒ Ⓓ	27. Ⓐ Ⓑ Ⓒ Ⓓ	35. Ⓐ Ⓑ Ⓒ Ⓓ
4. Ⓐ Ⓑ Ⓒ Ⓓ	12. Ⓐ Ⓑ Ⓒ Ⓓ	20. Ⓐ Ⓑ Ⓒ Ⓓ	28. Ⓐ Ⓑ Ⓒ Ⓓ	36. Ⓐ Ⓑ Ⓒ Ⓓ
5. Ⓐ Ⓑ Ⓒ Ⓓ	13. Ⓐ Ⓑ Ⓒ Ⓓ	21. Ⓐ Ⓑ Ⓒ Ⓓ	29. Ⓐ Ⓑ Ⓒ Ⓓ	37. Ⓐ Ⓑ Ⓒ Ⓓ
6. Ⓐ Ⓑ Ⓒ Ⓓ	14. Ⓐ Ⓑ Ⓒ Ⓓ	22. Ⓐ Ⓑ Ⓒ Ⓓ	30. Ⓐ Ⓑ Ⓒ Ⓓ	
7. Ⓐ Ⓑ Ⓒ Ⓓ	15. Ⓐ Ⓑ Ⓒ Ⓓ	23. Ⓐ Ⓑ Ⓒ Ⓓ	31. Ⓐ Ⓑ Ⓒ Ⓓ	
8. Ⓐ Ⓑ Ⓒ Ⓓ	16. Ⓐ Ⓑ Ⓒ Ⓓ	24. Ⓐ Ⓑ Ⓒ Ⓓ	32. Ⓐ Ⓑ Ⓒ Ⓓ	

Reading

1. Ⓐ Ⓑ Ⓒ Ⓓ   9. Ⓐ Ⓑ Ⓒ Ⓓ   17. Ⓐ Ⓑ Ⓒ Ⓓ   25. Ⓐ Ⓑ Ⓒ Ⓓ   33. Ⓐ Ⓑ Ⓒ Ⓓ
2. Ⓐ Ⓑ Ⓒ Ⓓ   10. Ⓐ Ⓑ Ⓒ Ⓓ   18. Ⓐ Ⓑ Ⓒ Ⓓ   26. Ⓐ Ⓑ Ⓒ Ⓓ   34. Ⓐ Ⓑ Ⓒ Ⓓ
3. Ⓐ Ⓑ Ⓒ Ⓓ   11. Ⓐ Ⓑ Ⓒ Ⓓ   19. Ⓐ Ⓑ Ⓒ Ⓓ   27. Ⓐ Ⓑ Ⓒ Ⓓ   35. Ⓐ Ⓑ Ⓒ Ⓓ
4. Ⓐ Ⓑ Ⓒ Ⓓ   12. Ⓐ Ⓑ Ⓒ Ⓓ   20. Ⓐ Ⓑ Ⓒ Ⓓ   28. Ⓐ Ⓑ Ⓒ Ⓓ   36. Ⓐ Ⓑ Ⓒ Ⓓ
5. Ⓐ Ⓑ Ⓒ Ⓓ   13. Ⓐ Ⓑ Ⓒ Ⓓ   21. Ⓐ Ⓑ Ⓒ Ⓓ   29. Ⓐ Ⓑ Ⓒ Ⓓ
6. Ⓐ Ⓑ Ⓒ Ⓓ   14. Ⓐ Ⓑ Ⓒ Ⓓ   22. Ⓐ Ⓑ Ⓒ Ⓓ   30. Ⓐ Ⓑ Ⓒ Ⓓ
7. Ⓐ Ⓑ Ⓒ Ⓓ   15. Ⓐ Ⓑ Ⓒ Ⓓ   23. Ⓐ Ⓑ Ⓒ Ⓓ   31. Ⓐ Ⓑ Ⓒ Ⓓ
8. Ⓐ Ⓑ Ⓒ Ⓓ   16. Ⓐ Ⓑ Ⓒ Ⓓ   24. Ⓐ Ⓑ Ⓒ Ⓓ   32. Ⓐ Ⓑ Ⓒ Ⓓ

Math

1. Ⓐ Ⓑ Ⓒ Ⓓ   11. Ⓐ Ⓑ Ⓒ Ⓓ   21. Ⓐ Ⓑ Ⓒ Ⓓ   31. Ⓐ Ⓑ Ⓒ Ⓓ   41. Ⓐ Ⓑ Ⓒ Ⓓ
2. Ⓐ Ⓑ Ⓒ Ⓓ   12. Ⓐ Ⓑ Ⓒ Ⓓ   22. Ⓐ Ⓑ Ⓒ Ⓓ   32. Ⓐ Ⓑ Ⓒ Ⓓ   42. Ⓐ Ⓑ Ⓒ Ⓓ
3. Ⓐ Ⓑ Ⓒ Ⓓ   13. Ⓐ Ⓑ Ⓒ Ⓓ   23. Ⓐ Ⓑ Ⓒ Ⓓ   33. Ⓐ Ⓑ Ⓒ Ⓓ   43. Ⓐ Ⓑ Ⓒ Ⓓ
4. Ⓐ Ⓑ Ⓒ Ⓓ   14. Ⓐ Ⓑ Ⓒ Ⓓ   24. Ⓐ Ⓑ Ⓒ Ⓓ   34. Ⓐ Ⓑ Ⓒ Ⓓ   44. Ⓐ Ⓑ Ⓒ Ⓓ
5. Ⓐ Ⓑ Ⓒ Ⓓ   15. Ⓐ Ⓑ Ⓒ Ⓓ   25. Ⓐ Ⓑ Ⓒ Ⓓ   35. Ⓐ Ⓑ Ⓒ Ⓓ   45. Ⓐ Ⓑ Ⓒ Ⓓ
6. Ⓐ Ⓑ Ⓒ Ⓓ   16. Ⓐ Ⓑ Ⓒ Ⓓ   26. Ⓐ Ⓑ Ⓒ Ⓓ   36. Ⓐ Ⓑ Ⓒ Ⓓ   46. Ⓐ Ⓑ Ⓒ Ⓓ
7. Ⓐ Ⓑ Ⓒ Ⓓ   17. Ⓐ Ⓑ Ⓒ Ⓓ   27. Ⓐ Ⓑ Ⓒ Ⓓ   37. Ⓐ Ⓑ Ⓒ Ⓓ   47. Ⓐ Ⓑ Ⓒ Ⓓ
8. Ⓐ Ⓑ Ⓒ Ⓓ   18. Ⓐ Ⓑ Ⓒ Ⓓ   28. Ⓐ Ⓑ Ⓒ Ⓓ   38. Ⓐ Ⓑ Ⓒ Ⓓ
9. Ⓐ Ⓑ Ⓒ Ⓓ   19. Ⓐ Ⓑ Ⓒ Ⓓ   29. Ⓐ Ⓑ Ⓒ Ⓓ   39. Ⓐ Ⓑ Ⓒ Ⓓ
10. Ⓐ Ⓑ Ⓒ Ⓓ   20. Ⓐ Ⓑ Ⓒ Ⓓ   30. Ⓐ Ⓑ Ⓒ Ⓓ   40. Ⓐ Ⓑ Ⓒ Ⓓ

Test 3 Answer Sheet

Verbal

1. Ⓐ Ⓑ Ⓒ Ⓓ	9. Ⓐ Ⓑ Ⓒ Ⓓ	17. Ⓐ Ⓑ Ⓒ Ⓓ	25. Ⓐ Ⓑ Ⓒ Ⓓ	33. Ⓐ Ⓑ Ⓒ Ⓓ
2. Ⓐ Ⓑ Ⓒ Ⓓ	10. Ⓐ Ⓑ Ⓒ Ⓓ	18. Ⓐ Ⓑ Ⓒ Ⓓ	26. Ⓐ Ⓑ Ⓒ Ⓓ	34. Ⓐ Ⓑ Ⓒ Ⓓ
3. Ⓐ Ⓑ Ⓒ Ⓓ	11. Ⓐ Ⓑ Ⓒ Ⓓ	19. Ⓐ Ⓑ Ⓒ Ⓓ	27. Ⓐ Ⓑ Ⓒ Ⓓ	35. Ⓐ Ⓑ Ⓒ Ⓓ
4. Ⓐ Ⓑ Ⓒ Ⓓ	12. Ⓐ Ⓑ Ⓒ Ⓓ	20. Ⓐ Ⓑ Ⓒ Ⓓ	28. Ⓐ Ⓑ Ⓒ Ⓓ	36. Ⓐ Ⓑ Ⓒ Ⓓ
5. Ⓐ Ⓑ Ⓒ Ⓓ	13. Ⓐ Ⓑ Ⓒ Ⓓ	21. Ⓐ Ⓑ Ⓒ Ⓓ	29. Ⓐ Ⓑ Ⓒ Ⓓ	37. Ⓐ Ⓑ Ⓒ Ⓓ
6. Ⓐ Ⓑ Ⓒ Ⓓ	14. Ⓐ Ⓑ Ⓒ Ⓓ	22. Ⓐ Ⓑ Ⓒ Ⓓ	30. Ⓐ Ⓑ Ⓒ Ⓓ	38. Ⓐ Ⓑ Ⓒ Ⓓ
7. Ⓐ Ⓑ Ⓒ Ⓓ	15. Ⓐ Ⓑ Ⓒ Ⓓ	23. Ⓐ Ⓑ Ⓒ Ⓓ	31. Ⓐ Ⓑ Ⓒ Ⓓ	39. Ⓐ Ⓑ Ⓒ Ⓓ
8. Ⓐ Ⓑ Ⓒ Ⓓ	16. Ⓐ Ⓑ Ⓒ Ⓓ	24. Ⓐ Ⓑ Ⓒ Ⓓ	32. Ⓐ Ⓑ Ⓒ Ⓓ	40. Ⓐ Ⓑ Ⓒ Ⓓ

Quantitative

1. Ⓐ Ⓑ Ⓒ Ⓓ	9. Ⓐ Ⓑ Ⓒ Ⓓ	17. Ⓐ Ⓑ Ⓒ Ⓓ	25. Ⓐ Ⓑ Ⓒ Ⓓ	33. Ⓐ Ⓑ Ⓒ Ⓓ
2. Ⓐ Ⓑ Ⓒ Ⓓ	10. Ⓐ Ⓑ Ⓒ Ⓓ	18. Ⓐ Ⓑ Ⓒ Ⓓ	26. Ⓐ Ⓑ Ⓒ Ⓓ	34. Ⓐ Ⓑ Ⓒ Ⓓ
3. Ⓐ Ⓑ Ⓒ Ⓓ	11. Ⓐ Ⓑ Ⓒ Ⓓ	19. Ⓐ Ⓑ Ⓒ Ⓓ	27. Ⓐ Ⓑ Ⓒ Ⓓ	35. Ⓐ Ⓑ Ⓒ Ⓓ
4. Ⓐ Ⓑ Ⓒ Ⓓ	12. Ⓐ Ⓑ Ⓒ Ⓓ	20. Ⓐ Ⓑ Ⓒ Ⓓ	28. Ⓐ Ⓑ Ⓒ Ⓓ	36. Ⓐ Ⓑ Ⓒ Ⓓ
5. Ⓐ Ⓑ Ⓒ Ⓓ	13. Ⓐ Ⓑ Ⓒ Ⓓ	21. Ⓐ Ⓑ Ⓒ Ⓓ	29. Ⓐ Ⓑ Ⓒ Ⓓ	37. Ⓐ Ⓑ Ⓒ Ⓓ
6. Ⓐ Ⓑ Ⓒ Ⓓ	14. Ⓐ Ⓑ Ⓒ Ⓓ	22. Ⓐ Ⓑ Ⓒ Ⓓ	30. Ⓐ Ⓑ Ⓒ Ⓓ	
7. Ⓐ Ⓑ Ⓒ Ⓓ	15. Ⓐ Ⓑ Ⓒ Ⓓ	23. Ⓐ Ⓑ Ⓒ Ⓓ	31. Ⓐ Ⓑ Ⓒ Ⓓ	
8. Ⓐ Ⓑ Ⓒ Ⓓ	16. Ⓐ Ⓑ Ⓒ Ⓓ	24. Ⓐ Ⓑ Ⓒ Ⓓ	32. Ⓐ Ⓑ Ⓒ Ⓓ	

Reading

1. Ⓐ Ⓑ Ⓒ Ⓓ	9. Ⓐ Ⓑ Ⓒ Ⓓ	17. Ⓐ Ⓑ Ⓒ Ⓓ	25. Ⓐ Ⓑ Ⓒ Ⓓ	33. Ⓐ Ⓑ Ⓒ Ⓓ
2. Ⓐ Ⓑ Ⓒ Ⓓ	10. Ⓐ Ⓑ Ⓒ Ⓓ	18. Ⓐ Ⓑ Ⓒ Ⓓ	26. Ⓐ Ⓑ Ⓒ Ⓓ	34. Ⓐ Ⓑ Ⓒ Ⓓ
3. Ⓐ Ⓑ Ⓒ Ⓓ	11. Ⓐ Ⓑ Ⓒ Ⓓ	19. Ⓐ Ⓑ Ⓒ Ⓓ	27. Ⓐ Ⓑ Ⓒ Ⓓ	35. Ⓐ Ⓑ Ⓒ Ⓓ
4. Ⓐ Ⓑ Ⓒ Ⓓ	12. Ⓐ Ⓑ Ⓒ Ⓓ	20. Ⓐ Ⓑ Ⓒ Ⓓ	28. Ⓐ Ⓑ Ⓒ Ⓓ	36. Ⓐ Ⓑ Ⓒ Ⓓ
5. Ⓐ Ⓑ Ⓒ Ⓓ	13. Ⓐ Ⓑ Ⓒ Ⓓ	21. Ⓐ Ⓑ Ⓒ Ⓓ	29. Ⓐ Ⓑ Ⓒ Ⓓ	
6. Ⓐ Ⓑ Ⓒ Ⓓ	14. Ⓐ Ⓑ Ⓒ Ⓓ	22. Ⓐ Ⓑ Ⓒ Ⓓ	30. Ⓐ Ⓑ Ⓒ Ⓓ	
7. Ⓐ Ⓑ Ⓒ Ⓓ	15. Ⓐ Ⓑ Ⓒ Ⓓ	23. Ⓐ Ⓑ Ⓒ Ⓓ	31. Ⓐ Ⓑ Ⓒ Ⓓ	
8. Ⓐ Ⓑ Ⓒ Ⓓ	16. Ⓐ Ⓑ Ⓒ Ⓓ	24. Ⓐ Ⓑ Ⓒ Ⓓ	32. Ⓐ Ⓑ Ⓒ Ⓓ	

Math

1. Ⓐ Ⓑ Ⓒ Ⓓ	11. Ⓐ Ⓑ Ⓒ Ⓓ	21. Ⓐ Ⓑ Ⓒ Ⓓ	31. Ⓐ Ⓑ Ⓒ Ⓓ	41. Ⓐ Ⓑ Ⓒ Ⓓ
2. Ⓐ Ⓑ Ⓒ Ⓓ	12. Ⓐ Ⓑ Ⓒ Ⓓ	22. Ⓐ Ⓑ Ⓒ Ⓓ	32. Ⓐ Ⓑ Ⓒ Ⓓ	42. Ⓐ Ⓑ Ⓒ Ⓓ
3. Ⓐ Ⓑ Ⓒ Ⓓ	13. Ⓐ Ⓑ Ⓒ Ⓓ	23. Ⓐ Ⓑ Ⓒ Ⓓ	33. Ⓐ Ⓑ Ⓒ Ⓓ	43. Ⓐ Ⓑ Ⓒ Ⓓ
4. Ⓐ Ⓑ Ⓒ Ⓓ	14. Ⓐ Ⓑ Ⓒ Ⓓ	24. Ⓐ Ⓑ Ⓒ Ⓓ	34. Ⓐ Ⓑ Ⓒ Ⓓ	44. Ⓐ Ⓑ Ⓒ Ⓓ
5. Ⓐ Ⓑ Ⓒ Ⓓ	15. Ⓐ Ⓑ Ⓒ Ⓓ	25. Ⓐ Ⓑ Ⓒ Ⓓ	35. Ⓐ Ⓑ Ⓒ Ⓓ	45. Ⓐ Ⓑ Ⓒ Ⓓ
6. Ⓐ Ⓑ Ⓒ Ⓓ	16. Ⓐ Ⓑ Ⓒ Ⓓ	26. Ⓐ Ⓑ Ⓒ Ⓓ	36. Ⓐ Ⓑ Ⓒ Ⓓ	46. Ⓐ Ⓑ Ⓒ Ⓓ
7. Ⓐ Ⓑ Ⓒ Ⓓ	17. Ⓐ Ⓑ Ⓒ Ⓓ	27. Ⓐ Ⓑ Ⓒ Ⓓ	37. Ⓐ Ⓑ Ⓒ Ⓓ	47. Ⓐ Ⓑ Ⓒ Ⓓ
8. Ⓐ Ⓑ Ⓒ Ⓓ	18. Ⓐ Ⓑ Ⓒ Ⓓ	28. Ⓐ Ⓑ Ⓒ Ⓓ	38. Ⓐ Ⓑ Ⓒ Ⓓ	
9. Ⓐ Ⓑ Ⓒ Ⓓ	19. Ⓐ Ⓑ Ⓒ Ⓓ	29. Ⓐ Ⓑ Ⓒ Ⓓ	39. Ⓐ Ⓑ Ⓒ Ⓓ	
10. Ⓐ Ⓑ Ⓒ Ⓓ	20. Ⓐ Ⓑ Ⓒ Ⓓ	30. Ⓐ Ⓑ Ⓒ Ⓓ	40. Ⓐ Ⓑ Ⓒ Ⓓ	

Test 4 Answer Sheet

Verbal

1. Ⓐ Ⓑ Ⓒ Ⓓ	9. Ⓐ Ⓑ Ⓒ Ⓓ	17. Ⓐ Ⓑ Ⓒ Ⓓ	25. Ⓐ Ⓑ Ⓒ Ⓓ	33. Ⓐ Ⓑ Ⓒ Ⓓ
2. Ⓐ Ⓑ Ⓒ Ⓓ	10. Ⓐ Ⓑ Ⓒ Ⓓ	18. Ⓐ Ⓑ Ⓒ Ⓓ	26. Ⓐ Ⓑ Ⓒ Ⓓ	34. Ⓐ Ⓑ Ⓒ Ⓓ
3. Ⓐ Ⓑ Ⓒ Ⓓ	11. Ⓐ Ⓑ Ⓒ Ⓓ	19. Ⓐ Ⓑ Ⓒ Ⓓ	27. Ⓐ Ⓑ Ⓒ Ⓓ	35. Ⓐ Ⓑ Ⓒ Ⓓ
4. Ⓐ Ⓑ Ⓒ Ⓓ	12. Ⓐ Ⓑ Ⓒ Ⓓ	20. Ⓐ Ⓑ Ⓒ Ⓓ	28. Ⓐ Ⓑ Ⓒ Ⓓ	36. Ⓐ Ⓑ Ⓒ Ⓓ
5. Ⓐ Ⓑ Ⓒ Ⓓ	13. Ⓐ Ⓑ Ⓒ Ⓓ	21. Ⓐ Ⓑ Ⓒ Ⓓ	29. Ⓐ Ⓑ Ⓒ Ⓓ	37. Ⓐ Ⓑ Ⓒ Ⓓ
6. Ⓐ Ⓑ Ⓒ Ⓓ	14. Ⓐ Ⓑ Ⓒ Ⓓ	22. Ⓐ Ⓑ Ⓒ Ⓓ	30. Ⓐ Ⓑ Ⓒ Ⓓ	38. Ⓐ Ⓑ Ⓒ Ⓓ
7. Ⓐ Ⓑ Ⓒ Ⓓ	15. Ⓐ Ⓑ Ⓒ Ⓓ	23. Ⓐ Ⓑ Ⓒ Ⓓ	31. Ⓐ Ⓑ Ⓒ Ⓓ	39. Ⓐ Ⓑ Ⓒ Ⓓ
8. Ⓐ Ⓑ Ⓒ Ⓓ	16. Ⓐ Ⓑ Ⓒ Ⓓ	24. Ⓐ Ⓑ Ⓒ Ⓓ	32. Ⓐ Ⓑ Ⓒ Ⓓ	40. Ⓐ Ⓑ Ⓒ Ⓓ

Quantitative

1. Ⓐ Ⓑ Ⓒ Ⓓ	9. Ⓐ Ⓑ Ⓒ Ⓓ	17. Ⓐ Ⓑ Ⓒ Ⓓ	25. Ⓐ Ⓑ Ⓒ Ⓓ	33. Ⓐ Ⓑ Ⓒ Ⓓ
2. Ⓐ Ⓑ Ⓒ Ⓓ	10. Ⓐ Ⓑ Ⓒ Ⓓ	18. Ⓐ Ⓑ Ⓒ Ⓓ	26. Ⓐ Ⓑ Ⓒ Ⓓ	34. Ⓐ Ⓑ Ⓒ Ⓓ
3. Ⓐ Ⓑ Ⓒ Ⓓ	11. Ⓐ Ⓑ Ⓒ Ⓓ	19. Ⓐ Ⓑ Ⓒ Ⓓ	27. Ⓐ Ⓑ Ⓒ Ⓓ	35. Ⓐ Ⓑ Ⓒ Ⓓ
4. Ⓐ Ⓑ Ⓒ Ⓓ	12. Ⓐ Ⓑ Ⓒ Ⓓ	20. Ⓐ Ⓑ Ⓒ Ⓓ	28. Ⓐ Ⓑ Ⓒ Ⓓ	36. Ⓐ Ⓑ Ⓒ Ⓓ
5. Ⓐ Ⓑ Ⓒ Ⓓ	13. Ⓐ Ⓑ Ⓒ Ⓓ	21. Ⓐ Ⓑ Ⓒ Ⓓ	29. Ⓐ Ⓑ Ⓒ Ⓓ	37. Ⓐ Ⓑ Ⓒ Ⓓ
6. Ⓐ Ⓑ Ⓒ Ⓓ	14. Ⓐ Ⓑ Ⓒ Ⓓ	22. Ⓐ Ⓑ Ⓒ Ⓓ	30. Ⓐ Ⓑ Ⓒ Ⓓ	
7. Ⓐ Ⓑ Ⓒ Ⓓ	15. Ⓐ Ⓑ Ⓒ Ⓓ	23. Ⓐ Ⓑ Ⓒ Ⓓ	31. Ⓐ Ⓑ Ⓒ Ⓓ	
8. Ⓐ Ⓑ Ⓒ Ⓓ	16. Ⓐ Ⓑ Ⓒ Ⓓ	24. Ⓐ Ⓑ Ⓒ Ⓓ	32. Ⓐ Ⓑ Ⓒ Ⓓ	

Reading

1. Ⓐ Ⓑ Ⓒ Ⓓ	9. Ⓐ Ⓑ Ⓒ Ⓓ	17. Ⓐ Ⓑ Ⓒ Ⓓ	25. Ⓐ Ⓑ Ⓒ Ⓓ	33. Ⓐ Ⓑ Ⓒ Ⓓ
2. Ⓐ Ⓑ Ⓒ Ⓓ	10. Ⓐ Ⓑ Ⓒ Ⓓ	18. Ⓐ Ⓑ Ⓒ Ⓓ	26. Ⓐ Ⓑ Ⓒ Ⓓ	34. Ⓐ Ⓑ Ⓒ Ⓓ
3. Ⓐ Ⓑ Ⓒ Ⓓ	11. Ⓐ Ⓑ Ⓒ Ⓓ	19. Ⓐ Ⓑ Ⓒ Ⓓ	27. Ⓐ Ⓑ Ⓒ Ⓓ	35. Ⓐ Ⓑ Ⓒ Ⓓ
4. Ⓐ Ⓑ Ⓒ Ⓓ	12. Ⓐ Ⓑ Ⓒ Ⓓ	20. Ⓐ Ⓑ Ⓒ Ⓓ	28. Ⓐ Ⓑ Ⓒ Ⓓ	36. Ⓐ Ⓑ Ⓒ Ⓓ
5. Ⓐ Ⓑ Ⓒ Ⓓ	13. Ⓐ Ⓑ Ⓒ Ⓓ	21. Ⓐ Ⓑ Ⓒ Ⓓ	29. Ⓐ Ⓑ Ⓒ Ⓓ	
6. Ⓐ Ⓑ Ⓒ Ⓓ	14. Ⓐ Ⓑ Ⓒ Ⓓ	22. Ⓐ Ⓑ Ⓒ Ⓓ	30. Ⓐ Ⓑ Ⓒ Ⓓ	
7. Ⓐ Ⓑ Ⓒ Ⓓ	15. Ⓐ Ⓑ Ⓒ Ⓓ	23. Ⓐ Ⓑ Ⓒ Ⓓ	31. Ⓐ Ⓑ Ⓒ Ⓓ	
8. Ⓐ Ⓑ Ⓒ Ⓓ	16. Ⓐ Ⓑ Ⓒ Ⓓ	24. Ⓐ Ⓑ Ⓒ Ⓓ	32. Ⓐ Ⓑ Ⓒ Ⓓ	

Math

1. Ⓐ Ⓑ Ⓒ Ⓓ	11. Ⓐ Ⓑ Ⓒ Ⓓ	21. Ⓐ Ⓑ Ⓒ Ⓓ	31. Ⓐ Ⓑ Ⓒ Ⓓ	41. Ⓐ Ⓑ Ⓒ Ⓓ
2. Ⓐ Ⓑ Ⓒ Ⓓ	12. Ⓐ Ⓑ Ⓒ Ⓓ	22. Ⓐ Ⓑ Ⓒ Ⓓ	32. Ⓐ Ⓑ Ⓒ Ⓓ	42. Ⓐ Ⓑ Ⓒ Ⓓ
3. Ⓐ Ⓑ Ⓒ Ⓓ	13. Ⓐ Ⓑ Ⓒ Ⓓ	23. Ⓐ Ⓑ Ⓒ Ⓓ	33. Ⓐ Ⓑ Ⓒ Ⓓ	43. Ⓐ Ⓑ Ⓒ Ⓓ
4. Ⓐ Ⓑ Ⓒ Ⓓ	14. Ⓐ Ⓑ Ⓒ Ⓓ	24. Ⓐ Ⓑ Ⓒ Ⓓ	34. Ⓐ Ⓑ Ⓒ Ⓓ	44. Ⓐ Ⓑ Ⓒ Ⓓ
5. Ⓐ Ⓑ Ⓒ Ⓓ	15. Ⓐ Ⓑ Ⓒ Ⓓ	25. Ⓐ Ⓑ Ⓒ Ⓓ	35. Ⓐ Ⓑ Ⓒ Ⓓ	45. Ⓐ Ⓑ Ⓒ Ⓓ
6. Ⓐ Ⓑ Ⓒ Ⓓ	16. Ⓐ Ⓑ Ⓒ Ⓓ	26. Ⓐ Ⓑ Ⓒ Ⓓ	36. Ⓐ Ⓑ Ⓒ Ⓓ	46. Ⓐ Ⓑ Ⓒ Ⓓ
7. Ⓐ Ⓑ Ⓒ Ⓓ	17. Ⓐ Ⓑ Ⓒ Ⓓ	27. Ⓐ Ⓑ Ⓒ Ⓓ	37. Ⓐ Ⓑ Ⓒ Ⓓ	47. Ⓐ Ⓑ Ⓒ Ⓓ
8. Ⓐ Ⓑ Ⓒ Ⓓ	18. Ⓐ Ⓑ Ⓒ Ⓓ	28. Ⓐ Ⓑ Ⓒ Ⓓ	38. Ⓐ Ⓑ Ⓒ Ⓓ	
9. Ⓐ Ⓑ Ⓒ Ⓓ	19. Ⓐ Ⓑ Ⓒ Ⓓ	29. Ⓐ Ⓑ Ⓒ Ⓓ	39. Ⓐ Ⓑ Ⓒ Ⓓ	
10. Ⓐ Ⓑ Ⓒ Ⓓ	20. Ⓐ Ⓑ Ⓒ Ⓓ	30. Ⓐ Ⓑ Ⓒ Ⓓ	40. Ⓐ Ⓑ Ⓒ Ⓓ	

Test 5 Answer Sheet

Verbal

1. Ⓐ Ⓑ Ⓒ Ⓓ	9. Ⓐ Ⓑ Ⓒ Ⓓ	17. Ⓐ Ⓑ Ⓒ Ⓓ	25. Ⓐ Ⓑ Ⓒ Ⓓ	33. Ⓐ Ⓑ Ⓒ Ⓓ
2. Ⓐ Ⓑ Ⓒ Ⓓ	10. Ⓐ Ⓑ Ⓒ Ⓓ	18. Ⓐ Ⓑ Ⓒ Ⓓ	26. Ⓐ Ⓑ Ⓒ Ⓓ	34. Ⓐ Ⓑ Ⓒ Ⓓ
3. Ⓐ Ⓑ Ⓒ Ⓓ	11. Ⓐ Ⓑ Ⓒ Ⓓ	19. Ⓐ Ⓑ Ⓒ Ⓓ	27. Ⓐ Ⓑ Ⓒ Ⓓ	35. Ⓐ Ⓑ Ⓒ Ⓓ
4. Ⓐ Ⓑ Ⓒ Ⓓ	12. Ⓐ Ⓑ Ⓒ Ⓓ	20. Ⓐ Ⓑ Ⓒ Ⓓ	28. Ⓐ Ⓑ Ⓒ Ⓓ	36. Ⓐ Ⓑ Ⓒ Ⓓ
5. Ⓐ Ⓑ Ⓒ Ⓓ	13. Ⓐ Ⓑ Ⓒ Ⓓ	21. Ⓐ Ⓑ Ⓒ Ⓓ	29. Ⓐ Ⓑ Ⓒ Ⓓ	37. Ⓐ Ⓑ Ⓒ Ⓓ
6. Ⓐ Ⓑ Ⓒ Ⓓ	14. Ⓐ Ⓑ Ⓒ Ⓓ	22. Ⓐ Ⓑ Ⓒ Ⓓ	30. Ⓐ Ⓑ Ⓒ Ⓓ	38. Ⓐ Ⓑ Ⓒ Ⓓ
7. Ⓐ Ⓑ Ⓒ Ⓓ	15. Ⓐ Ⓑ Ⓒ Ⓓ	23. Ⓐ Ⓑ Ⓒ Ⓓ	31. Ⓐ Ⓑ Ⓒ Ⓓ	39. Ⓐ Ⓑ Ⓒ Ⓓ
8. Ⓐ Ⓑ Ⓒ Ⓓ	16. Ⓐ Ⓑ Ⓒ Ⓓ	24. Ⓐ Ⓑ Ⓒ Ⓓ	32. Ⓐ Ⓑ Ⓒ Ⓓ	40. Ⓐ Ⓑ Ⓒ Ⓓ

Quantitative

1. Ⓐ Ⓑ Ⓒ Ⓓ	9. Ⓐ Ⓑ Ⓒ Ⓓ	17. Ⓐ Ⓑ Ⓒ Ⓓ	25. Ⓐ Ⓑ Ⓒ Ⓓ	33. Ⓐ Ⓑ Ⓒ Ⓓ
2. Ⓐ Ⓑ Ⓒ Ⓓ	10. Ⓐ Ⓑ Ⓒ Ⓓ	18. Ⓐ Ⓑ Ⓒ Ⓓ	26. Ⓐ Ⓑ Ⓒ Ⓓ	34. Ⓐ Ⓑ Ⓒ Ⓓ
3. Ⓐ Ⓑ Ⓒ Ⓓ	11. Ⓐ Ⓑ Ⓒ Ⓓ	19. Ⓐ Ⓑ Ⓒ Ⓓ	27. Ⓐ Ⓑ Ⓒ Ⓓ	35. Ⓐ Ⓑ Ⓒ Ⓓ
4. Ⓐ Ⓑ Ⓒ Ⓓ	12. Ⓐ Ⓑ Ⓒ Ⓓ	20. Ⓐ Ⓑ Ⓒ Ⓓ	28. Ⓐ Ⓑ Ⓒ Ⓓ	36. Ⓐ Ⓑ Ⓒ Ⓓ
5. Ⓐ Ⓑ Ⓒ Ⓓ	13. Ⓐ Ⓑ Ⓒ Ⓓ	21. Ⓐ Ⓑ Ⓒ Ⓓ	29. Ⓐ Ⓑ Ⓒ Ⓓ	37. Ⓐ Ⓑ Ⓒ Ⓓ
6. Ⓐ Ⓑ Ⓒ Ⓓ	14. Ⓐ Ⓑ Ⓒ Ⓓ	22. Ⓐ Ⓑ Ⓒ Ⓓ	30. Ⓐ Ⓑ Ⓒ Ⓓ	
7. Ⓐ Ⓑ Ⓒ Ⓓ	15. Ⓐ Ⓑ Ⓒ Ⓓ	23. Ⓐ Ⓑ Ⓒ Ⓓ	31. Ⓐ Ⓑ Ⓒ Ⓓ	
8. Ⓐ Ⓑ Ⓒ Ⓓ	16. Ⓐ Ⓑ Ⓒ Ⓓ	24. Ⓐ Ⓑ Ⓒ Ⓓ	32. Ⓐ Ⓑ Ⓒ Ⓓ	

Reading

1. Ⓐ Ⓑ Ⓒ Ⓓ
2. Ⓐ Ⓑ Ⓒ Ⓓ
3. Ⓐ Ⓑ Ⓒ Ⓓ
4. Ⓐ Ⓑ Ⓒ Ⓓ
5. Ⓐ Ⓑ Ⓒ Ⓓ
6. Ⓐ Ⓑ Ⓒ Ⓓ
7. Ⓐ Ⓑ Ⓒ Ⓓ
8. Ⓐ Ⓑ Ⓒ Ⓓ

9. Ⓐ Ⓑ Ⓒ Ⓓ
10. Ⓐ Ⓑ Ⓒ Ⓓ
11. Ⓐ Ⓑ Ⓒ Ⓓ
12. Ⓐ Ⓑ Ⓒ Ⓓ
13. Ⓐ Ⓑ Ⓒ Ⓓ
14. Ⓐ Ⓑ Ⓒ Ⓓ
15. Ⓐ Ⓑ Ⓒ Ⓓ
16. Ⓐ Ⓑ Ⓒ Ⓓ

17. Ⓐ Ⓑ Ⓒ Ⓓ
18. Ⓐ Ⓑ Ⓒ Ⓓ
19. Ⓐ Ⓑ Ⓒ Ⓓ
20. Ⓐ Ⓑ Ⓒ Ⓓ
21. Ⓐ Ⓑ Ⓒ Ⓓ
22. Ⓐ Ⓑ Ⓒ Ⓓ
23. Ⓐ Ⓑ Ⓒ Ⓓ
24. Ⓐ Ⓑ Ⓒ Ⓓ

25. Ⓐ Ⓑ Ⓒ Ⓓ
26. Ⓐ Ⓑ Ⓒ Ⓓ
27. Ⓐ Ⓑ Ⓒ Ⓓ
28. Ⓐ Ⓑ Ⓒ Ⓓ
29. Ⓐ Ⓑ Ⓒ Ⓓ
30. Ⓐ Ⓑ Ⓒ Ⓓ
31. Ⓐ Ⓑ Ⓒ Ⓓ
32. Ⓐ Ⓑ Ⓒ Ⓓ

33. Ⓐ Ⓑ Ⓒ Ⓓ
34. Ⓐ Ⓑ Ⓒ Ⓓ
35. Ⓐ Ⓑ Ⓒ Ⓓ
36. Ⓐ Ⓑ Ⓒ Ⓓ

Math

1. Ⓐ Ⓑ Ⓒ Ⓓ
2. Ⓐ Ⓑ Ⓒ Ⓓ
3. Ⓐ Ⓑ Ⓒ Ⓓ
4. Ⓐ Ⓑ Ⓒ Ⓓ
5. Ⓐ Ⓑ Ⓒ Ⓓ
6. Ⓐ Ⓑ Ⓒ Ⓓ
7. Ⓐ Ⓑ Ⓒ Ⓓ
8. Ⓐ Ⓑ Ⓒ Ⓓ
9. Ⓐ Ⓑ Ⓒ Ⓓ
10. Ⓐ Ⓑ Ⓒ Ⓓ

11. Ⓐ Ⓑ Ⓒ Ⓓ
12. Ⓐ Ⓑ Ⓒ Ⓓ
13. Ⓐ Ⓑ Ⓒ Ⓓ
14. Ⓐ Ⓑ Ⓒ Ⓓ
15. Ⓐ Ⓑ Ⓒ Ⓓ
16. Ⓐ Ⓑ Ⓒ Ⓓ
17. Ⓐ Ⓑ Ⓒ Ⓓ
18. Ⓐ Ⓑ Ⓒ Ⓓ
19. Ⓐ Ⓑ Ⓒ Ⓓ
20. Ⓐ Ⓑ Ⓒ Ⓓ

21. Ⓐ Ⓑ Ⓒ Ⓓ
22. Ⓐ Ⓑ Ⓒ Ⓓ
23. Ⓐ Ⓑ Ⓒ Ⓓ
24. Ⓐ Ⓑ Ⓒ Ⓓ
25. Ⓐ Ⓑ Ⓒ Ⓓ
26. Ⓐ Ⓑ Ⓒ Ⓓ
27. Ⓐ Ⓑ Ⓒ Ⓓ
28. Ⓐ Ⓑ Ⓒ Ⓓ
29. Ⓐ Ⓑ Ⓒ Ⓓ
30. Ⓐ Ⓑ Ⓒ Ⓓ

31. Ⓐ Ⓑ Ⓒ Ⓓ
32. Ⓐ Ⓑ Ⓒ Ⓓ
33. Ⓐ Ⓑ Ⓒ Ⓓ
34. Ⓐ Ⓑ Ⓒ Ⓓ
35. Ⓐ Ⓑ Ⓒ Ⓓ
36. Ⓐ Ⓑ Ⓒ Ⓓ
37. Ⓐ Ⓑ Ⓒ Ⓓ
38. Ⓐ Ⓑ Ⓒ Ⓓ
39. Ⓐ Ⓑ Ⓒ Ⓓ
40. Ⓐ Ⓑ Ⓒ Ⓓ

41. Ⓐ Ⓑ Ⓒ Ⓓ
42. Ⓐ Ⓑ Ⓒ Ⓓ
43. Ⓐ Ⓑ Ⓒ Ⓓ
44. Ⓐ Ⓑ Ⓒ Ⓓ
45. Ⓐ Ⓑ Ⓒ Ⓓ
46. Ⓐ Ⓑ Ⓒ Ⓓ
47. Ⓐ Ⓑ Ⓒ Ⓓ

Test 6 Answer Sheet

Verbal

1. Ⓐ Ⓑ Ⓒ Ⓓ	9. Ⓐ Ⓑ Ⓒ Ⓓ	17. Ⓐ Ⓑ Ⓒ Ⓓ	25. Ⓐ Ⓑ Ⓒ Ⓓ	33. Ⓐ Ⓑ Ⓒ Ⓓ
2. Ⓐ Ⓑ Ⓒ Ⓓ	10. Ⓐ Ⓑ Ⓒ Ⓓ	18. Ⓐ Ⓑ Ⓒ Ⓓ	26. Ⓐ Ⓑ Ⓒ Ⓓ	34. Ⓐ Ⓑ Ⓒ Ⓓ
3. Ⓐ Ⓑ Ⓒ Ⓓ	11. Ⓐ Ⓑ Ⓒ Ⓓ	19. Ⓐ Ⓑ Ⓒ Ⓓ	27. Ⓐ Ⓑ Ⓒ Ⓓ	35. Ⓐ Ⓑ Ⓒ Ⓓ
4. Ⓐ Ⓑ Ⓒ Ⓓ	12. Ⓐ Ⓑ Ⓒ Ⓓ	20. Ⓐ Ⓑ Ⓒ Ⓓ	28. Ⓐ Ⓑ Ⓒ Ⓓ	36. Ⓐ Ⓑ Ⓒ Ⓓ
5. Ⓐ Ⓑ Ⓒ Ⓓ	13. Ⓐ Ⓑ Ⓒ Ⓓ	21. Ⓐ Ⓑ Ⓒ Ⓓ	29. Ⓐ Ⓑ Ⓒ Ⓓ	37. Ⓐ Ⓑ Ⓒ Ⓓ
6. Ⓐ Ⓑ Ⓒ Ⓓ	14. Ⓐ Ⓑ Ⓒ Ⓓ	22. Ⓐ Ⓑ Ⓒ Ⓓ	30. Ⓐ Ⓑ Ⓒ Ⓓ	38. Ⓐ Ⓑ Ⓒ Ⓓ
7. Ⓐ Ⓑ Ⓒ Ⓓ	15. Ⓐ Ⓑ Ⓒ Ⓓ	23. Ⓐ Ⓑ Ⓒ Ⓓ	31. Ⓐ Ⓑ Ⓒ Ⓓ	39. Ⓐ Ⓑ Ⓒ Ⓓ
8. Ⓐ Ⓑ Ⓒ Ⓓ	16. Ⓐ Ⓑ Ⓒ Ⓓ	24. Ⓐ Ⓑ Ⓒ Ⓓ	32. Ⓐ Ⓑ Ⓒ Ⓓ	40. Ⓐ Ⓑ Ⓒ Ⓓ

Quantitative

1. Ⓐ Ⓑ Ⓒ Ⓓ	9. Ⓐ Ⓑ Ⓒ Ⓓ	17. Ⓐ Ⓑ Ⓒ Ⓓ	25. Ⓐ Ⓑ Ⓒ Ⓓ	33. Ⓐ Ⓑ Ⓒ Ⓓ
2. Ⓐ Ⓑ Ⓒ Ⓓ	10. Ⓐ Ⓑ Ⓒ Ⓓ	18. Ⓐ Ⓑ Ⓒ Ⓓ	26. Ⓐ Ⓑ Ⓒ Ⓓ	34. Ⓐ Ⓑ Ⓒ Ⓓ
3. Ⓐ Ⓑ Ⓒ Ⓓ	11. Ⓐ Ⓑ Ⓒ Ⓓ	19. Ⓐ Ⓑ Ⓒ Ⓓ	27. Ⓐ Ⓑ Ⓒ Ⓓ	35. Ⓐ Ⓑ Ⓒ Ⓓ
4. Ⓐ Ⓑ Ⓒ Ⓓ	12. Ⓐ Ⓑ Ⓒ Ⓓ	20. Ⓐ Ⓑ Ⓒ Ⓓ	28. Ⓐ Ⓑ Ⓒ Ⓓ	36. Ⓐ Ⓑ Ⓒ Ⓓ
5. Ⓐ Ⓑ Ⓒ Ⓓ	13. Ⓐ Ⓑ Ⓒ Ⓓ	21. Ⓐ Ⓑ Ⓒ Ⓓ	29. Ⓐ Ⓑ Ⓒ Ⓓ	37. Ⓐ Ⓑ Ⓒ Ⓓ
6. Ⓐ Ⓑ Ⓒ Ⓓ	14. Ⓐ Ⓑ Ⓒ Ⓓ	22. Ⓐ Ⓑ Ⓒ Ⓓ	30. Ⓐ Ⓑ Ⓒ Ⓓ	
7. Ⓐ Ⓑ Ⓒ Ⓓ	15. Ⓐ Ⓑ Ⓒ Ⓓ	23. Ⓐ Ⓑ Ⓒ Ⓓ	31. Ⓐ Ⓑ Ⓒ Ⓓ	
8. Ⓐ Ⓑ Ⓒ Ⓓ	16. Ⓐ Ⓑ Ⓒ Ⓓ	24. Ⓐ Ⓑ Ⓒ Ⓓ	32. Ⓐ Ⓑ Ⓒ Ⓓ	

Reading

1. Ⓐ Ⓑ Ⓒ Ⓓ	9. Ⓐ Ⓑ Ⓒ Ⓓ	17. Ⓐ Ⓑ Ⓒ Ⓓ	25. Ⓐ Ⓑ Ⓒ Ⓓ	33. Ⓐ Ⓑ Ⓒ Ⓓ
2. Ⓐ Ⓑ Ⓒ Ⓓ	10. Ⓐ Ⓑ Ⓒ Ⓓ	18. Ⓐ Ⓑ Ⓒ Ⓓ	26. Ⓐ Ⓑ Ⓒ Ⓓ	34. Ⓐ Ⓑ Ⓒ Ⓓ
3. Ⓐ Ⓑ Ⓒ Ⓓ	11. Ⓐ Ⓑ Ⓒ Ⓓ	19. Ⓐ Ⓑ Ⓒ Ⓓ	27. Ⓐ Ⓑ Ⓒ Ⓓ	35. Ⓐ Ⓑ Ⓒ Ⓓ
4. Ⓐ Ⓑ Ⓒ Ⓓ	12. Ⓐ Ⓑ Ⓒ Ⓓ	20. Ⓐ Ⓑ Ⓒ Ⓓ	28. Ⓐ Ⓑ Ⓒ Ⓓ	36. Ⓐ Ⓑ Ⓒ Ⓓ
5. Ⓐ Ⓑ Ⓒ Ⓓ	13. Ⓐ Ⓑ Ⓒ Ⓓ	21. Ⓐ Ⓑ Ⓒ Ⓓ	29. Ⓐ Ⓑ Ⓒ Ⓓ	
6. Ⓐ Ⓑ Ⓒ Ⓓ	14. Ⓐ Ⓑ Ⓒ Ⓓ	22. Ⓐ Ⓑ Ⓒ Ⓓ	30. Ⓐ Ⓑ Ⓒ Ⓓ	
7. Ⓐ Ⓑ Ⓒ Ⓓ	15. Ⓐ Ⓑ Ⓒ Ⓓ	23. Ⓐ Ⓑ Ⓒ Ⓓ	31. Ⓐ Ⓑ Ⓒ Ⓓ	
8. Ⓐ Ⓑ Ⓒ Ⓓ	16. Ⓐ Ⓑ Ⓒ Ⓓ	24. Ⓐ Ⓑ Ⓒ Ⓓ	32. Ⓐ Ⓑ Ⓒ Ⓓ	

Math

1. Ⓐ Ⓑ Ⓒ Ⓓ	11. Ⓐ Ⓑ Ⓒ Ⓓ	21. Ⓐ Ⓑ Ⓒ Ⓓ	31. Ⓐ Ⓑ Ⓒ Ⓓ	41. Ⓐ Ⓑ Ⓒ Ⓓ
2. Ⓐ Ⓑ Ⓒ Ⓓ	12. Ⓐ Ⓑ Ⓒ Ⓓ	22. Ⓐ Ⓑ Ⓒ Ⓓ	32. Ⓐ Ⓑ Ⓒ Ⓓ	42. Ⓐ Ⓑ Ⓒ Ⓓ
3. Ⓐ Ⓑ Ⓒ Ⓓ	13. Ⓐ Ⓑ Ⓒ Ⓓ	23. Ⓐ Ⓑ Ⓒ Ⓓ	33. Ⓐ Ⓑ Ⓒ Ⓓ	43. Ⓐ Ⓑ Ⓒ Ⓓ
4. Ⓐ Ⓑ Ⓒ Ⓓ	14. Ⓐ Ⓑ Ⓒ Ⓓ	24. Ⓐ Ⓑ Ⓒ Ⓓ	34. Ⓐ Ⓑ Ⓒ Ⓓ	44. Ⓐ Ⓑ Ⓒ Ⓓ
5. Ⓐ Ⓑ Ⓒ Ⓓ	15. Ⓐ Ⓑ Ⓒ Ⓓ	25. Ⓐ Ⓑ Ⓒ Ⓓ	35. Ⓐ Ⓑ Ⓒ Ⓓ	45. Ⓐ Ⓑ Ⓒ Ⓓ
6. Ⓐ Ⓑ Ⓒ Ⓓ	16. Ⓐ Ⓑ Ⓒ Ⓓ	26. Ⓐ Ⓑ Ⓒ Ⓓ	36. Ⓐ Ⓑ Ⓒ Ⓓ	46. Ⓐ Ⓑ Ⓒ Ⓓ
7. Ⓐ Ⓑ Ⓒ Ⓓ	17. Ⓐ Ⓑ Ⓒ Ⓓ	27. Ⓐ Ⓑ Ⓒ Ⓓ	37. Ⓐ Ⓑ Ⓒ Ⓓ	47. Ⓐ Ⓑ Ⓒ Ⓓ
8. Ⓐ Ⓑ Ⓒ Ⓓ	18. Ⓐ Ⓑ Ⓒ Ⓓ	28. Ⓐ Ⓑ Ⓒ Ⓓ	38. Ⓐ Ⓑ Ⓒ Ⓓ	
9. Ⓐ Ⓑ Ⓒ Ⓓ	19. Ⓐ Ⓑ Ⓒ Ⓓ	29. Ⓐ Ⓑ Ⓒ Ⓓ	39. Ⓐ Ⓑ Ⓒ Ⓓ	
10. Ⓐ Ⓑ Ⓒ Ⓓ	20. Ⓐ Ⓑ Ⓒ Ⓓ	30. Ⓐ Ⓑ Ⓒ Ⓓ	40. Ⓐ Ⓑ Ⓒ Ⓓ	

Test 7 Answer Sheet

Verbal

1. Ⓐ Ⓑ Ⓒ Ⓓ	9. Ⓐ Ⓑ Ⓒ Ⓓ	17. Ⓐ Ⓑ Ⓒ Ⓓ	25. Ⓐ Ⓑ Ⓒ Ⓓ	33. Ⓐ Ⓑ Ⓒ Ⓓ
2. Ⓐ Ⓑ Ⓒ Ⓓ	10. Ⓐ Ⓑ Ⓒ Ⓓ	18. Ⓐ Ⓑ Ⓒ Ⓓ	26. Ⓐ Ⓑ Ⓒ Ⓓ	34. Ⓐ Ⓑ Ⓒ Ⓓ
3. Ⓐ Ⓑ Ⓒ Ⓓ	11. Ⓐ Ⓑ Ⓒ Ⓓ	19. Ⓐ Ⓑ Ⓒ Ⓓ	27. Ⓐ Ⓑ Ⓒ Ⓓ	35. Ⓐ Ⓑ Ⓒ Ⓓ
4. Ⓐ Ⓑ Ⓒ Ⓓ	12. Ⓐ Ⓑ Ⓒ Ⓓ	20. Ⓐ Ⓑ Ⓒ Ⓓ	28. Ⓐ Ⓑ Ⓒ Ⓓ	36. Ⓐ Ⓑ Ⓒ Ⓓ
5. Ⓐ Ⓑ Ⓒ Ⓓ	13. Ⓐ Ⓑ Ⓒ Ⓓ	21. Ⓐ Ⓑ Ⓒ Ⓓ	29. Ⓐ Ⓑ Ⓒ Ⓓ	37. Ⓐ Ⓑ Ⓒ Ⓓ
6. Ⓐ Ⓑ Ⓒ Ⓓ	14. Ⓐ Ⓑ Ⓒ Ⓓ	22. Ⓐ Ⓑ Ⓒ Ⓓ	30. Ⓐ Ⓑ Ⓒ Ⓓ	38. Ⓐ Ⓑ Ⓒ Ⓓ
7. Ⓐ Ⓑ Ⓒ Ⓓ	15. Ⓐ Ⓑ Ⓒ Ⓓ	23. Ⓐ Ⓑ Ⓒ Ⓓ	31. Ⓐ Ⓑ Ⓒ Ⓓ	39. Ⓐ Ⓑ Ⓒ Ⓓ
8. Ⓐ Ⓑ Ⓒ Ⓓ	16. Ⓐ Ⓑ Ⓒ Ⓓ	24. Ⓐ Ⓑ Ⓒ Ⓓ	32. Ⓐ Ⓑ Ⓒ Ⓓ	40. Ⓐ Ⓑ Ⓒ Ⓓ

Quantitative

1. Ⓐ Ⓑ Ⓒ Ⓓ	9. Ⓐ Ⓑ Ⓒ Ⓓ	17. Ⓐ Ⓑ Ⓒ Ⓓ	25. Ⓐ Ⓑ Ⓒ Ⓓ	33. Ⓐ Ⓑ Ⓒ Ⓓ
2. Ⓐ Ⓑ Ⓒ Ⓓ	10. Ⓐ Ⓑ Ⓒ Ⓓ	18. Ⓐ Ⓑ Ⓒ Ⓓ	26. Ⓐ Ⓑ Ⓒ Ⓓ	34. Ⓐ Ⓑ Ⓒ Ⓓ
3. Ⓐ Ⓑ Ⓒ Ⓓ	11. Ⓐ Ⓑ Ⓒ Ⓓ	19. Ⓐ Ⓑ Ⓒ Ⓓ	27. Ⓐ Ⓑ Ⓒ Ⓓ	35. Ⓐ Ⓑ Ⓒ Ⓓ
4. Ⓐ Ⓑ Ⓒ Ⓓ	12. Ⓐ Ⓑ Ⓒ Ⓓ	20. Ⓐ Ⓑ Ⓒ Ⓓ	28. Ⓐ Ⓑ Ⓒ Ⓓ	36. Ⓐ Ⓑ Ⓒ Ⓓ
5. Ⓐ Ⓑ Ⓒ Ⓓ	13. Ⓐ Ⓑ Ⓒ Ⓓ	21. Ⓐ Ⓑ Ⓒ Ⓓ	29. Ⓐ Ⓑ Ⓒ Ⓓ	37. Ⓐ Ⓑ Ⓒ Ⓓ
6. Ⓐ Ⓑ Ⓒ Ⓓ	14. Ⓐ Ⓑ Ⓒ Ⓓ	22. Ⓐ Ⓑ Ⓒ Ⓓ	30. Ⓐ Ⓑ Ⓒ Ⓓ	
7. Ⓐ Ⓑ Ⓒ Ⓓ	15. Ⓐ Ⓑ Ⓒ Ⓓ	23. Ⓐ Ⓑ Ⓒ Ⓓ	31. Ⓐ Ⓑ Ⓒ Ⓓ	
8. Ⓐ Ⓑ Ⓒ Ⓓ	16. Ⓐ Ⓑ Ⓒ Ⓓ	24. Ⓐ Ⓑ Ⓒ Ⓓ	32. Ⓐ Ⓑ Ⓒ Ⓓ	

Reading

1. Ⓐ Ⓑ Ⓒ Ⓓ   9. Ⓐ Ⓑ Ⓒ Ⓓ   17. Ⓐ Ⓑ Ⓒ Ⓓ   25. Ⓐ Ⓑ Ⓒ Ⓓ   33. Ⓐ Ⓑ Ⓒ Ⓓ
2. Ⓐ Ⓑ Ⓒ Ⓓ   10. Ⓐ Ⓑ Ⓒ Ⓓ   18. Ⓐ Ⓑ Ⓒ Ⓓ   26. Ⓐ Ⓑ Ⓒ Ⓓ   34. Ⓐ Ⓑ Ⓒ Ⓓ
3. Ⓐ Ⓑ Ⓒ Ⓓ   11. Ⓐ Ⓑ Ⓒ Ⓓ   19. Ⓐ Ⓑ Ⓒ Ⓓ   27. Ⓐ Ⓑ Ⓒ Ⓓ   35. Ⓐ Ⓑ Ⓒ Ⓓ
4. Ⓐ Ⓑ Ⓒ Ⓓ   12. Ⓐ Ⓑ Ⓒ Ⓓ   20. Ⓐ Ⓑ Ⓒ Ⓓ   28. Ⓐ Ⓑ Ⓒ Ⓓ   36. Ⓐ Ⓑ Ⓒ Ⓓ
5. Ⓐ Ⓑ Ⓒ Ⓓ   13. Ⓐ Ⓑ Ⓒ Ⓓ   21. Ⓐ Ⓑ Ⓒ Ⓓ   29. Ⓐ Ⓑ Ⓒ Ⓓ
6. Ⓐ Ⓑ Ⓒ Ⓓ   14. Ⓐ Ⓑ Ⓒ Ⓓ   22. Ⓐ Ⓑ Ⓒ Ⓓ   30. Ⓐ Ⓑ Ⓒ Ⓓ
7. Ⓐ Ⓑ Ⓒ Ⓓ   15. Ⓐ Ⓑ Ⓒ Ⓓ   23. Ⓐ Ⓑ Ⓒ Ⓓ   31. Ⓐ Ⓑ Ⓒ Ⓓ
8. Ⓐ Ⓑ Ⓒ Ⓓ   16. Ⓐ Ⓑ Ⓒ Ⓓ   24. Ⓐ Ⓑ Ⓒ Ⓓ   32. Ⓐ Ⓑ Ⓒ Ⓓ

Math

1. Ⓐ Ⓑ Ⓒ Ⓓ   11. Ⓐ Ⓑ Ⓒ Ⓓ   21. Ⓐ Ⓑ Ⓒ Ⓓ   31. Ⓐ Ⓑ Ⓒ Ⓓ   41. Ⓐ Ⓑ Ⓒ Ⓓ
2. Ⓐ Ⓑ Ⓒ Ⓓ   12. Ⓐ Ⓑ Ⓒ Ⓓ   22. Ⓐ Ⓑ Ⓒ Ⓓ   32. Ⓐ Ⓑ Ⓒ Ⓓ   42. Ⓐ Ⓑ Ⓒ Ⓓ
3. Ⓐ Ⓑ Ⓒ Ⓓ   13. Ⓐ Ⓑ Ⓒ Ⓓ   23. Ⓐ Ⓑ Ⓒ Ⓓ   33. Ⓐ Ⓑ Ⓒ Ⓓ   43. Ⓐ Ⓑ Ⓒ Ⓓ
4. Ⓐ Ⓑ Ⓒ Ⓓ   14. Ⓐ Ⓑ Ⓒ Ⓓ   24. Ⓐ Ⓑ Ⓒ Ⓓ   34. Ⓐ Ⓑ Ⓒ Ⓓ   44. Ⓐ Ⓑ Ⓒ Ⓓ
5. Ⓐ Ⓑ Ⓒ Ⓓ   15. Ⓐ Ⓑ Ⓒ Ⓓ   25. Ⓐ Ⓑ Ⓒ Ⓓ   35. Ⓐ Ⓑ Ⓒ Ⓓ   45. Ⓐ Ⓑ Ⓒ Ⓓ
6. Ⓐ Ⓑ Ⓒ Ⓓ   16. Ⓐ Ⓑ Ⓒ Ⓓ   26. Ⓐ Ⓑ Ⓒ Ⓓ   36. Ⓐ Ⓑ Ⓒ Ⓓ   46. Ⓐ Ⓑ Ⓒ Ⓓ
7. Ⓐ Ⓑ Ⓒ Ⓓ   17. Ⓐ Ⓑ Ⓒ Ⓓ   27. Ⓐ Ⓑ Ⓒ Ⓓ   37. Ⓐ Ⓑ Ⓒ Ⓓ   47. Ⓐ Ⓑ Ⓒ Ⓓ
8. Ⓐ Ⓑ Ⓒ Ⓓ   18. Ⓐ Ⓑ Ⓒ Ⓓ   28. Ⓐ Ⓑ Ⓒ Ⓓ   38. Ⓐ Ⓑ Ⓒ Ⓓ
9. Ⓐ Ⓑ Ⓒ Ⓓ   19. Ⓐ Ⓑ Ⓒ Ⓓ   29. Ⓐ Ⓑ Ⓒ Ⓓ   39. Ⓐ Ⓑ Ⓒ Ⓓ
10. Ⓐ Ⓑ Ⓒ Ⓓ   20. Ⓐ Ⓑ Ⓒ Ⓓ   30. Ⓐ Ⓑ Ⓒ Ⓓ   40. Ⓐ Ⓑ Ⓒ Ⓓ

Test 8 Answer Sheet

Verbal

1. (A) (B) (C) (D)	9. (A) (B) (C) (D)	17. (A) (B) (C) (D)	25. (A) (B) (C) (D)	33. (A) (B) (C) (D)
2. (A) (B) (C) (D)	10. (A) (B) (C) (D)	18. (A) (B) (C) (D)	26. (A) (B) (C) (D)	34. (A) (B) (C) (D)
3. (A) (B) (C) (D)	11. (A) (B) (C) (D)	19. (A) (B) (C) (D)	27. (A) (B) (C) (D)	35. (A) (B) (C) (D)
4. (A) (B) (C) (D)	12. (A) (B) (C) (D)	20. (A) (B) (C) (D)	28. (A) (B) (C) (D)	36. (A) (B) (C) (D)
5. (A) (B) (C) (D)	13. (A) (B) (C) (D)	21. (A) (B) (C) (D)	29. (A) (B) (C) (D)	37. (A) (B) (C) (D)
6. (A) (B) (C) (D)	14. (A) (B) (C) (D)	22. (A) (B) (C) (D)	30. (A) (B) (C) (D)	38. (A) (B) (C) (D)
7. (A) (B) (C) (D)	15. (A) (B) (C) (D)	23. (A) (B) (C) (D)	31. (A) (B) (C) (D)	39. (A) (B) (C) (D)
8. (A) (B) (C) (D)	16. (A) (B) (C) (D)	24. (A) (B) (C) (D)	32. (A) (B) (C) (D)	40. (A) (B) (C) (D)

Quantitative

1. (A) (B) (C) (D)	9. (A) (B) (C) (D)	17. (A) (B) (C) (D)	25. (A) (B) (C) (D)	33. (A) (B) (C) (D)
2. (A) (B) (C) (D)	10. (A) (B) (C) (D)	18. (A) (B) (C) (D)	26. (A) (B) (C) (D)	34. (A) (B) (C) (D)
3. (A) (B) (C) (D)	11. (A) (B) (C) (D)	19. (A) (B) (C) (D)	27. (A) (B) (C) (D)	35. (A) (B) (C) (D)
4. (A) (B) (C) (D)	12. (A) (B) (C) (D)	20. (A) (B) (C) (D)	28. (A) (B) (C) (D)	36. (A) (B) (C) (D)
5. (A) (B) (C) (D)	13. (A) (B) (C) (D)	21. (A) (B) (C) (D)	29. (A) (B) (C) (D)	37. (A) (B) (C) (D)
6. (A) (B) (C) (D)	14. (A) (B) (C) (D)	22. (A) (B) (C) (D)	30. (A) (B) (C) (D)	
7. (A) (B) (C) (D)	15. (A) (B) (C) (D)	23. (A) (B) (C) (D)	31. (A) (B) (C) (D)	
8. (A) (B) (C) (D)	16. (A) (B) (C) (D)	24. (A) (B) (C) (D)	32. (A) (B) (C) (D)	

Reading

1. Ⓐ Ⓑ Ⓒ Ⓓ
2. Ⓐ Ⓑ Ⓒ Ⓓ
3. Ⓐ Ⓑ Ⓒ Ⓓ
4. Ⓐ Ⓑ Ⓒ Ⓓ
5. Ⓐ Ⓑ Ⓒ Ⓓ
6. Ⓐ Ⓑ Ⓒ Ⓓ
7. Ⓐ Ⓑ Ⓒ Ⓓ
8. Ⓐ Ⓑ Ⓒ Ⓓ

9. Ⓐ Ⓑ Ⓒ Ⓓ
10. Ⓐ Ⓑ Ⓒ Ⓓ
11. Ⓐ Ⓑ Ⓒ Ⓓ
12. Ⓐ Ⓑ Ⓒ Ⓓ
13. Ⓐ Ⓑ Ⓒ Ⓓ
14. Ⓐ Ⓑ Ⓒ Ⓓ
15. Ⓐ Ⓑ Ⓒ Ⓓ
16. Ⓐ Ⓑ Ⓒ Ⓓ

17. Ⓐ Ⓑ Ⓒ Ⓓ
18. Ⓐ Ⓑ Ⓒ Ⓓ
19. Ⓐ Ⓑ Ⓒ Ⓓ
20. Ⓐ Ⓑ Ⓒ Ⓓ
21. Ⓐ Ⓑ Ⓒ Ⓓ
22. Ⓐ Ⓑ Ⓒ Ⓓ
23. Ⓐ Ⓑ Ⓒ Ⓓ
24. Ⓐ Ⓑ Ⓒ Ⓓ

25. Ⓐ Ⓑ Ⓒ Ⓓ
26. Ⓐ Ⓑ Ⓒ Ⓓ
27. Ⓐ Ⓑ Ⓒ Ⓓ
28. Ⓐ Ⓑ Ⓒ Ⓓ
29. Ⓐ Ⓑ Ⓒ Ⓓ
30. Ⓐ Ⓑ Ⓒ Ⓓ
31. Ⓐ Ⓑ Ⓒ Ⓓ
32. Ⓐ Ⓑ Ⓒ Ⓓ

33. Ⓐ Ⓑ Ⓒ Ⓓ
34. Ⓐ Ⓑ Ⓒ Ⓓ
35. Ⓐ Ⓑ Ⓒ Ⓓ
36. Ⓐ Ⓑ Ⓒ Ⓓ

Math

1. Ⓐ Ⓑ Ⓒ Ⓓ
2. Ⓐ Ⓑ Ⓒ Ⓓ
3. Ⓐ Ⓑ Ⓒ Ⓓ
4. Ⓐ Ⓑ Ⓒ Ⓓ
5. Ⓐ Ⓑ Ⓒ Ⓓ
6. Ⓐ Ⓑ Ⓒ Ⓓ
7. Ⓐ Ⓑ Ⓒ Ⓓ
8. Ⓐ Ⓑ Ⓒ Ⓓ
9. Ⓐ Ⓑ Ⓒ Ⓓ
10. Ⓐ Ⓑ Ⓒ Ⓓ

11. Ⓐ Ⓑ Ⓒ Ⓓ
12. Ⓐ Ⓑ Ⓒ Ⓓ
13. Ⓐ Ⓑ Ⓒ Ⓓ
14. Ⓐ Ⓑ Ⓒ Ⓓ
15. Ⓐ Ⓑ Ⓒ Ⓓ
16. Ⓐ Ⓑ Ⓒ Ⓓ
17. Ⓐ Ⓑ Ⓒ Ⓓ
18. Ⓐ Ⓑ Ⓒ Ⓓ
19. Ⓐ Ⓑ Ⓒ Ⓓ
20. Ⓐ Ⓑ Ⓒ Ⓓ

21. Ⓐ Ⓑ Ⓒ Ⓓ
22. Ⓐ Ⓑ Ⓒ Ⓓ
23. Ⓐ Ⓑ Ⓒ Ⓓ
24. Ⓐ Ⓑ Ⓒ Ⓓ
25. Ⓐ Ⓑ Ⓒ Ⓓ
26. Ⓐ Ⓑ Ⓒ Ⓓ
27. Ⓐ Ⓑ Ⓒ Ⓓ
28. Ⓐ Ⓑ Ⓒ Ⓓ
29. Ⓐ Ⓑ Ⓒ Ⓓ
30. Ⓐ Ⓑ Ⓒ Ⓓ

31. Ⓐ Ⓑ Ⓒ Ⓓ
32. Ⓐ Ⓑ Ⓒ Ⓓ
33. Ⓐ Ⓑ Ⓒ Ⓓ
34. Ⓐ Ⓑ Ⓒ Ⓓ
35. Ⓐ Ⓑ Ⓒ Ⓓ
36. Ⓐ Ⓑ Ⓒ Ⓓ
37. Ⓐ Ⓑ Ⓒ Ⓓ
38. Ⓐ Ⓑ Ⓒ Ⓓ
39. Ⓐ Ⓑ Ⓒ Ⓓ
40. Ⓐ Ⓑ Ⓒ Ⓓ

41. Ⓐ Ⓑ Ⓒ Ⓓ
42. Ⓐ Ⓑ Ⓒ Ⓓ
43. Ⓐ Ⓑ Ⓒ Ⓓ
44. Ⓐ Ⓑ Ⓒ Ⓓ
45. Ⓐ Ⓑ Ⓒ Ⓓ
46. Ⓐ Ⓑ Ⓒ Ⓓ
47. Ⓐ Ⓑ Ⓒ Ⓓ

Test 9 Answer Sheet

Verbal

1. A B C D	9. A B C D	17. A B C D	25. A B C D	33. A B C D
2. A B C D	10. A B C D	18. A B C D	26. A B C D	34. A B C D
3. A B C D	11. A B C D	19. A B C D	27. A B C D	35. A B C D
4. A B C D	12. A B C D	20. A B C D	28. A B C D	36. A B C D
5. A B C D	13. A B C D	21. A B C D	29. A B C D	37. A B C D
6. A B C D	14. A B C D	22. A B C D	30. A B C D	38. A B C D
7. A B C D	15. A B C D	23. A B C D	31. A B C D	39. A B C D
8. A B C D	16. A B C D	24. A B C D	32. A B C D	40. A B C D

Quantitative

1. A B C D	9. A B C D	17. A B C D	25. A B C D	33. A B C D
2. A B C D	10. A B C D	18. A B C D	26. A B C D	34. A B C D
3. A B C D	11. A B C D	19. A B C D	27. A B C D	35. A B C D
4. A B C D	12. A B C D	20. A B C D	28. A B C D	36. A B C D
5. A B C D	13. A B C D	21. A B C D	29. A B C D	37. A B C D
6. A B C D	14. A B C D	22. A B C D	30. A B C D	
7. A B C D	15. A B C D	23. A B C D	31. A B C D	
8. A B C D	16. A B C D	24. A B C D	32. A B C D	

Reading

1. Ⓐ Ⓑ Ⓒ Ⓓ	9. Ⓐ Ⓑ Ⓒ Ⓓ	17. Ⓐ Ⓑ Ⓒ Ⓓ	25. Ⓐ Ⓑ Ⓒ Ⓓ	33. Ⓐ Ⓑ Ⓒ Ⓓ
2. Ⓐ Ⓑ Ⓒ Ⓓ	10. Ⓐ Ⓑ Ⓒ Ⓓ	18. Ⓐ Ⓑ Ⓒ Ⓓ	26. Ⓐ Ⓑ Ⓒ Ⓓ	34. Ⓐ Ⓑ Ⓒ Ⓓ
3. Ⓐ Ⓑ Ⓒ Ⓓ	11. Ⓐ Ⓑ Ⓒ Ⓓ	19. Ⓐ Ⓑ Ⓒ Ⓓ	27. Ⓐ Ⓑ Ⓒ Ⓓ	35. Ⓐ Ⓑ Ⓒ Ⓓ
4. Ⓐ Ⓑ Ⓒ Ⓓ	12. Ⓐ Ⓑ Ⓒ Ⓓ	20. Ⓐ Ⓑ Ⓒ Ⓓ	28. Ⓐ Ⓑ Ⓒ Ⓓ	36. Ⓐ Ⓑ Ⓒ Ⓓ
5. Ⓐ Ⓑ Ⓒ Ⓓ	13. Ⓐ Ⓑ Ⓒ Ⓓ	21. Ⓐ Ⓑ Ⓒ Ⓓ	29. Ⓐ Ⓑ Ⓒ Ⓓ	
6. Ⓐ Ⓑ Ⓒ Ⓓ	14. Ⓐ Ⓑ Ⓒ Ⓓ	22. Ⓐ Ⓑ Ⓒ Ⓓ	30. Ⓐ Ⓑ Ⓒ Ⓓ	
7. Ⓐ Ⓑ Ⓒ Ⓓ	15. Ⓐ Ⓑ Ⓒ Ⓓ	23. Ⓐ Ⓑ Ⓒ Ⓓ	31. Ⓐ Ⓑ Ⓒ Ⓓ	
8. Ⓐ Ⓑ Ⓒ Ⓓ	16. Ⓐ Ⓑ Ⓒ Ⓓ	24. Ⓐ Ⓑ Ⓒ Ⓓ	32. Ⓐ Ⓑ Ⓒ Ⓓ	

Math

1. Ⓐ Ⓑ Ⓒ Ⓓ	11. Ⓐ Ⓑ Ⓒ Ⓓ	21. Ⓐ Ⓑ Ⓒ Ⓓ	31. Ⓐ Ⓑ Ⓒ Ⓓ	41. Ⓐ Ⓑ Ⓒ Ⓓ
2. Ⓐ Ⓑ Ⓒ Ⓓ	12. Ⓐ Ⓑ Ⓒ Ⓓ	22. Ⓐ Ⓑ Ⓒ Ⓓ	32. Ⓐ Ⓑ Ⓒ Ⓓ	42. Ⓐ Ⓑ Ⓒ Ⓓ
3. Ⓐ Ⓑ Ⓒ Ⓓ	13. Ⓐ Ⓑ Ⓒ Ⓓ	23. Ⓐ Ⓑ Ⓒ Ⓓ	33. Ⓐ Ⓑ Ⓒ Ⓓ	43. Ⓐ Ⓑ Ⓒ Ⓓ
4. Ⓐ Ⓑ Ⓒ Ⓓ	14. Ⓐ Ⓑ Ⓒ Ⓓ	24. Ⓐ Ⓑ Ⓒ Ⓓ	34. Ⓐ Ⓑ Ⓒ Ⓓ	44. Ⓐ Ⓑ Ⓒ Ⓓ
5. Ⓐ Ⓑ Ⓒ Ⓓ	15. Ⓐ Ⓑ Ⓒ Ⓓ	25. Ⓐ Ⓑ Ⓒ Ⓓ	35. Ⓐ Ⓑ Ⓒ Ⓓ	45. Ⓐ Ⓑ Ⓒ Ⓓ
6. Ⓐ Ⓑ Ⓒ Ⓓ	16. Ⓐ Ⓑ Ⓒ Ⓓ	26. Ⓐ Ⓑ Ⓒ Ⓓ	36. Ⓐ Ⓑ Ⓒ Ⓓ	46. Ⓐ Ⓑ Ⓒ Ⓓ
7. Ⓐ Ⓑ Ⓒ Ⓓ	17. Ⓐ Ⓑ Ⓒ Ⓓ	27. Ⓐ Ⓑ Ⓒ Ⓓ	37. Ⓐ Ⓑ Ⓒ Ⓓ	47. Ⓐ Ⓑ Ⓒ Ⓓ
8. Ⓐ Ⓑ Ⓒ Ⓓ	18. Ⓐ Ⓑ Ⓒ Ⓓ	28. Ⓐ Ⓑ Ⓒ Ⓓ	38. Ⓐ Ⓑ Ⓒ Ⓓ	
9. Ⓐ Ⓑ Ⓒ Ⓓ	19. Ⓐ Ⓑ Ⓒ Ⓓ	29. Ⓐ Ⓑ Ⓒ Ⓓ	39. Ⓐ Ⓑ Ⓒ Ⓓ	
10. Ⓐ Ⓑ Ⓒ Ⓓ	20. Ⓐ Ⓑ Ⓒ Ⓓ	30. Ⓐ Ⓑ Ⓒ Ⓓ	40. Ⓐ Ⓑ Ⓒ Ⓓ	

Test 10 Answer Sheet

Verbal

1. Ⓐ Ⓑ Ⓒ Ⓓ
2. Ⓐ Ⓑ Ⓒ Ⓓ
3. Ⓐ Ⓑ Ⓒ Ⓓ
4. Ⓐ Ⓑ Ⓒ Ⓓ
5. Ⓐ Ⓑ Ⓒ Ⓓ
6. Ⓐ Ⓑ Ⓒ Ⓓ
7. Ⓐ Ⓑ Ⓒ Ⓓ
8. Ⓐ Ⓑ Ⓒ Ⓓ

9. Ⓐ Ⓑ Ⓒ Ⓓ
10. Ⓐ Ⓑ Ⓒ Ⓓ
11. Ⓐ Ⓑ Ⓒ Ⓓ
12. Ⓐ Ⓑ Ⓒ Ⓓ
13. Ⓐ Ⓑ Ⓒ Ⓓ
14. Ⓐ Ⓑ Ⓒ Ⓓ
15. Ⓐ Ⓑ Ⓒ Ⓓ
16. Ⓐ Ⓑ Ⓒ Ⓓ

17. Ⓐ Ⓑ Ⓒ Ⓓ
18. Ⓐ Ⓑ Ⓒ Ⓓ
19. Ⓐ Ⓑ Ⓒ Ⓓ
20. Ⓐ Ⓑ Ⓒ Ⓓ
21. Ⓐ Ⓑ Ⓒ Ⓓ
22. Ⓐ Ⓑ Ⓒ Ⓓ
23. Ⓐ Ⓑ Ⓒ Ⓓ
24. Ⓐ Ⓑ Ⓒ Ⓓ

25. Ⓐ Ⓑ Ⓒ Ⓓ
26. Ⓐ Ⓑ Ⓒ Ⓓ
27. Ⓐ Ⓑ Ⓒ Ⓓ
28. Ⓐ Ⓑ Ⓒ Ⓓ
29. Ⓐ Ⓑ Ⓒ Ⓓ
30. Ⓐ Ⓑ Ⓒ Ⓓ
31. Ⓐ Ⓑ Ⓒ Ⓓ
32. Ⓐ Ⓑ Ⓒ Ⓓ

33. Ⓐ Ⓑ Ⓒ Ⓓ
34. Ⓐ Ⓑ Ⓒ Ⓓ
35. Ⓐ Ⓑ Ⓒ Ⓓ
36. Ⓐ Ⓑ Ⓒ Ⓓ
37. Ⓐ Ⓑ Ⓒ Ⓓ
38. Ⓐ Ⓑ Ⓒ Ⓓ
39. Ⓐ Ⓑ Ⓒ Ⓓ
40. Ⓐ Ⓑ Ⓒ Ⓓ

Quantitative

1. Ⓐ Ⓑ Ⓒ Ⓓ
2. Ⓐ Ⓑ Ⓒ Ⓓ
3. Ⓐ Ⓑ Ⓒ Ⓓ
4. Ⓐ Ⓑ Ⓒ Ⓓ
5. Ⓐ Ⓑ Ⓒ Ⓓ
6. Ⓐ Ⓑ Ⓒ Ⓓ
7. Ⓐ Ⓑ Ⓒ Ⓓ
8. Ⓐ Ⓑ Ⓒ Ⓓ

9. Ⓐ Ⓑ Ⓒ Ⓓ
10. Ⓐ Ⓑ Ⓒ Ⓓ
11. Ⓐ Ⓑ Ⓒ Ⓓ
12. Ⓐ Ⓑ Ⓒ Ⓓ
13. Ⓐ Ⓑ Ⓒ Ⓓ
14. Ⓐ Ⓑ Ⓒ Ⓓ
15. Ⓐ Ⓑ Ⓒ Ⓓ
16. Ⓐ Ⓑ Ⓒ Ⓓ

17. Ⓐ Ⓑ Ⓒ Ⓓ
18. Ⓐ Ⓑ Ⓒ Ⓓ
19. Ⓐ Ⓑ Ⓒ Ⓓ
20. Ⓐ Ⓑ Ⓒ Ⓓ
21. Ⓐ Ⓑ Ⓒ Ⓓ
22. Ⓐ Ⓑ Ⓒ Ⓓ
23. Ⓐ Ⓑ Ⓒ Ⓓ
24. Ⓐ Ⓑ Ⓒ Ⓓ

25. Ⓐ Ⓑ Ⓒ Ⓓ
26. Ⓐ Ⓑ Ⓒ Ⓓ
27. Ⓐ Ⓑ Ⓒ Ⓓ
28. Ⓐ Ⓑ Ⓒ Ⓓ
29. Ⓐ Ⓑ Ⓒ Ⓓ
30. Ⓐ Ⓑ Ⓒ Ⓓ
31. Ⓐ Ⓑ Ⓒ Ⓓ
32. Ⓐ Ⓑ Ⓒ Ⓓ

33. Ⓐ Ⓑ Ⓒ Ⓓ
34. Ⓐ Ⓑ Ⓒ Ⓓ
35. Ⓐ Ⓑ Ⓒ Ⓓ
36. Ⓐ Ⓑ Ⓒ Ⓓ
37. Ⓐ Ⓑ Ⓒ Ⓓ

Reading

1. Ⓐ Ⓑ Ⓒ Ⓓ
2. Ⓐ Ⓑ Ⓒ Ⓓ
3. Ⓐ Ⓑ Ⓒ Ⓓ
4. Ⓐ Ⓑ Ⓒ Ⓓ
5. Ⓐ Ⓑ Ⓒ Ⓓ
6. Ⓐ Ⓑ Ⓒ Ⓓ
7. Ⓐ Ⓑ Ⓒ Ⓓ
8. Ⓐ Ⓑ Ⓒ Ⓓ

9. Ⓐ Ⓑ Ⓒ Ⓓ
10. Ⓐ Ⓑ Ⓒ Ⓓ
11. Ⓐ Ⓑ Ⓒ Ⓓ
12. Ⓐ Ⓑ Ⓒ Ⓓ
13. Ⓐ Ⓑ Ⓒ Ⓓ
14. Ⓐ Ⓑ Ⓒ Ⓓ
15. Ⓐ Ⓑ Ⓒ Ⓓ
16. Ⓐ Ⓑ Ⓒ Ⓓ

17. Ⓐ Ⓑ Ⓒ Ⓓ
18. Ⓐ Ⓑ Ⓒ Ⓓ
19. Ⓐ Ⓑ Ⓒ Ⓓ
20. Ⓐ Ⓑ Ⓒ Ⓓ
21. Ⓐ Ⓑ Ⓒ Ⓓ
22. Ⓐ Ⓑ Ⓒ Ⓓ
23. Ⓐ Ⓑ Ⓒ Ⓓ
24. Ⓐ Ⓑ Ⓒ Ⓓ

25. Ⓐ Ⓑ Ⓒ Ⓓ
26. Ⓐ Ⓑ Ⓒ Ⓓ
27. Ⓐ Ⓑ Ⓒ Ⓓ
28. Ⓐ Ⓑ Ⓒ Ⓓ
29. Ⓐ Ⓑ Ⓒ Ⓓ
30. Ⓐ Ⓑ Ⓒ Ⓓ
31. Ⓐ Ⓑ Ⓒ Ⓓ
32. Ⓐ Ⓑ Ⓒ Ⓓ

33. Ⓐ Ⓑ Ⓒ Ⓓ
34. Ⓐ Ⓑ Ⓒ Ⓓ
35. Ⓐ Ⓑ Ⓒ Ⓓ
36. Ⓐ Ⓑ Ⓒ Ⓓ

Math

1. Ⓐ Ⓑ Ⓒ Ⓓ
2. Ⓐ Ⓑ Ⓒ Ⓓ
3. Ⓐ Ⓑ Ⓒ Ⓓ
4. Ⓐ Ⓑ Ⓒ Ⓓ
5. Ⓐ Ⓑ Ⓒ Ⓓ
6. Ⓐ Ⓑ Ⓒ Ⓓ
7. Ⓐ Ⓑ Ⓒ Ⓓ
8. Ⓐ Ⓑ Ⓒ Ⓓ
9. Ⓐ Ⓑ Ⓒ Ⓓ
10. Ⓐ Ⓑ Ⓒ Ⓓ

11. Ⓐ Ⓑ Ⓒ Ⓓ
12. Ⓐ Ⓑ Ⓒ Ⓓ
13. Ⓐ Ⓑ Ⓒ Ⓓ
14. Ⓐ Ⓑ Ⓒ Ⓓ
15. Ⓐ Ⓑ Ⓒ Ⓓ
16. Ⓐ Ⓑ Ⓒ Ⓓ
17. Ⓐ Ⓑ Ⓒ Ⓓ
18. Ⓐ Ⓑ Ⓒ Ⓓ
19. Ⓐ Ⓑ Ⓒ Ⓓ
20. Ⓐ Ⓑ Ⓒ Ⓓ

21. Ⓐ Ⓑ Ⓒ Ⓓ
22. Ⓐ Ⓑ Ⓒ Ⓓ
23. Ⓐ Ⓑ Ⓒ Ⓓ
24. Ⓐ Ⓑ Ⓒ Ⓓ
25. Ⓐ Ⓑ Ⓒ Ⓓ
26. Ⓐ Ⓑ Ⓒ Ⓓ
27. Ⓐ Ⓑ Ⓒ Ⓓ
28. Ⓐ Ⓑ Ⓒ Ⓓ
29. Ⓐ Ⓑ Ⓒ Ⓓ
30. Ⓐ Ⓑ Ⓒ Ⓓ

31. Ⓐ Ⓑ Ⓒ Ⓓ
32. Ⓐ Ⓑ Ⓒ Ⓓ
33. Ⓐ Ⓑ Ⓒ Ⓓ
34. Ⓐ Ⓑ Ⓒ Ⓓ
35. Ⓐ Ⓑ Ⓒ Ⓓ
36. Ⓐ Ⓑ Ⓒ Ⓓ
37. Ⓐ Ⓑ Ⓒ Ⓓ
38. Ⓐ Ⓑ Ⓒ Ⓓ
39. Ⓐ Ⓑ Ⓒ Ⓓ
40. Ⓐ Ⓑ Ⓒ Ⓓ

41. Ⓐ Ⓑ Ⓒ Ⓓ
42. Ⓐ Ⓑ Ⓒ Ⓓ
43. Ⓐ Ⓑ Ⓒ Ⓓ
44. Ⓐ Ⓑ Ⓒ Ⓓ
45. Ⓐ Ⓑ Ⓒ Ⓓ
46. Ⓐ Ⓑ Ⓒ Ⓓ
47. Ⓐ Ⓑ Ⓒ Ⓓ

Made in the USA
Monee, IL
19 September 2021